JUVENILE JUSTICE IN SCOTLAND

Twenty-five Years of the Welfare Approach

JUVENILE JUSTICE IN SCOTLAND

Twenty-five Years of the Welfare Approach

ANDREW LOCKYER

Senior Lecturer, Department of Politics, University of Glasgow

FREDERICK H. STONE

Emeritus Professor of Child and Adolescent Psychiatry, University of Glasgow

T&T CLARK
EDINBURGH
1998

T&T CLARK LTD
59 GEORGE STREET
EDINBURGH EH2 2LQ
SCOTLAND

ISBN 0 567 00528 3

British Library Cataloguing-in-Publication Data
A catalogue record for this book is available from the British Library

Typeset by Fakenham Photosetting Limited, Fakenham, Norfolk
Printed and bound in Great Britain by MPG Books, Bodmin

Contents

Table of Cases

Table of Statutes

Table of Statutory Instruments

Preface

It is just over a quarter of a century since the children's hearings system was inaugurated – which provides us with a useful milestone for a major review of Scotland's welfare approach to children who come to public attention with problems. The central question we seek to address is whether the ideas and principles upon which the system was founded continue to provide a coherent basis in practice for the treatment of children and their families. We question whether the changes that have taken place during these twenty-five years, culminating in the Children (Scotland) Act of 1995, represent a consolidation or a transformation of the approach adopted by the Kilbrandon Committee in its innovative Report of 1964. It was its recommendations that provided the framework embodied in the Social Work (Scotland) Act 1968. The fact that this legislation peculiar to Scotland came to be approved by a British government was in itself remarkable. Its endurance in the face of trends in the United Kingdom and in North America unsympathetic to the 'welfare approach' makes it worthy of attention beyond Scotland.

Momentum for change

From the start the Scottish children's hearings system exhibited an internal dynamic. Practice has developed in the light of experience and in response to the demands of twenty-five years of social change. However, the need for significant legislative reform has generally been resisted. The disposition to conserve the body and spirit of what was put in place in 1971, especially by the central participants in the system, has been a prime motivation. Yet during the 1990s there was increasing momentum for new legislation in Scotland, the pressure for which was both internal and external. The Review of Child Care Law in Scotland, reporting in 1990, was a response to the demand for legislative reform in England and Wales. This was immediately followed by a number of events on both sides of the border revealing problems in child-care provision and practice which led to a further series of reviews. The events in Scotland which gave rise to the Fife and Orkney Inquiries are dealt with in the text in some detail as they had a major impact on proposals for change. Pressures also arose from concern about juvenile crime in the United Kingdom, and from the international rights agenda in Europe and the United Nations. The reforms of the Children (Scotland) Act 1995 were a product of these pressures on the government of the day. The significance of the changes brought about by the new legislation and whether the 'improvements' will be in harmony with the Kilbrandon legacy remain to be seen.

Setting the scene

For overseas readers and others who are unfamiliar with the Scottish scene, a few general facts may be useful. Although Scotland has nearly a third of the total land area of the United Kingdom, it has only 9 per cent of the population. The population is about five million and, as elsewhere in Europe, it is becoming progressively older since more people are living longer and fewer children are born. Children (up to fifteen years of age) account for one million, ie, one fifth of the total population. Ethnic minority groups make up about 1.5 per cent of the population, residing mainly in the densely populated areas of the Glasgow and Edinburgh conurbations.

A brief word is called for regarding the major changes in Scottish family life during recent decades, especially as these have affected the roles of parents and the experiences of children. About one in four marriages ends in separation or divorce and one in five households is headed by lone parents. As a result of parents' new liaisons, children often have to cope with multiple relationships and lack continuity of care. There is less secrecy and inhibition about sexual matters, and early sexual experience is common among boys and girls. The abuse of alcohol remains a major problem. Many schoolchildren are cigarette smokers, and drug and solvent abuse is no longer rare, even at primary-school level. Recent decades have been characterised by poor employment prospects for many young people and although family discord and disruption are not confined to lower-income groups, poverty is a commonly associated factor (Stone, Introduction, Kilbrandon Report, 1995).

Under the 1707 Act of Union Scotland retained many of its own institutions, including its church and education and legal systems. Therefore, the United Kingdom Parliament has usually passed separate Scottish Acts – differing only marginally from the Acts applying south of the border – in areas which affect distinctive Scottish institutions. As we shall see, the Social Work (Scotland) Act 1968 was exceptional in departing in a major way from legislation applying in England and Wales and Northern Ireland. Scotland has had its own administrative structure, with the Scottish Office in Edinburgh presided over by a Secretary of State, with a group of separate Scottish departmental ministers. It has also had a distinctive political culture. During much of the lifetime of the children's hearings system there was a Conservative government which had only minority support in Scotland. A Labour government came to power in May 1997 with a commitment to introduce a separate Scottish Parliament.

The publication of this book therefore comes at a time of major constitutional significance for Scotland. With the enabling legislation for a Scottish Parliament underway, the future for the hearings system, and the children it serves, will be more firmly in the hands of the government and people of Scotland. The present Secretary of State for Scotland, who has the major responsibility for implementing the new constitutional arrangements, has a long-standing association with the children's hearings system. In his recent Kilbrandon lecture (November 1997) he affirmed the government's commitment to the Kilbrandon principles and expressed his belief that they should continue to provide the basis for the treatment of children in Scotland. For supporters of the children's hearings system there are grounds for optimism. It is our contention that a critical understanding of the Kilbrandon legacy – that is, how the principles have been, and should be, put into practice – remains crucial if the welfare approach to children in trouble is to continue to flourish.

Acknowledgements
We wish to express our gratitude to Kathleen Murray for her assistance in planning this project; to Brian Kearney for guidance in all matters legal; and to Avril Johnstone, Jeanette Berrie and Sally Kuenssberg for help with producing and proof-reading the text.

Andrew Lockyer
Fred Stone
University of Glasgow
March 1998

SECTION I

Foundations and Development

Andrew Lockyer and Fred Stone

1 : The Kilbrandon Origins

IN 1961 a working party under the chairmanship of Lord Kilbrandon, a Scottish Law Lord, was appointed by the Secretary of State for Scotland 'to consider the provisions of the law of Scotland relating to the treatment of juvenile delinquents and juveniles in need of care or protection or beyond parental control and, in particular, the constitution, powers and procedure of the courts dealing with such juveniles' (Kilbrandon Report, 1964, para 1).[1]

The outcome of this initiative was remarkable. First, the Kilbrandon Report, as it came to be known, was of a breadth and depth which could hardly have been anticipated. Secondly, four years after the publication of the report, its main recommendations had become enshrined in statute by Act of Parliament, in the Social Work (Scotland) Act 1968.

Since the Act of Union, when major legislation has been introduced which has relevance for the whole of the UK, the usual process is for an English Act to be passed, followed with relatively minor adjustments by a Scottish Act. In this instance, the Scottish Act had no English precedent, an unusual circumstance which is analysed from a political and administrative aspect by Cowperthwaite (1988).

The central aim of the Kilbrandon Report was to spare children and adolescents the rigours of the adult criminal justice system by dealing with them, as well as their parents, in a setting which, by its informality and generous allocation of time, would ensure, as far as possible, effective participation by child and adults in the search for appropriate and realistic remedies. In essence what the Kilbrandon recommendations achieved was the separation of the judgment of evidence (or the 'adjudication of the allegation issue') from the judgment of welfare (or 'consideration of the measures to be applied' (para 72). The former remained the province of the law courts; welfare considerations became the responsibility of a lay tribunal of three members, the nucleus of volunteers who came to form the Scottish children's hearings system.

Whether dealing with young offenders or with children offended against, the primary consideration was to be the welfare needs of the child. This meant that, with the exception of those committing very grave offences, children and juveniles in Scotland were removed from the jurisdiction of the courts. Children's hearings, under arrangements which were essentially those proposed by the Kilbrandon

---

[1] The Report of the Committee on Children and Young Persons: Scotland, prepared under the chairmanship of Lord Kilbrandon – referred to in this book as 'the Kilbrandon Report', 'Kilbrandon' or 'the Report'. The Committee which produced the Report is referred to as 'the Kilbrandon Committee' or 'the Committee'. The Report was republished by HMSO in 1995, with an introduction by Stone.

Report, were convened for the first time in April 1971 and have continued with only minor modifications (we will argue) to the present.

The pre-Kilbrandon scene

A useful starting-point for a brief overview of attitudes, concerns and theories about children and child development is the aftermath of two World Wars. Both periods, though in very different ways, were characterised by massive disruption of family life in Europe and in the United States. In both post-war periods there was a sharp rise in 'juvenile delinquency', especially in adolescents, and particularly in boys. The response tended to be polarised: on the one hand 'corrective' measures and institutions; on the other, psychological approaches. In Boston, in the Twenties, William Healey pioneered a team approach to behaviourally disordered youngsters and their families – the beginnings of 'child guidance' in America. Similar developments followed in the UK, especially during and after the Second World War, an important impetus being the prevalence of emotional and behavioural disturbance in many of the children in wartime Britain evacuated to rural areas, often at considerable distance from their homes. It was some time before it was realised that the frequently occurring pilfering, bedwetting and absconding were not necessarily a continuation of previous behaviour, but a reaction to the separation from home, whatever its limitations.

The nature nurture controversy was unresolved; it has carried on down to the present. There were those who, recognising the frequency with which juvenile delinquency occurs in disorganised families – often repeating similar behaviour patterns in previous generations – tended to discount the disadvantaged environment as a significant factor. The researches of John Bowlby, begun in the late Thirties and continued after the 1939–45 War, undoubtedly added weight to the importance of a secure, caring environment for later healthy emotional development. Bowlby's review of world literature, *Maternal Care and Mental Health*, on behalf of the World Health Organisation in 1951, highlighted the concept of 'early emotional deprivation' and made a considerable impact on child-care practices in Europe and America. His emphasis on continuity of early affectionate mothering, while probably an over-simplification and later attacked as a reactionary view of 'motherhood', nevertheless acted as a catalyst for valuable observation: research into behavioural disturbance in early childhood. A practical outcome, largely attributable to the studies of his colleague James Robertson, was the sensitisation of the care of young children in hospital and other residential establishments (Robertson, 1952).

During the three years of its work, from 1961 to 1964, the Kilbrandon Committee took written and oral evidence from many associations and individuals. On one issue only was there general agreement, namely the inadequacy of existing arrangements. 'Care and protection' procedures were not severely criticised, though it is evident that they were not subjected to the intense scrutiny of measures directed towards juvenile offenders. There was no uniformity in the type of court attended; procedures there were often unintelligible to the offender and family; and there was little guarantee of the special knowledge and skills required by those presiding. In his report to the Carnegie Trust, John Mack (1953) analysed the court decisions as follows:

> 'In about a third there was "no action"; a third were placed on probation; a smaller number were fined, and in a few cases the parents were fined. About 5% of young offenders were sent to approved schools, residential units administered by the education authorities, and a fewer number still were detained in remand homes for 28 days.'

Some comment is required about both of these institutions. In his historical review of child-care services in Scotland, Murphy (1992) observes that, compared with England and Wales, records are decidedly scanty. Nevertheless the main trends are clear enough. The traditional Scottish recipe for dealing with large numbers of children 'in care' was 'boarding out' – that is, placement on a voluntary basis with private families, mainly in rural areas in the highlands or offshore islands. This scheme was administered by local authorities under the provisions of the Poor Law (Scotland) Act 1934, on behalf of children under sixteen years who were orphaned, deserted or separated from their parents, and it was generally accepted that the location of the residence should be such that contact between child and parents would be infrequent! It is difficult if not impossible to assess in retrospect the success of these measures, almost certainly a mixed picture. When, however, the report on homeless children appeared (Clyde, 1946) perceptions had begun to change, 'boarding out' being viewed rather critically because of the children's remoteness from their homes, and the use of many of them as useful hands in croft industries!

Alongside family placements there had developed piecemeal a number of large residential institutions variously termed 'orphanages' or 'children's villages', many of them initiated by church and other charitable organisations. Dr Guthrie of Edinburgh's 'ragged schools' and William Quarrier who founded Quarrier's Homes in the west of Scotland were outstanding nineteenth-century pioneers of such developments. These institutions of variable size and quality were the precursors of the 'approved schools' which aimed to provide a more organised and skilled resource, usually in a residential setting, for children and adolescents with special scholastic and behavioural needs. The story of the 'remand homes' is altogether more dismal. These 'places of detention', established by the Children Act 1908, were used variously by the courts for offenders between eight and eighteen years of age, for assessment prior to admission to approved schools, for the containment of absconders, as 'places of safety', and for disturbed youngsters awaiting admission to psychiatric hospitals. The level and quality of staff were poor, the physical environment wretched and overcrowding frequent (Remand Homes, 1961). Not until 1968, under the provisions of the Social Work (Scotland) Act, were they replaced by purpose-built assessment units.

Before leaving this brief overview of child legislation and provision prior to the Kilbrandon Report, it is important to reflect on how the needs of children were understood. 'Care and protection'[2] was almost exclusively confined to the physical

---

[2] The Kilbrandon Report refers to 'care *or* protection', and this formula is sometimes adopted elsewhere. No great significance attaches, so we speak of care *and* protection throughout.

aspects of development, nutrition, cleanliness, housing, warmth and health. The emotional welfare of the child, using present-day terminology, came to notice, if at all, only on the evidence of cruelty or neglect, and although this was at times a police responsibility, and education authorities had powers to intervene, the only agency which for many years was active in its concern about the treatment of children in their own homes was a voluntary one, the Royal Scottish Society for the Prevention of Cruelty to Children (RSSPCC). It is true that by the early Sixties Kempe (1962) and others had begun to describe the 'battered-baby syndrome' and other features of deliberate injury to young children, but sexual abuse of children was hardly recognised, and emotional abuse not even conceptualised. Yet the officers of the RSSPCC – the 'Cruelty', as they were colloquially designated in many localities – intervened on behalf of numerous neglected or maltreated children with benevolent authority or more stringent measures as situations demanded, at times leading to police involvement. A further safeguard of child welfare was the home-visiting service provided by health visitors with statutory supervisory duties throughout infancy, and whose aims by the 1940s had broadened from exclusive concern with physical health and development to encompass the child's emotional welfare and the quality of parenting.

We now consider the role of the school. For many decades educational provision in Scotland was held in high regard throughout Britain and beyond. The school atmosphere was mostly formal; discipline tended to be strict and corporal punishment the accepted norm. Education authorities employed attendance officers who investigated absenteeism by visiting families, and parents could be prosecuted for persistent truancy by their children. This picture, a rather austere one, is a fair description of nineteenth- and early twentieth-century Scottish schooling, and, moreover, was so, irrespective of social class or neighbourhood. During the same period in England it was fashionable for families with means to send their children to private boarding schools (paradoxically called public schools). This never became a common practice in Scotland even among those who could have afforded to do so.

Special categories of children did, however, require separate provision – for example, the mentally or physically handicapped. Mostly they attended 'special schools', separate categories of handicap having their own day schools. Only in exceptional circumstances was residential education provided. Resources for children with severe behavioural and emotional problems developed more slowly in the form of 'residential schools for maladjusted children', and later still the value of specialised day centres or day schools began to be appreciated, especially in the larger towns. All of the day, and some of the residential, units were administered and staffed by the education authorities; others were developed on the initiative of a variety of independent, charitable organisations, supported to a variable extent by local authority and government grants. Relationships between the statutory and voluntary sectors were not always or consistently harmonious, owing to ideological and financial considerations.

But the difficulties of 'maladjusted children' have never been confined to those displaying learning delay, unruly behaviour or truancy. These children often come to notice because of somatic symptoms – sleep disturbance, disorders of appetite, poor bowel or bladder control, recurrent pain – and are dealt with in the first instance by family doctors. Still others, especially boys, demand attention because of persistent antisocial behaviour – aggression, stealing, absconding – and come to the notice of the police, and so to the courts, the probation services and, as previously mentioned, to approved schools. It is not, therefore, surprising that questions arose as to whether these youngsters were the responsibility of the education authority, the health service, the police or, when social factors were prominent, the child welfare services.

What in fact happened was that each agency followed its own initiatives. In the early Thirties, school psychological services and child-guidance clinics were inaugurated, mostly by the education authorities. In several parts of Scotland police liaison schemes were introduced, specially trained officers working at community level with 'difficult' youngsters. Juvenile offenders whom the courts considered were in need of ongoing surveillance could be placed under the supervision of the probation service inaugurated by the Criminal Justice Act 1949. Psychiatric services for children and adolescents began to develop in the Forties, with various patterns of out-patient and in-patient provision. None of these services was able to keep pace with the level of demand, a situation which has not changed radically to the present time.

So far we have made little mention of social work services for the good reason that in the pre-Kilbrandon era there existed only various disparate groups working in a variety of settings. Initially a volunteer service, primarily in general hospitals, the lady almoners provided a listening ear and practical benevolence to needy patients. Psychiatric social workers, few in number but with recognised training and professional status, worked alongside medical and nursing colleagues in the mental hospitals, an even smaller number as members of child-guidance and child-psychiatric teams. Almost all were women. The probation officers, account-able to local authority committees, and working almost exclusively with young offenders, were predominantly men. The elderly, the infirm and the handicapped were the responsibility of general duty welfare officers, where they existed. With the Children Act 1948, whose recommendations applied to the whole of the UK, local authorities were required to set up children's committees and to appoint children's officers. Their main function was to protect children deprived of a normal home life. Murphy (1992) gives a vivid account of the vicissitudes of this potentially important service, which remained patchy, and poorly resourced, frequently with part-time officers. Any integration that occurred between the various, uneven elements of service was almost entirely due to the initiative of determined, enthusiastic individuals.

The Kilbrandon Committee Report

In order to trace the origin of the Committee, we must look to the publication in 1960 of the Report of the Committee on Children and Young Persons which applied to England and Wales (Ingleby, 1960). The terms of reference of that committee, under the chairmanship of Lord Ingleby, were to inquire into and make recommendations on:

- the powers and proceedings of the courts in respect of juveniles, delinquent or in need of care and protection;
- the workings of juvenile courts;
- remand homes and approved schools;
- prevention of cruelty to, and exposure to moral danger of juveniles; and
- whether local authorities should be given new powers to prevent suffering and neglect of children in their own homes.

Among its recommendations was the proposal to raise the age of criminal responsibility from eight to twelve years (with the possibility of a later rise to thirteen or fourteen years). It was in fact raised to ten years of age and has so remained until the present, whereas in Scotland it has remained eight years. Ingleby further recommended that a power and duty should be conferred on local authorities to prevent suffering and neglect of children in their own homes and, looking to the future, the development of 'a unified family service'.

Not surprisingly there was considerable pressure, in Parliament and elsewhere, for similar issues to receive formal consideration in Scotland. Cowperthwaite (1988) describes the political process leading to the establishment of the Kilbrandon Committee in 1961. Whereas the Ingleby proposals were cautious and largely concerned with procedures, those of Kilbrandon were radical, something that could hardly have been predicted from the wording of its official remit.

The Kilbrandon Report begins by dealing with several 'basic' considerations, recognising the need to prepare the reader for what are likely to be regarded as unexpected conclusions. A principal aim is to develop methods of reducing or even preventing juvenile delinquency. From the vantage point of prevention, no essential distinction is seen between offenders and those in need of care or protection. The emphasis on the 'needs' of such children and of 'preventive measures' is quite remarkable for its time. Moreover, the legal distinction between these two main categories of children which had held sway until then was declared to be 'of little practical significance' (para 13). It is difficult to grasp, in the climate of today's orientation, how radical such views were. Indeed, it is worth noting that a separate working party, the McBoyle Committee, had been initiated in 1961 by the Scottish Advisory Council in Child Care to consider necessary measures to combat 'the suffering of children through neglect in their own homes', an aspect which though not included in the remit of the Kilbrandon Committee, in no way inhibited its discussions. We should note how the Kilbrandon Report conceptualised the needs of children and how these might be met.

> 'The basic similarity of the underlying situation far outweighs the differences, and from the point of view of treatment measure, *the true distinguishing factor, common to all the children concerned, is their need for special measures of education and training, the normal upbringing processes having, for whatever reason, fallen short'* (emphasis added) (para 15).

It is important to grasp the very broad concept of 'education' as used here.

'It is intended, wherever possible, not to supersede the natural beneficial influences of the home and the family, but wherever practicable to strengthen, support, and supplement them. . . . [C]oercive powers in relation to parents of juvenile delinquents . . . are ultimately incompatible with the nature of educational process itself, more particularly in the context of the parent-child relationship' (para 35).

The Report then goes on to emphasise the importance of involving parents and child in a non-coercive manner. This process the Report designated 'social education'. Seemingly, the logical recommendation was that this service be provided by a department of social education within the education authority, but as we shall discover it was one of the few recommendations which did not materialise in subsequent legislation. However, the central Kilbrandon recommendation was accepted, and passed into legislation in remarkably short time, namely that young offenders as well as children offended against be dealt with, not by courts of law, nor even by juvenile courts (which in any case had never been widely instituted in Scotland), but by panels of three lay members, the children's hearings. Treatment had to be geared to the needs of the individual child and family, so that assessment called for sensitive and intuitive understanding.

There is an interesting passage on the aetiology of delinquency where, although recognising that poverty and what we would now term 'disadvantage' are important factors, it was observed that 'Many children from such backgrounds do not become delinquent, nor had improvement in living standards brought the improvement that would be expected' (para 77). And, of course, this was written in the early Sixties, a period of economic growth. Equal weight is given to the individual factor, the 'maladjustment' present in many delinquents. But the discussion stops short of ideas regarding the origins of 'maladjustment', a term, incidentally, used primarily by educational administrators who for convenience place it alongside other forms of handicap! In considering the approach to 'treatment', however, much emphasis is given to the child as a member of a family, and the need to work not only with the child but also with the parents, where sometimes the major effort has to be directed. Indeed a particular point is made of emphasising the need to work in the closest co operation with parents whether the child continues to live at home or in a residential setting. In reviewing the work of juvenile courts, the supervision and fining of parents are regarded as incompatible with family casework. 'In practice,' it is asserted, 'all social casework proceeds on the basis of persuasion and so co-operation. . . .' The inadequacy of the arrangements and services then existing, especially when residential placement was involved, is tellingly summarised as follows.

'It was represented to us' – by those giving evidence – 'that too often the results of the present arrangements . . . amount to a process of shuffling from one agency to another, in which at various transient points in time the intervention of the courts is momentarily invoked' (para 38).

The Report discusses at some length the dual function of every criminal court, whether dealing with adults or children: first the establishment of the alleged offences, and secondly the action to be taken once the facts are established. These two functions, it is asserted, call for 'quite different skills and qualities', and it is the attempt to combine these two activities 'within the present juvenile court system' that is a cause of 'dissatisfaction' (para 71).

As to the notion previously mentioned that a child can be considered capable of a criminal act above a specific age – the so-called 'age of criminal responsibility' – the Report is outspokenly critical.

'No witness who gave evidence before us was prepared to say that by clinical observation or otherwise it was possible to come to a conclusion that chronological age as such has any direct bearing on the capacity to form a criminal intent and to commit a crime' (para 64).

The discussion makes it clear that such an age – eight years in Scotland – has been laid down 'for purely legalistic reasons', primarily to protect young children from the 'the rigours of the criminal law applicable in earlier times' (para 62). The practical consideration, the Report maintains, is whether young offenders above, say, the age of eight years should, in the interests of preventive measures, be dealt with by some form of non-criminal procedure. As to the dichotomy of court function, we should note that at the outset the Kilbrandon Committee was made aware of the practice in Scandinavia of separating them completely. In those countries the courts' concern was solely with the establishment of the truth or otherwise of allegations; the treatment of juvenile offenders had become the responsibility of an entirely separate agency, the child welfare committee. This pattern had clearly influenced the thinking of the Kilbrandon Committee. Criminal procedures, however modified it was argued, affect the atmosphere in a manner not conducive to the relaxed informality which was considered essential to effective participation of child and parents in helping the hearing reach an appropriate decision.

In about 95 per cent of cases where children came before the courts there was no dispute as to the facts, there was a plea of 'guilty', so in the great majority of cases the primary function for which courts were equipped was not required. None the less, there would continue to be cases where alleged offences would be denied and an adjudication of evidence required. It was always accepted that the court would continue to fulfil this necessary role when the facts were contested. However, these cases would be passed on to the 'children's panel' to decide what measures should be taken, if the allegation was proved.[3]

With the separation of functions it was possible for the panel hearing not to resemble a court 'in any accepted sense', even though its decisions would have legal force, its sole function being to determine what course of action would be in the best interests of the child.

---

[3] There was a change in nomenclature in that the 'children's panel' was subsequently designated the 'children's hearing' and the 'children's panel' came to refer to the appointed group of 'panel members' from whom members of children's hearings were drawn.

'Bearing in mind that discussions at the panel will almost in all cases be directed solely to the treatment measures which can most appropriately be applied we do not consider that it is either necessary or desirable to seek to lay down any rigid framework governing the panel's proceedings' (para 109).

There would be something of a 'committee' atmosphere, involving all parties, including child and parents.

One further issue remained, however: how to proceed if the offence committed by the child was of a particularly grave nature. This, it was decided, would remain at the discretion of an independent Minister of the Crown, the Lord Advocate, whose traditional role in Scots law is to decide when public prosecution is indicated. While this was no doubt reassuring both to the public and to the legal profession, it created a certain inconsistency in the argument that offence itself was not a reliable indicator of the seriousness or complexity of the child's overall situation. This duality of procedure, as we shall see, has become a focus of criticism.

These then were the main considerations which influenced Lord Kilbrandon and his committee in forming their recommendations. It is rather remarkable that this group, widely representative of the Scottish legal profession, and including a chief constable, a headmaster, a professor of Scots law, a children's psychiatrist, a chief inspector of child care and probation, two sheriffs, two justices of the peace – several of whom had experience of voluntary work with children and families, locally and nationally – and the Chairman himself, a Scottish Law Lord, were all willing to consider measures well beyond the strictly legalistic and procedural, as might have been anticipated. Moreover, they produced a unanimous report.

The main recommendations of the Kilbrandon Committee may be summarised as follows.

- To establish throughout Scotland a system of children's hearings which would decide whether the needs of the child or adolescent (up to the age of sixteen years) justified compulsory measures of education and training. 'Compulsory' measures would be required when available helping agencies and methods had failed or when voluntary co-operation by child or parents had proved inadequate.
- The decision to refer a child to a hearing would be the responsibility of a newly created official, 'the reporter to the children's panel', to whom all cases would be directed, whether from a member of the 'helping professions' – teacher, social worker, doctor, police officer – the courts, a member of the public, or the child's own parent or parents. The reporter's role would be somewhat analogous to the local representative of the public prosecutor, the procurator fiscal.
- The children's hearing would consist of three lay members, including both sexes. Service would be part-time and voluntary.
- The decisions of the hearing would be enforceable, child and parents having the right of appeal to the sheriff against any decision of the hearing, and a statutory right of appeal at annual intervals.

- There would be a routine review procedure to ensure that the decisions had been carried out, and to assess their efficacy.
- The hearing would decide, on the basis of a social background report and, if required, other specialist reports, whether the child required a period of assessment and supervision while continuing to live at home or exceptionally in a residential setting; or whether the case should be discharged.
- The preparation of social background reports, recommendations for treatment and their application would be the responsibility of a new statutory 'Social Education Department' of the local authority.
- These arrangements would result in children no longer attending courts other than in quite exceptional circumstances.

Beyond the Report
In April 1964 the senior Minister responsible for Scottish affairs, the Secretary of State for Scotland, announced the publication of the Kilbrandon Report and, by means of a written parliamentary answer, indicated his intention to seek the views of interested bodies and the public generally. The Report was received warmly by the media – even enthusiastically by some sections of the Scottish press. Its recommendations were debated in Parliament by the Scottish Grand Committee, with general approval, though reservations were expressed regarding the proposed social education department.

Shortly after the Kilbrandon Report appeared, a report entitled Crime – A Challenge to us All was published by a study group of the Labour Party (Longford, 1964) which represented a commitment by that party to introduce legislation on juvenile offenders. Cowperthwaite quotes a passage from the study group's report which was cited by advocates of the Kilbrandon proposals.

> 'It has not been possible for us to examine the Scottish position in detail; but we have learned enough to realise Scotland has an opportunity unique within the United Kingdom to give a lead to the rest of us in testing new penal methods' (Cowperthwaite, 1988, p29).

When, as a result of a general election in the autumn of 1964, the Conservative Party was defeated, the incoming Labour Government acknowledged that this would involve reorganisation of the social work services. It may well be, as Cowperthwaite suggests, that this fortuitous sequence of political events at this particular time was highly favourable to this Scottish initiative. Certainly it is worth noting that the Home Office proceeded with a different set of proposals for juvenile offenders in England and Wales, without embarking on social work reorganisation (Seebohm, 1968).

The White Paper: Social Work and the Community
For the reader who is not familiar with British parliamentary procedure, it may be useful to explain the nature of a White Paper. This type of document occupies an intermediate position between a proposal for change (such as the Kilbrandon Report) and new legislation embodied in an Act of Parliament (in this case the Social Work (Scotland) Act 1968). The details are set out in a manner compatible

with legislative procedure and terminology, a task ordinarily undertaken by the Civil Service. The 'study group' which was set up in this instance was, rather unusually, augmented by three specialist advisers from the fields of sociology and social work.[4] The contents of Social Work and the Community (1966) were presented under three headings:

- The government's proposals.
- The local authority social work department.
- Social work with children.

Part I traces the background of the review, beginning with the Kilbrandon recommendations. It acknowledges that all the services involved are under-manned, and recognises the need for improved recruitment and training. It notes the valuable contributions of a variety of voluntary agencies and emphasises the importance of co-operation with local authorities. It then states the case for a new type of local authority social work department with wide-ranging responsibilities, 'to provide community care and support, whether for children, the handicapped, the mentally and physically ill or the aged ... within a single organisation' (para 10). While recognising that certain basic skills are common to all forms of social work, the importance of specialist skills is noted, a principle that became subordinated to the concept of 'generic social work' for many years! Attention is rightly drawn to the multiplicity of agencies often involved in helping families, as well as the overlapping and poorly co-ordinated activities of workers in health, education and various forms of social work.

This new department would be headed by a director of social work. Clearly this was the central issue of the White Paper. What the Kilbrandon Report had described as 'the matching field organisation' in support of the proposed children's hearings became a welcome opportunity for the study group to present a blueprint for a single local authority resource, available not merely to children but to the needy members of the whole community – in short, the reorganisation of all social services.

The section on social work with children, outlining the procedures and responsibility of the children's hearings system, is relatively brief, and tallies closely with the recommendations of the Kilbrandon Report, except that the proposal for a social education department is rejected in favour of an autonomous social work department. This department would, it was stated, provide for the majority of children and families where 'shortcomings in a child's upbringing become apparent', on a voluntary basis. Sometimes, however, voluntary measures would be 'unsuccessful' or voluntary help would not be enough. The role of the children's hearing would begin at the discretion of the reporter when 'compulsory measures of care' were required (para 62).

---

[4] They were Richard Titmuss, Professor of Social Administration, London School of Economics; Megan Browne, Department of Social Study, University of Edinburgh; and Kay Carmichael, Department of Social Administration, University of Glasgow.

As for the details:

- Both parents would be expected to attend, and could be cited if they did not.
- A review hearing to assess progress must be held in not more than twelve months.
- Detention of children as a punishment would be abolished.
- Provision would be made for appeal procedures against both the findings and the hearing's decisions.
- It would be the responsibility of the local authority, through the director of the social work department, to ensure that the decision of the children's hearing 'was effectively implemented'.

One particular administrative problem discussed at some length, and which gave rise to considerable controversy, was the future of the probation service. Rather than dividing the service into two new sections, one for adults and one for those under sixteen years of age, the White Paper concluded that 'it would be better if all the functions of the probation service in Scotland were undertaken by the new Social Work Department' (para 29). This particular proposal was opposed, as might have been anticipated, by the probation services, as well as by the sheriffs who considered that it would weaken the effectiveness of the courts and were doubtful about the competence of the proposed 'all-purpose' social workers to deal effectively with adult offenders. As we shall see, this issue was readdressed thirty years later.

Criticism of the White Paper also came from the medical profession, partly because of the inevitable curtailment of many of its responsibilities, but also because of concern about the separation of local health and welfare services. Such a view was resisted by social work bodies who were clearly determined to acquire professional independence, the opportunity for which was presented by the Kilbrandon proposals.

There was strong resistance from local authorities on the planned arrangements for the administration of the new social work departments; indeed the arrangements were modified in favour of large burgh responsibility (Murphy, 1992).

It will be noted that there was in fact little serious opposition to the proposals for the Scottish children's hearings, which became embodied in the subsequent legislation very much as detailed in the original report of the Kilbrandon Committee.

In England a White Paper was published in 1965, The Child, the Family and the Young Offender, which paid tribute to the Kilbrandon Report, and proposed the setting up of 'family councils' where the child's needs would be discussed and agreement sought on appropriate action. Where such progress was not made, the family would be referred to a modified juvenile court, designated a 'Family Court'. Unlike the proposals in Scotland, these were strongly opposed, especially by magistrates and probation officers. As a result there was a second White Paper, Children in Trouble (1968), stating that the juvenile court would be used only when informal procedures by the social agencies had failed. These measures were embodied in the Children and Young Persons Act 1969.

The outcome in Scotland was very different. In spite of some opposition from the probation services, the sheriffs and the police, but with the support of the Association of Procurators Fiscal, the Kilbrandon proposals, in their essentials, passed into legislation as the Social Work (Scotland) Act 1968.

At this point our account could simply proceed to focus on Part III of the Act, 'Children in Need of Compulsory Measures of Care', by noting that the Kilbrandon Report was debated in both Houses of Parliament and emerged as legislation with only minor modifications. But that would not do justice to the far-reaching implications of the remainder of the Scottish Act, an all-embracing programme of social care.

This comprehensive service would make provision not only for children, but also for the elderly, the physically and mentally handicapped and for offenders – in short, as the White Paper, Social Work and the Community, had anticipated, it would have the 'power to provide for all citizens of whatever age and difficulties and problems', including the organisation of home helps and the provision of residential and day-care establishments, as well as the monitoring of appropriate voluntary organisations. Yet even this does not encompass in full this radical programme, for we must note that in s 12 the Act places upon local authorities a duty to 'promote social welfare'. This is spelled out in a guidance note.

'The new duty is not, however, related only to the needs for advice or social support which may be felt by individual people. The duty to promote social welfare must include concern for groups of people. ... Moreover, the duty is not merely that of reacting to known needs. It implies that the local authority should seek out existing needs, which have not been brought to the authorities' attention, identify incipient needs and try to influence social and environmental developments in such ways as will not only prevent the creation of social difficulties, but will positively lead to the creation of good social conditions' (Circular No SW6, December 1968, quoted by Murphy, 1992, p166).

It will come as no surprise to the reader to learn that, faced with such Herculean tasks, the early years of the newly established services were fraught. With limited resources, few reliable guidelines and many inexperienced staff, it was hardly surprising that the endeavours of this new breed of social worker frequently failed to live up to their own and others' expectations. And of course prominent, indeed inescapable, among these demands was the newly established children's hearings system whose needs for background reports and supervision of children was the responsibility of the directors of social work. Yet paradoxically it was the Kilbrandon initiative that acted as a catalyst in the reorganisation of Scotland's social services. Between the publication of the White Paper and the appearance of the Social Work Act two years later, these new services were placed under the administrative supervision of a new Scottish Office department, the Social Work Services Group (SWSG).

The scene was now set for the inauguration of the children's hearings system. Curiously, however, none of the aforementioned documents gave any guidance on procedures for the recruitment and selection of members of the children's panels. Regional committees – Children's Panel Advisory Committees (CPACs) – were therefore set up with the task of recommending to the Secretary of State the names of applicants for appointment. Rules for the conduct of the hearings were issued by the Secretary of State in March 1971, and in April of that year the first hearings took place.

2 : The Kilbrandon Philosophy Revisited

IT is our purpose in this chapter to re-evaluate the ideas embodied in the Kilbrandon Report, not from the perspective of how they have been put into practice, which will be examined later, but from the point of view of the criticisms that have been made of their theoretical content. Our procedure here will be to outline the principles in the Report and rehearse the criticisms to discover what issues they expose for further scrutiny.

In treating the Kilbrandon Report as the embodiment of a 'welfare philosophy' we run some risks. Describing the ideas in the Report as a 'philosophy' may lead to inflated expectations. It may urge us on the one hand to reconstruct its content at a level of systematic theory unintended and unattained. On the other hand, we may criticise the Report for not achieving this high level of theoretical rigour.

Throughout our analysis, therefore, we must be reminded that looking for a fully articulated systematic body of social, psychological or criminological theory might be misplaced. The text is the work of a committee. It was comprised of members from a variety of professions and disciplines, doubtless with varied preconceptions and motives. In addition they were working within a politically sensitive policy area, where consideration of what might be acceptable to government and public (to say nothing of their professional interests) is likely to have had a bearing on their deliberations.

We shall find that there are some ambiguities, some points of tension, and some areas where the Report is either silent or short on explanation. Therefore, in places, our discussion may need to amplify or tease out the implications of the Committee's thinking. However, we will see that the ideas embedded in the Kilbrandon Report do constitute the outline of a coherent framework capable of being viewed as a conceptual whole. Underlying the series of institutional innovations there is a body of principles which justify being described as the 'welfare approach', or as embracing the 'welfare philosophy'.

Primary principles
The philosophy of the Kilbrandon Committee is constituted by a number of interrelated key principles. These can be presented as embodying five propositions which contain both normative and empirical elements. The first and central normative position is the adoption of the *welfare criterion*. The proposition it embodies is that all young people, for whatever reason they come within the ambit of the state's law, ought to be treated according to their 'best interests'. Formally

at least this entails the position that the interests of others, or society as a whole, must be secondary. The adoption of the welfare principle is modified only in the case of very serious young offenders. In the case of most young offenders they should be treated (as it is popularly said) with regard to 'their needs rather than their deeds', once they have become legitimate candidates for state intervention.

In the first instance there is mention of the pre-existing duty of juvenile courts 'already recognised in statute' which 'required in every case to have regard for the welfare of the child' (Kilbrandon, para 12). In the second place necessary treatment 'to prevent further harm to the individual child and society' (para 13) is mentioned. However, the welfare stance becomes the clear and dominant theme when the question of 'practical action' is discussed. Once 'the basis for judicial action' is established (in terms of the later legislation, the 'grounds' for referral to the hearing have been 'established') the decision whether and in what manner to intervene should be taken entirely by reference to the young person's need. An offence, after proof, 'has significance only as a pointer to the need for intervention' (para 71).

The second plank in the Kilbrandon philosophy can be called the *general aetiological proposition*. It arises from what the Committee said was the 'consensus of experienced opinion' from which it took evidence, that despite the different reasons for young people coming to public attention, including both where they were offenders and where they were victims of neglect or abuse, 'they could not in practice be usefully considered as presenting a series of distinct and separately definable problems'. When viewed in terms of their needs, their 'basic similarity of underlying situation far outweighs the differences ... common to all the children concerned is their need for special measures of education and training, the normal upbringing processes having, for whatever reason, fallen short' (para 15).

The Report does not claim that in every case the particular cause and remedy are the same. Rather, it suggests there is no necessary correspondence between the reason for the case coming before the courts and the 'problems' which need to be dealt with. Children referred on the same grounds might have different specific needs and children referred for different reasons might have similar problems and needs. The causal generality as negatively formulated above is almost a truism. It is that, in all cases, home and other influences have failed to provide something that might have prevented whatever is untoward in the child's circumstances or behaviour. This does not assume that the home or wider environment are solely responsible for the difficulties, but it does imply they are relevant influences, for better or worse.

The third core proposition of the Kilbrandon philosophy is that the remedies for individual problems are generally to be found with something they called *social education*. The underlying aim is wherever possible 'to strengthen and further those natural influences for good which assist the child's development into a mature and useful member of society'. In the 'great majority of cases' this will involve the child 'remaining within the home' where the 'most powerful and direct influences lie' (para 17). The most important potential source of influence was the family itself. Where social education and training required to be provided by agencies of the state, it would 'necessarily imply working in the closest co-operation with the parents'. Although remedial social education and training might include some children being away from home for 'limited periods', sustaining parental involvement and returning children to their families is the normal expectation.

The central emphasis on the family was not simply a recognition of its causal importance in socialisation. It was equally a powerful normative statement. The Report both reinforces the concept of parental responsibility and underscores the presumption of the desirability of preserving children in their natural families. This of course must be reconcilable with the welfare principle. There is room for debate about how the Kilbrandon philosophy copes with the possibility of conflict between the ideal of sustaining natural families and the primacy of individual child welfare.

The fourth element of the Kilbrandon principles, which is linked to the welfare of young people, is the *principle of prevention*. This concept contains some element of ambiguity. The 'preventive approach' is clearly forward-looking; but it might be orientated either to securing the welfare of the individual recipient or to avoiding harm to others. Commonly the concept of prevention suggests forestall-ing a potential cost both to particular individuals and to society generally. Within the idea of 'prevention' the Committee brought together the needs of the child with the interests of society. In fact it sought to identify (rather than balance) 'the future protection of society' with 'the child's own interests' (para 13). This was linked with a rejection of some of the key assumptions associated with the use of punishment (para 57). There are a number of issues which arise from this. Suffice for now to say that both child protection and the prevention of future delinquency were seen to be facets of the same welfare approach.

Secondary principles

The institutional innovations proposed by the Committee logically follow the adoption of the principles so far outlined. We might regard these as embodying second-order principles which can be derived from the foregoing. However, in practice the critique of existing arrangements was equally the basis for articulating the institutional innovations which the Report proposed.

In fact the starting-point of the Committee's deliberations was dissatisfaction with courts as the main place for dealing with children in trouble. It is sometimes suggested that 'keeping children out of court' was seen as desirable *per se* and perhaps we should regard it as a fundamental principle of the system outlined. However, there is insufficient evidence for this being a position adopted in the Report, even though it might be an aim worth defending in its own right.

Yet the Committee was clear that a court was not the best forum for decisions to be made about what measures of education and training were needed. The 'first function' of courts is determination of guilt or innocence; their rules and procedure are specifically designed for hearing evidence and adjudicating on matters of fact (para 52). This function was not needed in the vast majority of cases, where guilt or fault was accepted. The secondary function of the courts is 'that of sentencing'. This was only deemed to be needed in cases of the 'the gravest crimes' where 'major issues of public interest must necessarily arise'. Courts are not therefore best suited for making decisions which aimed at co-operation and consensus.

We may notice three points in passing. (1) The Committee, here and elsewhere, took criminal proceedings as the paradigm of court practice. (2) Retaining exceptional cases within the ambit of the court compromises the universality of the welfare criterion. (3) The validity of the courts having the jurisdiction for appeals while not deemed approriate to make the initial welfare disposal, is questionable in principle.

The above reflections gave rise to the key institutional principle of *separation of adjudication of proof from disposal*. The 'adjudication of the allegation issue' was properly seen to be the court's business, whereas the 'consideration of the measures to be applied', the welfare judgment, should be made by the newly created institution of 'the panel' (para 72). The agency of the panel 'would thus exercise jurisdiction on the basis of facts established either by acceptance of the child in the parents' presence and with their agreement, or after an adjudication in a court of law' (para 73).

The informal and non-adversarial proceedings were designed to allow all parties to be involved in determining the best disposal for the child. The institution of the panel hearing was to encourage *participation* of all parties. The process of a hearing might in itself serve to facilitate *co-operation* which would assist the success of the outcome. The task of the panel hearing was to decide on the 'need for measures of education and training' and on 'what measures were most appropriate to the child's needs' (para 73). Underlying the hearing is the aim to involve all influential parties, including the child and parents, in finding a solution to the problem. This could best be achieved without the imposition of a 'rigid framework'. The issues were likely to 'emerge most clearly only in an atmosphere of full, free and unhurried discussion' (para 109).

The model of decision procedure suggested is one of seeking *consensus*. The Committee 'would expect that in many cases it would be possible to enlist the co-operation of parents from the outset', which they imply might obviate the need for compulsion. However, while participation in the process and co-operation with the outcome should be sought, it would not always be forthcoming. The Committee accepted that parents, and to a greater extent children, will continue sometimes to see measures 'for a child's protection and future welfare' as 'amounting to compulsion and punishment' (para 57). The adoption of the consensual model as ideal does not imply either that conflict can always be avoided or that panel members can avoid the ultimate decision-making responsibility.

One of the distinctive features of the hearings system is its reliance on unpaid citizens to conduct and adjudicate children's hearings. The case for using lay decision-makers is not clearly made in the Kilbrandon Report. It says that persons appointed should be those with 'knowledge or experience ... considered to be specially qualified to consider children's problems'. They were thought likely in practice to include 'members of the legal profession, doctors, teachers, and local authority members'; in fact people rather like those who served on Lord Kilbrandon's Committee – not necessarily chosen for their expertise, but for their 'personal qualities' (para 74).

As we have seen, the case for the panel being composed of 'representatives of the community' was introduced by the White Paper, Social Work and the Community (1966), and was not part of the original Kilbrandon conception. It is sometimes said that the two sources pointed to conflicting criteria, which suggested personnel with different social characteristics (May and Smith, 1980; Curran, 1977; Jones and Adler, 1990). In truth the attribute which the Report pronounced to be 'important' was *independence* of other agencies. This was also to be a major virtue of the reporter, who must make the initial referral decision (para 102).

Other ideas of the Kilbrandon Committee can be regarded as embodying lesser matters of principle. A number of them derive directly from the adoption of the primary commitment to welfare and prevention. These include support for the exercise of the *widest* and *unfettered discretion* both in determining initial measures and in modifying, varying and extending the time scale (until the age of eighteen) as necessary (paras 73 and 79).

The Committee proposed that the creation of a *social education department*, with a director and 'suitably qualified staff'; these were described as the 'executive agent' of the panel. Placing the primary responsibility for advice and supervision on the single agent was intended to ensure the objective of the director of the service being answerable to the panel for all children subject to panel orders. 'Apart from any specific review of cases made by the panel itself', the director would have discretion to report back at any time where circumstances required a review (para 91). Through the director the panel would have 'continuous access to and oversight of the full range of measures at its disposal'. Whether or not the relationships envisaged here form the precise basis of those put into legislation and further, into practice, remains for later consideration. In the Kilbrandon Report at least, the hearing's control of 'its executive arm' is regarded as necessary to ensure a 'clear and continuous' chain of responsibility.

Criticisms

Objections to the Kilbrandon Report and criticisms of the juvenile justice system in place are not the same thing. Faults may be found with the legislation or operation of the children's hearings system which are not traceable to the original conception, and deficiencies may be found in the Report which have not led to problems in practice. However, many of the criticisms of the hearings system are founded on objections to the ideas of the Kilbrandon Committee, whether or not this is recognised by critics. The most fundamental criticisms, ambiguities or alleged 'contradictions', do have their origin in the Kilbrandon philosophy. Two types of criticism we will treat separately: those which raise issues about the 'justness' of the principles and those which question their 'coherence'.

Under the first heading we can include arguments which appeal to some competing ideas about justice. There are three main lines of criticism, which can be loosely associated with different components of justice found in Western liberal democracies. The first is the notion of 'equity' – or equality of treatment before the law. The welfare approach can be viewed as offending the principle of equity because it fails to treat like cases in a like manner, and may treat different cases similarly. 'Liberty' is the second constituent principle of justice held to be in conflict with the Kilbrandon approach. The objection is that welfare justifies too much intrusion or intervention in family life. This complaint is grounded on the notion that the essence of liberty is to be left alone, and that compulsion of children and parents ought to be minimised. The third challenge to the justice of the welfare approach is that it pays too scant regard to public protection, and the interests of victims.

A second type of criticism finds fault not on normative grounds, but on the basis that the report is 'contradictory', 'ambiguous', or lacking in substance. Fault finding here centres on the Report's understanding of delinquency and its remedial prescriptions. The most common targets here are the concept of social education and the idea of treatment, which are found to be both lacking in specification and misleading. Linked to this is doubt about how to determine what constitutes appropriate measures and whether the authority to judge them is properly located in the hands of lay decision-makers.

While the range of issues identified here have arisen and been discussed throughout the lifetime of the hearings system, some have become more acute in recent times as a result of the contemporary agenda discussed in the preface. In particular, criticisms which invoke the idea of children's or parents' rights have become more frequently voiced. This has coincided with the shift in the balance of referrals to deal with more 'care or protection' cases, which in itself has led to an increased questioning of the validity of the Kilbrandon philosophy.

Justice for children

Before examining what the appeal to 'justice' might mean, let us first be clear that contrasting it with 'welfare' by stipulative definition will not do. Whether or not the position adopted by the Kilbrandon Committee embodies justice for children (and for others) is an open question, to be judged no doubt in the light of debate. What has to be set aside at the start is the implicit value judgment that 'welfare' is opposed to, or can be contrasted with, or must be balanced with, 'justice'. This juxtaposition is often made (Morris *et al*, 1980; Scotland's Children, 1993; Fraser, 1993). Those who make it are ostensibly using the term 'justice' to invoke principles and practice associated with the judicial system. However, this is an unwarranted appropriation of the term, which takes for granted much of what the Kilbrandon approach challenges. For our purposes the term 'justice' cannot be used to describe any set of arrangements in advance of analysis. What can be called 'just' is essentially contestable.

The Kilbrandon Committee itself set out the contrast between what it said was 'a system resting primarily on ideas of crime, responsibility and punishment' and the approach which focused on 'preventive' and 'treatment measures'. It did not begin by entirely rejecting the former in preference to the latter on the grounds of justice. Rather it pointed out that the two offered a different set of ideas which tended to 'militate against each other' (para 54). The contrast drawn between the 'crime-responsibility-punishment concept' and the 'preventive' and 'treatment' concepts were explicitly set out in the Report, and can be summarised as follows.

- Punishment is restricted to proven offenders. It may not be applied to potential offenders. This militates against taking *early preventive measures* against potential delinquency. Treatment which carries no stigma of criminality can be applied early to prevent criminality.

- Punishment cannot be extended 'to any substantial degree' (*sic*) beyond the offender. Treatment can be applied to others whose life has a bearing on the offender, such that a change in a delinquent's behaviour may be brought by changing his or her *environment*.

- Punishment must fit the crime. Treatment on the other hand can be chosen to fit the needs of the individual which facilitates the aim of prevention.

- Punishment must be definitive and 'once and for all'. *Alteration of treatment* is permissible; so it may be modified, terminated or extended in the light of its effects and according to changing needs and circumstances.

Advocates of punishment, as well as those who endorse the preventive treatment approach, could accept that the above is a fair account of some of the important differences between punishment and treatment. The Kilbrandon Report does not then proceed to argue for the justness of the preventive treatment approach. Rather it begins by casting doubt both on the efficacy and the justice of the punishment of children.

Responsibility
The fundamental weakness of the criminal justice model is that its central doctrine of punishment presupposes that children should be regarded as individually responsible and culpable for their illegal acts. In focusing on the offending act of the individual it takes a too narrow and formalistic view of responsibility.

The Report first notes that the criminal law 'assumes a high degree of personal responsibility'. It recognises 'youth as a mitigating factor' but criminal responsibility is 'still inherent and fundamental' to any proof of guilt (para 60). The authors of the Report then proceed to cast doubt on the application of the full-blown doctrine of criminal responsibility to immature young people. They observe that the age limit of eight years is arbitrary and has no sound basis in 'legal theory' nor 'observable fact' about children. In truth the age of criminal responsibility is 'largely a meaningless term' (para 65). The Committee was therefore moved to propose that 'any rule of law or statutory provision establishing a minimum age of criminal responsibility should be abolished' (para 138).

This meant the proof of capacity for 'a guilty mind' would be left for the court to determine in respect of any age. While the Committee may have believed that this would serve to assist the defence against finding children culpable, it would also have allowed the prosecution of children below the present minimum age.

The direction of discussion in the Report is to question the moral validity of treating young people as no different from adults in respect of criminal responsibility. The authors observe that the idea fits very uncomfortably with the presumption of incompetence in other fields of law. Children were not generally regarded as 'free agents' and 'over a wide variety of fields of civil responsibility are debarred from rights of choice available to adults' (para 67).

This line of argument suggests the possibility of abandoning completely the notion of juvenile crime. Indeed this is hinted at when the Report considers the 'Suggested Alternative' of proceeding in all cases on care or protection grounds (paras 68–70). This would allow the notion of the criminal responsibility of children to be set aside. Actions which would be criminal if performed by adults could be treated as grounds for care or protection. Some commentators have observed that this would have been the logical position for the Committee to have settled for (Adler, 1985).

However, it was not prepared in the end to decriminalise law-breaking by young people by converting it to a civil wrong. The main reason given is that the requirement of proof (beyond reasonable doubt) of an offence still affords a protection against unwarranted intervention. The Committee says that the lower standard of proof required of civil proceedings (the balance of probabilities), would be 'both artificial and inherently unstable' (para 69) – it means anomalous and unfair. Whether this was the Committee's motive for continuing to deal with children over eight years old as offenders might be doubted, but relying on the standard-of-proof argument brings into question the validity of the civil standard for the same range of interventions in respect of non-offence referrals.

The Report compromises by not challenging the concept of juvenile crime, but by divorcing it from liability to punishment, except in 'the gravest cases'. Adopting the preventive treatment approach after proof allows the reversion to a wider notion of responsibility – one which can implicitly be shared between children and those responsible for their upbringing. A virtue of the treatment approach is that it operates without the need to focus on individual responsibility, involving culpability or even the necessity to apportion moral blame.

The Kilbrandon Committee insisted that holding parents legally culpable for their children's action was unjustifiable and would be counter-productive. It argued at length against both the legal propriety of fining parents for their children's actions and requiring them to make compulsory restitution (paras 30–33). It maintained that co-operation was unlikely to be forthcoming if parents themselves were directly subject to supervision (para 21).

However, the Committee was clear that children's 'standards' were in part a consequence of their 'upbringing', or socialisation. The influences 'in the home' and among 'immediate associates' (subculture and peer group) must have a bearing on a young person's ideas of right and wrong, and standards of behaviour. The Report strives to adopt a middle course between blaming parents and according significance to the home environment in explaining the behaviour of young people. By implication at least some degree of moral responsibility will normally lie beyond the young persons themselves. The Report says that 'educative influences', including the measures for dealing with young people, are equally unavoidably 'society's responsibility' (para 81).

Equity and liberty objections

We may now address the principles of justice from which the Kilbrandon approach can be criticised. Equality before the law means that there ought to be impartiality in the application of legal rules and that certain procedural rights should be observed. It does not of course imply that there will be identity of outcomes of the judicial process; rather that differences in decision must arise from the fair application of relevant criteria.

There is nothing intrinsic to the doctrine of legal equality which requires that sameness or differences in treatment to be determined by any particular set of criteria. Although 'seriousness' of harm caused, 'cost' to the injured party, degree of 'culpability', and 'corrigibility' might be relevant according to one set of principles, what is needed for reform, or to provide remedial social education, might equally constitute the basis for legitimate discrimination. Therefore, the claim that the decisions of a hearings system are inherently unjust cannot be founded alone on the concept of legal equality. It is necessary either to make a convincing case for the criteria associated with punishment being uniquely valid or to show that remedial 'social education' provides no clear criterion for legitimate discrimination. The Kilbrandon Committee gives solid reasons for substantial doubt about the former applying to young people. We will return to consider the coherence of its ideas about treatment. Let us next consider the libertarian critique.

Separation of the judgment of proof and the adjudication of welfare in principle permits intervention in the lives of families only where there are publicly stated proven or accepted grounds. The legal entitlement to challenge the basis for intervention, we have seen, was recognised to be an important safeguard. However, even if this is supported by children and parents having access to court (with legal representation) at proof and appeal, it is unlikely to satisfy those who see privacy in family life to be fundamental. Some libertarians regard family life as near to sacrosanct, an area into which the agencies of the State (or uninvited others) should almost never go.

The Kilbrandon Committee was conscious that its proposals might permit more or earlier compulsory intervention than a system of punishment would allow. As we have seen, it had no illusions that both adults and children would sometimes view the measures taken as unwarranted interference or punishment, especially when children were removed from home (para 57). This did not of course mean that their perceptions should be decisive. The Report at this juncture fails sufficiently to insist that the perception of being punished does not make what is done punishment.[1]

As we have seen, the Kilbrandon Committee hoped at all stages to gain the co-operation of parents without compulsion. It cannot be denied that compulsory supervision, education or training of children (beyond that universally required by compulsory schooling) was a direct invasion of parental control. The loss of liberty in terms of formal rights in any compulsory measures is, in terms of legal rights, principally a loss to parents. While children may be the principal recipients of 'intervention', and in the main it is their conduct and associations which are subject to interference, the legal entitlement to decide who provides day-to-day care and supervision, or where a child is domiciled, normally lies with parents or legal guardians.

The Committee appeared to recognise that parents might be the principal objectors and that invasion of family autonomy might be a major public concern. This is not to say that the welfare approach must concede that it entails the greater loss of real liberty to children. It could be argued that the negative conception of liberty – the liberty to be left alone or only punished – may be overridden by a deeper conception of liberty which is concerned with empowerment that comes through social education and self-development. However, the paternalism of the Kilbrandon approach must be recognised.

The Kilbrandon Committee was fully aware of the 'liberal' objection. Following the 'educative principle' might in practice make an 'appreciable inroad into personal and family life, amounting to loss of liberty' which might be 'unaccept-able in our society'. If this view is taken, it says, 'it is necessary to have a practical alternative'. The Committee believed that the *status quo* which tries to combine the competing models is not a possible option, the only alternative being to return to a purer form of the 'crime-punishment' concept, which it regarded as 'altogether unacceptable' (para 80).

Protection of society and deterrence
The criticism that the Kilbrandon Committee gave too little consideration to those harmed by children, or to the interests of society as a whole, is implicitly made by the popular view that the children's hearings system is too soft on young offenders. On the face of it, this is a claim about the workings of the system and as such should be left for consideration later. However, it has seldom been a judgment based on an actual assessment of the operation of the system; rather it is an objection to the adoption of the welfare philosophy itself.

We have noted already that the Kilbrandon Committee at a number of points mentioned the place of public protection. Its primary task was to propose measures which would 'effect, so far as this can be achieved by public action, the reduction, and ideally the elimination, of delinquency' (para 12). While it was

---

[1] This is more fully argued in 'Justice and Welfare' (Lockyer, 1982). However, the Committee recognises that its position might be at odds with those who regarded minimum intervention as the greatest good.

clear that public interest in combating delinquency was not the Committee's only concern, it was the criterion by which it recognised that its recommendations would be judged. It should also be noticed that the fact that ordinary members of the public were adopted as the critical decision-makers would give some measure of assurance that the public interest would not in practice be left out of account.

Some radical critics of the system have argued that in fact the welfare criterion allows for too much 'social control'. The unlimited discretion to intervene in the upbringing of children makes possible an excessive imposition of the public upon the private, more so than a system of punishment would permit (Morris and McIsaac, 1978). While the needs of the child might be formally paramount, the needs of society not to be offended against may in fact take precedence (Watson, 1980).

Despite both the reference to combating delinquency in the Report and the view taken by some libertarian critics that too much imposition of society's values or interests is possible, it cannot be denied that the central doctrine placed the interests of the child alone at the centre of its rationale for intervention. We should notice that the Social Work (Scotland) Act 1968 uniquely made no reference to public protection as a legitimate criterion for making dispositional decisions.

It is open to debate how far the preventive approach of the Kilbrandon Committee incorporates or is at odds with the protection of society. A full examination would require an in-depth analysis of the complex relationship between the interests of children and those of society as a whole in all our child-rearing practice and family law. Suffice for now to say, in general terms, that it is difficult to conceive of any genuine long-term conflict of interest between children and adult society. This does not mean that there are no genuine conflicts of interest between individuals, or individuals and society as a whole. The law is one mechanism for regulating and harmonising these. The critical question is whether the principles of the children's hearings system provide for the just treatment of individual children, which is in step with the general protective purposes of the criminal and civil law.

While there is no absence of concern for the public interest, nor lack of reference to public protection, there is what amounts to an implicit rejection of one of the major arguments which justify the use of criminal sanctions, namely the deterrence argument. At no point does the Report suggest that the loss or suffering caused by compulsory intervention might have value either in deterring the individual from further offences or, more importantly, deterring other potential young offenders. Deterrence is of course an intended object of punishment. Its absence may provide grounds for the view that public protection is being sold short.

Of course any threatened form of 'intervention' if unwanted by the recipient will influence conduct under conditions where calculation of consequences comes into play. Therefore, it is not only punishment which might deter. The prospect of compulsory measures might equally provide a reason or an inducement to modify behaviour of parents and children. The difference between punishment and compulsory measures of care is that the deterrent effect of the former is part of the purpose, while in the latter it is a latent function (Lockyer, 1982).

In general the approach was to reform by education rather than to control by threat of consequences. The Report suggests that proceeding by seeking co-operation is always to be preferred. The most constructive way of influencing children and parents is through 'social education'. Either the efficacy or the morality of deterrence, or both, may be being doubted where children are concerned. What is clear is that state-authorised punishment is an unacceptable method of socialising the generality of delinquent children.

Exceptional cases

The Kilbrandon Committee seemed to believe that protecting society was on all fours with the welfare approach to juvenile justice, without generally needing the threat of punishment to deter. However, this must be qualified by the Committee's acceptance that where some of the most serious offences were involved there would remain a public interest in prosecuting children in the courts. The offences which the Committee put into this category were 'murder, attempted murder, culpable homicide, wounding with intent to cause grievous bodily harm and rape' (para 124).

This might be viewed as an implicit recognition either that deterrence after all has its place or that the public desire for retribution must be heeded in the gravest cases. The decision to continue the traditional discretion of the Lord Advocate (the Crown's chief law officer in Scotland) is intoned in a manner which makes clear only the Committee's deference to the Scottish legal establishment. Whether this demonstrates its conservatism or its astute pragmatism is open to debate, but there is little doubt that the support of the Scottish legal establishment was crucial to the acceptability of the proposals within the Scottish Office.

The discretion to bring some young offenders into the jurisdiction of the adult court allows that the character of 'evil deeds' may after all take precedence over the young offenders' needs. This involves the operation of a double standard which threatens the integrity of the welfare approach (Spencer and Bruce, 1976). Defining 'seriousness' or 'gravity' in terms of the characteristics or consequences of the antisocial act reverts to an adoption of criminal justice criteria. It creates a distinction between two categories of young offender based on deeds rather than needs, which was what the Kilbrandon philosophy began by consciously setting aside.

The treatment model

Leaving aside appeals to traditional ideas about justice, the area in which the Kilbrandon philosophy has been found most deficient is in the substance of what is proposed to replace punishment. The complaint is that no coherent alternative is proposed. It has been suggested that this has something to do with the lack of clarity in thinking about juvenile crime. This has the consequence of creating ambiguity over what is meant by treatment and leads to a lack of substance in the idea of remedial social education.

Many of the early commentators claimed that the Kilbrandon Committee favoured a 'medical model' of treatment. Taken literally, this would suggest that offending behaviour was something akin to physical or mental illness. The implications of this are far-reaching. It would imply that antisocial behaviour was determined by some malady or malfunction of the individual beyond his or her will to control. This would suggest that appeals to reason or seeking agreement to alter conduct would be inappropriate methods of attempting to bring about change. Diagnosis and cure would be matters of expert analysis, judgment and application. There are a great many objections to any system constructed on these assumptions, not least of which have been evinced by totalitarian political régimes.

There is very little evidence that in fact the Kilbrandon Committee did adopt a medical model. There is just one point in the Report where an analogy between medical treatment and treating the offender is used. In a section sub-headed 'Alteration of Treatment' it is said:

> 'Even were our knowledge about causes of crime and the reformation of offenders much fuller than it is, it is inconceivable that a court could guarantee to have chosen, at the moment of the commencement of the sentence, the exact treatment ... appropriate to the individual person before it. The doctor prescribes a course of treatment and observes the patient's response to it over a period. On the basis of his observations he continues the treatment or prescribes a different course, more drastic or less as the situation appears to him to require' (para 54).

The above argument is the basis for hearings having the discretion to review, continue, change or terminate treatment measures. The use of a medical analogy does not of course entail that hearings' judgments are modelled on decisions in medicine, nor that a clinical paradigm is lurking in the background. The alacrity with which commentators have attributed the medical model to the Kilbrandon Committee, it has been suggested, is explained by the ease with which the position can be dispatched by the academic (Martin, *et al*, 1981, p4). However, suspicion of the influence of the medical paradigm arises in part because of its weight in crude and discredited early theories of delinquency.

The Kilbrandon Committee made no attempt to declare a position with regard to the debate about the causes of delinquency. Whether or not this is a weakness depends on how fruitful we regard the products of this debate to be. If we allow that none of the general accounts, whether biological, psychodynamic, sociological, or class related, are singularly acceptable, then not electing among them would seem the wisest strategy. That the Kilbrandon Committee failed to consider or make reference to the substantial literature on delinquency was perhaps no great loss, but a clearer statement of theoretical neutrality, or causal eclecticism, might have gone some way to scotch the idea that delinquency was being regarded as an 'illness', which required something akin to medical treatment in response.

Social education

We have noted that 'something having gone wrong with the upbringing process' was the general aetiological position adopted by the Kilbrandon Committee. This is compatible with almost any theory of delinquency, except those which are singularly deterministic. Whatever factors have contributed to any particular child's problems (whether manifest in their antisocial behaviour, or in any kind of failure to thrive), their occurrence is prima facie evidence of some of the 'influences to the good' having 'fallen short'. Insofar as 'upbringing' in all cases is a relevant factor which might have made a difference, its failure to do so may be regarded as the most general cause.

This does not commit the Kilbrandon Committee to the belief that upbringing is the single or most weighty contributory factor in all cases where something goes wrong. It means only that for anyone concerned to bring about change, the significant practical 'cause' is the factor or condition which is amenable to change – or that which can be 'manipulated' and to which blame can be attached (Hart and Honore, 1959). Governments may be able to affect all manner of conditions relevant to delinquency, and therefore it is appropriate to identify social causes of delinquency within the ambit of their policy-making. Any factors whose absence or presence makes a difference to the general phenomenon can constitute a general cause. But concentration on the family and other agents of social education usually offers the best chance of bringing about change in the lives of individual young people. Therefore, the Kilbrandon Committee's general aetiological claim rightly focuses attention on where the juvenile justice system might make a difference.

What Kilbrandon meant by 'education for social living' was both wide and rather vague. It incorporated 'training measures' but could include anything that might influence care and upbringing, to meet a child's physical, emotional and intellectual needs. We have seen that where influences at home and normal schooling had proved inadequate, a new agency was expected to supplement and co-ordinate resources, 'to help others help themselves'. Clearly, the children's hearing was envisaged as an integral part of a process of social education. It was not only the occasion for deciding upon and activating the necessary intervention; it was expected to elicit the co-operation of the family in the 'appropriate measures'. Lay members of the public, professional educators and specialists in child care were each apparently expected to work with families.

The nature of decisions
We have seen that the 'matching field organisation' which had the primary duty to meet the needs of children dealt with by hearings was the local authority social work department with a director. This was the agency to carry out what the Kilbrandon Committee described as 'social education'. Specifying what this might encompass was a task taken on largely by a body of newly created social workers. The Social Work (Scotland) Act 1968 created the generic social worker in Scotland as well as the system which they were to service. However, from the start there was particular uncertainty about how the role of social work was to be differentiated from other professions, the reporter and lay members.

When those who had to define the social workers' territory and specify their training needs examined the Kilbrandon Report, they found it inadequate for their purposes. It gave no clear guidance on when to propose intervention and how to conduct remedial action. This led some to conclude that there was no basis in principle for separating the lay panel member's frame of reference from that of the social worker. In the view of some commentators social workers had their professional judgment usurped by amateurs (May, 1977; May, 1979; May and Smith, 1980).

We shall examine later how the different parties came to view their roles and what tensions this created in practice. Suffice for now to consider what can be derived from the Report. It must be said that the Kilbrandon Committee did not specify clearly distinct tasks for panel members and those who were to carry out the social education they envisaged. The failure to articulate the justification for vesting the central decision with lay members of the public was a significant omission. This does not mean that none was possible, only that none was made explicit.

It can be argued that both the validity of ordinary opinion and the essentially non-technical character of the intervention decision were in fact implicit in the very conceptions of 'proper upbringing' and 'social education'. It is debatable how much specialist knowledge and expertise is required in identifying children's needs, or identifying the deficiencies in child rearing and family life style. Clearly, psychiatrists and paediatricians have a valuable contribution to make. Equally, commonsense, knowledge and insight into how families function are also pertinent. However, the crux of the matter is that whatever expert or commonsense views may be put forward about how to effect changes, both what is acceptable upbringing, and how far the state is entitled to interfere with the autonomy of families, essentially involve a moral judgment. That is to say, it is a judgment not reducible to any kind of specialist or technical knowledge. Therefore, in principle it is not the preserve of any profession, or body of experts. This does not mean that professionals can have no opinion about when it is desirable to interfere in the normal life of children, or override parental rights; only that their opinions should have no privileged or ultimate authority. Also there may be good reason for not leaving paid officials with the final power to decide on such matters (Asquith, 1983; Watson, 1982; Lockyer, 1989).

The Kilbrandon Committee did not spell out the criteria on which participants in the hearings system must take decisions. However, its acknowledgement of the part to be played by children, and their families, was recognition that 'social education' is something which cannot be entirely externally determined and imposed. It is essentially a co-operative enterprise, where the decision about what is to be done must be part of the learning process. The system envisaged allows the determination of acceptable upbringing for a particular child to be arrived at by discussion among family, professionals and representatives of the community. Moreover, giving the final decision to ordinary citizens, recognises the open, public, and democratic character of setting standards in such matters. The fact that the Kilbrandon Committee avoided laying down specific content and standards for 'social education' need not be regarded as a fault.

3 : The 1968 Act and the Actors

The hearings system

What follows in this section is an outline of the workings of the hearings system under the legislation which, with minor amendment, was in operation between April 1971 and April 1997. It will serve as an introduction to its current functioning, because the Children (Scotland) Act 1995 involves relatively few changes in practice. The significant modifications introduced by the 1995 Act will be discussed in Chapter 7[1] and later chapters.

Grounds for referral

Part III of the Social Work (Scotland) Act 1968 which sets out the provisions for the children's hearings system is entitled Children in Need of Compulsory Measures of Care. For the purposes of this part of the Act, 'care' is defined as including 'protection, control, guidance and treatment' (s 32(3)).[2] A child 'may be in need of compulsory measures of care' if any of eight 'conditions', amended to eleven, mentioned in s 32(2), was satisfied. These were:

(a)   being beyond the control of parents;
(b)   falling into bad associations or exposure to moral danger;
(c)   being caused unnecessary suffering by neglect or lack of parental care;
(d)   being offended against or being a member of a household of a child offended against;
(dd) being, or likely to become, a member of a household of a child offender;[3]
(e)   being female and a victim of incest, or female and in a household of such a victim;
(f)   having failed to attend school (without reasonable excuse);
(g)   having committed an offence;
(gg) having misused a volatile substance by deliberately inhaling;[4]
(h)   being referred from another jurisdiction or court;
(i)   being in the care of the local authority and requiring special measures for care and control.[5]

The above are commonly called the *grounds of referral* but it should be noted

---

[1]   This section can be passed over by those familiar with the children's hearings system. B. Kearney's *Children's Hearings and the Sheriff Court* (1987) provides the fullest and most authoritative account of the legislation.
[2]   Section numbers refer to the Social Work (Scotland) Act 1968, as amended.
[3]   Added by the Children Act 1975.
[4]   Added by the Solvent Abuse (Scotland) Act 1983.
[5]   Added by the Health and Social Services and Social Security Adjudications Act 1983.

that any of the 'conditions' must be supported by a 'Statement of Facts' which together constitute the 'grounds for referral of the case to a hearing' and which are made available to the family prior to a hearing.

Anyone who has reasonable cause to believe a child may be in need of compulsory measures of care may give the reporter ('an officer, whole-time or part-time' (s 36)) such information as they are able to discover (s 37(1)). The largest number of initial referrals come (in descending order) from the police, social work departments and schools. The reporter will make such additional investigation as he or she 'may think necessary', then determine on one of three options: take 'no further action' (s 39(1)); refer the case to the social work department for them to provide 'advice, guidance and assistance' on a voluntary basis (s 39(2)); refer the case to a children's hearing (s 39(3)). The first option means no *official* action by the reporter but it might involve the family being seen by the reporter, or an arrangement with the police to give a formal warning, if appropriate. Referral to a children's hearing will take place 'where it appears that the child is in need of compulsory measures of care' and there is sufficient evidence to establish at least one of the grounds for referral.

Where a reporter has decided to initiate a children's hearing a series of tasks follow. These include arranging the time and place of the hearing; giving due notice to family, panel members and the social work department; and providing appropriate documents to relevant parties. The local authority must provide suitable accommodation for the hearing (s 34(3)) and a 'report on the child and his social background' (s 39(4)); the chairman of the children's panel must arrange for three members to hear the case, usually through the provision of a service roster (HR 5).[6] The child and parents must receive notification and, unless a review with no new grounds, copies of the grounds for referral with seven clear days' notice. Hearing members must receive relevant specified documents within a minimum of three days before the hearing (HR 6,7,8,16, 27).

The reporter has also to arrange children's hearings to review existing supervision, either to comply with the time-limit of one year (s 48(3), (4A) or sooner at the behest of the local authority, child or parent (s 48(2), (4)), or to consider making or reviewing warrants to detain a child in a place of safety (ss 37, 40, 43, 58E), or to consider cases referred by courts or transferred from other jurisdictions, or to provide advice to court on request (HR 21), or to continue the consideration of cases suspended for further information (s 44(3), (4)). These types of hearings follow a similar pattern except that the grounds for 'warrant hearings' are different, remitted cases from the court cannot be challenged, and 'advice hearings' have no decisions to be appealed.

Persons present at a children's hearing
At the standard hearing there will normally be three panel members, a reporter, a child or children, parents (or guardian), and a member of the social work

---

[6] HR is the abbreviation used here for the Children's Hearings (Scotland) Rules 1971, as amended in 1986 (SI 1986/2291). These were replaced in December 1996.

department. There may also be other participants and observers. Provisions covering those who have absolute or qualified rights and duties to be present are quite complicated. Any recognised 'parent' or 'guardian' (excluding fathers of 'illegitimate' children unless afforded guardian status) shall attend the children's hearing at all stages unless the hearing members decide it would be 'unreasonable' to require it, or their attendance is 'unnecessary' to consideration of the case (s 41(2)). Prosecution of a parent for failing to attend without dispensation is a possibility (s 41(3)), but has been largely used as a threat to secure attendance at a rescheduled hearing. The children's hearing does have the authority to proceed without an absent parent's agreement to the grounds (s 42(8)), and this provision is taken advantage of if his or her presence is deemed unnecessary.

Children referred are obliged to attend unless a children's hearing is satisfied that their attendance 'is not necessary for a just hearing of that case', particularly one of alleged abuse, or in a case where it would be 'detrimental to the interest of the child to be present' (s 40(2)). The entitlement to proceed 'in the absence of the child' had two difficulties, one theoretical the other practical. First, the authority of the hearing to dispense with the child's presence left unclear whether, none the less, a child had a right to attend. Second, there was a major practical problem in the exercise of discretion over the child's or parents' obligation to attend lying with the hearing which considers the case. Parties needed to know in advance whether or not they must attend, but there was no statutory means of making an authoritative decision in advance. A variety of conventions were adopted involving either reporters exercising a preliminary discretion, usually with prior consultation with the nominated hearing chairman, or by a 'business meeting' of hearing members – a doubtful practice before being endorsed by the 1995 Act (s 64).

There has never been an absolute requirement for either reporter or social worker to be present at a children's hearing. The reporter's only duty at the hearing specified by the rules is to 'keep or cause to be kept' a record of proceedings (HR 30), which implies that the presence of a qualified reporter is not essential. However, in practice most hearing chairmen would view reporters as 'required or expedient for the proper conduct of the proceedings of the children's hearing' (HR 14(e)).

The extent to which reporters participate in hearings varies with individual styles and local practice. For the most part, they act as legal advisers to the hearing, but they may be asked to explain what led them to consider the need for compulsory measures or why they are seeking a warrant. In some places it has been normal for the reporter to draft the hearing's 'reasons for decision' for the chairman to sign (HR 9(3)), though elsewhere this practice has not been endorsed.

The presence of a member of the social work department is normally regarded as essential. The person preferred is the author of the report for an initial hearing, or, in cases being reviewed, the key worker with the main responsibility for carrying out supervision. Other care providers (foster parents, residential staff, intermediate treatment workers) and authors of other reports – psychologists, child-guidance staff or teachers – may also be present. In practice any representative of an agency which has had an involvement with the child and family and has a contribution to make might be invited to attend by the reporter.

Children and parents are entitled to be accompanied by a 'representative' at a hearing. The rule states that a representative 'shall assist' the person or persons they represent 'in the discussion of the case' (HR 11(2)). A representative may be anyone, including a lawyer, though contentiously no legal aid has been available for this purpose. That family members may share their representative accords with the consensual rather than the adversarial model of the hearing. Most importantly, representatives are not permitted to act as agents in the sense of being permitted to speak instead of the parties they represent.[7]

In 1986 hearing chairmen and sheriffs acquired the power to appoint, and the duty to consider appointing, safeguarders in circumstances where they believe 'there is or may be a conflict ... between the interest of a child and those of his parent' to safeguard the child's interests 'in the proceedings' (s 34A). Safeguarders are entitled to attend the hearing with a right to all documents and to participate fully; they are also expected to provide a report (Social Work Services Group, 1985). They have the power to appeal the decisions of hearings on behalf of the child. Safeguarders have been used sparingly by courts and hearings (for reasons explained later). It remains to be seen whether this will change as a result of the wider terms under which they may be appointed under the 1995 Act.[8]

Children's hearings are conducted in private and nobody shall be present unless 'necessary for the proper consideration of the case' or permitted by the chairman. Bona fide representatives of the press cannot be excluded. However, to date the general prohibition on any reporting which leads to identification of children (s 58(1)) has meant that there has been very little media interest in attending hearings – with a few notorious exceptions. The people who may be permitted to observe at the chairman's discretion include Children's Panel Advisory Committee members, trainee panel members and social workers, researchers, or anyone else whose presence may be justified 'by special circumstance' (HR 14(a)–(e)). In the first place the reporter and sometimes the panel chairman may in fact vet those wishing to approach the hearing; a widespread practice is for families to be asked whether they object to observers. However, the hearing chairman has an overall duty to 'take all reasonable steps to ensure that the number of persons present at a children's hearing at any one time are kept to a minimum' (s 25(2)).

Conduct of the hearing
The conduct of the children's hearing is largely in the hands of the hearing chairman. It is both the chairman's duty to ensure compliance with the specified procedure and his or her brief to exercise discretion in procedural matters within the law. However, the Act and the rules were not entirely consistent in differentiating between the kinds of responsibilities which lie with the chairman

---

[7] This remains the case under the 1995 Act.
[8] See Chapters 5 and 7.

individually and those which lie with the 'children's hearing' (meaning the three panel members) collectively. For instance, the children's hearing shall make inquiry into the child's age (s 55) and the chairman shall consider the need to appoint a safeguarder (s 34A). In practice the formal aspects of the hearings are principally carried out by the person in the chair, and substantive decisions, even if procedural, are taken collectively, panel members sharing equally the responsibility for focusing on the required elements of discussion.

After all present are introduced and the child or children identified (usually by age, name and address), the purpose of the hearing is explained by the hearing chairman (HR 19(1)). If it is a first hearing, or there are new grounds, these will be 'explained' in a manner appropriate to the child's age. A common practice is for them first to be read verbatim as set out in the formal statement which the family have received, then put into simpler, more colloquial language (s 42(1)). If understood and accepted by the child and accepted by the parents, the hearing proceeds. If not understood or denied, the hearing members must decide either to instruct the reporter to make application for proof or discharge the case. Where one or some of a number of grounds are accepted, or part of a ground for referral is accepted, it must be decided whether to proceed on the basis of what has been accepted. Where the decision is to apply to the sheriff to consider whether the grounds are established the chairman explains the purpose of the application, the duty to attend and the possible consequences of not doing so (s 42(3)). Proof hearings before the sheriff are technically 'in chambers', which means there is no right of public access, but the normal rules for hearing evidence in court apply. The procedure is a 'civil proceedings *sui generis*' (*Kennedy* v *O* 1975 SC 308). The standard of proof is the civil standard of the 'balance of probability', except where the grounds for referral are an alleged offence, in which case the criminal standard of 'beyond reasonable doubt' applies. If the grounds are found established the case returns to a hearing for consideration of disposal.

While there is no standard course that the hearing must take, the rules specify certain elements of what a fair consideration of the case must include (HR 19(2)). Commonly the starting-point at a hearing with new grounds will be a discussion of the circumstances which led to the referral. Consideration must be given to 'the report on the child and his background' (the 'social background' or 'social enquiry report'). Any judicial remit or other relevant document must also be considered; as should any other report, including one requested or provided by the manager of a residential establishment, by a school, a safeguarder, or an assessment requested by a previous hearing. Under the original rules, children and their parents had no entitlement to a copy of reports. Their contents should normally have been 'shared' between authors and family members prior to hearings as a matter of good practice, but this will not necessarily have happened. According to the rules, it is the hearing chairman's duty 'to inform the child and his parent *of the substance* of any report or documents' if it appears 'material to the manner in which the case of the child should be disposed of, and that its *disclosure would be not detrimental to the interests of the child*' (emphasis added) (HR 19(3)). The absence of an entitlement of children and parents to see copies of reports was a controversial issue. It was supported by the court (*Kennedy* v *A* 1986 SLT 358), but overtaken by an adverse judgment of the European Court (*McMichael* v *United Kingdom* (1995) 20 EHRR 205). The current rules now give adults entitled to be at hearings copies of reports, but the entitlement of children has not been clarified (CHR 5(3)).[9] There are major issues associated with access to reports and these are discussed in later chapters.

The hearing must 'discuss the case' with the child, parents, any safeguarder and representative attending and endeavour to obtain their views on possible disposals (HR 19(2)c, d). There is no prompt statutory requirement to include the social worker, or any other author of a report in the discussion, but invariably, if present, they will be invited to speak to their reports and take a full part in the consideration of the disposal. There is no set time on the length of hearings. The average time per case has been estimated at forty minutes, though hearings lasting over an hour are quite common and this is probably the norm in less busy rural areas (Lockyer, 1992, para 7.7). A hearing may be adjourned and resumed on the same day, typically, for example, to identify an emergency placement (HR 9(2)). A case may be continued 'for further investigation' and a child could be required to attend or reside in any place for up to twenty-one days for the purpose of assessment (s 43(3), (4)).

After the hearing 'have considered the case' but 'before the conclusion of the hearing', the decision must be made and communicated to the parties. The established practice is to reach a decision in front of the family without adjournment. Each panel member in turn gives his or her judgment with reasons for it. It can be a majority verdict. At the conclusion of the hearing the chairman is required to (a) explain the decision, (b) summarise the reasons for it, (c) inform the child, parent and safeguarder (if there is one) of their entitlement to appeal against the decision, and (d) inform them of the right to receive a statement of the decision in writing. It is standard practice to advise on the entitlements and time scales for seeking a review when a compulsory requirement has been made. The chairman makes 'or causes to be made' a statement of written reasons for the decision immediately after the hearing, usually when the family have left, but on some occasions while the family are present (HR 9(3)(d)).

Disposals, reviews and appeals

Children's hearings can either discharge the case or make a supervision requirement. Under the 1968 Act supervision requirements are divided into two classes: requiring the child to 'submit to supervision in accordance with such conditions as they [the hearing] may impose' (s 44(1)(a)); and requiring the child to reside in a named 'residential establishment' with the same possibility of 'conditions' attached (s 44(1)(b)). In reality the more important distinction is whether the child is permitted to remain at home, or is to be placed away from the parental home. The away-from-home option may be in a residential school or children's home managed by the local authority, defined as a 'residential establishment'

[9] CHR is the abbreviation used here for the Children's Hearings (Scotland) Rules 1996 (SI 1996/3261).

(s 44(1)(b)); or it may be a substitute family home provided by approved foster carers or community parents, which are requirements under s 44(1)(a) with 'a condition of residence'. Thus the division in section s 44(1) does not neatly correspond to the 'at home' and 'away from home' distinction, which for the purposes of gathering statistics was unhelpful.

Theoretically, there is no restriction on what could be a 'condition' of a requirement, except that it must apply to the child who is the subject of the order. In practice requirements of *attendance* at day centres, clinics, intermediate treatment programmes, and limitations on *access* or *contact* with family or other specified persons, have most frequently been the type imposed. The use of conditions by hearings to specify what 'supervision' should entail has been an area of potential conflict with what some social workers regard as professional discretion. The 1968 Act gave the local authority both the duty 'to give effect to a supervision requirement made by a children's hearing' (s 44(5)) and the duty 'to provide and maintain such residential and other establishments as may be required' (s 59(1)).

In 1983 (as a result of the Health and Social Services and Social Security Adjudications Act) provisions were introduced for the placement of children in 'secure accommodation'. This departed significantly from the established division of principle that social workers recommend and implement and that hearings dispose. The new provisions permit children's hearings to make a condition which only *authorises* the use of secure accommodation (where it is necessary to prevent a child from 'absconding' or 'he is likely to injure himself or other persons'), whereas the director of social work and the head of the residential establishment have the final discretion as to whether secure provision will be used (s 58E). There are arguments for and against this arrangement.[10]

All decisions taken by hearings which prescribe positive intervention are of limited duration. No supervision requirement can remain in force without review beyond one year (s 48(3)) and a local authority must seek a review of supervision as soon as it is deemed unnecessary or inappropriate (s 47(1)). The parents or the child may require a review of any new requirement after three months, or of an existing requirement after six months (s 48(4)). Where a disposal cannot be made but it is necessary to issue a warrant to retain a child in a place of safety, either for their own protection or to prevent them running away, the maximum duration of the order is twenty-one days, renewable once by a children's hearing, and for a further two periods by the sheriff on cause shown by the reporter (s 37(2), (4), (5), (5A)).

All substantive decisions, including those concerning warrants, can be appealed against in the first place by the child or parent, or safeguarder (on the child's behalf) to the sheriff in chambers (s 49(1); CPR 12(2)).[11] The wording of the 1968 Act is that 'where the sheriff is satisfied that the decision of the children's hearing is not justified in all the circumstances he shall allow the appeal' (s 49(5)).

---

[10] See Chapter 5.
[11] CPR is the abbreviation used here for the Social Work (Sheriff Court Procedure Rules) 1971.

It has been suggested that while the primary onus is on the appellant to satisfy the sheriff, extensive powers to call for additional information suggest that he or she may adopt something more of an 'inquisitorial approach' than is usual in our adversarial tradition (Kearney, 1987, p328). The sheriff may see all reports and statements available to the children's hearing, along with reports of their proceedings and their reasons for decision, and may examine the reporter and other compilers of reports. The sheriff can also 'call for any further reports which he considers may assist him in deciding the appeal' (s 49(3)). This allows not only the possibility of the appeal considering evidence of irregularities in the hearings' proceedings, but also obtaining information relevant to the disposal not available to the hearing. If upholding the appeal, the sheriff has the option to discharge (or recall a warrant), or return the case to a hearing for reconsideration.[12]

A further appeal from the sheriff to the Court of Session is possible, not on the merits but by way of a stated case on a point of law, or any irregularity in the conduct of a case (s 50(1)). This is the final level of appeal. As well as the parties with a right to appeal to the sheriff, the reporter 'acting on behalf of the hearing', may appeal to the Court of Session. While there is no mechanism for the hearing to instruct the reporter to contest the sheriff's adjudication, this implies perhaps that only where the sheriff on appeal overturns a hearing's decision should a reporter contemplate an appeal to the Court of Session. When an appeal to the sheriff is lodged a hearing may be requested by parent or child to suspend the operation of the decision appealed. The interim decision is not itself appealable.

The numbers of appeals at both levels within the hearings system have annually been at a low level. In most years fewer than 100 cases are appealed to the sheriff and stated cases are annually in single figures. The infrequency of appeals is sometimes considered a cause for concern, implying that children and parents are unwilling to exercise their rights. It might be indicative of a passivity, lack of faith in the judicial process, or poor representation. However, it must be remembered that the facility to seek a review hearing in most cases provides an equal or more effective means of having a decision reversed, without the possible expense or the heightened anxiety of judicial proceedings. Therefore, comparisons with numbers of appeals in other jurisdictions where appeals are the only means of seeking a review are misleading. The relative scarcity of stated cases has meant a slower development of informative case-law than might have been desirable. However, it has had the effect of producing a largely consistent body of authoritative interpretation by which professionals and lay decision-makers have been guided.[13]

The principal actors
Before the new system became operational the personnel to serve in the two entirely new offices had to be recruited and, so far as was possible, trained. Since neither reporters nor panel members had any forerunners or close equivalents in

---

[12] Notably the sheriff's power of examination and disposal are expanded by the 1995 Act. For discussion, see Chapters 7, 10 and 17.
[13] For the important judgments in this regard, see Chapter 10.

other jurisdictions, nobody had any exactly relevant experience upon which to base selection and training. The appointment criteria for both offices had to be constructed with reference largely to what people imagined were the qualities needed. Although local authority social work departments did obtain senior staff who had formerly worked in children's departments and the probation service, there were few social workers who had the breadth of experience to carry out the range of work required. The body of central government with the responsibility for establishing mechanisms and providing the guidance for implementing the Act was the Social Work Services Group (SWSG). They were a group of professional civil servants and social work advisers formed in 1967 and attached to the Scottish Education Department.

Reporters
The appointment of reporters was made the joint responsibility of local authorities and central government. The former employed them and bore their operational costs, but their independence was secured by reserving to the Secretary of State the power to dismiss or suspend them. The Secretary of State was also empowered to prescribe qualifications, but this was an option not exercised. The Kilbrandon Committee had suggested that the reporter 'should preferably be an officer combining a legal qualification with a period of administrative experience relating to child welfare and educational services' (para 98). However, the requirement for the reporter to be a hybrid, with skills in administration, knowledge and judgment of children's needs (not just administration of 'child welfare'), as well as knowledge of the law, led to a reluctance to prescribe specific qualifications. Whether or not reporters ought to have a qualification in law has remained an issue of contention throughout the history of the hearings system (McLean, 1983; Grant, 1975; Kearney, 1992; Finlayson, 1992).

Among the first appointees (men and women in equal numbers) about half were solicitors with experience in private practice or local authority work; the rest mainly had backgrounds in work with young people, a significant group having formerly been probation officers. Preliminary 'training' was organised by SWSG at which the new reporters received a varied diet of speakers, visits and an eclectic reading list.[14] The diversity of skills required by the model reporter could not be expected to have been possessed by each in advance of appointment; at best they were possessed only collectively, by the pre-service group. No doubt the hope was that individuals with varied backgrounds would learn from each other at preliminary training. The Scottish Children's Reporter Association provided a valuable forum for sharing experience once the system was in operation. Only the large authorities could boast anything like a team with a diversity of relevant skills and experience, and even here the tendency was for individuals to be lone decision-makers. Yet it would be a mistake to depict the official at the centre of

---

[14] For an entertaining account of the beginnings of the reporter service, see *A Distinctive Task: Reflections on the Reporter Service 1970–1996*, edited by Sally Kuenssberg (1996).

the hearings system as operating in isolation. In essence, the job brought immediate contact with established agencies like police, procurators fiscal, courts and schools, and a close association with social workers and panel members.

What gave the holders of the new office so crucial an influence in establishing the character of the hearing system were two factors. First, their judgments were pivotal in deciding which children and families entered the system. Therefore, in large measure they orchestrated the demands on other agencies. Secondly, reporters took a leading role in determining the character and practice of hearings. Here they were the full-time officers working in close liaison with a large and diverse group of part-time volunteers. As the 'professionals' they were active in supporting, advising and even part training 'their' panel members – as reporters in the early days were inclined to regard the local panel (for example, see Margaret Kernohan in Kuenssberg (ed), 1996). The close relationship between reporters and panel members was largely considered a strength, though it came to be viewed in some quarters as an undesirable lack of independence. Whether the lay members were too reliant on the reporter within the hearing itself was a moot point, but their dependence on the full-time official for administrative purposes was inevitable, the more so given the policy of panel recruitment and the focus of early panel training.

Panel recruitment and Children's Panel Advisory Committees

As we have noted, the Kilbrandon Committee gave no deep consideration to justifying a particular policy of selection from volunteers, but suggested they were likely to be drawn from the professions who were 'specially qualified to consider children's problems'. However, the White Paper, Social Work and the Community (1966), stressed the importance of community involvement; thus panel members were to be 'representatives of the community' with 'personal knowledge of the community to which the child belongs' (para 81). Both the Kilbrandon Committee's view of individual qualifications and the White Paper's emphasis on community representation had some influence on the initial policy of selection. There was an extensive debate in the academic literature, and among those responsible for guiding and implementing policy, as to how these two approaches were to be reconciled.

The 1968 Act adopted one proposal of the White Paper by assigning the job of recommending members for appointment by the Secretary of State to locally established Children's Panel Advisory Committees (CPACs), rather than to sheriffs as the Kilbrandon Committee had proposed. These advisory committees were hybrids composed of Secretary of State appointees and local authority representatives, reflecting not only the partnership of central and local government, but also a balance between expertise and representativeness.

Recruitment and selection were the most pressing task for the newly appointed CPACs. The success or failure of the hearings system, it was thought, would depend on whether 'suitable members of the community are willing and able to serve on the panels in adequate numbers' (Guidance, SW 7/1969, para 76). We are informed by a leading ex-civil servant at the Scottish Office that one of the main objections to the proposed system was the doubt that Scotland could provide the appropriate number of 'citizen volunteers'. He refers us to the fact that 'Scotland did not have the tradition of voluntary government service exemplified by the Justices of the Peace in England and Wales' (Cowperthwaite, 1988, pp 42–43). This begs the question of whether the Scottish system was looking for 'citizens' who were the equivalent in background to the lay magistracy in England and Wales. Their tradition of service has its origins among the ruling classes whose administration of justice (as the Lord Chancellor's office reminds potential recruits) goes back 'at least to the fourteenth century' (Lord Chancellor's Department, 1984).

The first authoritative guidance from SWSG on panel member selection suggested that 'the success of the system depended' on reaching 'people whose occupation and circumstances have hitherto prevented them from taking part in helping and advising young people or who might not have previously thought of themselves as candidates for public service' (SW 7/1969, Appendix A, para 1). This gave the clear message that the new system intended to engage a wider cross-section of the Scottish public than was the case either with magistrates or with traditional volunteers. This suggested that the work might not be too demanding of time, that there would be adequate support and remuneration, and even that membership need not to be confined to those who saw themselves as 'pillars of the establishment'. These considerations may have had a bearing on how the task and the system were perceived by those who came forward for selection and those who selected them.

The same SWSG circular went on to suggest criteria for selection based on a balance between the ideas of expertise (or competence) and representativeness to be found in the two authoritative sources. The first suggested 'knowledge and experience in dealing with families'; the second suggested that members should be 'drawn from a wide range of neighbourhood, age group and income group'. However, the predominant thrust of the guidance which was to carry most weight in the selection process was its invocation of 'personal qualities'. These included 'an absence of bias and prejudice'; 'genuine interest in the needs of children in trouble and their relationship to the community'; and an ability to sympathise and communicate in order to 'get through to children and their parents' to 'understand their feelings' and 'gain their confidence'. In short, the qualities looked for in panel members were in large measure determined by the philosophy of the system. Potential panel members would need to be in harmony with the Kilbrandon approach, or at least capable of being 'converted' to it. The ability to recruit panel members was the first test of public acceptability of the welfare-based system.

The first recruitment of panel members showed that there was no shortage of citizens willing to serve. Eight hundred and fifty members were appointed in the fifty-two panel areas, in most parts the numbers applying being three or four times greater than those appointed. The initial numbers appointed were a substantial underestimate of those needed to cover the caseload and some areas required a second recruitment in the first year. Within five years the total number of panel members stabilised at around 1,500, with a turnover of between 300 and 400 hundred a year (Murray, 1976).

As we have seen, the major responsibility of CPACs was to determine who were selected to serve on hearings. Their formal duties, as set out in Schedule 3 to the 1968 Act, were as follows.

- To submit names of possible panel members to the Secretary of State.
- To advise the Secretary of State, as required, on the suitability of persons referred to him as possible members.
- To advise the Secretary of State on such matters relating to the general administration of panels as he may refer to them.

Though the methods of selection varied from region to region, the essential components laid down by guidelines were the traditional ones of factual application forms supported by references and face-to-face interviews. There was also a requirement for screening for any criminal record, though this was not an automatic bar to appointment. A variety of additional aids to selection were gradually introduced – for example, group discussions based on case material or in response to attitude-provoking assertions.

Having satisfactorily completed the preliminary training, panel members' initial appointments were usually for three years, at the end of which the individual who so wished could be considered for reappointment. To provide the basis for this reassessment an extended duty was introduced in 1971, namely that CPAC members should attend hearings to observe 'the manner in which panel members carry out their work' and to meet periodically with panel members to discuss any general problems. Like other observers at hearings, CPAC members required the approval of the hearing chairman. These visits were not enthusiastically welcomed by all panel members, particularly those appointed in the early years who had no initial expectation of being observed.

Discomfort was greatest in areas where the panel and the CPACs had not established regular personal contacts, so that panel members did not know those who observed them. CPAC members who had not previously served as panel members were often those whose role was less readily accepted. Though the observers' comments were kept in confidential files, which every panel member was entitled to peruse, this was seldom done. This process of observation, a continuous one over a period of time and carried out by more than one CPAC member, came to be known as 'monitoring', but it was only one strand of relevant information regarding the panel member's progress. Weight was also attached to availability for hearings, attendance at training sessions, knowledge of the system and the views of the panel chairman.

Considering the importance attached to methods of selecting panel members, little attention has been given to the criteria for the appointment of members of the CPACs. On each committee a majority are appointed by the Secretary of State, whose policy it has always been to have a mixture of former panel members and others on the basis of personal qualities and experience, the remaining committee members being nominated by the local authority. Though not universally the case, the local authority appointees tended be councillors who served on the council's social work committee. This has had the advantage of providing a link between the panel and those responsible for child-care services in their area; the disadvantage being that the 'link persons' might well be absent on more urgent council business.

There has been no national study of CPAC members, but it is clear that they have included members from a variety of backgrounds. The balance to be struck between those with panel experience and those without has been a keenly debated issue. Previous panel experience was not always an advantage. The transition from active hearing participant to observer often proved to be a testing experience. Equally, previous specialised work with children and families, a seemingly appropriate recommendation for appointment, has sometimes necessitated considerable 'unlearning' in the process of discovering that a hearing is not a counselling interview, not a family therapy session, nor a courtroom dialogue.

The responsibility of CPACs to advise the Secretary of State on matters he may refer to them is frequently overlooked. For the chairpersons of CPACs this has often proved to be an arduous task, as these 'matters', though raised infrequently, tended to be concerned with the intransigent aspects of interpersonal relationships which from time to time occur in any large organisation. To the Scottish public the existence and activities of the CPACs were certainly less well known than those of the children's panels. Yet, like the latter, membership has been readily if somewhat anxiously accepted, and duties have been carried out with enthusiasm and commitment.

Representativeness and suitability

The composition of the panel was the major topic of interest and debate both before and immediately after the system came into operation. Two studies of the selection process, Mapstone in Fife (1973) and Smith and May in Aberdeen (1971), noted that although selectors were aware that community representativeness was one of the desirable characteristics of the panel as a whole, individual 'suitability for the task' was the main criterion upon which selection was actually made. This focus, the identification of people with the desired personal qualities, attitudes and values, led to a predisposition to favour 'middle-class' professionals. Mapstone suggested that the ideal qualities were the same as those required by a 'good social worker', and Smith and May claimed that this gave rise to a predictable 'homogeneity' among them. The unsurprising outcome was that of those selected, there was an over-representation of professional 'middle-class' panel members, and an under-representation of manual skilled, semiskilled and unskilled.[15]

Since referral to hearings came predominantly from areas of disadvantage, this meant that neighbourhoods with a high proportion of families attending hearings had few panel members, whereas areas with low levels of referrals had a high

---

[15] These finding are confirmed by Rowe (1972), Moody (1976) and Higgins (1979), who are summarised in Curran (1977).

proportion. This mismatch was largely a function of self-selection of panel members at the application stage rather than a consequence of judgments of 'suitability' by selectors. The social class distribution of the applicants was very similar to that of the group appointed, which means there was an approximately equal chance of being selected whatever the social class of the applicant. If the sought-after 'qualities and attitudes' are in fact to be found more in the professional classes, then either the lower social class applicants were untypically competent and enlightened or the selectors did discriminate positively in favour of less well equipped non-professionals, which would imply that CPACs attached some weight to the 'representativeness' of the panel as a whole.

The response to the early composition of the panels was divided between those who were satisfied with having been able to get sufficient numbers of committed and able citizens and those who believed that the panels had not achieved the ideal of 'community representativeness'. What counted as the relevant 'community' and what was meant by 'representativeness' were vague, ambiguous and variously interpreted.[16]

The idea of representativeness which carried most practical weight was simply that there should be some *correspondence* between the characteristics of the panel and the Scottish population as a whole. Panel membership could not of course be a complete microcosm of Scottish society. The criteria of eligibility confined membership to the 18 to 65 age range, and certain occupation groups were excluded – for example, criminals and police. It was not realistic or desirable for panels to be statistically representative or to correspond proportionately to the population at large, even though this seems to be implied by the judgment that some categories of people were 'under' or 'over' represented (Jones and Adler, 1990). The sense of representativeness which was suggested by the SWSG guidance was nothing more precise than that panels should reflect the social *diversity* to be found in Scottish society. While the official literature did not mention social class (it rarely does), it talked of 'a range' of 'income groups', 'occupations', and 'neighbourhoods'. Clearly a social mixture was deemed desirable, as was 'a range' of other characteristics – including age, family experience and a gender balance. What is not quite clear is whether this diversity was to be pursued for its own sake, or simply to open up the field of potential recruits from which to select the best. The social composition of panels may well have had its greatest importance in enhancing the public acceptability of the new system (Lockyer, 1992).

Panel training

The Act empowered both the Secretary of State and local authorities to make provision for training panel members, though it imposed no requirement on either to do so. Nobody doubted that some training would be needed, though there was no formal agreement on the extent or content of the curriculum. The

[16] For a discussion of how these terms have been ambiguously and variously interpreted, see Lockyer (1992), section 1.

division of responsibility was for central government to fund and support three training organisers attached to university departments of adult education, with local authorities funding and approving their programmes. The content of pre-service training in the early years seems to have had a dual focus: to orientate panel members within the system by discovering what each of the other agencies did, and to learn about the needs of maladjusted, disadvantaged and delinquent children. This meant that the contributors tended to be professionals working with children or in the legal system, and academics, especially those with a knowledge of child development, an interest in paediatrics, social policy or law. These were the most readily available training resources.

The character of early training was inevitably influenced by the background and understanding of the first generation of trainers. The only full-time appointee, Kathleen Murray, who was responsible for training in Glasgow and the surrounding area, was an educational psychologist. Her understanding was that panel members were being asked to perform a quasi-professional task, where no specialist knowledge could be assumed. The challenge for training was in bringing members from contrasting cultural and educational backgrounds into a shared understanding of their common purpose within the hearings system (Murray, 1976).

A criticism often made of the initial training programmes was that they were 'too academic'. Some claimed the association with the universities might discourage the less-well educated from serving. It was even suggested that the very idea of 'training' detracted from the intended 'layness' of the panel (May, 1977). Much of this comment is lacking in substance. Certainly, the idea that resistance to training would come from the less formally educated was especially wide of the mark.[17] However, it can be said that the early emphasis in panel training was predominantly on 'understanding' rather than the acquisition of practical skills or technical competence in the rules of procedure. The dual focus referred to above might be better described not as training but as a mixture of social education and the inculcation of the welfare approach – in short, an orientation experience.

Kathleen Murray spoke for the generality when she expressed the view that the opportunity presented by panel training had significance much beyond preparing a diverse group of volunteers for a specific task. It was equally an exercise in community education and public enlightenment.

> 'Nowhere is there such a unique opportunity for confronting the general public with the whole range of social and individual problems, for encouraging the development of understanding not only of anti-social behaviour but also of the institutions and of society against which that behaviour is a reaction. The community is encouraged to find within itself greater humanity and the strength to offer relevant support to those with less fortunate life experiences' (Murray, 1976, p65).

Although the first pre-service sessions may have been heavily dependent on the

---

[17] The survey of panel members carried out on behalf of the Children's Panel Chairmen's Group showed that the least well formally educated panel members showed the greatest commitment to, and enthusiasm for, panel training (Lockyer, 1992, pp108–111).

input of professionals and academics (who might be regarded as a proselytising liberal élite), it was not long before panel members themselves began to take a major role in their own training. At local level area and district panel chairs organised follow-up in-service programmes. Tutors and specialist contributors were increasingly recruited from among the high proportion of teachers and others with relevant vocational experience or local knowledge who served on hearings. A feature of local training was a programme of visits to a variety of facilities – schools, children's homes, assessment centres, and also to the local social work team – with the purposes not only of seeing but discussing and scrutinising the services available. Enthusiasm and occasionally dismay sometimes led panel members to become agitators for resources and even initiators of some provisions. Not all panel members once appointed devoted time to activities beyond sitting on hearings, but many who did took an expansive view of what counted as training. It is fair to say that the prevailing interest was to know more about what could be done for children in trouble, rather than sharpen procedure in the conduct of hearings.

The matching field organisation

This was the term used in the Kilbrandon Report to identify the agencies which would be required to carry out the recommendations of the children's panel (its term for hearings). As we have seen, while the structure and functions of the lay tribunal passed into legislation very much as the Report outlined, the one element which encountered opposition from several professional groups, in Parliament itself, was the proposed 'Social Education Department'. Doubt was expressed that social casework pursuing a welfare approach was likely to flourish within the Scottish educational environment. It was further argued, quite explicitly in the White Paper, Social Work and the Community, that to provide for a children's service was too narrow a focus for a reorganisation of Scottish social work when a unique opportunity existed to create a comprehensive community-based service – a 'single door' through which all those seeking help could enter. At one legislative stroke, most of the separate, uncoordinated social work elements from hospital, child care and probation could be brought within one agency, the social work service. Moreover, for such an enterprise to flourish, the director of the envisaged autonomous department would of necessity require to be a qualified, experienced, social work practitioner if the new directorship was to merit respect. This then was the plan adopted and outlined in the Social Work (Scotland) Act 1968.

There were, however, a number of major difficulties. First, this was happening at a period of financial restriction and secondly, as we have noted, there was a dearth of suitably qualified personnel at all levels. There was, moreover, a reluctance among many contemporary social workers to acknowledge that casework, as envisaged by Kilbrandon, might call for special aptitudes, skills and experience in working with children and parents. This reflected a change in the direction of social work orientation towards what came to be known as the 'generic approach'. Under the influence of Wootton (1959), Younghusband (1959), Donnison (1954) and others, the late 1950s had seen a move towards a shared basic training of social workers in Britain which sought to prepare them for a wide range of work with individuals, groups and communities – a move towards a pragmatic approach to social and personal problems. This was partly a reaction against specialisation which had prevented the development of a unified social work profession, with nationally recognised training and qualifications. It was also a distancing from the psychodynamic approach to case-work with its psychoanalytic orientation which had acquired considerable status in the USA, especially in the child guidance field.

It can be readily understood, therefore, against such a background of professional development, that the consultant group who advised on the implementation of Kilbrandon saw it as an opportunity to reorganise Scottish social work in the 'generic' mould.

The implementation of the 1968 Act was no easy or straightforward matter. As we have seen, reservations were expressed by the judiciary, by the police, by the medical profession and especially by the well-established probation service who, with justification, doubted the ability of the new-style, all-purpose social worker to cope with the demands likely to emerge in particular with the older children and adolescent offenders. Nor were all the local authorities enthusiastic about the new arrangements which afforded the newly appointed social work committees and their directors a potential importance comparable with the powerful health and education departments.[18]

In spite of all the difficulties and with much *ad hoc* thinking, the changes were initiated. Scotland, with a total population of five million, was divided into fifty-two local authorities, inaugurated in April 1952. The formula of allocating ten to twelve social workers to serve a population of 50,000 was recommended – that is, a social work cohort of 1,000 for the whole of Scotland. A similar estimate was arrived at in England by the Seebohm Committee in 1968, though this influence and its rationale are unclear (Murphy, 1992).

Along with their manifold duties, the social workers were required to provide social background reports for the children's hearings. These, along with school reports, were to assist in the decision-making. In most cases referred to hearings, 'supervision' of the child was likely to seen by social workers as beneficial, although the concept of offering help on a compulsory basis was for some a difficult concept to come to terms with. We may well conjecture how the supervisory task was envisaged, recalling that neither the Kilbrandon Report nor the Social Work (Scotland) Act gave detailed guidance on this crucial activity. It seems likely that previous experience was significant. The former probation officer, who had worked mainly with older adolescents and adults, tended to adopt a benevolent authoritarian role on a one-to-one basis, whereas previous child care experience, especially with younger children, favoured a supportive approach towards child and family. Much depended on how the individual worker viewed this new system, and what lead was given by their own department.

---

[18] For a detailed account of the stage-by-stage implementation of the Social Work (Scotland) Act, the reader is referred to *British Social Services. The Scottish Dimension* (Murphy, 1992).

There is little doubt that, at the outset, the expectations of all concerned regarding the resources for the home-based and residential assessment and 'treatment' of children were unduly optimistic, as were the estimated demand for services and the financial implications. Experience showed that the creation of the new service produced its own demand. Therefore, a major issue from the start was how a social worker with a widely diverse caseload managed his or her priorities. Hearings and courts made demands which placed a statutory duty on the social worker and interfered with the principle of responding to clients purely on the basis of the urgency of their need. This was a source of some tension. The competing demands on the social worker's time necessitated a realistic assessment of what was practically possible under the aegis of supervision. The need to manage scarce resources produced the climate in which social work departments became important creators of policy.

4 : The First Decade: Establishing Standards

URING the first decade, from 1971 to 1981, the chief imperative for all of the participating actors was to put into practice the alternative to the juvenile courts which the Kilbrandon Committee had envisaged. Each of the key agencies had to establish norms of practice responsive to the new legislation, and to the institutions created by it. In the case of agencies which had functioned in parallel with the juvenile court, some modifications of practice and adjustment of attitudes were required. For example, the police, procurators fiscal and sheriffs incorporated the children's hearings system into their business with differing degrees of enthusiasm. Workers and managers in residential establishments dealing with young offenders required some 're-education' to the non-punitive approach. The same shift in emphasis was less obviously required, but was still needed to some degree, in schools and other institutions which dealt with young people. The business of grafting the provisions of the hearings system on to pre-existing institutions was more easily done where the welfare approach to young people was already in part accepted, as it was by the juvenile courts.

For the new actors – reporters and panel members – the process was not one of assimilation but of creating an original identity, like Rome (despite Kilbrandon and Romulus) to be achieved by degrees. The task was to adopt standards and conventions of practice which both complied with the letter of the Social Work (Scotland) Act 1968 and encapsulated the spirit of the Kilbrandon philosophy.

Informality of the setting

Panel members and reporters were conscious that the children's hearings system had been introduced to replace the formalism of the court and the judicial process. It was in the spirit of the legislation to create a climate of informality in which children and families would be sufficiently at ease to discuss matters openly. However, this had to be set against the fact that a hearing is none the less a rule-governed judicial proceeding. Therefore, a careful balance had to be struck between acting in the spirit of the legislation and keeping to the letter of the law. Many of the issues which arose during the first decade of practice can be regarded as facets of an ongoing conflict between the demands of 'due process' and the commitment to establish a new type of informal, flexible and family-friendly proceeding.

Before considering the conduct of hearings their physical setting was a major issue. Local authorities were required by the 1968 Act to provide 'suitable accommodation and facilities dissociated from criminal courts and police stations' (s 36(3)). Most authorities found rooms in more or less suitable public buildings, which in main centres also housed the reporter's department, but in rural locations any room in a general-purpose building might be put to occasional use. It is significant that accounts of the new system usually remarked on the variety of premises (see Fox, 1974, pp81–82). An examination of the 'Comments Books' kept by local panels suggests that the 'variety' was not always appreciated. Panel members complained of the lack of privacy, security and heat; roofs leaked; there was 'nowhere to make a cup of tea'; and invading noise 'from country dancing next door' sometimes detracted from the serious business.[1]

Accommodation was only one among a range of topics upon which panels and reporters had words. Much of their discussion was about how to facilitate an appropriate balance between formality and informality. Many issues were relatively trivial. Should panel members stand up and shake hands with family members? When should families be invited to sit? Should smoking be permitted? Might (quiet) toys be provided? Should the hearing see the baby?

Some panel members 'dressed up' like (most) reporters; others 'dressed down' like (most) social workers. How much effort should go into putting families at their ease was a major issue. However, it had to be acknowledged that hearings were also occasions of high tension, where non-trivial offences, harmful conduct and serious problems would be discussed; often significant disapproval must be registered and unpalatable decisions taken. There could be no guarantee of a constructive dialogue or a cosy consensus being reached. Setting the appropriate atmosphere and physical surrounding had to take both ideal and reality into account.

A topic which symbolically embodied this ambivalence was the question of the shape and size of the hearing table. The starting-point was the idea of equality embodied in the civilised notion of a round-the-table discussion. The table needed to be large enough to accommodate normally seven or eight people. (Observers, if any, would sit at the back or side of the room.) A large table gave a certain amount of protection from assault – best if it could not be easily reached across or overturned. Personal safety was a real consideration in equipping and arranging the hearing room, because the ethos was against having police or security personnel present. But the table could equally be a barrier to desirable interaction. This was especially so with young children, who would have most of their bodies below the table top. (As their interest waned it was not unknown for small children to disappear entirely beneath it.) Experiments were conducted where a small coffee table was used for cases where intimacy was at a premium. In such ways panel members and others found methods of exercising discretion, depending on the character of the cases before them.

Observing the rules

Informality was a question of higher stakes when it became a matter of flexibility or rigid adherence to the prescribed rules. A major criticism of children's hearings

---

[1] These remarks are extracted from *Comments Books* from area panels in the early days, examined in the Strathclyde Regional Chairman's Office in 1990.

which gained credence during the first decade was that generally too little regard
was paid to keeping to the rules. This was often expressed as a 'laxity' which might
lead to the infringement of children's and parents' rights (Grant 1982, 1976).
Although there was a clear shift in the focus of training to emphasise the
importance of following the statutory requirements of the hearing, when the first
major observational research into the conduct of hearings was carried out in
1978–79, it found there to be major shortcomings in their compliance with
procedural requirements (Martin *et al*, 1981, Chapter 7).

In 301 hearings observed, of the eight procedural elements identified, the
average 'score' was 4.5, and a quarter of hearings scored 3 or less. It could be
argued that the research method exaggerated the departure from the rules, and it
certainly failed to differientiate between the trivial and the substantive. However,
there is no doubt that significant deficiencies were found, and the general level of
compliance with the rules gave genuine cause for concern. A common response of
panel members to the findings was that they were not concerned with the rules for
their own sake. A training experiment with panel members observing each other
with a procedural check list showed they were much more interested in the
dynamic of successful communication than in the legal 'formalities' (Lockyer,
1983). However, the research had also shown there to be a positive correlation
between procedurally correct hearings and those where panel members were
successful 'in creating an atmosphere in which their clients [*sic*] feel that they can
speak freely and be heard sympathetically' (Martin *et al*, 1981, p110).

Despite reluctance among some parties within the hearings system to accept
the validity of the criticism, most influential commentators saw the need to
improve adherence to the rules. Few agreed with Grant that the solution lay in
legally trained chairmen for hearings (Grant, 1975). Nor was there much support,
even among reporters, for the idea that the reporter should take a more
intervening part in the hearing (Martin *et al*, 1981, p277). To an American
observer the attraction of the children's hearings system in providing an alternative to a court-based justice model was greatly diminished if it meant 'due
process' rights had to be sacrificed.[2] It will be remembered that the welfare
approach of the juvenile courts in the USA was largely discredited by its neglect of
children's rights. Although the analogue suggested here is very superficial, the
capacity of children's hearings to pay due regard to rights was and remains an
issue affecting its international standing (Fox, 1991).[3]

Procedure and practice
From the mid-1970s onwards training on practice and procedure became an
important element in all pre-service and in-service programmes. What became
increasingly clear was not just that there were inherent tensions between the
letter and the spirit, but that there was considerable scope for legitimate diversity

[2] The research conducted by Martin, Fox and Murray, reported in *Children Out of Court*, was,
through the auspices of Sanford Fox, funded by the US Justice Department.
[3] The influence of the International Rights agenda is discussed in Chapter 17.

of interpretation of the law and the rules. One of the consequences of informality and flexibility was the diversity of practice which it allowed and encouraged.

In the absence of firm guidance from the centre there was a tendency for areas and (after regionalisation in 1975) regions, to develop their own divergent norms of practice. Getting together at inter-area level, and (after 1974) at national panel training events, provided important opportunities for comparing practice, even though the typical first response from each locality was to lament the way hearings were conducted elsewhere (Martin, 1983a). The development of standard practice within areas or regions was a means of limiting discretion, but this usually fell short of uniformity of practice even among panels served by the same training organiser. Still less were there agreed national conventions.

The national gatherings of reporters had the potential to resolve differences of interpretation, but they rarely did so. Even when they met behind closed doors regional reporters maintained their independent practices (Grieve, 1981). Permissible variations of practice tended to develop between areas and regions rather than among hearings within them. This arguably embodied the worst of both worlds. While there was not much uniformity across Scotland, there was an increasing tendency to routinise the informal rather than encourage flexibility in the handling of individual cases. There were maverick chairmen who had the confidence to innovate, and some area panels were willing to try different approaches, perhaps inspired by a training session, or an idea picked up from practice elsewhere. The first decade was characterised by a continuing lively debate about what was permissible.

Grounds and reasons

The part of the hearing which gave rise to the greatest difficulty was the opening sequence in which the *grounds for referral* had to be explained and responded to. There were several problems here. The Act required the hearing chairman to 'explain the grounds' before ascertaining whether they were 'understood' and 'accepted' by the child and a parent (s 42(1)(2), (7)). There was first the difficulty of giving an explanation which was both accurate and not inclined to lead or prompt acceptance.

An often-cited difficulty was in explaining the concept of 'art and part' to a child who was alleged to have committed an offence when acting with others. This avers that the party 'acting along with' the principal actor is also culpable, but requires some 'intent' on the part of the accomplice. It was asserted that hearings sometimes treated as an acceptance a reply which indicated no more than an admission of being at the scene of the crime (Godwin, 1976).

There was an equal though less-noticed difficulty in explaining absence from school without 'reasonable excuse'. There being no legal definition of what might count as 'reasonable', the attempt to 'explain' too easily led to the chairman introducing his or her own conception of what was reasonable, thereby usurping the role of the sheriff (Meek, 1982).

In some places it was the normal practice for chairmen to read word for word the grounds for referral, both conditions and facts, and to invite the reporter to give any required legal explanation. Although there is no provision in the rules for devolving this duty, it was perhaps a tolerable arrangement, if the party bringing the accusation could be relied upon not to take advantage in advising the 'accused'. The root problem was that too often children and parents were undecided on whether to accept the grounds for referral, even though they had received due notice of them. The informality of the initial introduction to the hearing ill-prepared the family for making a formal response. It was commonly the case that instead of a straight acceptance or denial, a child or parent would launch into an explanation of what happened, which might amount to a defence or a plea in mitigation, neither of which ought to have been heard.

One suggested solution was to have the pleading diet before the sheriff who could refer 'acceptances', like cases with grounds established, to children's hearings for disposal (Godwin, 1976). However, most of the difficulties were resolved by the child and family receiving legal advice prior to hearings. In the first year of operation this was acknowledged by families being granted legal aid to contest grounds for referral, but it was a long time before it became the normal practice for families to be prepared for responding appropriately to the grounds for referral.

A further criticism was that hearing chairmen illegally amended the grounds (Grant, 1976; Godwin, 1976), but this was open to interpretation. Only sheriffs can alter grounds for referral by finding established different grounds from those averred if warranted by the evidence (CR 10), but hearings are permitted to proceed if grounds are partially accepted (s 42(2)(b)). However, it is not always clear where partial acceptance implies or requires amendment. Moreover, at what point does the denial of particular facts invalidate the acceptance of a condition? Suppose a child accepts that he or she is 'beyond parental control' but denies most of the facts advanced in support; or in a 'breach of the peace' where 'shouting' is accepted but 'swearing' denied. On questions such as these, where there is room for doubt, the legal commentator advises sending for proof (Kearney, 1987, Chapter 10), but this presumes an adherence to the pre-eminence of the due process model of justice. This is just what most panel members and many reporters did not accept. Appearing before the sheriff meant delay and anxiety, both of which were to be avoided if at all possible. The provision of partial acceptance was surely intended to facilitate this. Moreover, given that the decision of the hearing was to be in the child's best interests based on an evaluation of all that was known about the family, how much of the grounds, or precisely which offence was accepted, may often be considered immaterial.

This raised a much more general question of practice for reporters and panel members. Since the acceptance or proof of any ground for referral was sufficient to permit compulsory measures of any sort, did it matter what grounds the reporter presented or the family accepted? It was quite legitimate for reporters to have other reasons than the grounds for judging there to be a need for compulsory intervention; in only one-third of offence cases did reporters say the grounds themselves were the main reason for bringing the child to a hearing (Martin *et al*, 1981, pp84–85). There was also no explicit requirement for the reporter to bring the case under the grounds most relevant to his or her concerns. Sometimes when the major concern was something else, which would constitute a different ground if it were able to be proved, minor offences or failure to attend school might be used to bring children to hearings. Similarly, hearings could proceed on the basis of any ground accepted, while discharging denied grounds which might have been more pertinent to the reasons for bringing the case.

Court's opinion

The hearing's reasons for decision may or may not include reference to the ground for referral. In an early judgment on appeal (*K* v *Finlayson* 1974 SLT (Sh Ct) 51) Sheriff Sinclair argued not only that hearing members must give 'adequate reasons' for their decision, but that they were entitled to base their decisions only on 'facts' accepted or established. It was against 'natural justice', she concluded, for the hearing 'to take into account any other matters whatsoever that they choose, including grounds which were not placed before the parent'. At least one legal commentator (Sheriff Gordon) took the view that this judgment 'could have far-reaching effects' on the extent to which allegations in reports required to be incorporated into grounds (Gordon, 1976, p13). Although Sheriff Sinclair's judgment was widely regarded as errant, it was not rejected by the Court of Session until 1992 (*O* v *Rae* (IH) 1992 SCLR 318; 1993 SLT 570); therefore it carried a salutary warning of the possible success of an appeal against any decision which was made without adequate opportunity to challenge the facts or opinions on which it was based.

Most reporters came to recognise the importance of formulating the most relevant ground and the need to bring new grounds when possible because significantly different and disputed concerns had come to light. Panel training emphasised the undesirability of discharging the critical ground, and the need to identify and discuss disputed matters.

In an opinion given by Sheriff Mowat in 1973 an approach to the appellate jurisdiction was taken which limited the extent to which appeals might re-examine the substance of the hearing's decision. A sheriff should not set aside a hearing's decision 'simply because he felt another form of treatment might be preferable'; accordingly he should not allow an appeal unless there was a flaw in procedure or he was satisfied that the hearing 'had not given proper consideration to some factor in the case' (*D* v *Sinclair* 1973 SLT (Sh Ct) 47). The reasoning in this opinion became the standard approach adopted by most sheriffs and it was supported in the main by the Court of Session. In the first decade only about 10 per cent of the few appeals to the sheriff were upheld; in most years they referred twice as many cases back to hearings for disposal. In 1980 (a typical year) there were 67 appeals: 43 were rejected, four were upheld by the case being discharged, 20 were remitted back (1980 Children's Hearings Statistics).[4]

---

[4] 'Statistics', unless otherwise stated, refer to Children's Hearings Statistics published annually by the Scottish Office. The date is the year to which the Statistics refer rather than their date of publication.

Statistical evidence

During the first decade the hearings system dealt predominantly with young offenders.

With the usual caveats about how much statistics conceal, the evidence suggested that over the period the welfare approach performed no less well in terms of public protection than anything that had gone before. In the ten years prior to 1971 there had been a steady increase in the number of juvenile offenders (aged 16 and under) appearing before the courts. In 1960, for the first time, over 20,000 juveniles were proceeded against. By 1965 the number was more than 25,000 and it was almost 30,000 in the last year of the old system (1970 Criminal Statistics Scotland). In 1972, the first full year for which figures are available, referrals to reporters were just over 24,000 which related to just under 18,000 children (1981 Statistics). Various factors complicate comparison, but it is likely that the offences reaching the reporter were roughly the number which came to court before the introduction of the hearings system. Since reporters passed to hearings only just over half the referrals they received, to begin with there was a significant reduction of cases subject to judicial process.

TABLE 1

Number of Referrals to Reporter and Number of Children Involved, 1972–81

Year	Number of referrals	Number of children to whom referrals related
1972	24,219	17,950
1973	29,566	21,017
1974	31,876	21,907
1975	30,022	22,207
1976	29,514	18,638
1977	28,551	18,537
1978	26,583	17,308
1979	25,842	16,924
1980	28,950	19,035
1981	30,786	20,111

Referrals to the reporter increased between 1972 and 1974 when they reached almost 32,000; then for the next five years they fell steadily to below 26,000 in 1979 (see Table 1). The percentage of referrals relating to offences by children reduced modestly but steadily over the same period from 89 per cent to 80 per cent of all referrals. This meant that the actual number of referrals on offence grounds fell between 1974 and 1979 by 25 per cent for Scotland as a whole. Over the same period, offences committed by juveniles referred to the court, following the Lord Advocate's instructions, were reduced by nearly two-thirds to 1,055. So the decline in offence referrals to reporters took place despite their taking 96 per cent instead of 91 per cent of the total (Martin *et al*, 1981, Table 3.2).

The figures for offence referrals increased again during the next two years, and referrals to the reporter on all grounds were back to 1974 levels. However, in 1981 the number of offences referred were still only three-quarters of what they had been five years earlier; the similar referral figures for 1974 and 1981 were produced by the steady increase in non-offence referrals over the period.

TABLE 2

Referrals to Reporter According to Alleged Grounds for Referral

Grounds for referral	1972 %	1974 %	1976 %	1979 %	1981 %
(a)　Beyond parental control	745 (3.0)	771 (2.4)	556 (1.9)	677 (2.6)	923 (3.0)
(b–e)　Neglect, abuse and at risk	801 (3.2)	1,126 (3.5)	1,281 (4.3)	1,916 (7.4)	2,620 (8.6)
(f)　Failure to attend school	1,469 (6.0)	2,345 (7.2)	2,870 (9.7)	2,514 (9.7)	2,920 (9.6)
(g)　Offences by child	21,594 (87.5)	28,184 (86.8)	24,823 (84.1)	20,873 (80.2)	23,912 (78.6)
Others (transfers)	47 (0.2)	49 (0.2)	37 (0.1)	31 (0.1)	46 (0.2)
TOTAL	24,650	32,475	29,570	26,011	30,421

(Derived from Table 3a, 1981 Children's Hearings Statistics.)

During the first decade of the system truancy accounted for about half the non-offence grounds brought to the reporter. Children referred for 'being beyond parental control' remained fairly constant throughout the decade. Those referred for 'lack of parental care' more than doubled from 2.1 per cent (506) to 4.2 per cent (1,339) between 1972 and 1981. However, the most dramatic rate of growth was in children who were victims of offences. They increased tenfold over the decade and by 38 per cent between 1979 and 1981. By the end of the period 21 per cent of referrals were on non-offence grounds and over half of these were other than for truancy – that is neglect, abuse, at risk or beyond control.

It should be remembered that classifying cases by grounds has its limitations. We already know that a reporter might have brought a case on grounds of a minor offence or truancy when the major concern was something else. A reporter's reasons for bringing cases to a hearing might be identical despite the grounds being different. Some cases include more than one referral and different types of grounds; commonly offending and truancy arise together. The practice (adopted by the Scottish Office) of classifying in terms of 'offences' and 'non-offences' reinforces a simplistic dichotomy. That said, there are significant general differences which consistently correlate respectively with the offence and non-offence referrals.

There were the usual marked variations between males and females with respect to offending. In 1973 boys were between eight and twelve times more likely than girls to be referred on offence grounds for the age cohorts eight to fifteen. At the peak age of offending one in seven fifteen-year-old males in the population were referred compared with one in sixty females. Nine-year-old boys were more likely to be referred than fifteen year-old-girls. The proportion of one female in every eight offence referrals was virtually constant from 1972 to 1981. However, in relation to non-offence referrals the gender differences were slight. There were marginally more boys when truancy is included and marginally more girls when not.

Over the decade the gender balance and the age distribution among referrals to the reporter both changed significantly as a consequence of the increasing proportion of non-offence referrals. Among referrals the ratio of male to female shifted from 7:1 in 1972 to 3:1 in 1981. The increasing numbers of younger children meant that by 1981 there were 30 per cent of twelve years old or younger and nearly 10 per cent under eight (1981 Statistics).

The other main difference between offence and non-offence referrals concerned the proportion of each referred on to hearings: less than half of the former and over two-thirds of the latter in 1981. The effect in that year was that 30 per cent of first hearings were considering non-offence grounds. Moreover, whereas 43 per cent of offence-related hearings led to some form of supervision requirement, over two-thirds of non-offence referrals did so. Therefore, the latter type were a higher proportion of second hearings. Since children needing care and protection are likely to remain on supervision longer, this increases their presence at review hearings. The total effect was to amplify the proportion of non-offence-related hearings. While it is still not wildly inaccurate to view the first decade of the system as 'dealing mainly with offenders', it is easy to underestimate the trends already at work which led towards the major shift in types of cases which characterised the second decade.

Reporters' discretion

With regard to any particular referral the reporter's decision as to whether or not to bring a child to a hearing is final; that is, not subject to review or appeal. From time to time this has led to criticism, particularly from referring agencies – police and social workers – especially in relation to 'no action' decisions. Reporters, for their part, staunchly defended their 'independence', arguing that their duty to provide detailed statistical returns to central government makes them subject to a great deal of general scrutiny (Finlayson, 1992, para 4.21). This granted, the facility to scrutinise and compare statistics relating to various reporters' decision-making may be considered a poor substitute for being able to challenge their individual judgments.

A particular judgment whether or not to refer a child to a hearing depends on there being a sufficiency of evidence to establish one of the grounds for referral and whether compulsory measures (technically) are, or (in practice) may be, needed (s 39(3)). We have noted that during the first ten years throughout Scotland about half the referrals to the reporter led to hearings. (The figures are slightly more or less than half depending on whether we count children referred or referral reports.) The reporter of course has other formal options. During the first decade about one in twenty children were referred by reporters back to social work departments to receive 'advice, guidance and assistance' on a voluntary basis; a similar proportion received a police warning or agreed to take part in a police liaison scheme. The remaining 35–38 per cent were formally classified as 'no action', though reporters were quick to point out that this belied the fact that they took a range of informal measures, sometimes including personal interviews with family members. Also some 'no actions' related to children already receiving compulsory supervision.

Our discussion of statistics has so far dealt with Scotland as a whole, without paying regard to local differences. There were of course variations in the volume and type of referral depending, for example, on population areas – conurbations, small towns and rural communities. However, local differences in the rates of referral to hearings by reporters merit attention. They are not explicable without reference to the way different reporters exercised discretion. Table 3 compares rates of referral to hearings by regions in 1978 with those for the same territories prior to regionalisation in 1975. (Imperfect secondary sources are used because these figures are not available in officially published statistics.) Both the inter-regional variations and the differences within localities before and after the reorganisation in 1975 should be noted. While the changes over the six years were most dramatic where there was a reduction in the proportion going to hearings (Central Region, for example, from over three-quarters to under a half), the regions were roughly equally divided between those with rising and falling rates. Clearly the reorganisation of reporters after regionalisation led to some con-vergence, but there is not enough to suggest that reporters adopted or sought to adopt uniform guidelines or standards.

In 1981 for the first time reporters' reasons for 'no action' were recorded and

TABLE 3
Percentage of Referrals to Reporter Referred to Hearings,
by Region, 1973 and 1978

	1973	1978
Borders	50	35
Central	76	47
Dumfries/Galloway	34	46
Fife	41	51
Grampian	34	36
Highland	53	57
Lothian	54	48
Strathclyde	52	58
Tayside	65	46
Orkney	–	51
Shetland	–	40
Western Isles	–	38

(Derived from Martin and Murray, *Children's Hearings*, 1976, and Martin, Fox and Murray, *Children Out of Court*, 1981.)

published. In 57 per cent of referrals the reporter simply deemed a hearing 'unnecessary'; in a quarter the child was already under supervision. In only one in eight of all referrals was there said to be 'insufficient evidence'; but in abuse, neglect and at risk cases this was the reason given in almost half the cases. Strictly speaking, reporters exercised discretion only when there was sufficient evidence to establish grounds, but this begs the question of how sound their judgments tended to be. Of the 15 per cent of cases where hearings required grounds to be sent for proof in 1981, two-thirds were due to non-acceptance and one-third was because of a child's lack of understanding. In the first category, where the family genuinely contested the grounds, under half were established in whole or in part. Moreover, one-third were 'abandoned' (1981 Statistics). At best reporters' judgments or their presentation of evidence left something to be desired. At worst the rate of abandonment suggests that grounds with insufficient evidence were too often presented in the hope of acceptance – no doubt motivated by concern for children's welfare.

Martin, Fox and Murray examined the discretion exercised by reporters. Their starting-point was 'all that can be said with certainty is that there is little justification for assuming from the outset that reporters share a common set of beliefs concerning the factors that indicate the need for compulsory measures' (Martin *et al*, 1981, p65). Looking at the characteristics of offence referrals, the number of offences committed and their relative 'seriousness' correlated positively with referral to hearings. This confirmed Morris's findings (Morris, 1987), but such factors were generally a less strong influence than the child's previous history of referrals. The evidence suggested that a reporter was much more likely to refer a child to a hearing where there had been a previous decision not to refer, to try voluntary measures, or where a hearing had made no order.

In 84 per cent of cases reporters had reports from the local authority on the family background before they made a decision whether or not to bring to a hearing. An analysis of the content of these reports showed a positive correlation between chances of referral and (a) 'unusual family situations' – children living with single parents, only one birth parent, five or more brothers and sisters; (b) 'non-economically active' parents; and (c) low social class. None of this is surprising. These factors correlate with low income, poor housing and other forms of material deprivation. However, such background facts were much less significant, and some of them insignificant, when it came to second referrals. Social class, for instance, is no straightforward predictor of decisions after the first referral. Children from 'non-manual families' had a higher rate of referral to hearings than unemployed parents in respect of subsequent referrals (Martin *et al*, 1981).

A history of family problems – traumatic events, divorce, separation, alcohol and drug problems – corresponds with a higher rate of referral to hearings, as do school-related problems, even if they have no part in the grounds. Among the diversity of reasons which reporters gave for their decisions to refer to hearings – apart from 'the referral itself' which applied in one-third of instances – 'the child's history' and 'home circumstances' were most prominent as first reasons and 'school circumstances', together with 'home circumstances', were the most frequent of second reasons (Martin *et al*, 1981, Table 5.19). The analysis concluded that the characteristics of present offences and factors connected with home and school were equally influential on decisions to refer to hearings, but most influential was whether there was a previous history either of offending or other known family problems.

There is of course no unequivocal way of measuring the effectiveness of reporters' decisions any more than that of hearings' decisions. However, if we can regard the absence of repeat offences as one measure of 'success', the data relating to reporters' decisions between 1973 and 1976 were promising. Between these dates the percentage of first-time offenders referred to hearings fell from 43 per cent to 27 per cent and the proportion who had reoffended within two years, among those referred to hearings and those not referred, had fallen. By 1976 three-quarters of first-time offenders diverted from hearings had no further offence referrals within two years, which compares with four in ten of those placed on supervision and six in ten of those discharged by hearings. Expressed differently, 80 per cent of those with no second offence were those whose first offence had led to no formal action (Longitudinal Study, 1980). This suggested that during the period between 1973 and 1976 reporters were getting better at recognising and diverting from hearings those children whose offences were 'one off'. What we cannot tell is how often children with no further referrals would none the less have benefited from receiving compulsory supervision, or how many of those who received it benefited from doing so.

Hearings: disposals

During the first decade of the system the number of children subject to a compulsory supervision requirement in Scotland was around 9,000, which was just over eight per thousand of the population under sixteen years. Of these, around 1,000 were in *residential schools* and a similar number were in *residential homes* run by voluntary organisations or local authorities. Six out of ten children were being supervised while staying in a parental home; one in ten were either living with relatives or friends or were in foster care. There were significant regional variations both in the proportion of children subject to compulsory supervision and in the types of disposal. Strathclyde had more children subject to all types of supervision than the rest of Scotland, both in total and in proportion to its population. This was partly as a consequence of having a higher percentage of children in the population referred to the reporter, but mostly because of the larger percentage referred on to hearings and the lower proportion they discharged. No doubt the socio-economic composition and geographic distribution of regional populations were major factors contributing to different rates of referral and types of dispositions, but policies relating to resources also had an effect.

Despite the fact that reporters passed on only about half their referrals to hearings, panel members as a whole continued to discharge a significant proportion. Superficially these could be considered cases where hearings rejected the reporter's judgment. However, in practice reporters and panel members might consider that the hearing itself was compulsory intervention enough. This was especially likely when a 'one-off' offence was the main reason for bringing the case to the hearing. However, hearings, unlike reporters, had to identify a specific resource when they decided on compulsory measures, and this entailed a binding commitment on the local authority.

It was a moot point among panel members whether they should take account of competing demands on the social work department when making specific decisions. In practice the problem of availability of an appropriate resource was acutely experienced in relation to residential provision. About two-thirds of children in residential assessment centres (120 on 5th April 1981) were waiting for an appropriate placement. There were also occasions when hearings were informed by social workers that if they made a home-supervision requirement the case 'would not be allocated', or would have a 'low priority'. Panel members were resistant in principle to allowing supply to determine demand; lack of an appropriate resource should not circumscribe their judgment of individual needs. However, limited availability of resources was part of the general context in which realistic decisions had to be made. Only in the next decade was the effect of resource constraints on decisions quantified.[5]

The Kilbrandon Report had been almost silent about what 'treatment' might entail. In practice what home supervision amounted to was in large measure left to individual social workers. Hearings seldom specified 'conditions' except to determine residence. This was partly in deference to the social worker's assertion of the need for 'professional discretion', partly indicative of the fact that recommendations and decisions were generally somewhat unspecific about means and ends.

For the social worker supervision normally involved establishing a 'helping relationship' with the individual child. In many cases the social workers had an 'operational philosophy' of being a 'sort of social policemen', where the objective was to keep the child out of trouble (Vernon, 1981). This approach suggests supervision modelled on probation, focusing on controlling the child's antisocial behaviour. Sometimes social workers saw the whole family as their clients, when their role might be that of supporting or enabling parents to provide care. At best the approach to supervision would be dictated by an assessment of need agreed at a hearing, but it was just as likely to be a product of the ideological orientation of the social worker (Ford, 1982). The generic social worker in the area team had to deal with the whole gamut of client groups and a whole range of individual needs. It was unlikely that they would be equally well equipped to deal with all.

Before the system came into operation there was no attempt made to estimate the demand for the services of the new social work departments (Martin, 1976). Had there been, it would doubtless have been woefully short of what came to be demanded. The scarcity of trained social workers from the start meant that the general standard of supervision was lower than anyone would have wished. Caseloads, especially in urban areas, often meant that little more than 'statutory' tasks

---

[5] See Chapter 5.

and 'crisis' work could be attended to (Bruce and Spencer, 1976). The dilemma for the social work department was portrayed as deciding how to spread a limited amount of jam: '[I]t is useless to spread it to the point of invisibility, where does one spread it so that it can be seen and tasted?' (Spalding, 1976). Against this background the resentment of some social workers at the 'unrealistic expectations' of hearings was understandable. Ideally home-supervision requirements gave the social worker a chance to contribute to the 'overall development of the child' – to offer 'new experiences which draw on his creative potential'. Minimally it gave the child and family 'another chance' to avoid a period of separation (Ford, 1982, p83). However, even the limited goal of keeping the family together will sometimes have been too great a burden on a hard-pressed social worker's time. Doubtless the lack of resources to assist with home supervision contributed to the high number of recommendations for residential supervision during the decade. The evidence is that hearings were generally more reluctant to remove children from home than social workers were to recommend it (Martin *et al*, 1981).

The 1966 White Paper proposed that all existing residential resources would be integrated and hearings would have access to 'a range of establishments providing a variety of régimes and special treatments'. The principle of integrating the available provision was in the main accepted and taken further when local authorities took over responsibility for *List D schools*[6] after regionalisation, but the variety of provision in terms of treatment régimes remained limited. Also the fact that residential schools continued to accommodate some offenders serving sentences from the court, alongside those on supervision, was at least anomalous in theory. In practice there was little difference in the needs or treatment of those subject to the different orders (Rushforth, 1977).

By 1981 there were just over 1,500 places in List D schools, just under 200 of which were for girls. Each school accommodated between twenty and 100. The occupancy level was close to 80 per cent for most of the time. The schools' designated populations were differentiated by sex, age group and religion. The kind of education varied, as did the emphasis placed on disciplined training as against therapeutic care. The large schools for senior boys were in the main former approved schools, with a tradition of providing vocational training as a solution to offending. Schools for junior boys were better able to provide small-group remedial education and give more attention to individual socialisation and personal developmental needs. The matching of children to placements often involved compromises: hearings sometimes refused inappropriate places and schools often modified their régimes to accommodate particular children. There were significant gaps in provision, especially for disturbed and maladjusted children (Newman and Mackintosh, 1975). The geographical distribution was such that many children were located at a distance, which made sustained contact with home difficult. Some regions (Highland, Borders, Dumfries and Galloway) had no List D schools, while Strathclyde imported children.

---

[6] 'List D' schools was the name given by the Scottish Education Department to the group of establishments known as 'approved schools' before the 1968 Act.

Returning children to the deprived home environment from which they had been extracted was a major limitation on schools having a lasting rehabilitative impact. The need to improve continuity of care and the transition to aftercare was recognised early on (McMichael, 1974). However, it took some time before the widespread policy of using loss of weekend leave as a sanction was questioned. On the other hand, extending home leave as a preparation for a permanent return home carried some dubiety about the child's interim care status and sometimes caused conflict with review hearings who, with some justification, saw their decisions being pre-empted.

The majority of children who lacked a satisfactory parental home during the 1970s were accommodated in *children's homes* or *hostels* run either by local authorities or churches or other voluntary organisations. Children within this sector included those placed there with the agreement of parents, short-term or long-term; those for whom the local authority had parental rights (in some cases awaiting adoption); and those subject to supervision requirements. The voluntary placements were usually the largest category. The more specialised provision tended to be in the non-local-authority sector, where admissions could be selective (Murray, 1976). A higher proportion of those in local authority homes were subject to supervision requirements; some might be there on the basis of a temporary 'place of safety' order. Generally staffing of residential homes was not adequate to meet the variety of demands made of them. Newman and Mackintosh found staff in children's homes to be unqualified, low paid, lacking training, having poor morale, being unsupported and suffering from a high rate of turnover. Their findings were based on South East Scotland, but would have been applicable to establishments throughout the country. It would be hard to disagree with their view that residential care needed to be improved and should not be used through lack of other resources (Newman and Mackintosh, 1975).

Concern about the quality of residential care led to the pursuit of alternatives rather than to dedicating expenditure to improve it. There was a sustained effort to increase the provision of *foster care*, especially for younger children. By 1981 there were almost half as many children subject to compulsory supervision in foster care as in children's homes, though there were major differences between regions (1981 Statistics). However, it is fair to say that by the end of the decade there was a growing preference for the use, where possible, of substitute parents, foster placements or 'community carers', rather than residential homes or schools. There was certainly an increasing body of influential opinion among liberal commentators and social work management that residential care ought to be avoided if at all possible. It was considered the most intrusive and therefore the least acceptable form of care. By implication this perception is endorsed by Martin, Fox and Murray when they tell us they were 'impressed by the reluctance of panel members' to send children to List D schools but rather to 'retain it as a last resort' (Martin *et al*, 1981 p170).

This finding is somewhat at odds with the SWSG study, which indicates that over half the children subject to residential supervision 'in the period 1976–78 were so placed at their first referral' (Longitudinal Study, 1980, p11). It is possible that most of the residential disposals on first referral were to children's homes rather than residential schools. But this is sufficient to show that while hearings might prefer the least intrusive alternative they would decide on residential supervision in the first place where deemed appropriate. The suggestion that hearings operated something like a 'tariff' based on the number of offence grounds or appearances at hearings was massively wide of the mark (Morris and McIsaac, 1978; Morris *et al*, 1980).

The family's experience

In any evaluation of what was achieved by the system in the first ten years, the experience of children and their families at hearings must be of major importance, not only because the forum was intended to be more family friendly than courts, but also because the consensual model saw the engagement of children and parents in the hearing's decision-making as part of the treatment process. The primary task of the hearing was understood to be that of making the 'right' decision. However, it was also important that, where possible, the manner in which it was made elicited the co-operation of the family and was perceived by them to be fair.

One obstacle to the perceived fairness of the hearing was the fact that families had no entitlement to see reports. Although good social work practice would normally have involved prior discussion of what social enquiry reports contained, and the 'substance' of what was 'material' must be disclosed at the hearing, families were bound to feel disadvantaged at not knowing with certainty in advance what information the panel members had. The lack of access to reports by families was a perennial subject of criticism. In interviews with parents Petch found that three-quarters 'argued strongly' that they should see all reports (Petch, 1988).

The predominant experience of parents attending hearings was positive. The generally favourable response of parents interviewed after hearings must have reflected in some measure their relief at the event being over – usually with a less-than-feared outcome. Willock's early study of parents who had attended hearings found them to have 'a satisfactory degree of understanding and acceptance of the objectives of the Children's Panel system' (Willock, 1973). Four out of five were satisfied with their treatment by the hearing and over three-quarters saw the hearing as attempting to help rather than punish their child (Curran, 1977).

Martin, Fox and Murray found a high level of understanding and an extremely favourable response among parents. Parents claimed overwhelmingly to have understood the proceedings, to have been able to put their point of view, to have been listened to, and most found hearings to have been fair. It is suggested that parents may have been generally somewhat uncritical, perhaps because being treated in a civilised manner with sympathy and respect 'may have been lacking in other agencies with which these parents may previously have been in contact' (Martin *et al*, 1981, p234). Petch casts doubt on attaching too much significance to classifying parents' views in terms of understanding or attachment to the system's philosophy. Some of their views might suggest adherence to a 'welfare ideology', others imply a punishment model. (In the language of the appropriate literature, they operated with 'multiple ideologies'.) The finding that one in four parents would have preferred to have been dealt with by a court may tell us less about their ideologies or values than how they felt about being answerable for their parenting. Only 58 per cent of Petch's parents (interviewed together, which would make a difference) were satisfied with their level of participation, though 80 per cent were satisfied with the disposal (Petch, 1988).

The only independent systematic evidence of the response of children to the hearing experience was as part of the Martin, Fox and Murray research (Chapter 12), which was reviewed separately by Erickson (Erickson, 1982). In just under a quarter of cases observed children participated only minimally; in slightly more than a quarter they took part fully, asked questions and spoke without being prompted; in the largest percentage they responded adequately when spoken to. One hundred and five children aged between twelve and fifteen were interviewed after disposal of their case. Their level of comprehension of most aspects of the hearing process was quite high. Children could identify the persons present and their roles; they showed a better understanding of the decision process than their counterparts in juvenile proceedings in England and Wales (Morris and Giller, 1977) and in North America (Catton and Erickson, 1975). Four out of five thought the panel members wanted to hear their views and 85 per cent were satisfied that they had said all they wanted to say. Although this implied that some children were satisfied with rather low levels of verbal participation, we should take the point that concern about the amount spoken reflects an adult's preoccupation rather than a child's (Martin et al, 1981).

Four out of five children thought the hearing was fair, including two-thirds of those subject to residential supervision (Erickson, 1982). There was generally found to be a positive correlation between high levels of participation by family members and decisions to discharge or terminate supervision, and low levels of participation and outcomes unwanted by families. This may not of course indicate causal connections. Low levels of participation may have reflected the family members' anxiety and distress at an anticipated removal from home. In these cases children and parents were more likely to view the decision as having been 'already made'; they may have been right to assume that anything they said would not make a difference to the outcome.

Given the prevailing concern (provoked by delinquency theorists such as Becker, 1963; Cohen, 1966; Goffman, 1968) that official processing runs the risk of stigmatising and self-labelling such that a 'criminal identity' and thus delinquent behaviour are reinforced, a key question was whether the hearings system avoided this. Only one in five children saw themselves to be different from others and one in four thought themselves 'criminal'. However, two-thirds thought the police would hold their panel appearance against them and three-quarters thought a future employer would. These immediate perceptions might be diminished in time.

One finding which Erickson wished to bring to the attention of panel members was that the 'style' which the hearing adopted made a difference to the child's self-perception. If the panel members were generally 'sympathetic' and 'encouraging' and made some 'positive' remarks, children were more likely to see themselves being helped and less likely to view themselves in terms of negative stereotypes. Panel members and social workers were to some extent influenced by these findings, especially since Erickson's chapter appeared in what was one of the standard training textbooks.

Other questions

Apart from the ongoing debate about the extent to which hearings followed the rules, there were two further critical question marks about panel members' conduct of hearings. Both were the subjects of adverse anecdotal comment, to which the Martin, Fox and Murray research added weight. One was the importance which panel members attached to schooling; the other was their alleged reluctance to discuss sensitive issues, especially when this involved confronting parents. These complaints could be linked in that hearings may have been inclined to turn quickly to the relatively 'safe' subject of school attendance, instead of discussing more awkward matters which might exact hostility from parents.

One highly anecdotal account presents panel members' 'primary concern with school attendance' and interest in 'academic potential' as an aspect of their predisposition to impose conformity to their own 'middle-class' values (Brown, 1979). The emphasis which panel members generally placed on school issues might well be contrasted both with the time given to discussing offences and with the relative neglect of education issues by social work. In defence of panel members it should be noted, first, that any future orientated disposal was bound to focus on continuing problems, which school matters invariably were; and, second, a large number of offences were committed while truanting. Maybe many panel members did view school attendance as the key to remedying much of what was missing in the home environment – no doubt sometimes unrealistically.

While the aim of seeking parental co-operation was laudable, the fact that none of the parents interviewed in the Martin, Fox and Murray study felt that his or her shortcomings were considered relevant by hearings was disturbing (Martin *et al*, 1981, Chapter 13). There can be no doubt that parents frequently responded aggressively to examination by hearing members; Petch cites cases where some parents reported themselves unjustly criticised. What the evidence suggests is that in relation to offence referrals, hearings were relatively unsuccessful in getting parents to acknowledge that they might have any responsibility for their children's behavioural problems. This was despite the fact that panel members generally rated the parental role as a major factor in the causes of delinquency.

There was no systematic observation during the first decade to enable us to tell whether it was a different picture where the grounds for referral identified fault with the conduct of parents. However, we could anticipate that the tendency of parents to regard the child as 'the problem' would not necessarily disappear, and that these hearings would be more difficult for parents and for panel members. We have noted that, by the end of the decade, the number of hearings which dealt with children who were neglected, abused or at risk was already substantial. These presented an increasing challenge, not only to panels and hearings but also to the work of all agencies which dealt with children.

In the first decade the hearings system established standards which enabled it to satisfy most of its external critics and fulfil many of the aspirations of its founders. In the second decade it attained the maturity for self-criticism of those standards and thus developed a capacity to meet in large measure the demands made of it.

5 : The Second Decade: Consolidation and Protection

A T the beginning of the 1980s the integrity of the hearings system faced a challenge quite as severe as anything that had arisen from criticisms expressed in the early 1970s. Although the institutions of panel, reporter and social work department were firmly enough planted to resist being dispersed by an ill wind, the welfare philosophy remained vulnerable to a change in climate. The threat came from two sources: political and academic; government and criminological theory raised the prospect of a return to punishment.

Consultation on Powers and Procedures

The General Election of May 1979 brought to power a Conservative administration which had made election commitments to 'tougher' measures on crime. Within a month of being in office the Secretary of State for Scotland informed the House of Commons that the government intended 'to strengthen' the children's hearings system. In April 1980 the promised Consultative Memorandum on Powers and Procedures was widely distributed among interested parties, including all 1,500 panel members. The memorandum reported the conclusion of the Secretary of State's 'initial examination' that hearings 'are performing a valuable function' and that no 'fundamental alterations need be made'. However, while resources to implement compulsory measures of care had been increased, 'a number of criticisms have been made to the effect that the hearings do not have sufficient measures of discipline and punishment' (para 5). Thus the main proposals on which the government sought views were for hearings to have the power to impose fines on children, to extract 'caution' from parents and to require children to make 'reparation' or do community service. Few people associated with the hearings system accepted the claim that the changes proposed were not fundamental. At the 1980 Children's Panel Summer School devoted to considering the possibilities of 'Change', Alan Finlayson, the much-respected Regional Reporter for Lothian, spoke for the majority present when he stated that 'the implementation of these provisions would destroy the system as we know it' (Change, 1980, p79).

What the government were proposing was to give hearings punitive powers. The Memorandum suggested that there was no difference between punishment and compulsory measures of care. Most of those within the hearings system, weaned on the Kilbrandon principles, saw the difference to be fundamental.[1] The

[1] For a discussion of the difference between 'punishment and treatment', see Chapter 2 and Lockyer, 1982.

majority of the responses submitted to the Scottish Office were heavily critical, especially of the proposed punitive powers.[2] A few submissions saw some possible advantages, but only the Scottish Police Federation wholeheartedly endorsed the punitive measures:

> 'Parents and their recalcitrant children are well aware of the range of punishments available to children's hearings and the conclusion arrived at by the previous government not to impose fines on children has, in our opinion, been one of the major contributory factors to the escalating crime and vandalism rate.'

Murray notes that this observation was at odds with the evidence that offence referrals had fallen in Scotland since 1971, whereas they had been markedly higher and increasing during the previous ten years when punitive powers had been available to courts (Murray, 1980, p 9).

Some respondents identified the 'insuperable difficulties' and 'negative consequences' of using fines and caution. They wanted to know who would fix the penalties, who would pay fines, what would be the sanction for those who defaulted, and asked, 'When were parents ever improved by threat of financial penalties?' Others, more profoundly, saw that the mere existence of these powers would undermine the entire basis of 'honest and frank discussion' and the aim 'to exercise a positive and constructive influence' on children and parents. It was pointed out that fining children and imposing financial penalties on parents had been explicitly rejected by the Kilbrandon Committee. They were (in the words of the Association of Reporters) 'quite inappropriate to the whole concept of the hearings system'. Two authoritative commentators argued that 'to graft elements of 'a crime and punishment approach' on to a basically welfare and prevention orientated system would produce the worst of both worlds. On the one hand panel members would be constantly forced into hypocritical stances; on the other there would be a lack of legal safeguards and procedural rigour normally held to be essential when punitive disposals are under consideration' (Murray, 1980, p16).

Strathclyde Regional Panel, which represented half the panel members in Scotland, began its submission by expressing 'serious doubt whether the government has any understanding of the philosophy of the system, or whether the Minister has given serious thought to the effect of his proposals on that philosophy'. One of the effects of introducing measures of punishment must be to discriminate between offence and non-offence referrals, which challenges the principle of dealing with all cases on the same basis of need. A widespread criticism was that the government appeared to have 'forgotten' or 'overlooked' the work of children's hearings in the field of child protection. If the government were concerned with 'public perceptions', it would do well to recognise and give publicity to this aspect of hearings business.

Feelings about the government's intentions led some to boycott the reception given at Edinburgh Castle to celebrate the tenth anniversary on 3rd April 1981. Those who attended heard George Younger, the Secretary of State for Scotland,

---

[2] The following account is based on 61 responses collected and reviewed by Kathleen Murray, reported in *The Hearing* 1 (1980), and our own examination of the files.

report that the response to the consultation had been 'overwhelming – something which in itself indicates just how important a place the hearings occupy in Scotland' (reported in *The Hearing* 3 (1981)). The usual formalities of thanks to the volunteers and proclamations of achievement were matched by some informal plain speaking to the Minister from a number of those he had appointed to serve. On 19th May, George Younger announced in the House of Commons the government's decision to drop the proposed additional powers and to consult further on a number of lesser matters which had some support in consultation. There was general relief, if not rejoicing, among those directly involved with the hearings system. It is hard to say how much enthusiasm there was for the punitive measures in government circles in Scotland, and thus to what extent they had been moved by argument or weight of opinion, but the force of opposition, especially from those whose voluntary service at least made the juvenile justice system relatively cheap, must have had an impact.

Other proposals: reparation and glue

In February 1982 readers of *The Hearing* were informed about the progress of the 'other proposals'. The Social Work Services Group 'had to do a good deal of rethinking' and were needing to seek views on their 'further thoughts' (Oliver, 1982). There were two main areas for further consideration. There had been significant support for the idea of *voluntary reparation* in responses to the Consultative Memorandum and advice would be issued on how this could be encouraged. Further consultation was required on the viability of having a new ground for referral relating to 'solvent abuse' or 'self-inflicted injury'. Both issues had to overcome the problem of passage from a criminal justice context.

The Dunpark Committee Report on Reparation by the Offender to the Victim in Scotland (Dunpark, 1977) had recommended that criminal courts in Scotland should have discretionary power to make compensation orders when sentencing, and this was implemented by the Criminal Justice (Scotland) Act 1980. Dunpark had considered giving hearings this power but after receiving submissions conceded that compulsory compensation orders here would be out of place (para 18.02), albeit that 'voluntary reparation by parents might serve a useful purpose in shaping the child's future' (para 18.19).

The idea of the voluntary reparation by children with parental supervision, rather than financial restitution by parents, was taken up by the SWSG circular, Powers and Procedures of Children's Hearings: Use of Voluntary Reparation as a Method of Treatment (SWSG, 1982). According to the circular, for the Dunpark Committee the primary object of voluntary supervision was 'to bring home to a child offender a proper sense of his or her wrongdoing and to give the child the opportunity of redressing the harm done'. However, the circular goes on to add the construction, found nowhere in Dunpark, that 'while "reparation" implies making amends to society, this does not necessarily imply recompensing of an individual victim or the repair of damage caused' (para 2). Under 'reparation', as well as activities which bring the offender into a personal relationship with their victims, 'sometimes community work can be arranged'. This suggests something like a voluntary community service order, or better called a 'community service request' (Martin, 1982a).

Not surprisingly, many of recipients of the circular on voluntary reparation were sceptical. It was another example of court practice being contorted to fit the welfare model. The suggestion that hearings might defer their decisions to see whether voluntary reparation had happened ran the risk of undermining it. This was modelled on the concept of a suspended court sentence. None the less hearings and reporters were enjoined by subsequent guidance to encourage voluntary reparation. There is little evidence of much taking place and even precious few anecdotes. There is, however, a story of a city boy who may eventually have learned something about gardening after a householder, originally a victim of vandalism, had become, by arrangement with the reporter, a victim the second time of over-enthusiastic double-digging.

The question of how to deal with the increasing problem of 'glue sniffing' was the subject of a further consultation paper in December 1981. Superficially the issue was about whether there was a need for a new ground of referral, but underlying this were two more fundamental questions: one about how 'solvent abuse' should be regarded; the other whether multiplication of specific grounds was necessary or desirable. An alternative to creating a new ground was to make 'solvent abuse' an offence – putting it on par with drug taking and underage drinking. However, this was to convert an activity which was a matter of concern almost entirely because of its potential for self-harm into societal harm or a threat to public order. The case for a new ground to cover 'self-inflicted injury' or being 'at risk' of self-harm was argued by those who insisted that the purpose of protecting the child should be recognised as the basis of referral (Borowski, 1982).

Matters were complicated by lack of consensus among groups of consultees. Some organisations like the Association of Children's Panels changed their mind between the two consultations. Some questioned the extent of the problem of glue sniffing. SWSG cast doubt on their understanding of the seriousness of the danger by proposing in the consultation paper that a referral to the reporter might only be appropriate on a second or third occasion, after a police warning. For a few children the first report of inhalation was too late to save their lives. Reporters generally were against the proliferation of grounds. The Association of Reporters argued that children involved in glue sniffing might be covered by being 'beyond parental control' (s 32(a)) or 'lack of parental care' (s 32(c)); but both of these involved laying responsibility on parents, which would sometimes be unfair and unhelpful. The issue was resolved in favour of a new specific ground covering the 'misuse of a volatile substance by deliberately inhaling, other than for medicinal purposes' created by the Solvent Abuse (Scotland) Act 1983, which amended the 1968 Act.

'Justice' for children

It was no coincidence that while the government's proposals to introduce punitive measures were under consideration, a group of criminologists were arguing in favour of bringing back punishment for children under the pre-emptive banner of 'justice'. A book by Morris, Giller, Szwed and Geach, *Justice for Children* (1980), represented a mode of thought that was increasingly holding sway elsewhere in the UK. It owed something to the reaction against the welfare approach in North America, but its context was crucially the perceived failure of the Children and Young Persons Act 1969 in England and Wales.

The nub of the critique was that treatment rather than punishment does not work; it leads to confusion, arbitrariness and injustice. The welfare approach is unsuccessful in protecting society and it is unfair to its recipients. It allows too much discretion and too much invasion into family lives. *Justice for children* requires the separation of offenders to be dealt with under criminal jurisdiction, with those in need of care coming under care proceedings. Effort should be made to divert children from court – for example, by greater use of police warnings. Juvenile courts should deal with offenders on the basis of their deeds, receiving determinate sentences proportionate to the 'seriousness' of their offences, not on a subjective assessment of their needs. Decisions about care should be taken with 'respect for parental autonomy' in a family court where there are rights of legal representation. Informal methods should be used where possible, but in both types of court the principle of 'the least restrictive alternative' should be adopted (Morris, *et al*, 1980).

We have already analysed the content of these ideas in Chapter 2. Suffice here to say that none of these ideas was new and none was instantly welcomed by agencies within the hearings system. Academic supporters of the hearings system in Scotland saw the dialogue with the advocates of a 'return to justice' movement to be desirable and necessary (Asquith, 1983). Even though their views were widely regarded as embodying a 'looking glass conception of Justice' (see Boroswski, 1981), they represented a set of beliefs and concerns which needed to be taken seriously, if for no other reason than that Scotland was part of the United Kingdom.

Although the principles which informed the 1969 Act in England and Wales were very similar to those of Kilbrandon, they lacked institutional embodiment and were very far from being implemented in spirit south of the border. It was perhaps surprising that the alleged 'failure' of the Act was attributed to principles that had never been accepted and applied. This closely parallels the experience of the 'rehabilitative Ideal' in the American juvenile court system. As Allen observed, it was held to have been proved to have failed without having been seriously attempted (Allen, 1973). In England, although care orders could be used for young offenders, Morris and Giller comment that 'the traditional punitive disposals, which were to have been abolished, are increasingly used by the juvenile courts ... there has been little change in the direction intended' (Morris, *et al*, 1980, p17).

The main reason why magistrates were unwilling to use care orders was that they gave complete discretion to local authority social workers on what measures to take, including whether children should stay at home or be placed in residential care, or other forms of care. Magistrates remained committed to public protection but lacked trust in and power over social workers. That recorded juvenile crime in England and Wales increased substantially between 1971 and 1977 – more rapidly than adult crime – was seen by many as the fault of the 1969 Act. Morris and Giller acknowledge the ways in which criminal statistics can be misleading and that the perception of a 'spiral of lawlessness' is part of a 'moral panic' which surrounds discussion of the 1969 Act. None the less, they take the 'failure' of the juvenile justice system in England and Wales to be real and a consequence of a treatment ideology that was never put into practice, rather than a consequence of 'traditional punitive disposals' which apparently continued much as before (Morris *et al*, 1980, pp21–25).

A consequence of the demand to deal with offenders on the basis of their offences, or record of offences, is that such offenders must be sharply differentiated from those whose need of care is the ground for intervention. There is bound to be contamination by association if non-offenders are to be treated within the same institutional setting. This was the conclusion drawn by the Black Report which had made proposals to separate the two in Northern Ireland (Black, 1979). As Asquith pointed out: 'The Black Report offers a practical embodiment of the philosophy presented by Morris, Giller *et al*' (Asquith, 1981). The separation of criminal justice and welfare, and its associated dual standard for dealing with what are often aspects of the same child, was a feature of each of the other jurisdictions in the British Isles. These were competing models with which the hearings system at the beginning of the second decade had politically and intellectually to contend (see Asquith, 1983).

Secure accommodation

By the early 1980s Scotland had in excess of fifty designated 'secure places' for under-sixteen-year-olds located in three purpose-built units attached to List D schools, plus a few 'secure beds' in Assessment Centres (SWSI, 1996). These secure places were geographically very unevenly distributed. Strathclyde contained two of the three List D secure units; half the regions had no secure places of their own. There was deep resistance to the existence of secure provision by some local authorities. Those who argued in their favour saw a need to be able physically to contain some young people who would otherwise abscond, and to rescue children from the other forms of unsuitable custodial provision. It should be said that a significant number of young people over fourteen years old, who were certified 'unruly' by a senior police officer, were held short term in police cells or, on the authority of a court, on remand in prison.[3]

In 1983 legislation was introduced (amending the 1968 Act) which required the use of secure accommodation to be specifically authorised in accordance with stated and challengeable criteria.[4] At the same time a new ground for referral was introduced enabling local authorities to refer children in their care who were not already subject to supervision, where their behaviour was such that special

[3] This was under the provisions of the Criminal Procedure (Scotland) Act 1975, ss 296 and 297.
[4] Introduced by the Health and Social Services and Social Security Adjudications Act 1983, s 8.

measures were needed for their adequate care and control. These provisions were introduced to comply with the European Convention on Human Rights, which required that persons should not be deprived of their liberty without a judicial hearing.[5] Until this time it was accepted that staff responsible for children in local authority care needed 'the additional facility of physical security ... as a very exceptional aid to care and control' (DHSS Circular, 1975). In Scotland, as in England, it was considered a matter of professional discretion as to whether children in the care of the local authority need to be in a locked place. An examination of the admissions process into one of the Scottish Secure Units just prior to the new legislation revealed that despite there being a referral group to scrutinise admissions, the provision was used by the head of the school to provide 'short-term disciplinary placements' (Kelly, 1992, p57).

The criteria according to which hearings were entitled to authorise the use of secure accommodation as a condition of a residential requirement or attaching to a place of safety warrant were either (a) a young person had a history of absconding, and they were likely to abscond and if they did their 'physical, mental or moral welfare' would be at risk or (b) they were likely to injure themselves *or other persons* unless kept in secure accommodation. If these conditions were judged to apply, this had the effect of rendering the child 'liable to be placed and kept in secure accommodation in the named residential establishment at such times as the person in charge of the establishment, with the agreement of the director of social work ... considers it necessary' (s 58A). The amended Act continued to leave much to professional discretion. Not only did the actual decision on the use of secure provision remain with the care professionals after 'authorisation', the Secretary of State gave them the power to use it for up to seven days without authorisation if they judged the criteria to be met, under what the regulations described as 'interim detention' (1983 Regulations).

There was criticism of the new provision from two opposite directions. First, the criterion of likely injury to 'other persons' formally departed for the first time from 'the best interests of the child' criterion. Second, panel members objected to the fact that they had no power to decide that secure provision would be used, even though the criterion for authorisation required a judgment that it was necessary, not that it might be necessary. In effect the professionals could override the hearings judgment. The SWSG rationale was, and still is (see SWSI, 1996), that the discretion was to allow 'flexibility' so that children need be in secure provision for no longer than necessary. But this does not explain why there was no obligation to act on the authorisation even at the point where the hearing made the decision. There was a widespread belief that the permissiveness of implementation was introduced because of scarcity of places. Certainly, the discretion allowed more young people to be authorised to be held in security than there were places available. Data produced for 1994 indicate that between two-thirds and three-quarters of authorisations led to placements (SWSI, 1996).

---

[5] It is a widespread international convention, none the less simplistic, that 'deprivation of liberty' is peculiarly associated with 'locking up'.

Most panel representatives accepted that the limited number of secure places was no bad thing; it reinforced the resolve to provide security without locking doors, and a certain amount of absconding had to be tolerated. What they found difficult to accept, when it came to the allocation of places, was what they saw to be 'unfair' competition with courts. This was not because of the excessive demand from children subject to court sentences (there were only a few long-term residents who had committed very serious offences); it was from the courts' demand for 'interim detention', even though none of the strict criteria applying to hearings authorisation were met. Although courts could not legally bind a child to be held in secure accommodation on remand, they could and sometimes did threaten to send young people on remand to prison, unless a place in secure accommodation was offered. This distorted prioritising on the basis of need.

The availability of secure accommodation, together with persuasive representations, had a major impact on the excessive use of unruly certificates. The number issued by the courts fell dramatically from over 140 in 1985 to under fifty in 1986, and to single figures in 1989 (SWSI, 1996). Unfortunately there are no figures available for children held in police cells, but we know that some children were rescued by the social work departments with the promise of secure places. Desirable though this was, it had an adverse impact on the planned use of secure accommodation to provide individual care programmes.

There were also practical difficulties over movement between a secure and open setting, including in one location the demolition of the open school, which led to some children remaining in a closed unit beyond the point dictated by the criteria. This said, there were very real efforts to make the régime within the secure environment educational and therapeutic, which led to some children not wishing to move into an open setting (Kelly, 1992).

Safeguarders
The legislative origin of safeguarders in the Children Act 1975 (s 66) was a response to the shortcoming in child protection identified by the inquiry into the death of Maria Colwell (Howells, 1974). The fact that ten years elapsed before measures were taken to incorporate the 'safeguarding' function into Scottish legislation is an indication of the doubt about its relevance and usefulness north of the border.

Although only a minority of organisations who responded to the SWSG consultation in May 1984 expressed 'strong reservations', there was a good deal of resistance as well as confusion about what role they might play (Curran, 1989, Chapter 1). Some supporters envisaged that they would supply a means of communication with the child, some saw them as a check on social work. Both these views were suggested by the Maria Colwell Inquiry Report and were echoed in the parliamentary debate on the Children Bill, which was conducted entirely with practice in England and Wales in mind. Professor Martin spoke for many involved in the children's hearings system when he 'suspected' that the concept 'fits very uncomfortably into the philosophy of the children's hearings system ... the clause in question was inserted into the Act for no better reason than that there was a corresponding English clause, and little thought has so far been given to the dilemmas and contradictions to which it is likely to give rise when put into practice' (Martin, 1983b, p6).

With effect from June 1985 an amendment to the 1968 Act (by the Children Act 1975) provided that a hearing chairman or a sheriff 'shall consider' in any case 'whether it is necessary for the purpose of safe-guarding the interests of the child in the proceedings, because there is or may be a conflict, on any matter relevant to the proceedings, between the interests of the child and those of his parent, to appoint a person to act for that purpose'(s 34A(c)(i)).[6]

It should be noticed that the judgment that there is or may be a conflict of interest between child and parent is a necessary condition of appointment. Contentiously, this implied that in the absence of a conflict of interests with parents, children's interests will be looked after satisfactorily in the proceedings. Appointments do not have to be made if there is such a conflict, nor is there a presumption in favour of appointing. What is presumed is that sheriffs and hearing chairmen (invariably in practice the panel members collectively) are able to judge the likely interests of child and parents, before they have considered the case. The conflict of interests criterion was clearly both problematic and deficient (Lockyer, 1994b), which is why it came to be abandoned by the 1995 Act. But the main reason for doubting the need for safeguarders was not dubiety about identifying a conflict of interest, rather it was the belief that other parties already had the duty to safeguard the interests of children.

In fact in the first twelve months there were only 142 appointments – two-thirds by courts, one-third by hearings. Each local authority established a panel of safeguarders which served both courts and hearings; about half of the 102 first appointees were practising solicitors, a quarter had a social work qualification and the remainder had a mixture of professional qualifications or were ex-panel members. Hearings were advised to appoint safeguarders on a rota basis, which SWSG thought was desirable to distribute experience, so hearings seldom exercised the entitlement to appoint individuals (SWSG, 1985, para 12). Courts on the other hand tended to appoint known persons, usually but not exclusively solicitors. The upshot was a very uneven distribution of cases; a few solicitors took the majority of cases in the three Strathclyde sheriffdoms and over half the first group of appointees had no cases in the first year. The Strathclyde regional panel chairman thought safeguarders ought to be trained, and advised her panel members not to use them until they were. Local authorities and solicitor safeguarders were inclined to think training unnecessary.

Despite the difficulties and very low level of usage, Curran's research showed a significant shift in attitude among panel members and social workers to a more favourable disposition towards safeguarders once they had experience of their work. Safeguarders were used by hearings in a variety of types of case; in the majority there were 'care or protection' grounds, but they included offence and

---

[6] The term 'safeguarder' is not used in the Act but in the Social Work (Sheriff Court Procedure Rules) 1971 (rule 2(1)).

truancy referrals. Among the reasons given for appointment, a conflict between the social work department and the parent was most common. In the second largest category the local authority had parental rights. The first implied that the social work department was identified with the child's interest; the second implied the opposite. A few appointments were made with the object of finding out the child's point of view (Curran, 1989, Chapter 4). A later survey of safeguarders showed that they saw assisting the child to express his or her view as part of their brief (Grieve, 1993); and this was compatible with their primary duty to present their view of the child's interest (Sutherland, 1995).

Safeguarders provided reports to hearings, and almost all attended and participated, although strictly there was no legal obligation on them to do either. While standardisation of reports was lacking, they were generally found to be valuable. There was considerable diversity of practice and of views about the sharing of the content of reports with family members and social workers in advance of the hearing. In most cases safeguarders endorsed and supported social work recommendations, but by no means always. The 'independence' of the safeguarder's assessment in the minds of parents and most social workers was seen to be an advantage where there had been tensions or mistrust in their relationships (Curran, 1989).

Sheriffs dealing with applications for proof made more appointments of safeguarders than did hearings. They used them in the main when dealing with young children alleged to have suffered neglect or abuse. However, it was easier to see the role a safeguarder might have in respect of an appeal, where the court might legitimately be assessing where a child's interest lay, than at a proof where the sheriff is essentially making a finding of fact. The Sheriff Court Procedure Rules gave the safeguarder, after receiving all the documents and making 'such enquiries as he may consider appropriate', the option whether or not to become party to the proof. If the safeguarder declines to become a party he must 'report in writing to the sheriff on the extent of his enquiries and his conclusions as to the interests of the child in the proceedings' (1971 Rules, rule 4A(5)). The purpose of this report was unclear. By all accounts safeguarders produced reports which were relevant to the finding and disposal, but as Sheriff Kearney warned, if the sheriff reads the report 'he runs the risk of learning of matters which may not appear in evidence and which may be prejudicial' (Kearney, 1987, p210). Some sheriffs therefore declined to read safeguarders' reports, which were further rendered redundant by there being no mechanism for passing them on to hearings. An obvious solution would have been for appointments to carry over from one jurisdiction to the other until the case was resolved (Lockyer, 1994b).

Safeguarders continued to be sporadically used during the first five years. Hearings appointments increased but in 1991 they were still appointed in less than 1 per cent of cases (1991 Statistics). Against this and the fact of very wide variation in numbers of appointments among regions, it is hard to believe that in every case hearings had considered whether a safeguarder was necessary. The use of safeguarders by sheriffs was similarly uneven and appointments fell overall. However, this was partly a consequence of sheriffs in some places opting to appoint *curators ad litem* instead (arguably with a very similar remit), because of the low level of fees for safeguardering. The events in Orkney provided an opportunity to reflect again on the use that might be made of safeguarders.

Statistical evidence

The three main features of the changing statistical pattern during the 1980s were (a) the great increase in proportion of 'care and protection' cases dealt with by the hearings system as a whole, (b) the increasing diversion of cases from hearings, and (c) the shift in resources used, especially away from residential care. Each made an impact on the work and the relationship between the agencies within the hearings system, none more so than the first of these.

Before we consider the extent of the increase of what is commonly called 'care and protection' or 'child protection', we should be cautious about labels. In following the convention of differentiating these cases by grounds for referral, we do not imply that 'offence referrals' are necessarily different in terms of needs. The endeavour to prevent children offending might also be held to be 'care and protection work'.[7]

During the second decade of the system, the total number of children referred to the reporter rose steadily from 30,786 in 1981 to 41,560 in 1991 (1991 Statistics) – an increase of 35 per cent. This was against the background of a decline in the child population, so that the rate of children under sixteen referred increased by nearly 50 per cent from 16.7 to 24.1 per thousand. The increase in the cases coming to the reporter was very largely the result of the dramatic increase in non-offence grounds for referrals. While offence referrals went up by 5 per cent over the decade, non-offence cases rose by a massive 182 per cent – a consequence of the large rise in care and protection grounds, especially those where the child was alleged to be a victim of an offence, or there was lack of parental care. Offences were 79 per cent of grounds at the beginning of the decade but had fallen to 58 per cent by 1991. Whereas offence referrals (and truancy) per thousand remained almost static, the care and protection rate rose from 4.8 to 13 per thousand. One of the implications was the increasing numbers of girls and younger children referred to the reporter.

The proportion of care and protection cases dealt with by hearings and subject to supervision was considerably higher than the proportion referred to the reporter. Despite the disposition of reporters to reduce the percentage of all cases referred on to hearings, they still diverted more offence referrals. (By 1991 they referred on three in ten offence referrals and four in ten non-offence referrals.) Also hearings were still more likely to discharge cases where there were offence grounds only, at the first or subsequent hearing; and, as noted before, where the

---

[7] The shorthand phrase 'care and protection' cases is used, unless otherwise stated, to refer to cases where the grounds for referral are those specified in s 32(2)(a)–(e) of the 1968 Act and s 52(2) of the 1995 Act, ie, where the child is beyond parental control; in moral danger; where there is a lack of parental care; or the child is a victim of an offence, or in the same household of a child offended against, or of a child offender.

TABLE 4
Referrals to Reporter According to Grounds for Referral

Grounds for referral		1991			1995		
		Boys	*Girls*	*Both*	*Boys*	*Girls*	*Both*
(a)	Beyond parental control	1,050 (3%)	714 (6%)	4%	1,347 (4%)	963 (6%)	5%
(b–e)	Neglect, abuse and at risk	6,076 (19%)	6,607 (54%)	29%	6,507 (20%)	7,225 (48%)	29%
(f)	Failure to attend school	2,014 (6%)	1,391 (11%)	8%	2,415 (7%)	1,821 (12%)	9%
(g)	Offences by child	21,851 (70%)	3,304 (27%)	58%	22,826 (69%)	4,780 (32%)	57%
	Others (including solvent abuse and transfers)	368 (1%)	146 (1%)	1%	149 (0.5%)	157 (1%)	1%
TOTAL		31,359 (100%)	12,162 (100%)	*43,521*	33,244 (100%)	14,946 (100%)	*48,140*

(From the Statistical Bulletin for 1991 and 1995–96 (SWK/CH/1993/16 and SWK/CH/1997/20).)

child had been a victim or was at risk, the supervision was more likely to be lengthy. Thus by 1985 the majority of children subject to supervision requirements had been originally referred on care and protection grounds, and by 1991 this proportion had reached over three-quarters. This meant that the majority of hearings during the second decade dealt with children who had originally been referred for reasons other than their own misconduct.

There were very considerable regional variations in the distribution of cases by grounds. In 1987, six out of ten hearings in Highland Regions dealt with cases under care and protection grounds and only three out of ten with offence grounds. At the other extreme was Fife with only 22 per cent care and protection hearings (or 15 per cent if beyond parental control grounds are extracted) with six out of ten hearings dealing with offences (Lockyer, 1988). These differences probably reflected variations in referral policies between regions rather than simply socio-cultural factors.

The total number of children subject to compulsory supervision followed a downward trend early in the decade, from around 9,000 in 1981 to 8,000 in 1984; thereafter they rose steadily to over 10,000 by 1991. The greater use of informal measures seems largely responsible for the fall in compulsory supervision and its limited growth compared with substantially increasing referrals to the reporter. The reduction of the proportion of care and protection referrals passed on to hearings was a major factor in keeping down the number of supervision requirements. This does not tell us whether there was much more informal 'advice, guidance and assistance' taking place, but clearly some regions made more strenuous efforts than others to introduce informal arrangements.[8]

During the decade, the numbers of residential disposals changed significantly. Children subject to residential supervision fell as a proportion of total requirements from 29 per cent in 1981 to 14 per cent in 1991. Despite the increase in care and protection cases the proportion of children remaining at home with parent or guardian increased from 59 per cent to 68 per cent. In fact the chance of remaining at home on supervision was almost the same whether the ground for referral was an offence or not. Over the period foster placements doubled, reaching the same proportion as those in residential placements. The number staying with relatives or friends followed the same pattern and thus remained constantly about half the number in foster care.

In 1985 Boarding Out and Fostering Regulations were introduced which required that the procedures for assessment and approval of foster parents be applied to relatives, family and friends before hearings could designate their homes as places for children to reside. The increasing concern about the prospects of children being looked after away from home during the 1980s led to greater efforts to keep children living with family members or substitute families and more scrutiny of possible alternative family homes.

Impact of the increase in care and protection: physical and sexual abuse
It will be recalled that the Kilbrandon Report had asserted that there was no essential difference between 'offender cases' and 'care and protection cases', the children in both having suffered 'a failure in upbringing'. There was the expressed hope that the introduction of the Kilbrandon proposals would create an opportunity for early preventive measures in relation to delinquency, and this was not unrelated to care and protection. It was recognised that for truly preventive work to take place, circumstances would require to be addressed in which no criminal offence had been committed. Situations which the Kilbrandon Committee viewed as likely to precipitate early intervention were limited to persistent truancy and children beyond parental control (Kilbrandon, para 59). There is no reference to 'battered babies' or to 'non-accidental injury', even though these phenomena undoubtedly existed and were known about.

In the Seventies, the *physical abuse of children*, after a prolonged phase of what can only be described as denial, even by the medical profession as well as the public at large, began to be increasingly recognised. Such cases tended to come before the hearings as 'emergency' referrals, calling for the infant or toddler (the majority being in that age range) to be removed without delay to a 'place of safety'. Initially, this was usually a hospital paediatric ward, which, in addition to its obvious function of treatment based on accurate diagnosis and careful recording of medical findings for possible forensic use, was of course a 'safe place' to which the child's admission was usually acceptable to the parents on a voluntary basis.

[8] The regional variations in referral rates to hearings were not published in the Statistical Bulletin, but SWSG figures showed marked difference between regions. For statistics and commentary on regional variations, see the Children's Panel Chairmen's Group's Study (Lockyer, 1988).

Place of safety orders were often precipitated at the point where removal from hospital was being contemplated. The less obvious forms of neglect and abuse were gradually becoming identifiable, as the professionals involved – paediatricians, social workers, reporters and police – increasingly worked together and learned from each other at 'case conferences', and as case-study literature accumulated.

By the mid-Eighties, the more complex and often bewildering cases of *sexual abuse of children* began to be recognised or, to be more accurate, began to be suspected. At that time, there was an extreme shortage of experienced workers in this difficult field. The occasional articles which had for some time begun to appear in the literature of the helping professions in the United States and later in Europe were initially regarded by many with extreme scepticism. What took even longer to acknowledge was that a high proportion of sexual abusers were known to their victims and often members of the child's or young person's family or extended family.

The main reason for reviewing such now widely known facts is to emphasise the effect that they had on often young social workers, and even more so on lay volunteers serving on children's panels. Though there was considerable overlap between physical and sexual abuse, the two types of case gave rise to very different responses. Given explanation and support it is not too difficult to have some understanding of the isolated uncontrolled aggression towards a child. But long-standing secretive sexual activity with a child tested to the limit the comprehension, let alone the objectivity, of many.

The effects of the increasing prominence of sexual abuse on the child-protection scene in Scotland were, as elsewhere, significant. Where sexual abuse was alleged there was little likelihood of it being admitted, much media interest and much public incredulity. The effect was heightened by the publicity associated with events in Cleveland at the end of the decade, and thereafter in Rochdale and Orkney.[9] The overall effect was to make the job of those working in child protection increasingly difficult. Well-intentioned preventive intervention ran the risk of being publicly denigrated; and repeatedly the main scapegoats were social workers. In this climate a reluctance energetically to pursue allegations of child sexual abuse without the evidence being incontrovertible was understandable. Children were often disbelieved, simply because the facts were not believable, and modifications of court procedures which took informed account of the needs of child witnesses were long in coming. Social workers and others leaned heavily on official procedures in all such cases, which unfortunately tended to inhibit personal initiative and often led to an unhelpful professional defensiveness.

One of the consequences of the increase in care and protection grounds was the greater involvement of children, parents and reporters appearing before sheriffs. Whereas an application to establish proof was made only in respect of one in ten offence grounds, partly because hearings discharged a significant number of

---

[9] Some of these events are covered in the next chapter.

offence referrals (20 per cent in 1991), the majority of non-offence grounds were sent for proof. Of care and protection grounds, six out of ten required an application for proof, and in two-thirds of these applications the grounds were contested by one or more of the parties, rather than being referred to the sheriff only because the child was too young to be able to understand the grounds. The fact that disposal had to await proof meant that more decisions relating to a child's interim welfare had to be taken. Emergency protection, concerned largely with whether to make or renew place of safety warrants, was an issue for reporters, hearings and sometimes courts. The number of place of safety orders made or renewed by hearings more than doubled during the decade, reaching just under 2,000 in 1991.

The additional burden that 'court work' placed on reporters arose not only from the higher number of cases going to proof hearings, but also from the nature of the cases to be proved. The evidence in such cases was likely to be more complex, tricky to investigate and to judge; and allegations being made against adults, often parents, were likely to be sternly contested. Cases which include alleged sexual abuse or emotional abuse where physical evidence is lacking are especially difficult and time consuming. Finlayson describes the demands which the increase in care and protection cases made on the reporter's job during the 1980s. He says: 'The estimate that these cases take 75% of a reporter's time is conservative' (Finlayson, 1992, pp10–12).

The courts themselves are more closely brought into determining child welfare in respect of care and protection cases. They are not only determining the facts but in effect increasingly determining the minimal standards of parenting, when they decide what is 'acceptable chastisement' or what amounts to 'impairing health and development'. Although appeals increased only modestly (to 121 in 1991) and remits for disposal from criminal cases begun in courts remained low (114 in 1991), there was generally a greater dialogue between sheriffs, reporters and panel members.

In 1981 the first systematic investigation into hearings dealing with care and protection cases was carried out by observation of hearings (Martin, Murray and Millar, 1982). Panel members displayed a heavy dependence on social workers' recommendations, were often reluctant to open up sensitive areas for discussion and even showed an apparent lack of curiosity about the arrangements made for children removed from their homes. 'Children's hearings,' the authors state, 'provide an opportunity for calm and considered judgement, away from any political and departmental pressures.' In too many cases the opportunity was not fully taken.

In retrospect, none of this was surprising. Even experienced professionals spoke of considerable stress in working with such families. This demanded a substantial effort to equip panel members to cope better with child abuse cases. Specially devised in-service training opportunities were introduced for panel members; and this was extended in some places to advisory committee members, whose supportive role was now more necessary than ever. Clearly, more attention needed to be given to training in chairmanship. Nevertheless, many experienced panel members took the view that care and protection cases were not all that different, the families being much the same as before. Offences or truancy cases often involved complex family situations, intractable problems and conflict at hearings. It was a mistake to suggest that there was a new paradigm for child abuse hearings (Lockyer, 1994a). This said, the increasing numbers of abuse and neglect cases did arouse anxiety, especially in localities where few such cases had come to light in the previous decade.

Conflict, resources and disposals

In the second half of the decade there was a growing tension between the representatives of panel members and those of social work management, ostensibly over the availability and control of resources. Fundamentally the issue was about who decides what children and families need. The Children's Panel Chairmen's Group (CPCG) argued that the decision-making powers of children's hearings were being constrained by the child care policies of local authorities, 'which paid little regard to the local authorities' duty to make provision to carry out the decisions of hearings'. The Association of Directors of Social Work defended the right of elected local authorities, with the benefit of their professional advisers, to develop what they judged appropriate child care strategies. In the background to tension at national level was the local conflict in Fife, which became a *cause célèbre* during the next five years.

The CPCG undertook to initiate a study to attempt to quantify 'the extent to which panel members at hearings saw themselves constrained in their decision-making by lack of resources'. This was produced as the *Study of Children's Hearings' Disposals in Relation to Resources* (Lockyer, 1988).[10] The main finding was that one in five hearings believed that decisions were or would be affected by a resource deficiency. This indicated a lower level of problems associated with resources and services required to carry out hearings decisions, and a higher level of satisfaction, than many panel members expected. Directors of social work took some comfort. Panel members' criticisms were put into the context of a generally positive view of the work done by local authority social work departments. The report served to provide some data which opened up areas of discussion. The following is a summary of some of the findings.

- Hearings dealing with offence or truancy referrals were twice as likely to be resource constrained as care and protection cases.
- There was a higher level of satisfaction with resources provided for younger children than older children.
- The most frequently identified lack of resources related to social work time devoted to home supervision.
- There was delay in seeking an early review when one had been promised.
- There was lack of command over local authority resources not 'owned' by social work, especially alternative education provision.

[10] The findings were based on an analysis of questionnaires completed by panel members after all hearings during the three months from November 1987 to January 1988. It yielded 2,803 returns – 85 per cent of possible hearings.

- Despite raised expectations, intermediate treatment remained a scarce resource, considered more a voluntary option than a hearing's disposal, still less an 'alternative to custody'.
- There was no overall national shortage of residential places, but there were problems with their geographical distribution, access to the most appropriate and delay in placements.
- There was a high level of satisfaction with foster care but there were problems with availability, especially to enable siblings to remain together.
- There was an unmet demand for secure accommodation, though panel members wished to see more children adequately contained in an open setting than more locked places.

The study also looked at the relationship between social work recommendations and hearing decisions. It found a positive correlation between recommendations and decisions in approximately 85 per cent of cases. This compares with the '81 or 82 per cent' correspondence found by Martin, Fox and Murray (Martin *et al*, 1981). There are many complications about calculating this figure, but it seemed to show that convergence was a consequence of the higher proportion of care and protection cases in which there was more agreement than in others. Where the disposal required a specific non-domestic resource the correspondence was between 90 and 95 per cent; whereas on the decision whether or not compulsory measures were needed at all, there was agreement in only two-thirds of cases. There were considerable regional variations; notably in Fife a particular disjunction between recommendations and decisions to discharge or terminate supervision was found.[11]

A question raised by this and other studies was whether there was a 'healthy' or 'unhealthy' level of agreement between social worker recommendations and hearings decisions. This fed into the long-standing debate as to whether panel members were sufficiently independent from social workers in their judgments (Asquith, 1977; May and Smith, 1980). A high level of agreement between recommendations and decisions is not in itself evidence of panel members acting as 'rubber stamps' (Watson, 1982). The important question is not so much concerned with the level of agreement between the views expressed by social workers prior to the hearing and the hearings' dispositals, but whether children and parents have a chance to influence the decision. If they cannot, their participation in the proceedings is gained on false pretences (Lockyer, 1989).

What the evidence did show was that during the decade there had been a shift in the relative views of social workers and panel members on the need for compulsory intervention, quite apart from whether there was agreement on actual cases. In the 1970s social workers recommended overall more compulsory intervention than hearings endorsed; by the end of the 1980s hearings terminated fewer supervisions and discharged fewer referrals than were recommended. These differences were not dramatic; hearings made about 10 per cent more requirements than the number recommended. But it did mean that when there

---

[11] This became relevant to the Fife Inquiry, covered in the next chapter.

was a disagreement it was more likely to be that hearings were demanding more rather than less compulsory intervention. They were more often wanting to use resources rather than decline them. It was in these circumstances that stresses developed.

The CPCG Study concluded with the observation that there was a 'need for more liaison' between panel members and social work management. This was in part a recognition that the social worker at the hearing had become a less independent agent and more a bureau professional representing the views of a case conference, 'admissions group' or department policy. It was now recognised that there needed to be dialogue outside the hearing room to discuss problems that arose inside it. The system, it was sometimes said, was becoming 'increasingly political'. It could equally be said that it was reaching the age of maturity and a state of realism.

6 : The 1990s'
Recommendations for Reform

URING the 1970s and 80s the children's hearings system evolved by adapting its practice to changing circumstances. There were modest legislative innovations, but only those which could be assimilated by its institutional framework and compatible with the Kilbrandon philosophy. This was no accident. Among the central actors within the system the impulse to innovate was generally confined to changes in practice checked by the disposition to conserve the core values and institutions which were put in place in 1971. However, during the 1990s there was a growing momentum for legislative reform, driven mainly by events within Scotland, but influenced by moves throughout the United Kingdom and beyond to recognise children's rights.

This chapter deals with the events and debate in Scotland, but it should be remembered that this took place against the background that Britain had signed the United Nations Convention on the Rights of the Child, and that the European Convention on Human Rights now applied a standard against which Scottish legislation could be judged.

The Child Care Law Review (CCLR)

The formal beginning to the process was the setting up of a group by the Secretary of State in 1988 to 'to identify, in the light of developments since the implementation of the Social Work (Scotland) Act 1968, options for change and improvement in child care law' (CCLR, 1990, para 1.1). In some quarters the instigation of the Review was thought to be an unnecessary sequel to the much-needed review in England and Wales which led to the Children Act 1989. The Scottish group claimed to be 'informed rather than guided' by the Children Act (para 1.11), though in fact its influence on the drafting of the Children (Scotland) Act 1995 was rather greater than the review group might have wished.

The review group was composed predominantly of individuals involved with the hearings system or child care services, though there was a notable absence of representatives from education and health, and perhaps an over-representation of social workers. The Review was chaired by the senior civil servant responsible for children's hearings at the Social Work Services Group (SWSG) and proceeded by co-opting additional members with practice experience and issuing a series of three consultation papers. Given its composition and approach, the group was likely to reflect both the existing tensions among participant agencies, including those between central and local government, and the achievable compromises. The ninety-five recommendations were accordingly conservative, realistic and mostly unanimously adopted. In the end they provided the basis for most of the legislative innovation in the Children (Scotland) Act 1995.

In announcing the Review the Secretary of State made it clear that no radical departure from the hearings system was envisaged. The report duly concluded that the existing law was 'fundamentally sound and met the main needs of children and their families'. Although 'there was no need for wholesale revision or restructuring', there was scope for 'improvement and simplification' and some changes were required 'in order to meet the social needs and pressures which have emerged or become more pronounced since 1968' (para 1.15). A series of principles were elaborated which the review group claimed gave coherence to their examination, along with a 'strong commitment' to the principles embodied in the European Convention on Human Rights and the United Nations Convention on the Rights of the Child (paras 1.13 and 1.14).

One of the most politically sensitive areas related to the general duty of local authorities to promote social welfare, and make available 'advice, guidance, and assistance' to persons in need (1968 Act, s 12). The group was keen to extend the duty to use resources, not just to prevent children being 'received into care' or assist them 'after a period of care' – the existing formula carried narrow and negative connotations – but to require local authorities to assist anyone through-out childhood by providing 'a range of support services', to prevent family breakdown, give respite care, and assist the most vulnerable group of sixteen- to eighteen-year-olds. Local authorities' support for destitute families, children who had left home and those in public care, or who had left public care, had to be considered in the context of central government's recent withdrawal of income benefits from young people who could be regarded as remaining the financial responsibility of their parents. Representatives of local authorities were at pains to resist the shift of young people from income entitlement to discretionary welfare, and the financial burden from central to local government. The Review had to settle for endorsing the principle of maintaining the division of responsibility of 'central government to provide income support and local authorities to ensure the availability of services and related assistance for children and families in need'.[1]

The Review made proposals to clarify the rights and responsibilities of local authorities in relation to children and their parents, depending on the different forms of care status to which the child may be subject. For instance, it recommended there be a presumption of reasonable parental access to children in voluntary care, and to those under supervision away from home, or in a place of safety, unless a hearing or court made a condition regulating or terminating access. It recommended:

- 'care reviews' at specified intervals for children in physical care, with rights of attendance for children and parents subject to certain safeguards (recom-mendations 16–22);
- specific responsibilities to take account of religious, racial and cultural identity when making provision (recommendation 27);

[1] Discussed in Chapter 9.

- a duty on care authorities to promote the health and education of children in local authority care, and give advice and assistance to children who have left care to age twenty-one (recommendations 24 and 34–36);
- the assumption of parental rights should be by determination of a court according to non-morally judgmental grounds, rather than by administrative order (recommendations 40–42).

One area where there was significant and unresolved disagreement was the 'care status' of children subject to a home supervision requirement. Most reporters and panel members wanted to preserve the general description of 'compulsory measures of care', because *care*, defined as 'protection, control, guidance and treatment', was how they wished all forms of supervision to be viewed. However, the argument unremittingly pursued by social work representatives was that to regard children at home as *in care* of the local authority was unreasonable and undesirable. It led to unrealistic demands of social work and it undermined the responsibility of parents. This view prevailed with the majority of the review group, so that children at home should 'unequivocally' be considered in the care of parents, or other named persons, and only those physically away from home (in residential or foster care) should be considered in the care of the local authority (recommendation 69). No doubt the dispute contributed to the term 'care' being disassociated from all forms of supervision in the 1995 Act – which we consider regrettable.[2]

The proposals which related to the children's hearings and the reporter were relatively modest. Some simply removed ambiguities or filled gaps left by the 1968 Act. The recommendations specifying maximum time periods in the referral process to the reporter and to the hearing probably make the most significant demands on personnel, and may make the greatest impact on children and families. This was a response to the recognition that delay in bringing cases defies a child's sense of time and undermines considerations of welfare (recommendations 65–68).

There was much discussion and consultation on the grounds for referral. The idea of a composite ground was floated but sank; social work members urged dropping the 'truancy' ground but this was rejected; a codification of offences against children was proposed but deemed impractical. In the end the main change recommended was to extend the ground relating to solvent abuse to drugs and alcohol and other conduct causing 'serious self-harm' (recommendation 53).[3]

Two proposals relating to what the Review called 'operational aspects' of the hearing gained general endorsement only with difficulty. These were that hearings 'should have the power to exclude a parent from a part or parts of a hearing, in order to obtain the views of a child' (recommendation 82), and that hearings should be 'empowered to prescribe in a supervision requirement a date for its review' (recommendation 83).

---

[2] See Chapter 7.
[3] The 1995 Act created a separate new ground to cover 'misuse of alcohol or drug' and dropped the 'serious self-harm' formula.

The need for the power to exclude parents was doubted by many respondents to the consultation, including submissions from panel members, who argued that parents could normally be persuaded to leave the hearing room voluntarily. However, it was known that a child's attendance was occasionally excused to avoid the trauma of meeting a parent who had an absolute right to be present throughout. Support for this proposal gained ground after the events in Orkney, and the more the voice of children who had experienced hearings was listened to.

The proposal that hearings should have the power to specify the date for a review was strongly opposed by social work representatives among the review members and consultees. They saw it as an 'interference with case management', implying a distrust of local authorities to exercise their duty to call a review when required. There was an element of truth in this, since the proposal was grounded on the evidence from the Children's Panel Chairmen's Group (CPCG) research where, as we have noted, in a significant number of cases a review promised to families had not taken place. This recommendation survived opposition, with a caveat that it would be an exceptional measure where reasons for a predetermined date could be given as part of a care plan (para 20.3).

A further area where divided opinion among the review group reflected tension in practice related to the interface between children's hearings and decisions about the long-term care of children. While hearings were concerned with short-term measures, predominantly with sustaining children in existing families, local authorities had a duty to consider the longer-term arrangements for substitute families by pursuing the assumption of parental rights, freeing for adoption, and adoption through the courts. In practice there had been significant conflict in cases where hearings were unwilling to comply with the long-term plans – for example, by denying parental access to children in foster care – simply on the grounds that plans were afoot to make application to the court.

The reporter and the panel member on the review saw the solution to lie in shifting approval of permanent plans to hearings, the courts dealing only with contested cases on appeal. However, the majority view was that the authority of the court was required for the formal transfer of parental status and that when the court took such decisions, supervision requirements should be set aside. What was at issue here was more than a contest of jurisdiction. There was a view among social workers that hearings were less willing than courts to sever moribund family connections and give a child a fresh family start.

The compromise adopted was that local authorities must continue to seek approval from hearings for all significant changes in care plans; they would not require *'permission'* (CCLR emphasis, para 17.4) to initiate an application for transfer of parental rights, 'freeing', or an adoption order, but hearings must have the opportunity to submit observations and advice to the court (recommendations 71–73). Whether subsequent to a change in family status it was for the court or for the hearing to review the supervision requirement remained unresolved (recommendations 74A and B).

The Review recommended some modest changes to the law relating to the appointment of safeguarders, which will be discussed elsewhere (recommendation

83). The important proposal to amend the rules to give children and parents the right to 'see copies of reports submitted to hearings' (recommendation 86) gained force by a decision of the European Court of Human Rights criticising the lack of access to reports by family members, including unmarried fathers (*McMichael* v *UK* (1995) 20 EHRR 205). The judgment in *Kennedy* v *A* 1986 SLT 358 made it clear that children and parents were not entitled to access to reports. However, the Review considered the Access to Personal Files Act 1987 to have created a presumption of access which ought to be extended to hearings.[4]

The Review rejected the proposal that there should be legal aid for attendance at hearings, despite significant support among consultees (para 20.7). This was an issue which remained alive beyond the Review. After considerable deliberation the idea of making public provision to exclude a 'suspected perpetrator' was rejected because 'such a course seems unlikely to offer greater protection to a child at risk than is currently possible' by voluntary agreement or private proceedings.[5] This conclusion was reversed mainly by the rethinking induced by the Orkney Inquiry.

Two areas where the Review confronted the limits of its remit were also matters of potential conflict with central government. In relation to referral policy affecting sixteen- to twenty-one-year olds, in particular the imperative to keep more sixteen- to eighteen-year-olds in the hearings system, and the proposal to introduce a Child Welfare Commission, which had broad support, further reviews were recommended.

It could be claimed that the 'in-house' approach of the Review led to a missed opportunity to deal with major issues which had later to be addressed by recourse to judicial inquiry and review. However, it could equally be said that had the recommendations of the Review been in place, some later problems would have been avoided. Its measured proposals were for a while overshadowed by other events, but with a few exceptions (the main being in relation to emergency protection) it provided the basis for the 1995 Act. The residual tensions which our account of the Review has described were contained within a general acceptance of the core of the Kilbrandon prescribed arrangements. This consensus was apparently less secure when the operation of the system became exposed to the public gaze and to quasi-judicial contests in Fife and Orkney.

The Fife Inquiry

The Judicial Inquiry into Child Care Policies in Fife was the longest-running inquiry in the field of child care in Britain, beginning in April 1989 and reporting three and a half years later.[6] The inquiry could have been avoided if the local

---

[4] The judgment in the *McMichael* case and article 13 of the United Nations Convention on the Rights of the Child endorse this (see Chapters 7 and 10).

[5] Under the Matrimonial Homes (Family Protection) (Scotland) Act 1981.

[6] The Fife Inquiry was conducted by Sheriff Brian Kearney, author of *Children's Hearings and the Sheriff Court* (1987) and a contributor to this book. His original appointment to the Child Care Law Review was interrupted for the purpose of conducting the inquiry. He was advised by Elizabeth Mapstone, Emeritus Professor of Social Administration at the University of Dundee.

authority had accepted and acted on an SWSG advisers' report delivered in December 1988. This report identified a serious loss of confidence by the children's panel in the child care policy adopted by Fife Council in November 1985, and which was being put into practice by the director of social work. (The advisers' report is referred to in the prologue to the Fife Inquiry Report.)

The objectives embodied in Fife's policy document were neither at odds with trends elsewhere nor implacably opposed in principle by other agencies in Fife. In essence the policy promoted 'minimum feasible intervention'. This involved a preference for voluntary measures rather than the use of compulsion, examining all alternatives before removing children from home, and returning them as soon as possible, residential care being regarded as a measure of last resort. Policies of this sort were increasingly to be found in local authorities' child care strategies across Scotland – part of a developing consensus within social work, and supported by many agencies, including some reporters and panel members. However, the complaint in Fife was that the policies were being pushed too far, that they put children at risk, and undermined or marginalised the role of children's hearings.

The inquiry proceeded to examine policy in practice by viewing case files and hearing evidence in relation to fourteen core cases, in which the director was 'almost uniformly' willing to endorse the work carried out (p111). The central conclusion was that the problems which had arisen were a consequence of a 'simplistic and mechanical' application of policy, which was imposed by senior management as an 'orthodoxy' which gave little scope for individual discretion or for taking account of views or judgments of parties.

> '[T]he central impetus in implementation of policy which we found to exist was the tendency to over-simplify the approach of the social worker to the intricate and difficult discipline of child care and impose this simplified approach in a rigid and dogmatic manner which, thus imposed, alienated others involved in child care such as, on the one hand, the Children's Panel and the Reporter, parts of the hearings system and, on the other hand, other professionals directly involved in child care, such as teachers, guidance teachers, educational psychologists, psychiatrists, clinical child psychologists and health visitors. It also gravely inhibited the discretion of the professional social worker who worked directly with the child and was in touch with the child's needs' (p616).

This created a climate of dogma in relation to diversion from all forms of compulsory measures, and where this failed, in keeping children at home and out of residential care, almost at any cost. Although the policy theoretically *allowed* residential care to be used as a last resort, the climate of opinion towards it was 'almost universally negative' (p589). In the atmosphere created by the orthodoxy, any social worker who proposed residential care before other options had been tried, tended to be branded as a heretic (p614). The single most 'serious and dangerous effect of the impetus towards simplicity was the erosion of the professional discretion of the social worker' (p613).

An indication of the extent of the gulf between the social work department and the reporter and panel members in Fife was shown by the statistical study which the inquiry commissioned. It examined the relationship between social work recommendations and decisions during 1989. Its findings confirmed those of the Children's Panel Chairmen's Group Study (Lockyer, 1988), namely that in Fife the largest area of disagreement was whether there was a need for compulsory measures at all. About half of the home supervision requirements were made against advice to discharge or terminate. Of the few residential requirements made, the majority were contrary to social work advice (p412).[7] These findings must be seen against the unusually low number of children in the physical care of the local authority in Fife and the relatively few care and protection referrals (p586).

The local authority blamed the peculiarity of the region's figures on the referral policy of the reporter. However, the inquiry was satisfied that the low level of care and protection referrals was principally due to the department's 'inappropriate diversion of cases' (pp413, 595). The cases studied showed some withholding of information from hearings which might have been relevant to the need for intervention; some reluctance to put children on the protection register and hold case conferences (which denied social workers the expertise of other agencies); and a tendency to be 'over-optimistic' about improvements which permitted 'a quick return home'. Altogether these indicated a loss of focus on the paramount welfare of the child (pp555–571).

The inquiry report averred that in some cases, referral to a hearing 'may be of intrinsic value to the child and play a part in securing the child's rights'. It recommended that the direct interest of the child, 'including his interest in having his rights to justice and welfare protected within the context of the Hearings System', be taken into account when social workers were considering referral to the reporter (p596). Hearings should receive reports on the whole situation of the child (not just matters relevant to the grounds or to the disposal recommended); alternative disposals should be discussed; and in appropriate circumstances hearings should be invited to consider the long-term interests of the child (pp569, 598, 618).

Although the inquiry made recommendations both to clarify the law and improve practice aimed at restoring the balance between the agencies within the children's hearings system, in essence a recovery of mutual trust and renewal of co-operation was required (p16). The starting-point for this process had to be the acceptance of the findings by the director of social work and the local authority (p623). A recommendation which served to test this was that the regional panel should have an input into the council's social work committee when child care policies were being considered (p593).[8]

The region's immediate response to the inquiry report was not promising. However, an examination conducted by the newly created Social Work Services

---

[7] The details of Dr Kendrick's study are given in Annexation C, pp667–695.

[8] In the longer term, it was recommended that panel representation should be mandatory when local authorities were considering policy and resources affecting children. This is adopted by the Children (Scotland) Act 1995 (s 19(5)) which requires the 'chairman of the children's panel', together with the 'Principal Reporter' and others, to be consulted when local authorities are planning services for children.

Inspectorate (itself in part a response to the Fife Inquiry), completed in May 1994, found that there had been substantial progress. The main recommendations had been implemented, policies had been modified and the atmosphere of trust and co-operation with the children's panel had been 'much improved'. The region still remained short of residential places (SWSI, 1995).

The tensions which gave rise to chronic conflict in Fife are to some degree endemic in the hearings system. Events in Fife served as a cautionary tale and other regions were encouraged to improve co-operation to avoid similar problems. The experience of Fife also served to indicate the tolerable boundaries of managerialism within social work. It showed the practical limits to the doctrine of radical non-intervention, whose origins lay in pessimism about juvenile justice and child care practice, incompatible with the Kilbrandon philosophy.

Orkney events
The events in Orkney centred on the removal from their homes on 27th February 1991 of nine children from four families on suspicion that they had been exposed to organised sexual abuse. The Orkneys are a group of islands north-east of the mainland, served by the smallest local authority in Scotland. The families of the children involved were from a group of incomers living on the island of South Ronaldsay. The nature of the allegations and the response of the families made the conduct of the case a matter of intense national media interest.

Focus centred on an alleged event or events around a local quarry at which there was 'ritualistic music, and dancing' and 'sexual intercourse and/or simulated sexual intercourse' between children and a hooded 'master' of ceremonies in the centre (Clyde, 1992, para 7.11). The grounds for referral did not identify the alleged perpetrator, but it was widely publicised that the local minister of religion was suspected. Extraordinary press, radio and television coverage was made possible by the families of the children removed, who gave information and used the media to refute the allegations and to protest about their treatment. Official parties, constrained by the obligation to confidentiality both in relation to matters *sub judice* and to preserve anonymity, were ill equipped to deal with the media. The reaction of the families was understandable, but the lack of circumspection of the media coverage and its failure to comprehend proceedings was disturbing.

The concerns which led to the emergency removal stemmed from disclosures made by three other children of a large family, who were already in local authority care as proven victims of sexual abuse, with whom some members of the families had continued contact. Police and social workers, with the authority of a place of safety warrant from a sheriff, decided it was necessary to carry out what the media described as 'dawn raids' to remove and isolate the children for the purpose of investigation.

During the five weeks when the children were in places of safety on the mainland and out of contact with their parents, they were subject to a series of interviews, many aspects of which were later criticised. After two children's hearings and two appeals to the sheriff which sustained the need for removal until evidence was heard, a sheriff in Kirkwall decided the proof of the grounds for referral could not proceed because the application was 'fatally flawed', because the children were not present at the hearing to have the grounds explained.

The sheriff allowed the press to be present to hear his judgment on the application, and went on to express critical views relating to productions made available to him (transcripts and tapes of interviews) which cast doubt on what might be presented as 'evidence'. The children were immediately returned home. An appeal to the Court of Session found against the sheriff. Lord President Hope, sitting with two colleagues, found the sheriff to have been in error in not hearing the application (the hearing had been entitled to dispense with the children's presence and there was no illegality about the 'business meeting' which advised the reporter not to have them brought from the mainland). The sheriff had been entitled to open his deliberations to the press, but was 'in breach of the elementary rules of natural justice' by commenting without hearing evidence led. The consequences of this action were 'incalculable'(*Sloan* v *B* 1991 SLT 530).

Before we consider some of them, we should note their Lordships' comment that it should be clear at the outset that 'although the case raised difficult and sensitive issues which aroused strong feelings on either side and have attracted much publicity, there was ample provision within the existing rules of procedure for the taking of the appropriate decisions in a judicial and orderly manner in the best interests of all parties with a minimum of delay' (*Sloan* v *B*, p539).

The way was cleared for the acting reporter to resume the application for proof before another sheriff, but he chose not to do so. Whether or not this was a necessary consequence of the Kirkwall sheriff's action, or of the fact that the children had been returned home, we cannot know. The reporter's counsel argued at the Court of Session that 'the damage caused to the evidence of potential witnesses had been very grave' and had 'prejudiced' the case.

The Orkney Inquiry
The inevitable public inquiry was conducted by Lord Clyde at great expense and lasted eight months.[9] Its findings were published and presented to Parliament on 27th October 1992, on the same day as those of the Fife Inquiry, which significantly detracted from the public impact of the latter.

The terms of reference of the Orkney Inquiry did not permit it to adjudicate on the central issue of 'the truth or falsity of the allegations of sexual abuse'. To the public at large, and in the submission of the parents, this was a major failing. This is acknowledged by Lord Clyde. He makes the point that the families risked passing up the opportunity to have the facts fully explored when they elected to oppose the application for proof on the competency of the application (para 1.11). Lord Clyde says that the decision by the acting reporter to abandon the proof was 'precipitate' and indicated 'a complete lack of confidence' in being able to

---

[9] The cost of conducting the Orkney Inquiry, estimated at £6–7 m, was heavily criticised. The inquiry was conducted in Orkney, which involved most of the legal representatives travelling there by plane, funded generously by the Scottish Office (Bissett-Johnson, 1994).

prove his case (para 14.104). In passing no comment on the import of the sheriff's remarks, the inquiry ignored the possible effect on potential child witnesses of having had their testimony implicitly dismissed in public before being heard.

There were other pertinent questions beyond the terms of reference of the inquiry, such as why there was an 'acting' reporter, seconded from Strathclyde, working part-time in Orkney, and what effect this had had.[10] The least well covered aspect of the terms of reference was the inquiry into the effect of the 'attendant publicity' on the 'actings' of the agencies.

The Clyde Report fully documents and amply demonstrates a catalogue of deficiencies in practice and procedure, not only within a stressed and over-stretched Orkney Islands Social Work Department, but within other agencies brought in to assist. The decision to seek places of safety orders and remove the children was precipitately taken without full consideration of the degree of risk or alternative means of testing the allegations (paras 13.34–13.37). The timing of the removal 'was beyond serious criticism'. However, the way the removal was conducted – which involved children being denied personal possessions, not being told what was happening and not being allowed family contact, due to concern about collusion – was found to be unjustified (paras 14.1–14.19). This added to the hostility of the parents and contributed to their receiving neither social work support nor adequate information.

Most of the far-reaching criticism applied to the planning, conduct, recording, reporting and frequency of so-called 'disclosure' interviews. A most serious finding was that of the interviewers who, believing that the abuse had taken place, were unwilling to give due weight to denials (paras 14.70–14.93). Some of these criticisms echoed the findings made by the Inquiry into Child Abuse in Cleveland in England in 1988. Parallels between Orkney and Cleveland can be overstated, as can the relevance of guidelines formulated without 'organised abuse' in mind. However, on the need to listen to children, to treat them as individuals, to keep clear records and for agencies to share information and to co-operate, it is fair to say that lessons which might have been learned had not been learned. Lord Butler-Sloss's much-quoted dictum that 'the child is a person not an object of concern' was equally relevant to reflections on events in Orkney.[11]

Most of the 194 recommendations proposing improvements in procedures and practice were familiar and unobjectionable. They included the need for the careful planning, recording and assessment of all the options, the necessity for inter-agency co-operation and giving support to those under suspicion, the avoidance of acting in haste, and the need to 'keep an open mind' when interviewing children. All these required the assistance of better written guidance, more social work training and centrally available expert advice. By way of balance,

---

[10] The Orkney reporter had been suspended by agreement of the Scottish Office and the local authority.

[11] Lord Butler-Sloss spoke of the 'depressing and disturbing resemblance' four years on at a conference convened to compare the findings of the two inquiries. Its proceedings were edited by Stewart Asquith, 1993.

it was recommended that steps should be taken to increase public awareness of the problem of child sexual abuse, and the press and public should give social workers the support they need to do their work (recommendations 3 and 188). Both these conclusions were echoed by Lord Butler-Sloss in her comments on Orkney. She added that the police had been lucky to escape criticism (Asquith, 1993).

The Clyde Report rightly found fault not only with persons and procedures but with the law associated with emergency protection. Some of the deficiencies with place of safety warrants had already been identified by the CCLR, but Lord Clyde departed from some of the Review's proposals. The thrust of his proposals was to make the emergency removal of children from the family home less likely and to make the right to challenge the procedure more readily available. The report proposed a new Child Protection Order, to be granted following a more exacting procedure, on narrower criteria and with tighter specified conditions. There is doubt whether the Clyde proposals would have given more realistic opportunity to challenge the grounds for removal, but they would have allowed a more immediate legal challenge, and given a clearer specification of rights and duties than under the existing arrangements (paras 18.16–18.20).

The most contentious proposal in the report was that all decisions relating to emergency protection should be transferred to the sheriff court (para 18.20, recommendation 142). The reasoning behind this proposal was multifaceted and somewhat confusing. It was based on three considerations:

- the need to separate the grounds for emergency protection from those of compulsory measures of care (para 18.1);
- the need to keep the forum for considering evidence separate from that determining welfare (para 18.19);
- the capacity of hearings to deal with 'complex cases' such as those involving sexual abuse (para 18.22).

Crucially, the report fails to address the critical question of whether decisions in respect of emergency protection are essentially matters of evidential judgment or welfare judgments.

In his commentary Lord Clyde says the reporter was 'in error' in advising the hearing not to consider the substance of medical reports, and he goes on to suggest that it would be competent 'when considering the question whether the continued detention of the child under the place of safety order is in the child's best interests to have regard to *evidence bearing on the strength of the grounds for referral*' (our emphasis) (para 13.72). This of course contradicts the first consideration identified above. If Lord Clyde was right in thinking that hearings should take a preliminary view of the evidence, he was right to propose the transfer of the decision to the sheriff (in accordance with the second consideration above). However, before the evidence on the grounds for referral is heard, hearings have understood that their role is *not* to exercise a judgment about its veracity but to decide the need for protection, *given the fact of the accusation*, its nature and seriousness, and the response of the family to it. Thus we defend the reporter and the hearing's approach against the view taken by the Inquiry.

The case for transferring emergency protection to sheriffs on the ground that they are better equipped to deal with disputes and conflict begs a number of questions about these 'complex cases'. The presumption seems to be that sexual abuse (and perhaps some other categories of child abuse cases) give rise to such special difficulties that reform of the hearings system is required to deal with them.

Lord Clyde recognised the danger of generalising from the extraordinary circumstances of these cases, yet he was willing to reach general conclusions influenced by a number of submissions to the Inquiry (para 18.24). However, these were taken to be authoritative without being subject to critical scrutiny. Apparently the most persuasive was the submission from the Association of the Directors of Social Work (ADSW) (Child Protection: Policy Practice and Procedure, 1992). In our view this gives an extremely partial view of the operation of the children's hearings based on 'hard cases'. It exaggerates the extent to which child protection cases are different from others and it fails to recognise the extent to which the consensual rather than the adversarial approach is still appropriate (Lockyer, 1994a). Correspondingly, the Clyde Report underestimates the extent to which co-operation with families is possible in a non-adversarial setting in child protection cases prior to proof, and overestimates the lack of conflict in all cases after proof. That the Directors of Social Work saw the 'way forward' to lie in treating care and protection cases differently from others, including individual representation and child advocates at hearings, is of no small significance (ADSW, 1992, pp50–52).

The submission of the Scottish Child Law Centre (SCLC) (Marshall, 1992) also took the opportunity to make the case for child advocates. The Inquiry proposed that it should first be seen whether the role of safeguarders could be developed to meet the needs of children both in and before court and hearings proceedings (recommendation 84). The Inquiry endorsed other recommendations of the Scottish Office Review of Child Care Law in Scotland (1990) but suggested that further consideration be given to the viability of removing from home the alleged abuser instead of the child. These ideas were taken up by the White Paper, Scotland's Children (1993).

In response to a Scottish Office consultation on Emergency Protection (SWSG, 1992) subsequent to the Clyde Report, it was forcefully argued by many that the proposal to transfer all emergency protection decisions to sheriffs was seriously misguided and if adopted would substantially undermine the role of children's hearings. Most significant perhaps was the opposition of the Sheriffs' Association. The proposal was dropped in the White Paper which followed.

Scotland's Children

The White Paper, Scotland's Children: Proposals for Child Care Policy and Law, published in August 1993, was a distillation of proposals from the three sources already discussed, and from the Scottish Law Commission Report, Family Law

(SLC, 1992), Finlayson's Reporters to the Children's Panels: Their Role, Function and Accountability (1992), Skinner's Report on Residential Child Care (1992) and the SWSG Review of Adoption Law in Scotland (1993). In addition to incorporating proposals from these sources, the White Paper claimed also to be a response to 'social trends' in relation to child care since the 1968 Act.

The White Paper began by emphasising 'parental responsibilities', reflecting the influence of the Scottish Law Commission's view that these were the basis of parental rights and must be shared by both parents. Listening to children and treating them as individuals were themes which echoed the words of Butler-Sloss, Clyde, and Kearney. The need to deal 'effectively with young offenders' was a somewhat discordant echo of politicians and public, but it reminded the reader of the other side of the children's hearings business. In setting out its guiding principles the White Paper cited the three areas covered by the United Nations Convention on the Rights of the Child: provision, protection and participation.

Of the provisions mentioned, the CCLR proposal to widen the scope of the general duty to help promote the welfare of young people (under s 12 of the 1968 Act) was reduced from being a requirement on local authorities to being a permission (para 3.3). Children with disabilities and those with a need for aftercare were given particular attention (paras 3.38 and 4.6).

The necessary provision of 'residential care (including secure accommodation) for children who need to live in a more controlled setting away from home', as Kearney and the Skinner Report suggest, had to be of high quality, and include educational provision, with trained, qualified and well-paid staff (para 3.9). This theme applied equally to staff undertaking care and protection work and working with offenders (paras 5.6 and 6.12), though there was no acceptance of Lord Clyde's proposal to make the basic social work qualifying course three years rather than two.

The proposed emergency protection arrangements were complicated. They followed Lord Clyde's criteria for granting child protection orders (CPOs) that there must be 'reasonable cause to believe that the child is likely to suffer significant harm' and that 'immediate removal' is necessary. 'Child assessment orders' (instead of Clyde's interim CPOs) were proposed to cover circumstances where access to children was needed to investigate a 'reasonable suspicion' of significant harm.

The initial CPO, which had to be authorised by a sheriff, to which ancillary orders relating to interviewing, examination and contact could be attached, would last for three days only, and could be directly appealed. A hearing had to review an order within a maximum of three days. Thus it would have to consider the need for emergency protection without knowing the grounds for referral and the family's response to them.

This proposal concurred with practice already adopted in part of Scotland where considering renewal of place of safety warrants occurred 'on the first lawful day'. The alternative practice was to delay the first hearing for up to seven days so that grounds for referral could be formulated and the response known before considering the need for a warrant. This was the approach adopted and criticised in Orkney, although endorsed by the CCLR (recommendation 57) and the Fife Inquiry (p597). There are merits in both approaches, and room to argue for the linkage or for separation of grounds for emergency protection and for referral, but there is no merit in continuing to tolerate such a fundamental diversity of practice between reporters.[12]

The proposed arrangements increased the already numerous possible occasions of hearings and judicial proceedings before grounds for referral could be tested. To these were added procedures relating to 'exclusion orders' which the White Paper proposed to introduce. The appointment of safeguarders from the initial stage of granting a CPO was envisaged (though this was abandoned in the 1995 Act). Certainly the demand for their services was significantly enhanced by the increasing opportunities to challenge and defend emergency removal. The CCLR's recommendations on safeguarders were accepted and the promise of a further review of their role (suggested by Lord Clyde) was endorsed.

The most important innovation relating to the reporter service was to place its administration under a 'chief reporter' rather than with local authorities.[13] Although this was at odds with the view taken by the Finlayson report, it was intended to achieve many of his objectives – such as establishing professional standards, consistency of procedures and training, and providing support for those working in small authorities. Decisive here was the expected reorganisation and increase in number of local authorities.

With regard to hearings, the proposed increased powers were modest. They included hearings specifying the date of a review, which it was indicated might be of particular use in relation to offence referrals (para 7.11). The suggestion was made, with some validity, that social workers had not always given offending behaviour the priority it deserved (para 7.2). An improvement in relation to home supervision could be the setting of 'national standards' – an idea derived from probation to encourage more use of the option. The concept of 'contracts' or agreements was suggested as a way of specifying clear goals and the expectations of all parties. Precisely how formal these 'contracts' might be was not spelt out, and how they might strengthen hearings was only hinted at.

Sheriff Kearney's suggestion that hearings should have a 'range of options' of possible disposals was endorsed, as was the CCLR's proposal to give hearings the power to speak to children in the absence of parents, and exclude third parties where they interfered with proceedings to the detriment of the child's interests. The role of hearings in relation to long-term planning, including the duty to advise the courts on parental rights and adoption, were their most significant enhanced responsibilities. In practice, the adoption of the Fife Inquiry's proposal to include the panel chair in deliberations about resources within local authorities might prove to have been the most important proposal in maintaining a 'range of options'.

In sum, the White Paper was impressive for being a political animal that did not

[12] The 1995 Act separates these issues and slightly simplifies the process (see Chapter 7).
[13] This office becomes the 'principal reporter' under the 1995 Act, the reporter service being centralised under the Scottish Children's Reporter Administration (see Chapter 11).

bark. Though in places suggesting that 'offenders' should be thought of differently from those in need of care and protection, it endorsed the overall philosophy of the system, which was not to separate children formally by grounds for referral. This was despite the increasing tendency in social work departments to think of them separately, and the government's continuing disposition not to be too 'understanding' towards young offenders.

The Ayrshire case

Just as events surrounding allegations of organised sexual abuse presented problems associated with 'proof' in Orkney, so they did in a related but more protracted way in Ayrshire.

In May 1990 the mother of three young boys alleged in statements to her doctor and her lawyer that her husband had sexually abused the children, aged five, eight and ten years. These children were admitted to a children's home first on a voluntary basis with their mother and then subject to a place of safety order. During interviews the boys named the children of two related families as further victims of sexual abuse. At various times in June and July 1990, eight children of three families were made subjects of place of safety orders and were medically examined and interviewed. The cases of the children were treated together ('conjoined') for the purpose of proof, and grounds for referral to children's hearings were found established in August 1990 following an eleven-day hearing. The sheriff stated in his summary that there had been 'systematic sexual abuse and corruption of the children over a period of eighteen months'. One parent appealed unsuccessfully to the Court of Session. The eight children were made subject to supervision requirements away from their parents.

During the following three years some twenty-five children's hearings were held to review supervision requirements. Most of the decisions were appealed and all except one relating to access were upheld. Throughout much of this period the parents and their representatives sought to have hearings consider matters relevant to challenging the grounds for referral. However, these hearings properly considered the current welfare of the children on the basis of the grounds established and the current attitudes of the children and parents.

In July 1993 the families successfully petitioned the Court of Session to exercise its extraordinary power (under the *nobile officium*) to provide a remedy in 'exceptional and unforeseen circumstances' on the basis that there was no provision in the 1968 Act for hearing new evidence which could not have been presented at the time of the original proof. It was averred that there was additional expert opinion which questioned some relevant medical evidence, that subsequent judgments had cast doubt on the sheriff's findings and, most significantly, that there was now 'a greater understanding of the importance of a number of features' which related to the interviewing of children, and which were not available prior to the findings in Rochdale and the Orkney Inquiry (*L, Petitioners (No 1)* 1993 SLT 1310; *L, Petitioners (No 2)* 1993 SLT 1342; (IH) 1993 SCLR 693 (*sub nom L v Kennedy*).

The Court of Session directed that there be a rehearing of the proof before a sheriff who had no previous involvement with the cases. This began in December 1993 and concluded a year later (more than four years after the first hearing of the evidence), after over 100 witnesses had been led. In his report the sheriff stated: 'I cannot with any certainty come to a view as to the truth of this whole complex, complicated and disturbing case' – not even, as was required, on a balance of probability. The Court of Session therefore set aside the earlier findings and directed the managed return of the children. During 1995, with the help of various supportive measures, the children were reunited with their families.

There are many disquieting features of this case. It was doubtful whether the evidence heard over a period of twelve months, three to four years after the relevant events, was better than that originally heard over eleven days within months of the alleged events. The mother who had made the original allegations did not again give evidence. The sheriff apparently had no power to summon witnesses or call for reports on his own initiative, it being a proof hearing rather than an appeal – though this was not tested. Criticisms of the way in which the children were interviewed by the social work staff and to some extent the police officers may well have been justified. Yet the court's expectations of child witnesses might be similarly questioned. A nine-year-old boy was subjected to several days of cross-examination by the advocates for three families on events alleged to have taken place when he was five. The sheriff found that the boy's evidence 'lacked credibility'.

There must be serious doubt about the entire process of rehearing a child's account of events after such a passage of time in circumstances likely to have aroused distress and conflicting emotions. The value to be attached to the testimony of expert witnesses who had had no professional contact with the children or their families proximate to the alleged events is equally questionable.[14]

Whatever the truth in this case, irredeemable harm was done to the children. The lessons to be learned from Orkney about the need for professional training in the investigatory interviewing of children in relation to alleged sexual abuse are further underscored here, and these have been accepted and partially acted upon. However, whether the appropriate judicial lessons will be learned remains to be seen. Social work staff were deficient and expert witnesses may have been in error, but one or other of the sheriffs was mistaken in his judgment – albeit that both may have been justified in reaching the conclusions they did on the evidence available to them. Yet we have seriously to question whether the adversarial procedure for consideration of proof, with the sheriff having no power to make his own inquiry or take independent advice, is an adequate mechanism for a re-examination in this kind of case.

Prelude to the new Act

The Children Scotland Bill, published in November 1994, though long in gestation, was clearly drafted in a hurry. An explanation if not a defence is that

---

[14] For a chronology of events related to the Ayrshire case and an expression of concern, see Sarah Nelson, 'Locking up Pandora's Box' *Scottish Child* (April/May, 1995).

parliamentary time became unexpectedly available when the government's plans to privatise the Post Office fell through. Much of the formulation which departed from the Social Work (Scotland) Act 1968 was borrowed from the Children Act 1989. While this led to significant, and some unwelcome, conceptual shifts (for example, in the definition of 'supervision' which will be discussed later), it carried a hidden benefit. Allowing the legislation to be considered the equivalent of the Children Act in England and Wales avoided parliamentary attention being drawn to the fact that the Scottish Act also covered most young offenders. In the political climate of the time this was perhaps fortunate.

The parliamentary process produced an Act which is a great improvement on the Bill, even though deficiencies remain (discussed in the next chapter). During the Committee Stage there was an important innovation, a Special Scottish Standing Committee which took oral evidence in Glasgow and Edinburgh from interested parties. Among the groups giving evidence were children who had had experience of being in the physical care of local authorities and who made points relevant to hearings, rights in care and aftercare. However, the issue on which they had a decisive impact related to the exclusion from home of an alleged abuser. The Bill allowed for an exclusion order to be challenged before implementation, which would mean that children would need to be removed first. Parliament was persuaded to allow an interim order which would avoid this, largely as a result of hearing the experience of young people (Hansard, 6th February 1995; 1995 Act, s 76(4)(b)). This was an exemplary instance of not only listening to children but of acting on their views.

7 : The Children (Scotland) Act 1995

THE Children (Scotland) Act 1995 received the Royal Assent on 19th July 1995 and came into full operation in April 1997.[1] The Act brings together for the first time in Scotland private law relating to the responsibilities and rights of parents and guardians (Part I), the promotion of children's welfare by local authorities and by children's hearings (Part II), and amendments to adoption law in Scotland (Part III). Embedding the children's hearings system into a body of more comprehensive child care legislation is generally to be welcomed. However, one consequence is that what have come to be referred to as its 'overarching principles' (Norrie, 1995, p36)[2] are those which must be applicable in a wider court setting than that envisaged by the Social Work (Scotland) Act 1968. Thus, as we shall see, these principles tend to reflect the court setting and increase formality compared with those which underpinned the Kilbrandon approach.[3]

The principles

The declared principles which apply generally, though not universally, to the courts and hearings are:

- the child's welfare should be paramount in all decisions;
- children must have the opportunity to express views and have them taken into account in decisions which affect them; and
- an order should only be made if it is better for the child than making no order.

These principles are set out in the middle of Part I (s 11(7)) and at the beginning of Part II (s 16(1)).

The welfare principle

This is expressed in Part I as 'the court shall regard the welfare of the child concerned as its paramount consideration' (s 11(7)).[4] The principle as stated in

---

[1] For this account of the provisions of 1995 Act we are indebted to Professor Norrie's excellent commentary in his annotated text of The Children (Scotland)Act 1995 and Sheriff Kearney's unpublished commentaries on the Act used in training sheriffs. The best non-technical summary is the Guide to the Children (Scotland) Act 1995 by Alison Cleland, published by the Scottish Child Law Centre. At the time of writing, Professor Norrie's Children's Hearings in Scotland was about to be published and was therefore not consulted.

[2] The term 'overarching principles' is slightly misleading, as we shall see.

[3] They can be compared with those set out in Chapter 2.

[4] This follows the formula used in the Law Reform (Parent and Child) (Scotland) Act 1986 and in the Children Act 1989).

Part II applying to courts and hearings adds the phrase 'throughout childhood', and in Part III the duty to promote the welfare of a child in decisions relating to adoption is 'throughout his life' (s 95(6)(a)).

The child's welfare being the 'paramount consideration' is more conducive to the rights of the child than the terms of the United Nations Convention on the Rights of the Child, where the 'best interests of the child shall be *a primary consideration*' (our emphasis) (art 3(1)). The Convention, of course, applies to all aspects of policy, law and administration, not just child care law and juvenile justice. However, paramountcy is arguably a dilution of the welfare principle in the 1968 Act which makes the child's best interest to be the sole criterion in disposal decisions – though this was breached by the amendment on secure accommodation, as we have noted (see Chapter 5).

A good case can be made for viewing the paramountcy of the child's welfare as *the* 'overarching' principle (despite the derogation mentioned below) because it explains the exceptions to seeking the child's views, and the 'no order' principle can almost be derived from it. Sheriff Kearney expresses a similar sentiment by referring to the welfare principle as 'the premier overarching principle' (Kearney, 1997).

The 1995 Act departs further from 'the interests of the child' criterion by making an explicit derogation from the principle of paramountcy of the child's welfare. It permits a court, hearing or local authority to set aside the principle 'for the purpose of protecting members of the public from serious harm (whether or not physical harm)' (ss 16(5) and 17(5)). We may wonder whether 'the public' includes other members of the child's household or fellow residents of home or school, and whether non-physical 'serious harm' includes harm to others' inter-ests, their property as well as their persons. We will discuss later how important this derogation is from the welfare principle.

Listening to children

Giving children the opportunity to 'express their views' and, where they choose to do so, 'having regard to them' when parents, local authorities (sometimes), courts and hearings make decisions which affect them, endorses article 12 of the UN Convention. The principle is far from new. Taking account of children's views is only one step towards the principle of interactive participation that has been recognised to be one of the 'foundation stones' of the children's hearings system which anticipated the UN Convention (Fox, 1991). Also, eliciting children's views in relation to domestic proceedings has increasingly become an established court practice. However, the statutory requirements to ascertain and take account of children's views in a range of court proceedings, and where parents, local authorities and adoption agencies are making decisions which affect children, are significant extensions of the principle.

Decisions in which sheriffs are directly required to consider the views of the child in relation to child protection are specifically set out in Part II. They include making, varying or discharging orders and warrants, and in considering appeals, where decisions of hearings might be replaced or set aside (s 16(b)). Significantly, an exception is made of child protection orders on their initial granting, though children's views must be sought when they are reviewed by a court or hearing.

In taking account of a child's views, the child's age and maturity, and the extent to which it is 'practicable', are relevant. The way in which this is given legal expression is less than ideal. The Act says that 'without prejudice to the generality ... a child of twelve years of age or more shall be presumed to be of sufficient age and maturity to form a view' (s 11(10)). This does not mean that courts or others making decisions which affect children should presume that those younger than age twelve lack the maturity to form views. However, the wording suggests an age and maturity threshold for 'forming a view' rather than allowing 'due weight' to any expression of views according to age and maturity. The difference is that young and immature children may be deemed incapable of forming a view rather than being found to have immature views which, none the less, may deserve some weight. The age-twelve threshold derives from a presumption relevant to a degree of legal capacity – for instance, it is deemed indicative of sufficient maturity to instruct a solicitor (see Schedule 4, para 53). The application of the age and maturity limitation, especially outside the court setting, is unnecessarily restrictive.

The Children's Hearings Rules previously required the views of children to be sought and taken into account without reference to age or maturity – they had to be given 'due weight' in all the circumstances of the case. The introduction of the age and maturity condition into the new rules (rule 15(5)) could be regarded as a retrograde step for hearings in terms of the principle of listening to children. This is an instance where applying an 'overarching principle' derived from a legal setting could have a negative consequence if taken to provide the appropriate standard. However, there is nothing to prevent children's hearings continuing to elicit and take appropriate account of the views of children of all ages – without first considering whether they are mature enough to 'form a view'.

An attempt has been made in the 1997 Sheriff Court Rules[5] to accommodate the views of children in circumstances where there is understandable reticence. Special provision has been made to enable children to express views in writing in *confidence* to the sheriff – views of which other parties will gain only such knowledge as the sheriff thinks appropriate to disclose (rule 3.5(4). However, this exposes sheriffs to a real dilemma. Their duty to give effect to allowing children the opportunity to address them in private opens the possibility of their being influenced by 'testimony' not admitted in evidence. It remains to be seen how sheriffs will deal with this provision in the rules.[6]

The 'no order' principle

The principle that *no requirement or order* should be made unless it would be better for the child than making no order follows the principle stated in the Children Act 1989. It has been described as the *'minimum intervention principle'*

---

[5] The Act of Sederunt (Child Care and Maintenance Rules) 1997.
[6] This provision is discussed by Brian Kearney in Chapter 10. The issue of confidentiality is returned to in Chapter 17.

(Norrie, 1995, p46), but it means this in only a very restricted sense. The 'no order' formula will not minimise intervention among interventions; it demands only that the order under deliberation is tested by what would be '*better* for the child', against no order being made at all. Acting 'in the *best* interest of the child' (as it used to be said) would more than subsume this principle. We suggest that it has the least good claim to be regarded as 'overarching' since it could be derived from the paramountcy of welfare, properly understood.

The term 'minimal intervention' is usually taken to include adopting the least restrictive alternative; but the 'no order principle' does not attempt to minimise intervention among compulsory orders and requirements – even though some might think it ought to. The problem with the doctrine of the least restrictive alternative is that it implies agreement on what counts as 'restrictive' and suggests that intrusions on liberty can be comparatively quantified. There is no doubt an underlying commitment to the idea that families should not be unnecessarily subject to external prescription, but this is not captured by the 'no order' principle. The principle should be interpreted in line with this, but not as an injunction to do as little as possible – as the minimal intervention principle is often taken to imply.[7]

Parental and local authority responsibilities
Parental responsibilities and rights
Part I of the Act, which took effect in November 1996, embodies the most significant conceptual shift in Scottish law relating to parenthood. It explicitly sets out parental responsibilities as the foundation of parental rights – that is, parental rights are possessed for the purposes of enabling parents or guardians to carry out their responsibilities to their children.

The responsibilities specified are as follows (s 1(1)):

(a) to safeguard and promote the child's health, development and welfare;
(b) to provide direction and guidance;
(c) to maintain regular contact (if the child is not living with the parent); and
(d) to act as the child's legal representative.

Both parents have rights which correspond to these responsibilities (s 2(1)), which continue until the young person is sixteen years of age, except 'guidance' which is to be given until the young person is eighteen years of age. ('This is consistent with the parents' duty to attend their children's hearings up to the age of eighteen.) There is a presumption that responsibilities and rights are shared by both parents even if they are separated or divorced, unless they are restricted by court order.

Contact and residence orders
Most significantly the concepts of 'custody' and 'access' are replaced by the orders relating to *contact* and *residence*, that is, *specific issue orders* (s 11). These changes in terminology represent a shift away from regarding children as passive

---

[7] Its operational impact in Fife is discussed in Chapter 6.

objects, and enable their interests to determine parental responsibilities and rights. Both parents or either parent may act as a child's representative in giving consent on their behalf – for example, in relation to medical treatment if children are incapable of understanding and giving consent themselves (s 15(5)(b)). Both parents, rather than previously only the parent with custody, have rights in respect of decisions made about a child's education. (The Education (Scotland) Act 1980 is appropriately amended by Schedule 4, para 28.) No doubt there is potential for conflict where estranged parents disagree about what is in a child's interests, but there is also potential for co-operation such that the court need only adjudicate between parents, or give precedence to one party over another in respect of particular responsibilities where the child's welfare demands it.

Where there are two parents there is a presumption that the active involvement of both is better than one. However, at odds with this is the fact that neither responsibilities nor rights apply to unmarried fathers, unless they have acquired them by an 'agreement' with the mother (s 4; see Implementation Newsletter, Scottish Office, 1996), or by a court order. The inferior status of unmarried fathers has remained despite the proposals of the Scottish Law Commission (Report 135, 1992) to abolish 'illegitimacy'. Insofar as children are denied two responsible parents by enactments related to marital status, this also contravenes the non-discrimination provisions of the UN Convention (Norrie, 1995, p13). Resistance to numerous submissions on this matter has probably to be explained by a narrow and anachronistic view of 'maintaining family values' prevailing within the government of the day.[8]

The new orders give the court sufficient flexibility to regulate the upbringing of children in response to their particular circumstances, taking account where possible of children's wishes, without having to make more substantial changes in a child's family status unless required. However, the Act does in other parts make significant changes to the arrangement for securing the long-term welfare of children, where their birth families are unable to provide it.

Parental responsibility orders

Most importantly, as promised, the Act introduces a *parental responsibilities order* which requires the court to determine the transfer of parental responsibilities and rights to the local authority, rather than this being done by administrative resolution, with the court only considering the issue if the resolution is challenged. The conditions for granting an order without the agreement of a parent (where there is one) are where the parent has persistently failed to fulfil his or her responsibilities to promote the child's health, welfare and development, or to keep in contact with the child; or he or she has seriously mistreated the child, such that the child's reintegration into the household is unlikely (s 86(2)). This replaces criteria which referred to length of separation and the 'life style' of the child's parents.

[8] We acknowledge there is something to be said for curtailing the rights of purely biological fathers, but matrimonial status is very far from differentiating between real fathers and nominal fathers.

Adoption

It is not our task here to consider the amendments which Part III makes to the Adoption (Scotland) Act 1978. However, since the interface of 'permanency planning' with hearings' decision-making is an issue which the legislation partly addresses, we should briefly note some significant features (s 95). The overarching principles each apply at the various stages of the adoption procedures include a duty on adoption agencies to consider seeking no order and a consideration of alternatives to adoption. It is made a formal requirement for courts and adoption agencies to consider a child's religion, racial origin and cultural and linguistic background at the stages of freeing for adoption and adoption placement. As a major concern in adoption is the time the process takes, especially when dispensing with parental agreement, the amendments place a duty on the court to provide a time scale to be adhered to (Schedule 2, para 18).

It is no longer necessary for a biological parent to become an adoptive parent to facilitate adoption by a step-parent (s 97). Step-parent adoptions may be encouraged by this measure, which is in keeping with the concept of promoting joint parental responsibility. However, the Act does not resolve the question of the status of the child subject to compulsory supervision when adopted. Step-parent adoptions are cases where it is usually implausible to argue that compulsory supervision should automatically cease, because a child is making a new family start.

Promotion of children's welfare by local authorities

The duty of local authorities to provide support for families and make provisions for assisting children with particular needs, including those who require to be looked after in local authority accommodation, are set out in significantly more detail (in ss 16–38) than they were in the 1968 Act. This in part reflects the growing responsibility of local authorities to provide and to regulate arrangements for sustaining children in their communities without bringing them into contact with hearings and courts. Associated with the reorganisation of local government, the opportunity was taken to specify the legal framework within which authorities were to meet their obligations to children.

Children's services plans

Each local authority is required to prepare and publish a children's services plan, in consultation with health boards, trusts, voluntary organisations, housing associations, the principal reporter and children's panel chair, to cover the provision of 'relevant services' for children in its area (s 19). In addition, it must provide information about existing services available to various categories of children, including those provided by voluntary organisations (s 20). The Act introduces a general concept of 'children in need', in respect of whom authorities have a duty to safeguard and promote their welfare by offering 'a range and level of services' appropriate to their needs, consistent with maintaining them so far as possible within their families (s 22). Specific provision is required to be made to assess and meet the needs of children with disabilities or affected by disabilities of others, with the aim of giving them 'the opportunity to lead lives which are as normal as possible' (ss 23 and 24).

Children 'looked after'
Provision to provide accommodation for children lacking a viable home, permanently or temporarily, replaces the concept of 'voluntary care'. Both the concept of being 'in care' of the local authority and the fiction of 'volunteering' have disappeared, although the views of children provided with accommodation must now be considered (s 25(5)). Those with parental rights to regulate residence must be unwilling or unable to provide or arrange it (s 25(6)(a)). Children who were in residential care or in foster care are now 'looked after' by the local authority, whether through s 25, under compulsory supervision, or under a child protection order. This is intended to leave parents with responsibilities and rights unless explicitly removed or suspended, and to avoid the possible stigmatisation of 'in-care' status. (See the discussion in Chapter 5.)

New terminology
Much of the substance of Chapters 2 and 3 of the Act recapitulates what was contained in the 1968 Act, although sometimes wordy redrafting disguises this. The changes in Part II of the Act are less fundamental than those in Part I. Only the arrangements for emergency protection could be considered substantial. However, not all the lesser changes are simply 'tidying up' or filling gaps; some which are apparently modest may turn out to have a significant impact in practice, or on the system's overall development. We will concentrate on identifying departures from the 1968 Act which have this potential.

'Relevant persons'
The substitution of terms in Part II of the Act, unlike those in Part I, are relatively superficial; none the less they need to be noted. Among the least felicitous is the use of the term 'relevant person' instead of 'parent' or 'guardian'. The explanation for this is that parties deemed to have the 'relevant' rights to be involved in decisions relating to children go beyond actual parents enjoying parental responsibilities or rights. The definition includes anyone who in law has, or in fact exercises, parental responsibilities (see s 93(2)(b)). There may be more than two 'relevant persons' with rights and duties relating to hearings and court proceedings.

Principal Reporter
Another obfuscation in terminology, which does nothing to make the Act more accessible, is its use of 'Principal Reporter' rather than 'the reporter'. Confusingly the Act defines 'reporter' as 'the Principal Reporter; or any officer of the Scottish Children's Reporter Administration to whom there is delegated ... any of the functions [of] the Principal Reporter' (s 40(5)). It then proceeds to designate the official who receives reports and carries out duties under the Act as the 'Principal Reporter', whereas in practice, of course, it is the local reporter. The shift in

terminology may be intended to mark the fact that reporters are now responsible to a central administration, but it does nothing to enhance the standing of the local officer or identify the appropriate person who should receive referrals and reports.[9]

'Compulsory supervision'

Children placed under supervision by a children's hearing are said now to be subject to 'compulsory measures of supervision' rather than 'compulsory measures of care'. This is in keeping with removing the concept of 'care' from the description of the status of children now 'looked after' by local authorities. Equally it corresponds to the term used in the Children Act 1989 and is the same as that used to describe probation. This change in terminology is significant; it has been noted that '*supervision* is a narrower concept than *care*' (Stone, 1995, p15). The Act says compulsory measures of supervision 'may include measures taken for the protection, guidance, treatment or control of the child' (s 52(3)). These are exactly the same four elements which together defined 'care' in the 1968 Act (s 32(3)), but the wording implied that 'care' included all the elements together. Now 'supervision' *may include* any from among them. 'Control', for instance, is no longer necessarily linked to protection, guidance and treatment.

Attendance at hearings

The changes relating to *attendance at hearings* were as expected. The child's right to attend his or her own hearing 'at all stages' is confirmed (s 45(1)(a)); though, as before, children can be released from the obligation to attend in any case where it would be detrimental to their interests to be present (s 45(2)). The absence of a child from a hearing presenting new grounds for referral would require an application for proof (unless the grounds were discharged), even were they accepted by 'relevant persons' present. By contrast, the absence of a 'relevant person' does not prevent grounds accepted by those present being proceeded upon (s 65(10)).

Powers to exclude

'Relevant persons' have a duty to attend a hearing (as had 'parents' previously) unless they are released from the obligation to attend. They also have a right to attend, but it is no longer an absolute right to be present throughout. The Children's Hearings Rules extend the right to be present to an unmarried father who is living with the mother, but he has no obligation to be present (rule 12(1)). Hearings can exclude a 'relevant person' and his or her representatives from part or parts of a hearing in order to allow a child to express views, or because their presence is causing, or is likely to cause, significant distress (s 46(1)). The chairman has a duty to explain to any of these excluded parties the substance of what took place in their absence.

As we have seen, this provision was one which gained support during the 1990s but there was a common view that it should be sparingly used since it detracted

---

[9] For simplicity we shall continue to speak of 'the reporter'.

from the ethos of openness. A presence 'likely to cause significant distress' is a lower threshold than would probably have been accepted at the time of the 1990 Review of Child Care Law in Scotland. On the other hand, the Review recommended that the duty to convey the substance of what was said in anyone's absence be qualified by 'unless that would be detrimental to the child's interest' (recommendation 82). The Act makes no such reservation. So this provision cannot be used to offer confidentiality to a child. Notably hearings do not have the privilege given to sheriffs to keep children's views confidential; anything submitted to hearings in writing must be made available to all (adults) who have a right to be present (see below).

The press

Hearings have gained the power to exclude a bona fide representative of the press for the same reasons as above (s 43(4)), though here the chairman has discretion whether to explain what took place in his or her absence. The previous restrictions on reporting and publishing material which is likely to lead to the identification of the child are strengthened. Norrie observes that the prohibition is more extensive than that which applies in England and Wales (Norrie, 1995, p76). The ban on publishing information which identifies children may be dispensed with by a sheriff or the Court of Session in relation to appeals, or, as before, by the Secretary of State in relation to hearings, 'in the interests of justice' (s 44(5)).

Business meeting

The Act places on a formal footing *business meetings preparatory to children's hearings* to enable some procedural matters to be determined and for the reporter to obtain any related direction or guidance. The issues to be decided are who should be cited as 'relevant persons' or others entitled to be present at the actual hearing, and whether a child or relevant person may be released from his or her obligation to attend (s 64; Children's Hearings Rules, rule 4(2)). It was the practice in some places for the reporter to anticipate these procedural decisions of hearings after seeking the advice of panel members, usually gathered to hear other cases in the area, but these 'meetings' had no place in law (even though they were found in *Sloan v B* 1991 SLT 530 to involve 'no illegality or unfairness'). Notification of authorised business meetings must be made to all relevant parties, who are entitled to present their views through the reporter on the procedural issues to be considered. All parties must be notified of the determinations made by the meeting (rule 4(8)). This provision elaborately fills a small but significant gap.

Safeguarders

The role of safeguarders was not substantially changed by the Act, but the scope of the cases in which they might be involved is extended and their duties are clarified. The main change is that appointments are no longer restricted to cases where there is deemed to be a conflict of interest between parent and child in the proceedings. Consideration must be given to appointing a safeguarder in any proceeding before a hearing or court, except those related to child protection orders. Appointments shall be on 'such terms and conditions as appear appropriate' (s 41(1)(b)). Hearings collectively now appoint, rather than the chairmen alone, and they must give their reasons for making the appointment (s 41(3)).

Safeguarders are required to make such written reports as hearings require and these are to be made available to the reporter, who will supply copies along with all other documents to panel members and parties to the hearing. As previously, safeguarders are entitled to all relevant documents and reports and to attend hearings at all stages, but they retain discretion over whether or not to attend. They must now return all documents when they have completed their duties (rule 14). The Sheriff Court Rules make it clear that the same safeguarder appointed in hearings proceedings will be adopted by the court unless there is good reason to make a new appointment (1997 Rules, rule 3.7(2)).

The 1995 Act has to be regarded as a conservative response to the review of the role and functions of safeguarders promised by the White Paper. Lord Clyde saw a potential role for the safeguarder providing support for the child in relation to child protection, 'following the child through the implementation and review of decisions, following up the case to ensure the child's needs are attended to and reviewed when necessary ... advising the child on the child's rights and interests. The safeguarder might on occasion be on hand when the child is interviewed' (Clyde, para 17.13).

However, providing support for the child from the 'earliest stage' of removal from home is ruled out, presumably on the grounds of practicality. Safeguarders would have to be immediately available on the same basis as an emergency social worker or duty solicitor, and this is incompatible with their part-time semi-voluntary status (Lockyer, 1994b). If there is a gap in the arrangements for looking after the interests of children in emergency protection, the opportunity to use safeguarders to fill it was passed over.

However, the law makes it clear that safeguarders have a duty to help children express their views (Children's Hearings Rules, rule 15(4)(c), Sheriff Court Rules, rule 3.5(2)(c)) as well as to make a judgment about their interests. Children's interests in having and expressing views are irrespective of whether acting on their views is endorsed by the safeguarder (Lockyer, 1994b, pp64–65). Broadening the terms for the appointment of safeguarders is bound to have an impact on their use by hearings.[10] Appointments made by sheriffs are affected by their parallel power to appoint common law *curators ad litem* whose role is similar to safeguarders. It remains to be seen whether remuneration levels will continue to affect the types of appointments sheriffs will make.

Representatives

The rules which relate to representatives at hearings are in essence unchanged although they are reformulated. Each child and 'relevant person' may be

---

[10] At this moment no official figures are available, but the numbers of appointments are said to have increased significantly.

'accompanied by one person' who may assist the person they represent in the discussion of the case. The same person may represent any of the parties entitled to be represented. A representative may be anyone, including another child or a lawyer, but there is still no legal aid for this purpose. There is rather more need to identify who a representative is representing than there was in the past where commonly a friend of the family would attend on the assumption that he or she was assisting everyone. Only representatives of relevant persons can now be excluded on the same grounds as relevant persons. In the past any representative could be excluded by the chairman if persistently behaving in a manner to disrupt the proceedings or in ways detrimental to the interests of the child (Children's Hearings Rules 1986, rule 11(4)). A child's representative cannot now be excluded, although presumably a child could 'disown' a representative if proving unhelpful.

Grounds for referral

The grounds on which the reporter may refer children to hearings are essentially the same, apart from the minor changes presaged by the 1990 Review of Child Care Law and the White Paper. The ground relating to incest is extended to boys as well as to girls (s 52(2)(g). As expected, the ground relating to the misuse of alcohol and drugs is added (s 52(2)(j)). Children 'beyond parental control' have become children 'beyond the control of any relevant person' (s 52(2)(a)). A small but significant change to the grounds permits children who are 'looked after' by the local authority without compulsory measures to be referred where their behaviour requires special measures 'in his interest or the interest of others' (s 52(2)(l)). The last phrase is a notable addition to the equivalent ground in the 1968 Act, as amended in 1983 (s 32(2)(i)).

Conditions

There is no substantial change in compulsory measures of supervision available to hearings but the extent to which they may impose 'conditions' is underlined. Gone is the unhelpful distinction between residential and non-residential requirements; now conditions attaching to a 'supervision requirement' may specify the place or places where the child shall reside, whether a residential establishment or any other form of home (s 70).

Hearings, apart from those relating to residence, have a specific duty to consider conditions regulating 'contact' with any person or class of person, and giving permission for medical or other examination or treatment (subject to the child's right to give or withhold consent according to the Age of Legal Capacity (Scotland) Act 1991, s 2(4)). Hearings can also decide not to disclose to any person or class of person the place where a child is required to reside on supervision (s 70(6)). This has proved to be needed in certain cases, both to protect children and those providing what used to be called 'care'.

Reviews and agreements

Hearings have the new power to determine the time at which a supervision requirement shall be reviewed (s 70(7)), without prejudice to the following: one year is the maximum duration of a requirement; the child and any relevant person may instigate a review after three months (s 73(6)); the local authority has a duty to seek a review whenever necessary (s 73(4)); the reporter is entitled to arrange a review in response to any new referral and has a duty to do so within three months of the date on which the existing requirement would expire (s 73(8)).

There is no attempt to incorporate into law the proposal for 'agreements' or 'contracts' between children, parents and service agencies, which were intimated in the White Paper, but these are none the less being promoted in social work and panel member training. It can be expected that hearings will sometimes wish to incorporate aspects of these agreements into 'conditions' attaching to supervision requirements. If there is improvement in goal setting and specification of expectations of supervision in practice (in the past this has been an illusive ideal), there may be more early reviews, both agreed in advance and triggered by any of the parties.

Access to reports

Probably the change which will prove to have made the greatest impact on the character of hearings is embodied not in the primary legislation but in the Children's Hearings Rules. It is the provision which requires a copy of any document which the reporter makes available to panel members prior to a hearing also to be made available to 'each relevant person' (and any unmarried father) entitled to be present at a hearing (rule 5(3)). This practice was actually implemented six months before the Act came into operation, as a result of the findings of the European Court of Human Rights in *McMichael* v *United Kingdom* (1995) 20 EHRR 205, but it was a measure, as we have seen, that was widely supported.[11]

The availability of reports does not at present apply to children. The hearing chairman retains the obligation to disclose the substance, unless it would be detrimental to the interests of the child (rule 20(4)), although the fact that other parties can have copies of reports rather diminishes the protective import of this provision. It is hard to justify children being the only parties not entitled to access to the reports. However, there is still virtue in the chairman conveying the substance, if only to focus the hearing on those matters in the reports which might influence the outcome of the hearing. The wider availability of reports, it is believed, will on balance advance the interests of children, but there are likely to be costs as well as benefits (see later discussion). At present the greatest concern is for the confidentiality of reports distributed to family members. Regrettably they are not covered by the strict rules which apply to panel members, safeguarders and other official parties for keeping secure and returning all case materials.

Warrants

Under the 1968 Act the secure accommodation authorisation was the only 'condition' which could be attached to a warrant to detain a child in a place of

---

[11] See also discussions in Chapters 10, 11, 12 and 17.

safety. Now hearings may impose 'such conditions as appear to be necessary or expedient', and without prejudice to this generality they may include those relating to contact, or medical examinations and treatment, and the discretion not to disclose where a child is being looked after (s 66(4), (7)). These changes may be seen as hearings placing restrictions on local authorities, but equally they give proper authorisation for the exercise of specific responsibilities to those looking after children in a place of safety as well as subject to compulsory supervision. Specifying conditions which can be separately appealed against and reconsidered when warrants or requirements are subject to renewal is also an enhancement of children's and parents' rights.

Hearings have the facility to issue warrants to find a child, and keep him or her in a place of safety until a hearing can be arranged quickly (ss 45(5), 63(5)). The maximum period for these warrants is seven days. Most warrants to keep a child in a place of safety are issued when a 'hearing is unable to dispose of the case' (s 66). This is usually either because a hearing cannot proceed because grounds have not been accepted or established, or further information is needed for disposal. Each warrant may last for up to twenty-two days. Sixty-six days is the maximum total period for the operation of such warrants. The 1968 Act provided for a series of four twenty-one-day warrants, the first two to be granted by hearings, the third and fourth by a sheriff. A consequence of the duration of a single warrant for an extra day is that the making and renewal of warrants can now conveniently take place on the same day of the week. This facilitates the case being reconsidered by all or some of the same three panel members (since the panel service rota tends to reflect the same weekday availability of individual members). Thus greater continuity of hearing personnel – generally regarded as desirable – is promoted by this change.

Although hearings can make a series of only three warrants, s 67 of the 1995 Act allows the reporter 'on cause shown' to make application to the sheriff for a further unspecified maximum period, at any time prior to the expiry of warrants issued by hearings. We can presume that the 'cause' will normally be imminent expiry where there has been extraordinary delay in the proof hearing. This is also the provision by which the sheriff may continue the place of safety between establishing grounds and the hearing's disposal of the case. The sheriff's warrant should 'specify the date on which it will expire', but there is no bar to its renewal. We are told that this section was a late addition to the Act (Norrie, 1995, p135). It has the unfortunate consequence of detracting from the general attempt to reduce maximum specified time-limits.

Review of grounds of referral

One of the innovations which has given serious cause for concern is the facility to permit a sheriff to review the establishment of grounds where there is new evidence which would have been admissible and likely to have affected the original finding, and where there is a 'reasonable explanation' for the evidence not being previously made available (s 85). If the finding is that none of the original grounds is established, and no different ground is established, the sheriff must terminate supervision immediately, or at a prescribed future date, or determine a variation for a period, or prescribe voluntary measures. This new section is entirely a result of the experience of the Ayrshire case.[12]

A provision which permits the readdressing of a past miscarriage of justice may be regarded as desirable. However, it is in potential conflict with the principle of the paramountcy of the child's welfare which becomes the central consideration once the grounds have been held to be established. A facility which permits re-examination of the justice of past decisions runs the risk of ignoring the reality of the child's experience from the alleged past injustice to the present. This is quite apart from the potential threat which this provision creates for the possible re-exposure of children to giving evidence, and of pressures on them to retract past testimony, which to date usually (but not always) subsides after a definitive judgment of proof. It is to be hoped that the courts interpret the terms of this provision to make its invocation extremely rare, not to encourage parents (and children) to attempt to resurrect and change the past rather than addressing the future.

The power to replace disposal on appeal

The most controversial and extensively criticised alteration concerns the powers of the sheriff on appeal of a hearing's decision. After hearing from parties on the decision, examining authors or compilers of any reports or statements, including the reporter and the hearing chairman, a sheriff may call for further reports and may, in addition to his previous powers to discharge or require reconsideration by a hearing, now substitute any disposal which might be made by a hearing for that made by the original hearing (s 51).

This provision is clearly at odds with the fundamental division of responsibility at the heart of the Kilbrandon philosophy. The entire rationale for the hearings system is grounded on the view that a court is not the most appropriate forum for deciding matters of disposal. To quote and endorse Norrie, 'Not only is the provision bad in principle but it is likely to prove bad in practice' (Norrie, 1995, p90). There is no requirement on the sheriff under the new provision to conduct something equivalent to a hearing's discussion with family members. The three 'overarching' principles must be complied with but, as Sheriff Kearney suggests, this may mean that sheriffs will adopt something like the less formal procedure of a hearing (Kearney, 1997). The Act places no requirement on sheriffs to give reasons for their disposals, but it is suggested that they ought to do so and that their decisions will be open to appeal.

The sheriff's new power to override the disposal of hearings, together with the new derogation to set aside the paramount welfare of the child in the public interest, has led some to suspect a covert reintroduction of a punitive disposition. However, this is an unjustified concern as it overlooks the fact that an appeal to the sheriff against a disposal of a hearing can be made only by a 'relevant person', or a child, or a safeguarder on behalf of a child, not by an official with a duty to

---

[12] See Chapter 6.

protect the public. The government's declared reason for making the court the final arbiter of disposals is to avoid falling foul of the European Convention on Human Rights and this should probably be accepted in good faith, though we shall argue later that it is undesirable and probably unnecessary. The Minister gave assurance that the power is likely to be sparingly used and that 'sheriffs should think carefully before interfering with the decision of a children's hearing' (quoted by Cleland, 1995, p28). The legislators' intention is not entirely irrelevant, since sheriffs may consult Hansard to interpret the law.[13] We have noticed (in Chapter 3) that Sheriff Mowat's view that the court should be wary of substituting its view for hearings' disposals has generally been followed. An indication is given by the 1995 Children's Hearings Statistics (the last available covering the previous legislation). Of 145 appeals against a hearing's disposal, 45 were upheld, of which 39 were returned to hearings for reconsideration, and six cases were discharged.

Appeal to the Sheriff Principal
The Act introduced a new level of appeal from a decision of a sheriff by way of a stated case, either on a point of law or in respect of a procedural irregularity, to the Sheriff Principal – the senior sheriff in each area jurisdiction (sheriffdom). This is in addition to, rather than replacing, the appeal to the Court of Session, which remains the final level of appeal. An appeal by the child, relevant person or reporter against the sheriff's finding may be heard by the Sheriff Principal or the Court of Session either directly (most likely where the case deals with an important point of principle) or after the finding of the Sheriff Principal with his or her leave (s 51(11)). The intermediary level of appeal was doubtless introduced to save time and money, but finds objectors among some sheriffs who regard the change as a departure from the doctrine that only a higher court should overturn the decision of a lower court (see, for example, Mitchell, 1997).

Advice from hearings
The Act makes amendments to clarify the circumstances where the courts (sheriff court and High Court) must seek advice or may seek advice from hearings on sentence, and may remit cases to hearings. The general effect is to tidy the arrangements but to leave the discretion with the courts as to how far sixteen- and seventeen-year-olds might be subject to welfare-based disposals (ss 49, 50). Cases involving child offenders which begin by being prosecuted in the criminal court continue to be under the general direction of the Lord Advocate's instruction.

Among the most important additions to the responsibility of children's hearings is in giving advice to courts dealing with children subject to applications which affect parental rights, responsibilities and family status. When children are already subject to compulsory measures of supervision, hearings must be consulted and provide a report which the court shall consider before coming to a decision in relation to parental responsibility orders, freeing for adoption, or adoption proceedings (s 73(13), (14)). Advice must also be given to local authorities or

---

[13] Sheriff Kearney has pointed this out to us.

adoption agencies in relation to placing a child for adoption under the Adoption (Scotland) Act 1978. Advice hearings have the same duty to share information, consider views, explain their advice and give reasons for it to all relevant parties. It is the hearing chairman's duty to 'make or cause to be made a report' (Children's Hearings Rules, rule 22) which must be distinguished from the reporter's report of proceedings (rule 31). This responsibility of hearings to give advice in the form of reasoned reports is a significant new demand on panel members, for which they require training.

Emergency protection
The law relating to emergency protection is a substantial improvement on previous provisions relating to places of safety orders, which were widely acknowledged to be too generally formulated and gave too little opportunity for challenge. At the centre of the new provisions are child protection orders, with child assessment orders and exclusion orders as alternative means of achieving lesser interventions.

Child protection orders
An initial child protection order (CPO) can be granted only by sheriffs; where none is available, a justice of the peace may only authorise a child being taken to a place of safety for up to twenty-four hours (s 61). The basic criteria for granting CPOs – the belief 'that a child ... is being so treated (or neglected) that he is suffering significant harm; or ... will suffer such harm if he is not removed to and kept in a place of safety' or kept where he is presently accommodated (s 57(1)) – are essentially those set out in the White Paper. If the order is being sought by the local authority the criteria are extended to include 'reasonable grounds to suspect ... significant harm'; 'enquiries are being frustrated by access to the child being unreasonably denied'; and such access is a 'matter of urgency' (s 57(2)).

An imperative of the new provisions is to increase the demand for prima facie 'evidence' before an initial order to remove a child can be granted. Applicants for CPOs are expected to produce 'supporting evidence' (the form for CPOs lists 'reports, statements, affidavits, or other evidence produced'). Sheriff Kearney suggests that this will require a 'searching scrutiny' by sheriffs to satisfy themselves that the criteria are met, although he accepts that it will be difficult to resist granting applications since the main weight of responsibility will continue to fall on the authorised applicants (Kearney, 1997). However, there is no doubt that the increased formality and scrutiny will mean that applications will not lightly be sought or granted.

The 1995 Act makes provision for application to the sheriff to review an initial CPO, to be heard within three working days of the application, as an alternative to a hearing considering the order on the second working day after it has been served. Although a hearing will take place if no application for the sheriff to review has been notified in the first two days, it is still open to the relevant parties to apply for the review after the second-day hearing. When considering an application to recall or review a CPO the sheriff must apply the three principles (s 16(2)–(4)), as must the hearing; and the appointment of a safeguarder must be considered in any application to the sheriff to recall or vary a CPO (s 41(1)). Those who may seek a review of the CPO are the child, relevant persons, any person who has to be notified of the initial CPO, or the original applicant. The reporter may 'wish to make representations' to the sheriff considering the review of a CPO and he may arrange a hearing to provide advice for this purpose (s 60(10), (11)). At a review of the CPO a sheriff will discharge, confirm or vary the order and continue or vary any directions given in relation to it (s 60(12)).

Substantially the same consideration of the grounds for making the CPO (that is the basis for granting it and any directions which attach to it), whether they are justified and remain valid, must be carried out by the second-day hearing as by the sheriff on review, subject to the consideration mentioned above that the sheriff must now apply the three principles. This raises doubts about whether courts and hearings are equally equipped to perform this task, the only difference being that the hearing's consideration is conducted without a challenging application from one of the parties. It cannot, however, be assumed that nobody at the hearing will oppose the continuation of the order, or the attached conditions or directions.

A hearing to consider the grounds for referral must take place on the eighth working day, which is the last day a CPO can have effect (s 65(2)). Thereafter, a child may if necessary remain in a place of safety subject to a series of twenty-two-day warrants issued by hearings and any additional warrant granted by a sheriff until a dispositional hearing takes place.

CPOs are much more flexible than the place of safety orders they replace. They are also designed to operate in a very narrow time frame, which presumably is the reason why the principle of hearing the child's views is not underwritten and safeguarders may not be appointed until and unless a recall or variation by the sheriff is sought. It could none the less be regarded as a fault that CPOs provide an enhanced facility for parental challenge but rather less than this facility for the young child. The alternatives to CPOs do not include the same suspension of the child's right to be heard, or the initial appointment of safeguarders, though it is not obvious why the alternative orders should be able to allow these extra considerations at their inception.

Child assessment orders

Child assessment orders (CAOs) are intended as a way of giving a local authority the means of discovering whether greater intervention is needed (s 55). An authority can direct any person responsible for a child to deliver him or her to an authorised person and carry out an assessment, which may require attendance at a specified place and accommodation for up to the maximum duration of the order, which is seven days. The order permits a sheriff to make a range of 'directions' relating to contact or the conduct of the assessment. The CAO may be used to allow medical examination and treatment without parental consent (not of course without the consent of a child old enough to understand).

Local authorities must have 'reasonable *cause* to suspect' that a child is being so treated or neglected that he or she is suffering or likely to suffer significant harm, and the order is needed to determine whether this is so. However, there is a major problem in deciding whether to use a CAO or a CPO. A CPO requires a local authority to have 'reasonable *grounds* to suspect' the same concerns as expressed in a CAO. We might expect local authorities or sheriffs to prefer the lesser intervention, or the one preferred by the child (although considering the child's view is only required by a CAO). However, the Act requires the sheriff to grant a CPO in preference to a CAO, even when the latter is applied for, where the conditions for granting a CPO are met (s 55(2)). This implies that CAOs can only be granted where the local authority has reasonable 'cause' to suspect, but not 'grounds' to suspect. This seems an extremely arcane distinction to make and to apply in judgment.

Our best legal authorities (Professor Norrie and Sheriff Kearney) agree that the legislators cannot have intended to deprive the sheriff of a discretion regarding which type of order to make. We agree with Professor Norrie that it seems likely that the CAO, which is modelled on the Children Act 1989, s 43, will, as in England, be little used, CPOs being favoured (Norrie, 1995, pp101–102). The experience at the time of writing – three months after the coming into force of the legislation – confirms this.[14]

Exclusion orders
Elaborate terms and conditions are set out for exclusion orders (EOs). Modelled on the provisions of the Matrimonial Homes (Family Protection) (Scotland) Act 1981, they enable local authorities to apply to exclude a named person from a child's home and to avoid the necessity of the child's removal (s 76). It is a criticism of EOs that they may only be applied for by local authorities, not by other parties (Sutherland, 1995). In addition to the threat of conduct or 'reasonably apprehended conduct' of the named person causing or being likely to cause significant harm, the sheriff must consider whether there is 'an appropriate person' to care for the child, and any other children, in the family home (s 76(2)). The sheriff must also consider whether making the order is 'unjustifiable or unreasonable' – taking account, for example, whether the home is tied to the alleged abuser's work (s 76(9)). An EO requires the named person to have the opportunity to be heard, but an interim order can be granted until this happens (s 76(4)).

A sheriff may make a CPO when an EO has been sought. Although EOs were conceived to avoid emergency removal of children from home, they may be viewed as a longer-term alternative to removal in that they remain in force for up to six months if not recalled. Certainly, they may serve usefully as an alternative to employing place of safety warrants, when CPOs have run their course. However, some of the considerations which the sheriff must take into account might suggest that an order be granted for a specified limited duration (s 79(2)) – for example, until an application for proof has been considered.

Doubts have been expressed about EOs, both on the grounds of their efficacy

---

[14] See the conclusion of Chapter 10.

and their infringement of civil liberties. Orders can be given some teeth by including the power of arrest attaching to interdicts barring entry to the home or neighbourhood or making contact (s 78). However, in practice enforceability is likely to depend on considerations such as the attitude of other family members. Perhaps, as some have suggested, the provision will be rarely used, but the mere existence of the power might serve to encourage the voluntary departure of suspected or threatening parties, especially if local authorities are prepared to make financial resources for alternative accommodation available to those whose absence makes possible a child remaining at home.

It has to be accepted that a court order removing a suspected abuser is an infringement of his liberty, but it is no more unjust than removing alleged child victims for their own protection. Whatever their use, EOs are at least symbolically important. They demonstrate a new willingness of legislators 'to go the extra mile' in giving weight to the views of the child (as demonstrated at the end of Chapter 6) and in making the welfare of the child 'the paramount consideration'.

Section II

The System Reviewed

8 : Families and Other Resources for the Children's Hearings System

Malcolm Hill

THE children's hearings system is able to call on a range of resources which may contribute to children's welfare, either on a voluntary or compulsory basis. Social background reports are expected to review the options available, including the child's nuclear and extended family and any supportive or substitute services which may be required (Social Work Services Inspectorate (SWSI), 1995a). Broadly these resources comprise two types: total living situations and non-residential services. Each of these can take various forms. The principal ones are:

Total living situation
- the child's original birth family;
- alternative families
  - foster care
  - adoption;
- residential care.

Non-residential services – for example
- social work support/counselling;
- group work of various kinds;
- learning support;
- befriending.

A child or family may receive a combination or sequence of these services, sometimes as a planned package, sometimes because the apparent failure of one can lead on to another, as when a young person who frequently absconds is placed in secure accommodation. Most children looked after away from home continue to have contacts with their original families and see them to varying degrees as sources of support, advice and help.

At the outset it is important to recognise that any of the above, besides frequently acting as positive resources, may in certain circumstances prove to be negative or even abusive for children. In certain circumstances, a small minority of children have suffered physical or sexual ill-treatment in their birth families, foster families or residential care. Non-residential interventions engage children for shorter periods of time, but they too can be experienced as useless, or expose children to bullying or harassment. Thus it is important to see any one type of resource as having potential for good, harm or ineffectiveness, depending on the precise nature of the particular intervention and its degree of fit with the needs and wishes of the child.

The principal organiser and provider of resources for the hearings following the 1968 Act was the social work department, which was obliged not only to provide information about the needs of children and the resources available, but also to implement compulsory measures of supervision. In doing so, the social work department often sought the assistance of education, housing and health services as well as voluntary organisations, but neither panel members nor social workers had powers to command use of their resources. Local authorities have also made use of voluntary-sector provision, ranging from family support services to residential schools. For some time, social work departments have had decision-making and case-review mechanisms for children placed away from home which ought to dovetail with those of the hearings, but sometimes give rise to conflicting goals and actions.

This position was modified in several ways during the mid-1990s. The Local Government etc (Scotland) Act 1994 introduced new unitary councils which are no longer required to have a social work department as such. Each authority must provide a social work service, but this is labelled and organised in various ways. For instance, several councils have joint housing and social work offices. Further, the Children (Scotland) Act 1995 places a corporate responsibility for children's services on the whole authority, not just the social work services.

Both the balance of local resource provision and recommendations for individual children have been affected by changeable and at times competing sets of professional beliefs and values about the relative desirability and effectiveness of different forms of intervention. Some of the most important of these will be outlined next. The second part of the chapter will review evidence about the potential benefits and hazards of each of the main types of resource.

Perspectives on children's services

Seven approaches will be considered: child rescue/child protection; permanency planning; alternative care as a positive choice; prevention; family support; diversion; listening to children.

These do not represent logically coherent or distinct categories, but rather complex and often overlapping combinations of principles. Moreover, each has been open to more than one interpretation, so that, as we shall see, there has sometimes been considerable divergence between theory and practice. Besides incorporating knowledge and values about specific types of intervention, they also embody differing orientations towards the triangle of responsibilities and rights held to belong to children, parents and the state (Adler, 1985; Fox Harding, 1991, 1996). While it is possible to identify individuals or agencies who espoused one particular 'philosophy', often ideas can be drawn from each, depending on the circumstances under consideration.

Child rescue/child protection

This is perhaps the oldest tradition in modern child welfare. It represents a wish to rescue children from dangerous or adverse family circumstances and remove them to an environment which is thought to be better for them. This was the rationale for early foster care and residential villages like that established in Scotland by Sir William Quarrier at Bridge of Weir (Hill *et al*, 1991; Murphy, 1993; see also Chapter 1). Rural settings were often preferred in the hope of keeping children healthier and away from urban corruption. In addition to saving children from neglect or ill-treatment, 'child rescue' also protected the more wealthy sections of society from the threats of delinquent youth (Hendrick, 1994).

This approach came to be much criticised for uprooting and isolating children, often with insufficient cause, and for ignoring the material and social circumstances which made it difficult for their original families to care for them. Nowadays panel members and professionals need much stronger grounds than formerly for initiating removal of children on a long-term basis. Emergency protection measures remain important parts of the statute, although modified following the controversial events in South Ronaldsay, Orkney, in 1992 (Asquith, 1993). The hearings are empowered to authorise transfer of a young person to secure accommodation, and protecting society from harm may override the child's welfare in decision-making (Children (Scotland) Act 1995, s 16(5)).

Permanency planning

Permanency planning was a movement which reached its heyday in the 1980s, but remains influential. It has been seen by its critics as a continuation of the 'child rescue' philosophy (Holman, 1988), partly because in the UK, much less than in the US, it came to be associated with policies which cut children off from their original families.

At the heart of permanency planning is the notion that family life is vital both for the long-term upbringing of children and for support in adulthood (Maluccio *et al*, 1986). The first priority should be to sustain children within their own families, but if this is not possible or in a child's interests, a permanent substitute family should be sought as quickly as possible. Longer-term placements in foster or residential care are thought generally to be unable to provide the lifetime relationships which people should have. Consequently it is important for children to have time-limited plans for return home or moving to an alternative – preferably adoption. In its more extreme form, proponents of permanency claimed that children were unable to attach satisfactorily to more than one set of parents. If birth parents were not providing adequate care and did not respond quickly to efforts to help, it was thought best for children to be placed for adoption without any further access to their original families, rather than stay with foster carers – not knowing how long they would remain and unsure whether they really belonged there or not. This position was later modified, so that permanent fostering and adoption with contact have increasingly been seen as desirable options, too (Smith, 1995; Morrison, 1996).

Lothian Region took the lead in Scotland to promote policies which focused on returning children home from care as speedily as possible, but when this failed, seeking adoptive homes (McKay, 1980; O'Hara and Hoggan, 1988). Permanency planning played an important part in reducing the numbers of children in care during the 1980s. Significant numbers of children who would otherwise have stayed indefinitely in care, without legal security and with risks of placement changes, were successfully adopted by existing foster carers or new families (Hill *et al*, 1989). Local authorities were more willing to place children for adoption even though parents opposed the plan, and courts more often dispensed with parental agreement (Lambert *et al*, 1991; Ryburn, 1994). This sometimes led to tensions between the hearings' role to consider the child's welfare in relation to the immediate grounds for referral and the duty of local authorities to plan in relation to the child's welfare throughout childhood. The problem was exacerbated by the power which authorities had to assume parental rights unilaterally without recourse to a court, unless parents appealed. This power was removed by the 1995 Act.

Permanency planning had been in part a reaction to the steady increase in the numbers of children in foster and residential care between the 1940s and 1970s, with significant numbers appearing to 'drift', having no definite plan, legal security or sense of belonging (Rowe and Lambert, 1973). Research evidence about the effects of institutionalisation in large establishments and on the generally poor outcomes of life in care led to a negative view of all but very short periods for children away from home. Besides being antithetical to residential care, permanency planning has had little to say about how to respond to adolescents whose original families had let them down, yet who did not want to have a new family or were unable to form new family attachments.

Alternative care as a positive choice

The idea that any placement away from home was likely to be damaging was challenged in the 1980s. It was pointed out that using care as a last resort could mean that problems at home were allowed to become so severe that they were very difficult to remedy when the child did eventually leave, whereas an earlier separation might have given the family space and time to improve its capacity to care for the child (Packman *et al*, 1986). The notion of 'respite' has been expanded from denoting a brief period of relief for families with a disabled child to cover a range of short-term placements to give 'breathing space' to families in crisis (Aldgate *et al*, 1996).

At the same time, reports on residential care for adults as well as children sought to counteract the prevailing negative image of residential establishments. They emphasised that sometimes this is a preferred or preferable option, so that it should be available as a 'positive choice' (Wagner, 1988; Skinner, 1992). It was noted that many older children in care did not want to live in a new family because of loyalties to their original family or because that family had hurt them so much they could not contemplate another. Teenagers account for approximately half of those who live away from home (Social Work Services Group (SWSG), 1996a). Idealisation of family life was seen as unfairly stigmatising residential care.

Prevention

The three approaches so far considered have mainly been concerned with the role of care arrangements outside a child's original family. However, the majority of children who are referred to the children's hearings system do not leave home and for many intervention is aimed at preventing the need for separation. Prevention has been an important concept for some decades. During the 1950s and 1960s child-care policy shifted from an emphasis on 'rescue' to preventing the need for a child to go away from home or appear before a court (Children and Young Persons Act 1963).

Subsequently ideas about prevention have widened to encompass preventing long-term family breakdown, abuse of children and law-breaking behaviour. Within this broader context, brief family separation may have a role in preventing immediate harm for the child or longer-term family difficulties. In a sense the whole thrust of the hearings system has been 'preventive' in that it aims to meet children's welfare needs and so prevent the recurrence of further offending, school non-attendance and so on. The Social Work (Scotland) Act 1968, s 12, placed a broad duty on local authorities to 'promote welfare', although guidance and limited budgets meant that in practice section 12 cases and expenditure were mainly about preventing family breakdown (Davidson, 1991). The 1995 Act, s 22, replaced this provision with a duty to promote and safeguard the welfare of 'children in need', ie, those whose health or development would otherwise be adversely impaired, and children affected by disability.

Thinking about prevention has been dominated by a public health model involving three levels (Hardiker *et al*, 1991):

- *primary prevention* aims to prevent social problems (like family stress or violence) arising by means of social policies directed at whole populations;
- *secondary prevention* aims to prevent a family problem becoming a major crisis – this involves helping vulnerable families who already have problems;
- *tertiary prevention* aims to prevent child abuse or family breakdown through intensive services to help 'high risk' families.

Primary prevention relies mainly on universal services such as health visiting, nursery schooling and child benefit, which are available to all. Secondary and tertiary prevention are targeted more at families with greatest need (however defined), but tend to be more variably accessible and stigmatised. While the 'prevention levels' approach helps to organise thinking about the range of services, their aims and target populations, it focuses entirely on changes in children and their families. A more ecological approach, as recommended by Boushel (1994), takes account of the influence of societal values (eg, about punishment, masculinity) and wider social networks, which can also be targets for change.

Family support

During the 1980s preventive ideas became reconceptualised as family support, which was contrasted with both substitute care and child-protection investigations. This perspective was critical of both permanency planning and the increasingly legalistic mode of child protection for their emphasis on compulsory actions in children's interests (Holman, 1988; Tunstill, 1995, 1996). The family-support perspective gives priority to positive services for families and urges co-operation with parents on a voluntary basis, except in extreme circumstances. This approach is encouraged by the Children (Scotland) Act 1995 – for example, in measures to promote the health and development of children and the stress on parental responsibility. A 'no order' presumption was also introduced. This means that hearings and courts should not make an order unless to do so is clearly better for the child than informal alternatives (1995 Act, ss 11, 16 and 96).

Although 'family support' has generally been visualised as embodying voluntary collaboration, it can operate as a more subtle form of social control, as health and welfare professionals engage with parents and children to achieve social conformity using varying degrees of persuasion or coercion (Hill *et al*, 1995; Rodger, 1996).

In the UK the idea of family support has generally been opposed to the principles of permanency planning with alternative families, although in its original form permanency planning embraced family support (Maluccio *et al*, 1986). Fox (1982) and Fox Harding (1991) characterised as 'kinship defenders' those who favoured keeping families together whenever possible and who opposed the powers used by local authorities to assume parental rights, to terminate access by children to their parents and to seek adoption against parental wishes. They pointed to parents' difficulties in coping in situations of material disadvantage and to the emotional significance to children of their biological families.

Few people disagree with the vital importance of having a range of family-support services, but the family-support approach is open to criticism. By using the global notion of 'family', it skates over potential conflicts of interest between adults and children, men and women. Moreover, supporting families should be seen as broader than helping intact birth families, since families need support when a child is in foster care and residential care, while advice, information and more specialist services can be vital for adoptive families too (Phillips and McWilliam, 1996).

Diversion

The principle and techniques of diversion originated within the field of criminal justice. Initially it referred to measures which divert young offenders from appearing in court or at a hearing 'and either do nothing or substitute some kind of informal intervention' (Morris and Giller, 1983, p138). Somewhat confusingly, diversion also came to refer to keeping young people out of residential institutions, with or without a legal order. In either sense it was premised on the view, supported by considerable empirical evidence, that legal and especially custodial intervention with offenders has often been at best ineffectual and commonly counter-productive, serving to reinforce a criminal identity rather than reform or deter from future misdemeanours. This idea has been supported by

• *labelling and deviance-amplification theories*, which suggested that responses to offending may encourage a criminal career by such mechanisms as alienating the offender further from 'mainstream society' and leading young people to feel they have little alternative but to conform to negative images of them held by those in authority;

• recognition that most young people *'grow out' of offending*, almost regardless of what is done to them;

• the concept of *net-widening*, ie, justice systems and their associated treatments had a tendency to capture large numbers of young people with relatively minor or even no offences who were more likely to be harmed than helped by formal intervention;

• the notion of *contamination in 'schools of crime'*, ie, putting young people together especially in the same establishment facilitates their continued associations with peers who are also offenders and who may teach them ways of committing further crimes.

Diversionary principles have been interpreted in various ways. They can entail selectively desisting from any official action at all in the expectation that guilt and shame are sufficient. All that is needed for this form of diversion is some kind of gate-keeping procedure to assess which individuals should be dealt with in the justice system and which ones without further action. Diversion has also been taken to mean informal action. It is interesting to note that the children's hearings system has built into it discretion for the reporter not to refer cases to a hearing when the responses of the child and the family seem adequate to deal with the problem, perhaps supported by voluntary (ie, informal) supervision (see Chapters 3 and 4). In fact, the majority of referrals to reporters do not lead on to hearings, although the percentage varies markedly from one part of Scotland to another (Asquith, 1992a; McGhee *et al*, 1996). There is, however, a tension between the welfare orientation of the hearings and diversionary principles, since 'the use of systems management to divert children and young people from welfare inter-ventions can seem to run the risk of failing to identify or meet welfare needs' (Ballantyne, 1995, p110).

However, diversion has also been applied to formal measures which act as alternatives to custody or indeed any placement away from home. Here the aim is a lower degree of intervention rather than non intervention. Most commonly this has involved *intermediate treatment* (IT), an ambiguous and hence unhelpful term which covers a range of group and individual activities. When diversion involves such services its nature and purpose may well overlap with those of prevention. Indeed some forms of IT are referred to as preventive (Robertson and McClintock, 1996).

Although mainly applied to arrangements for young offenders, diversion principles have also been used to shape broader child-care policies. For example, Strathclyde Region established Area Resource Groups to scrutinise and screen recommendations to the reporter and plans for reception into care. Use of these ARGs resulted in fewer recommendations for home supervision (Ballantyne, 1996). The most notable application in Scotland occurred in Fife during the late

1980s (see Chapter 5). The social work department achieved a large reduction in the numbers of children placed away from home, but panel members and others criticised the policy for ignoring the perceived needs of some children for formal intervention (Bilson and Thorpe, 1987; Kearney, 1992). Although this extreme application of diversionary principles was condemned by central government and other agencies, nevertheless the idea that it is desirable to respond with the minimum necessary intrusion in children's and families' lives remains strong and is reflected in the 'no order' principle in the Children (Scotland) Act 1995.

Listening to children
This final perspective differs from the others in not expressing preferences as regards different forms of living situation or intervention. Rather the emphasis is placed on taking account of children's own views. Children's rights can be examined in several ways and include rights to protection and services, but in this context it is children's participatory rights which are most relevant. Stimulated by the 'child liberationist' movement and later by the less radical but more widely accepted principles of the United Nations Convention on the Rights of the Child, increasing attention has been given to enabling children to express their opinions and to trying to ensure that adults take more account of them. The Children (Scotland) Act 1995 states that a child's views should be taken account of in any major decision which affects his or her welfare (ss 6, 11(7), 16(2), 17(3) and 95(2)).

The hearings have from the outset involved children actively in decisions and sought to facilitate communication by reducing formality and status differentials. It has also become customary for children in care to participate in review meetings and even sometimes in child-protection case conferences. Feedback from young people suggests that many feel able to express themselves at such meetings and do think their views are considered, but some feel inhibited, puzzled or alienated. A fair number think that decisions are predetermined, regardless of what they say (Kendrick and Mapstone, 1992; Triseliotis *et al*, 1995; Freeman *et al*, 1996). The 1995 Act allows for parents to be excluded from a hearing when this might intimidate a child (usually in cases of child abuse). This change has the general support of panel members, social workers and the police (Veitch, 1995).

The range of resources
In broad terms, child rescue, permanency planning and positive choice perspectives have mainly concentrated on substitute living arrangements, whereas prevention, family support and diversion emphasise actions to keep children at home. In reaching decisions for children to stay home or not and about the range of service options in either case, hearings need to take account of the context and consequences of each type of resource.

Birth families
Over 80 per cent of children with supervision requirements remain at home and most of those who are placed away from home eventually return there (Scottish Office, 1995b; Bullock *et al*, 1993). Thus birth families, as well as often having a part

to play in the grounds for referral, are usually also the primary locus for seeking to remedy the cause for concern, whether that relates to the child's welfare alone or also the child's behaviour. For instance, parents' willingness and capacity to monitor children's activities is a crucial influence on involvement in law-breaking activities (Wilson and Herbert, 1978; Laybourn, 1986). The availability of interest, stimulation and concern from key adults in a child's network (such as a teacher or grandparent) can be a vital help in overcoming adverse home circumstances (Cochran *et al*, 1990; Werner and Smith, 1992; Fonagy *et al*, 1994; Gilligan, 1997).

Demographic and socio-economic changes might suggest that stresses in families have increased, resulting in a greater likelihood of difficulties in meeting children's needs and decreased ability to act as a positive resource. Global figures indicate that households with dependent children have become more diverse in form and with higher proportions living in straitened circumstances (see also Chapter 7). Since family discontinuity and poverty are the two main features associated with child-care difficulties, as indicated by reported crime and referrals to the reporter (Bebbington and Miles, 1989; see also Chapter 3), it could be inferred that more families are now in a weaker position to act as a resource for their children. Though there is some evidence in support of this thesis, it is an oversimplification. Despite the increases in child poverty during the 1980s and 1990s (Long, 1995), the proportion of children placed away from home on either a voluntary or compulsory basis declined markedly (SWSG, 1994).

The basic facts of household changes involving children in Scotland over the last few decades are well enough known (Tisdall and Donaghie, 1995):

- fertility and average family size have fallen;
- the proportion of births to unmarried mothers had grown to 29 per cent in 1991 (although many such births were jointly registered, suggesting cohabitation by the parents);
- the number of households headed by a lone parent has increased to 16 per cent;
- the rate of divorce has become approximately one in three, and over 10,000 children each year are affected by the divorce of their parents;
- the numbers of remarriages and reconstituted families have increased.

There is evidence that a higher proportion of children in lone-parent households have scholastic or emotional/behavioural difficulties compared with those living with both parents, though the majority in both types of household do well (McLanahan and Booth, 1989). However, this apparently consistent and significant difference disappears when families in similar material circumstances are compared. Likewise children living in step-families *on average* experience more difficulties, achieve less well educationally and leave home earlier than those with both birth parents, but the differences are mostly small and again can be linked to material circumstances (Kiernan, 1992; Ferri, 1993). Hence it appears that household form in itself is not a crucial factor in families' capacities to support children, but material circumstances and the attitudes and sensitivities of others are important (Schaffer, 1990; Campion, 1995). A study of fifteen-year-olds found that there was 'little or no relationship between being in an intact, reconstituted or single-parent family and self-esteem, psychological well-being or physical symptoms' (Sweeting and West, 1995, p168).

Divorce is often associated with distress for children, although some feel relief (Mitchell, 1985; Ayalon and Flasher, 1993). In the long run most children adapt quite well and tend to see the divorce as either inevitable or for the best (Amato and Keith, 1991). Moreover, many of the apparently negative 'consequences of divorce' were in fact present before the marital relationship ended and so were more the result of pre-divorce conflict and tension than post-divorce trauma (Jenkins and Smith, 1991; Richards 1994). Now that divorce has become widespread, it may well be that children will feel less isolated and stigmatised, so that adverse effects will diminish.

It may be concluded that family and household patterns have definitely changed, but 'the family is not in terminal decline' (Richards, 1995, p49). It is not so much parental separation and divorce which affects children as conflict and it is by no means clear whether family conflict has become more common or not. While commentators from the left and right have argued that men, women or both are nowadays less committed to children (Halsey, 1993), the evidence is more that adults are less prepared to stay in unhappy relationships with other adults, but normally still do their best to provide good care for their children. Many children and young people are very positive about their parents (Noller and Callan, 1991; Hill *et al*, 1995). Nevertheless there are some casualties of family change and it is important for policies and services to give appropriate support. In the early days of the hearings, children living in lone-parent households were more likely to be placed on home supervision than those living with two parents (Martin, 1982b).

Since the inception of the hearings system, the population in many parts of Scotland has become ethnically more diverse. The Children (Scotland) Act 1995 introduced new requirements for local authorities and courts to have regard to a child's religious persuasion, racial origin, culture and linguistic background. Although the hearings were not specifically covered in this respect, their general duty towards the child's welfare can be seen as encompassing attention to a child's heritage and identity.

Children from ethnic minority backgrounds have, on average, more individuals to call on for support within their households. Most households contain at least one adult who is a fluent English speaker, though more older people – especially women and those of Chinese background – speak little or no English, so that interpreting assistance is required in dealings with officials (Smith, 1991).

Poverty, work and unemployment patterns
Definitions and interpretations of poverty are controversial, but it seems clear that large numbers of households with children have incomes significantly below those which allow for generally accepted needs to be met and social participation to occur. Over one-third of children in Scotland live in households with below 50 per cent of average income (after housing costs), including the one-quarter of all

children whose families are dependent on income support (Long, 1995). Standardised measures of costs and subjective reports from parents living in poverty demonstrate that income-support levels are insufficient to cover the costs of providing a healthy diet and caring for a child on a long-term basis (Kumar, 1993; Middleton *et al*, 1994).

The majority of children who attend hearings are living in poor families, where there is a high likelihood of debts, difficulties in meeting day-to-day costs (like travel) and educational disadvantage. If such families are to overcome their material and environmental hardship, they will often need a range of financial and social support, compensatory care and education, and individual or collective measures to improve their financial position (Gibbons, 1995; Long, 1995).

Among the main factors causing poverty in families with children are unemployment (combined with low benefit rates), low pay and inadequate child-support payments for lone parents. Female employment rates rose substantially between 1970 and 1985, less so since then. Although a woman's earnings are often crucial in keeping a family out of poverty, the highest levels of employment and earnings are among women with higher qualifications (Long, 1995). Two-thirds of married women in the UK are in paid employment. Over one in ten of mothers with a pre-school child works full time and one-third when the youngest child is aged ten or more (Kiernan and Wicks, 1990; Fox Harding, 1996). In many cases this means that both or the only parent at home is working full time. Since full-time day care and after-school care are in short supply, especially in rural areas, there is considerable reliance on informal social networks or paid help to supplement parental care (Hill, 1987; Cohen, 1995).

Foster care

When panel members consider requiring a child to live away from home, there are two main options: living with an alternative family (foster care) or in a non-family setting (residential care). Each form of care encompasses a variety of types and most also offer care for children looked after 'on a voluntary basis' as well as those with a supervision requirement. Decisions should be informed by knowledge of how the qualities of foster and residential care settings fit with children's particular needs and wishes and of 'risk factors' which affect the likelihood of a placement succeeding or failing.

Foster care refers to an individual, couple or family looking after a child not born to them without any legal transfer of parental rights and responsibilities to the carers (which occurs in adoption). It is legal to foster children on a private basis, with parents paying a regular fee, although statutory supervision is required. However, the great majority of children fostered under the auspices of the hearings will be placed by social work services, who also recruit, pay and support the foster carers. At the time of writing, just two voluntary agencies in Scotland have a foster-care scheme.

During the 1980s, in addition to their 'mainstream' fostering services, most local authorities established specialist fostering schemes (variously labelled). These provided planned, time-limited placements, with carers receiving a fee in addition to the usual allowance to cover costs. Specialist foster carers have catered mainly for teenagers, but may serve younger children, including those with disabilities. Some argue that this separation of special fostering from mainstream fostering is divisive and elitist, especially now that few children are placed in foster care for any length of time unless they have special needs. For this reason, Fife Region decided to pay all its foster families a salary (Ramsay, 1996). Foster homes tend to be more available outside big city centres, whereas disproportionate numbers of looked-after children come from urban areas (Lothian, 1994).

The number of foster placements in Scotland has remained fairly steady for a number of years (SWSG, 1995a), but since the overall number of children looked after away from home has declined, fostering has contributed an increased *proportion* of out-of-home placements. However, a number of agencies have expressed concern that it is becoming increasingly difficult to recruit and retain foster carers. This may be affected by the increased demands of the fostering task, together with deficiencies in the levels of remuneration and quality of support. More fundamentally, the demographic and economic changes noted above mean that there are now fewer of the kinds of family who traditionally engaged in foster care, with the father having a steady job and the mother wishing to work at home. As we have seen, more families are affected by male unemployment and poverty, while more women want paid employment outside the home. Such factors have affected availability and initiative for voluntary activities more generally (Knight, 1993).

The role of foster carers has changed substantially in recent years, so that providing good day-to-day care of children has become only one of their tasks. Family-support principles have largely displaced child-rescue considerations in agency policies. In most placements, emphasis is laid on helping to maintain contacts with the child's birth family (a statutory duty under s 17 of the Children (Scotland) Act, 1995) and on assisting birth parents so that the child may return home and be cared for effectively there. This is often not easy, since either party may feel a sense of rivalry, and some parents may be perceived by foster carers as unreliable, uncaring or aggressive (Waterhouse, 1992). Moreover, nowadays few children are placed away from home unless they have serious difficulties and fewer are placed in residential care than previously, so that the children's emotional needs and behaviour are frequently very demanding. For example, a young child who has been sexually abused may seek inappropriate physical contacts or use sexually explicit language in ways which distress or embarrass foster carers or their own children.

At best, foster care can offer a loving, supportive home for a child in a setting which, unlike residential care, resembles that of the great majority of their peers. Among the benefits recognised by children and young people are a sense of belonging, involvement in shared family activities and some degree of autonomy (Triseliotis *et al*, 1995).

A significant problem with fostering, though, is that there is a considerable risk of the placement breaking down. The concept of 'breakdown' (sometimes called a disruption) is a complex one. It refers to a premature placement ending, but this may mean too soon according to the child's needs, the child's wishes, the original plans, or later reviews, and judgments by foster carers, social workers, children and parents often differ as to when or even if a breakdown has occurred (Rowe *et al*, 1989; Hill *et al*, 1996). Also placements may continue beyond the point where they are helpful for a child, often because alternative arrangements do not materialise. In spite of policies which emphasise a speedy return home or finding a permanent alternative, many children remain overlong in temporary placements without such plans being fulfilled (Kosonen, 1993). Then children may become restless or, alternatively, so attached to the foster family that they are less willing or able to adjust to returning home or a planned permanent alternative.

Researchers have used different and sometimes simplified criteria for judging unsuccessful placements, but most have revealed that as many as one in three longer-term or specialist foster placements break down, and perhaps one in ten short-term placements (Berridge and Cleaver, 1987; Rowe *et al*, 1989; Fenyo *et al*, 1991), though the rates in Strathclyde in the 1980s were higher than this. Comparisons between breakdown rates in foster care and residential care indicate that there is little difference, allowing for the generally lower age of admission to foster care (Rowe *et al*, 1989; Kendrick, 1995a).

Researchers have identified a number of risk factors associated with a greater likelihood of breakdown. Not surprisingly the main 'child' factors associated with a high risk of breakdown are older age at placement and a history of serious emotional/behaviour problems. Most studies have found that more experienced foster carers have fewer breakdowns. An inclusive orientation by carers to birth families and social workers also seems to augur well for placement stability (Triseliotis *et al*, 1995). A consistent finding – less expected perhaps – has been that placements are significantly more likely to end prematurely if there is another child in the foster home close in age (Triseliotis, 1989; Department of Health, 1991). Although such an arrangement might seem to afford companionship, in practice rivalry and competing demands are more probable.

The implication of findings about foster-care risk factors is not necessarily to avoid placements when such factors are present, especially as the risks for residential placements are quite similar. Rather, greater caution is needed and more support may be required to deal with the likely greater stresses.

Residential care
Residential care takes place in a wide range of establishments where children are looked after by paid staff. Usually the number of children is significantly more than in the typical family, though in recent years there has been a trend towards housing no more than five to ten children. The two main forms of residential care are children's homes (now often referred to as residential units) and residential schools. The latter, as the name implies, combine both care and educational functions on the same premises. Also secure accommodation is available for young people who are considered a danger to themselves or others, usually on account of serious offending or repeated absconding (Littlewood, 1996). A recent development is 'crash pads' which offer short periods of respite and support for adolescents experiencing a family crisis (Swanson, 1988). Section 38 of the

Children (Scotland) Act 1995 allows local authorities and others to offer refuge (in an approved establishment) for children seeking shelter from situations of danger to themselves. This may last seven days, with the possibility of an extension for another week.

Since 1976 the numbers of children and young people placed in residential care has fallen from over 6,000 to just over 2,000, including about one-quarter in residential schools (SWSG, 1995a). Many establishments have closed or altered their functions, but also some mainly smaller units have been opened. Nevertheless, most cater for nine or more children (Skinner, 1992). The boundaries of residential care have deliberately become more permeable in recent times. With some exceptions, notably secure units, flexibility has increased about the time children may spend in their parental home, while some residential schools offer day places. There is an increasing trend for staff to work closely with families and to offer outreach on a preventive basis, though such developments are patchy.

It is often seen as desirable that residential care be provided in the same neighbourhood as the child's family home, so that children can maintain contacts with relatives and friends, and sometimes avoid a change of school. The principle of localisation is in tension with a common view that establishments should specialise according to age and the nature of children's needs or problems, rather than take all comers. In practice, most residential placements are arranged at very short notice and on the basis of availability, not necessarily suitability (Kendrick, 1995a; Triseliotis *et al*, 1995).

Most residents are aged eleven plus, but the proportion of younger children varies markedly from one part of Scotland to another. Offences or other behavioural difficulties are the primary factors which led to the admission of over two-thirds of young people in residential care (either admitted via the hearings or otherwise 'accommodated' by local authorities) (Kendrick, 1995a).

The great majority of care staff are untrained and there is a high turnover, but central government has invested considerably to improve training and status in the last few years (Skinner, 1992). As with foster care, judgments about 'success' in residential care depend on how it is assessed and who makes the judgment. Abuse and inadequate care do occur, but research evidence suggests that the majority of residents benefit, although sometimes in a limited way. On the whole, residential placements fare no better and no worse than foster placements. Developing trust with staff seems to be a vital ingredient for success (Kendrick, 1995a; Triseliotis *et al*, 1995).

Residential schools have often been viewed negatively, but recent research indicates that they are offering a service which is particularly appreciated by parents and young people. Furthermore, social workers recognise high levels of success in achieving behavioural and educational change, as well as enhancing maturity and social activities (Triseliotis *et al*, 1995). Critical factors which assist with these good outcomes are planned placements, coherent programmes, continuity of staff and individualised schooling on the premises.

Preparation, through care and support programmes, has been developed to enable those leaving care at around sixteen to cope more effectively. However, vulnerable young people with limited family contacts continue to face major difficulties of poverty, poor housing and social isolation (Biehal et al, 1995; Triseliotis et al, 1995a). It remains a basic problem that the responsibilities of the hearings system and the care system usually end at an age well before most young people are expected to manage on their own (Jones and Wallace, 1992).

Adoption

Lawmakers have not seen fit to extend the principles of informal, lay decision-making to adoption, which is dealt with in courts rather than at hearings. However, under the influence of permanency planning, over the last two decades increasing numbers of older children have been placed for adoption, when birth relatives appear to be unable to provide a satisfactory long-term home. Some of these children are subject to a supervision requirement. At times there have been divergences of opinion among social workers, panel members and parents about the suitability or otherwise of a plan for adoption.

Until the 1960s, decisions to place children for adoption were usually made by parents in relation to infants, but then local authorities began considering adoption for children previously considered unadoptable, whether because of parental opposition or matters which at that time were thought to make the child 'hard to place', like disability, behaviour difficulties or a family history of mental illness. First North American experience and then UK experience showed that adopters could be found for these children using active recruitment strategies, a greater readiness to dispense with parental consent and, in some cases, the availability of financial and other support (Hill et al, 1989; Triseliotis et al, 1997). Also the Adoption (Scotland) Act 1978 made it possible for children to be 'freed' for adoption before a suitable placement was found and the full adoption process initiated. This provision came to be used mainly in contested cases (Lambert et al, 1991).

Decisions by local authorities to place children for adoption are usually initiated in child care-reviews and then, by law, must be affirmed at adoption panels. When a child is subject to a supervision requirement, it is necessary for the hearing to agree to any change of residence by the child or alteration to adoption of a foster placement. During the 1980s and 90s complaints were made that local authorities sometimes presented hearings with a *fait accompli*, rather than reach a shared decision. Also panel members were often more reluctant than social work departments to sever families' ties in order to facilitate adoption plans, since this seemed to pre-empt the decision of the court about adoption (Marshall, 1994). As a result of these difficulties the Children (Scotland) Act 1995 gives hearings the right and duty to comment on plans for adoption and introduces obligations on local authorities or voluntary adoption agencies to advise the reporter when making a formal decision about adoption (s 73). A further shift back towards the approach of kinship defenders and minimal intrusion is embodied in the new requirement for agencies and courts to approve adoption only after consideration of alternatives or of making no order.

The placement of older children for adoption means that they have known and perhaps grown attached to pre-adoptive carers, including possibly one of their parents. As a result, decision-makers may fear that the children will not be able to establish effective bonds in a new family. In fact research has shown that many adoptions of older children are very successful. However, in general the older the child at placement the more likely that the child's history of interrupted and/or poor parenting will result in long-term difficulties and stresses (Borland *et al*, 1991; Rushton and Rushton, 1995; Howe, 1996). Methods based on attachment theory are used to help children 'move on' (Fahlberg, 1994). First, children are helped to understand and, if necessary, grieve for the people and places they have been separated from or are about to leave. As far as possible, people significant to the child should demonstrate their approval of the planned change. Secondly, new carers are helped to 'claim' the child by positively valuing the child, adapting to likes and interests, developing shared experiences and not expecting progress too soon.

Non-residential services

There is a wide range of non-residential social, educational and health services which can be deployed in conjunction with voluntary or compulsory supervision. These can be preventive or diversionary in orientation, or assist children in care. Some are directed at children and young people themselves, others are offered to parents, alternative carers or families as a whole. These services include social work support, various special measures of schooling, different kinds of group work, volunteer befriending and referral to specialist psychological or psychiatric services. The availability of group work, whether for young people at home or looked after away from home, varies greatly from one area to another (Triseliotis *et al*, 1995; SWSI, 1995a). Increasingly voluntary and statutory agencies have set up projects to help particular populations (eg, children with the same disability, children of ethnic minority backgrounds), or to assist with issues, such as child abuse, drug-taking or alcohol misuse. Since there are only a few of each type of project, access is often quite restricted geographically. In certain areas, social work, education and voluntary agencies have collaborated to tackle school-related problems, sometimes as part of a wider youth strategy (Kendrick, 1995b).

The core ingredient of home supervision is the face-to-face contact between social worker and children and their families. Initially, the avowed purpose was to support parental supervision or influence a young person through building a trusting counselling relationship (Ford, 1982; Kelly, 1996). More recently emphasis has been placed on explicit formal agreements, partly influenced by the introduction of National Standards with respect to adult offenders and by developments in 'child protection' work. Hardly any systematic information is available about the goals, processes and outcomes of these interactions. One study found that, with certain exceptions, the planning and sharing of expectations was generally not so clear or specific as with children placed away from home. Individual work with young people on supervision appeared to be most effective when workers took time to build trust, share their aims clearly and provide guidance about behaviour and relationships in a caring but firm manner (Triseliotis *et al*, 1995).

It is also part of the supervising social worker's role to arrange access for children to specialist groups and services. Feedback from young people suggests that they like informal arrangements, especially group activities, run by people they see as in tune with youth culture(s). Some quickly cease contact with psychologists, psychiatrists and other specialists who do not communicate on young people's wavelength, because they feel alienated and see little purpose (Triseliotis *et al*, 1995; Freeman *et al*, 1996). Others are greatly helped. For instance, a specialist counselling project for children who had been sexually abused was seen by referring agencies as offering sensitive and welcome support. The lesson seems to be that young people mainly respond to people they know and trust, so that referral to specialists who are strangers should be done sparingly and after careful assessment of the likelihood that the young person will readily engage.

Support services for families are mostly available pre-school and in the teen years, and there tends to be a dearth of provision in middle childhood. The value to children and parents in general of good quality pre-school care/education has been repeatedly demonstrated (Scarr and Dunn, 1987). Such services can also play a vital role in complementing the care of children whose development of health is impaired and in monitoring the progress of children thought to be at risk. Intensive pre-school education has been shown to have lasting benefits for disadvantaged children (MacDonald and Roberts, 1995; Young, 1995).

Increasingly staff working in early-years provision seek to support parents and carers as well as look after children. *Family centres* aim to provide help to families as a whole, though in practice the main users are mothers and children. Many offer professional services (eg, parent education, counselling); some are based more on mutual aid principles to tackle problems of isolation, poverty or lack of employment opportunities (Holman, 1988; Kirk, 1995; Long, 1995).

During the 1970s and 80s one of the central elements of supervisory interventions for teenagers was 'intermediate treatment' – an array of measures, usually involving group work, which were intermediate between home-based work and placement away from home. IT developed in the context of diversion principles and its aims are compensatory as well as controlling. Considerable evidence pointed to its success in enabling young people to avoid further involvement with the justice system (Pitts, 1988). A children's hearing may make a compulsory condition of a supervision requirement that a child attends at an IT programme or equivalent (1995 Act, s 73). Most commonly, though, attendance is voluntary.

The development of IT in Scotland has exhibited great diversity and innovation, with little co-ordination (Jones and Gallagher, 1985; Intermediate Treatment Resource Centre (ITRC), 1986). Although the term IT has fallen into disuse in some parts of Scotland, many local authorities and voluntary agencies offer activities, discussion and structured group activities, sometimes combined with individual or family counselling (Hill *et al*, 1997). An evaluation of IT in Scotland revealed that it seemed to have less impact on behaviour than individual supervision or residential care, but did lead to improvements in personal and social functioning. The best outcomes were achieved by intensive IT programmes, which are the most structured, require attendance for longer periods of time and are targeted at 'heavy end' groups, ie, those with persistent offending, school or family problems (Robertson and McClintock, 1996). Many parents of children attending groups think they should last longer and be held more frequently (Triseliotis *et al*, 1995; Robertson and McClintock, 1996).

Conclusions

A spectrum of resources is available for consideration by hearings. They range from one-to-one counselling at home to temporary or permanent placements away from home. Decisions about which options are appropriate should clearly take account of children's needs and expressed wishes, but recommendations and the availability of particular services are affected by prevailing or competing ideas about their relevance, as well as by resource constraints. Some approaches (eg, family support, diversion) emphasise minimal intrusion; others place more stress on compulsion or removal of children from home where necessary (eg, care as a positive choice; permanency planning). Although some people adhere to each of these viewpoints as their overriding orientation, most recognise that usually it is desirable to support children at home, but there are circumstances when removal is necessary to protect a child from danger or for the sake of his/her health and development. Thus, the debate mainly concerns how broadly or narrowly defined are the circumstances which make short-term or permanent placement away from home desirable. A children's rights perspective insists on the importance of affording children an opportunity to express their views and then giving careful consideration to them, both as a matter of right and also because otherwise any intervention may be rejected or undermined.

Decisions about the appropriate use of resources should also be informed by evidence about the effectiveness of different kinds of intervention. Unfortunately, the messages from research are not always straightforward. Some differences have been identified in the outcomes and popularity of particular kinds of service, but there are always individual exceptions to any general conclusions. Trusting relationships, clear plans, open and specific sharing of expectations and aims, structure and firmness are associated with success both at home and away from home. Opportunities for children and young people to build consistent and trusting relationships with their carers and workers are the foundation on which developmental and behavioural change becomes possible. Otherwise, alienation is likely to arise and a child's difficulties may well be compounded rather than alleviated. Also some factors are clearly associated with risk (eg, placing children in a foster home with a similarly aged child). However, each form of intervention may help some children, but not others. This highlights the importance of careful assessment and matching according to each child's situation, views and orientations (Cleaver, 1996), as indeed the legislation requires.

9 : The Changing Focus of Social Work

Ian Gilmour and Donal Giltinan

THIS chapter describes the development of social work services in Scotland, with particular emphasis on the Social Work (Scotland) Act 1968. It attempts to explain how the tasks of the social worker and the organisation of local authority social work departments have developed in response to the lessons of experience. The relationship between social work and the children's hearing system is set in the context of the range of competing demands placed on social work, together with other agencies, in supporting children and families. Some of the issues covered include changing ideas about what constitutes 'supervision', the status of children 'in care', and the division of responsibilities between parents and local authorities. The impact of increasing economic pressures and their implications for practice and priorities are discussed. Reference is made to the effect of the increasing emphasis on children's and parents' rights. The final section deals with the implementation of the Children (Scotland) Act 1995 in the context of recent reorganisation and its consequent effect on available resources.

Changing focus of social work

The concept and practice of social work has existed since time immemorial but has largely defied definition. The modern profession of social work has evolved around a set of values, beliefs and principles about society's responsibilities to its members. The concept is in a state of permanent evolution and it is unlikely that it ever will reach a state of final development. In our time the profession of social work is closely aligned with a set of values and principles about the role and importance of the family in society.

Families present a particular challenge for state intervention. They are independent and self-creating institutions which are beyond the scrutiny of the state, yet the state has a vested interest in ensuring that the proper social education of children which the family provides is carried out. How then can a state institution attempt to influence families in a way that does not compromise their primary characteristic of being private, ie, beyond the legitimate control of the state? The differing forms which families take in modern society add further dimensions to this complication. One of the fundamental principles of the Children (Scotland) Act 1995 is that the state should not intervene in the lives of families unless doing so would be to their obvious benefit – the principle of minimum intervention. No order should be made unless the court or a children's hearing considers that the making of an order would be better for the child than not making an order. This is not intended to mean that the making of an order should be a 'last resort' but that there is certainty that the order being made is necessary for the child's welfare and the best way forward for that child. If on the other hand the child's welfare can be secured, as the paramount consideration, without an order or other form of intervention, that is the appropriate decision.

Professor Marshall, in her inaugural lecture at Glasgow Caledonian University in May 1993, stated as her basic thesis that 'as the welfare principle has grown in prominence, the law's attitude to children has become less directive and more discretionary. The law has increasingly looked to social work for guidance in exercising that discretion'. While few would argue about the need for such discretion in the affairs of families, the challenge for social work has been how best to respond and in what circumstances and for what purposes. For some years now the profession of social work has struggled with the dilemma of how best to respond to the legitimate criticism of the press following over-zealous intervention on the one hand and what was sometimes perceived as hesitant intervention on the other.

The development of social work departments
The professionalisation of social work has been very much a modern phenomenon, largely consigned to the second half of this century. Child and family welfare has moved from being concerned with the provision of services to individuals and families to a powerful interventionist authority with the law placing limits on its actions. There is very little evidence to suggest that this change has been led by social work as a profession; indeed it has at times been forced reluctantly to accept this role.

To understand the changing focus of social work in Scotland it is necessary to re-examine some of the values and principles that were prevalent during the nascent years of statutory social work. Some of the greatest paradigm shifts in the development of social work have been initiated by tragic events. In England, following the death in 1945 of Denis O'Neil from neglect and starvation while in foster care, the Home Office appointed Myra Curtis to chair the Care of Children Committee. The remit of the Committee was '[t]o enquire into the existing methods of providing for children who from loss of parents, or any other cause whatsoever, are deprived of a normal home life with their own parents or relatives, and to consider what further measures should be taken to ensure that these children are brought up under conditions best calculated to compensate them for lack of parental care' (Curtis, 1946). The Curtis Report stressed the importance of home life for disadvantaged children and, where necessary, strongly preferred fostering to care in large, impersonal institutions. The report was highly critical of many residential homes, characterised by 'a lack of personal interest in and affection for the children'.

Scotland, with its separate judicial system, established a parallel committee under the chairmanship of J. L. Clyde, KC, later Lord President – father of J. J.

Clyde, who, a generation later, chaired the Orkney Inquiry (see Chapter 6). Both Curtis and Clyde, noting the absence of a government department specifically responsible for children, recommended the establishment of a single local authority committee, the Children's Committee, to be staffed by a Children's Officer, for whom training was considered essential, as it was for residential child-care staff. There seemed to have been a certain sense of complacency in Scotland, with a feeling that the system was largely satisfactory and that there was no urgent need for major changes in the delivery of social work services or the intervention of the state into the lives of families. However, the Clyde Report offers us an important insight into the public and professional understanding of child care at the end of the first half of this century. It expressed the broadly held views of Scottish society at that time regarding children in need of state care: 'There are cases where, owing to the conduct of parents, it is in the child's interest that it should reside where contact with its parents will not be easy and therefore infrequent.' Later the report states: 'We consider it inadvisable that backward or maladjusted children should be placed in homes where there are normal children. Neither tag is good for the other.' And later: 'There should be infants' homes for children up to two years' (Clyde, 1946).[1]

These selective vignettes give us an insight into the history of social work in Scotland. By the early 1950s the boarding out of children (and people with learning difficulties) from the cities to the healthy fresh air of the highlands and islands of Scotland had been well established. The prospect of sending them further afield, to the colonies, away from the negative influences of poor housing and inadequate families, to work in the open spaces and in the farmlands of the New World, was a logical extension of this philosophy. These were pre-Bowlby days, when there was little or no understanding of the feelings of loss and separation which these children might experience at the time or later (Bowlby, 1979).

Many of the most significant developments in British social policy have been generated not by the appreciation of empirical research findings but by events which stimulated public opinion, such as the tragic lives of young people in care. The 1966 television documentary, *Cathy Come Home*, had a similar effect on the public imagination. The powerful image was of a social care system which trapped families in a downward spiral where they eventually disintegrated. The major local authority departments of housing, welfare and children's services operated under different systems, constraints, forces and value bases and, as a consequence, failed to see the family in holistic terms.

The position in Scotland in the mid-1960s was such that a new initiative was needed that would offer a locally based and integrated service for children and their families, and would include protection from abuse. The development of social work in Scotland has, for most of its history, a habit of trying to mirror initiatives south of the border, despite the fact that Scotland has its own very

---

[1] For a full account of the background to the Curtis and Clyde Reports and the impact of their recommendations, see Murphy (1992).

distinctive history, culture and judicial system and the factors that motivate a re-examination of child care in England and Wales are often irrelevant in Scotland.

It was in such circumstances that the Kilbrandon Committee was established in 1960. Its remit was apparently similar to that of the Ingleby Committee in England, which had been set up in 1956 to advise on the law and procedures in respect of juveniles. The history and the outcome of the Kilbrandon Report are dealt with in great detail in Section I of this book and are addressed here only insofar as they affect the development of social work practice and the organisation of social work services in Scotland. We are particularly concerned with the relationship between the profession of social work and the system of juvenile justice as undertaken by the children's hearings system.

The language of treatment and service provision

There seems to have been a consensus within the Kilbrandon Committee that the time was right for a system of social justice which would give prominence to the 'needs' of young people rather than to their 'deeds'. The Committee considered that children who exhibited antisocial behaviour would benefit from the ministrations of the social work profession. As we have seen, the children's hearings system sought to provide help either on a voluntary basis or as 'compulsory measures of care', 'care' being defined by the 1968 Act as including 'protection, control, guidance and treatment'. There was general commitment to the Kilbrandon principles as they were embodied in the 1968 Act. That was to provide advice and counselling or practical assistance on request or on referral from the reporter, and to give compulsory 'guidance, protection and control' without viewing it as punishment. However, there was no common understanding about what was meant by 'treatment', and in reality the use of the term concealed genuine differences about the use of a spectrum of measures.

In Chapter 2 the term 'treatment' is discussed, and it is argued that although the Kilbrandon Committee used an analogy with medical treatment at some points, it did not in reality endorse or prescribe a medical model. However, there are many commentators who have pointed out that even if medicine was not intended as a serious model for social work, it provided a seductive analogy (Morris and McIsaac, 1978; Lockyer, 1982; Adler, 1985). Many social workers employed terms like 'diagnosis', 'symptom' and perhaps even 'cure', though it is doubtful whether anyone in the field seriously thought of delinquency as a disease with a known pathology and a discoverable remedy. Certainly the term 'treatment' was employed and the association of the term with medicine had its attractions. It fitted comfortably with the ethos in the 1960s and 70s of a morally non-judgmental approach to clients and, just as important, achieving professional status for casework.

The medical analogy could be pursued into the discussion of 'treatment' in practice. There was a real difference between those who thought removal from contaminating influences to a controlled environment with expert care for a period of 'cure' might be most appropriate. The alternative public health model was to change behaviour and improve the general 'health' of the home environment. By the 1980s care in the community was increasingly the preferred option in both medicine and social work, not least because the effects of institutional care and institutional dependency were recognised to be problems. However, the analogy with medicine should not be taken too far, except to say that social work, like general health care, might provide a variety of approaches. The gradual disappearance of the language of treatment from social work discourse was a consequence of the increasing recognition that the metaphor could be misleading, and that social work practice could stand on its own professional feet.

The debate over methods of dealing with children in a home setting within their own families, in residential care, or with foster parents, or by a range of methods called 'intermediate treatment', is about finding the most appropriate resources and the best approach to the needs of individual children. It is not about the terms in which such debate should be conducted.

The concept and exercise of statutory supervision requirements

The Social Work (Scotland) Act 1968 was revolutionary in the emphasis it placed on the importance of supervision as a means of providing help to families. However, there was not at that time, nor has there evolved since, a satisfactory understanding of what this concept of supervision really meant. It was ill defined and was explained in simple terms of advice and welfare support, and its effectiveness seemed to be dependent on avoiding too narrow or precise a definition. Despite a massive investment of resources in the undertaking of statutory and voluntary supervision, since the implementation of the 1968 Act there has been very little empirical analysis of the outcome and long-term effectiveness. It has involved a great deal of professional social work time, of guidance and procedure from central and local government, and has commanded widespread public support as being generally 'a good thing', but it has not been subjected to the test of close scrutiny or comparative analysis. There is therefore particular interest in the findings of the longitudinal research study recently inaugurated by the Social Work Services Group.

In the new social work departments established in 1968, the concept of supervision of children who were the subject of compulsory measures of care was an amalgam of the approaches adopted by former probation officers who had dealt with young offenders placed on probation by the juvenile court, and former child-care officers. Those with a probation background tended to view the supervision of young people in much the same way as the supervision of adults. In contrast, child-care officers' experience was with the supervision of children in residential care, foster care and, in some cases, in the community through supervision orders made for failure to attend school. The two approaches involved different methods and values. The 'probation' concept of supervision was mainly office-based, with the probationer 'reporting' to the officer to account for his or her behaviour. The 'child care' model viewed the child in the context of his or her family and community, and the problems requiring intervention across a range of family circumstances included poverty, alcohol dependency and relationship issues, as well as management of domestic finances. The distillation of the two approaches tended to favour the child-care model.

In 1971 two documents were issued which further defined supervision. One was the Assessment of Children guidance issued by the Social Work Services Group (SWSG). This contained a concept of assessment in the community which led to social work supervision addressing the needs of the child. The problems that had been identified in the assessment were to be presented to the children's hearing for the co-ordination of a plan that might involve other agencies. The second document was the report of a Working Party on Police Procedures which set out the relevant responsibilities of the police and social work services in relation to conveying young people to and from hearings, courts, or to residential establishments. A key feature was the responsibility for conveying recovered 'absconders' to residential establishments, which fell fully on social work departments unless the young person's behaviour was so unruly that police assistance was required. As a result, many young people saw social workers, including those who met them 'out of hours' in police offices, as akin to 'soft policemen'. This not only influenced the perception of a potential supervisor but presented to parents and the general public at large a different view of 'social work'.

The supervision of children in the community was undertaken by social workers, including many newly trained staff whose social work education and placements had involved a range of community attachments and practice experience in the area teams of the new social work departments. These departments sought to provide a comprehensive service, which meant that children who had been brought before the hearing for offending were seen in a wide context. As a result, workers were often involved in assisting families with a range of problems of crisis dimension such as debt issues – a very real concern since eviction for rent arrears was still a major problem until the development of community-based social work in the late 1970s.

The range of services which came to be known as 'intermediate treatment' has been mentioned. This approach was pioneered by a number of charismatic individuals, but the concept was well founded. Young people who required more than one-to-one supervision were afforded a range of community-based resources. Day-care provision, group work and task-focused activity at evenings and weekends often helped to prevent the breakdown of relationships in the family which could lead to the young person entering an approved school (List D school) or other form of residential care. Underpinning this was a commitment within supervision to try to keep the child with his or her own family and in his or her own community. This approach also recognised the fact that even a period of residential care was liable to be but a short episode between a child leaving home and returning there. The developing range of services that can and should be provided within the concept of supervision has continued and is reviewed in the previous chapter.

Reservations about the children's hearings system
It is a precept of jurisprudence that the law should generally reflect the values of the society in which it operates and that it should pursue rather than lead its beliefs. The Social Work (Scotland) Act 1968, particularly Part III of the Act, had

the support of a democratically elected Parliament, but it was not viewed throughout the land as the 'beautiful new-born' of Scottish legislation. Thirty years seems to have filtered out much of the dismay, criticism and cynicism that surrounded the setting up of the children's hearings system and the integrated social work departments.

Alan Finlayson, an experienced reporter to the children's panel, described the situation as follows:

'At the time the hearings system was the butt of considerable and continued media criticism. Some of that criticism related to suggestions that children, because of the difficulties in getting placements, could commit offences with impunity. Some of the criticism emanated from the hard-pressed police and some from high court judges who predicted that, with the passage of responsibility on child offenders from the courts to the individuals, crime would rise and the new organisation was unsuited to the responsibilities of taking decisions in regard to allegations of offences. At a time when the hearing system badly required the support of outside agencies, and in particular needed encouragement by agencies such as courts, that support was badly lacking. People, however, struggled on and in some ways the criticism was a spur to their doing so' (Finlayson, Care Justice and Protection (paper presented at children's panel national weekend school), 1991).

The newly formed social work departments were unequivocal in their support for the system and, with the enthusiasm of the new panel members, were able to ride the storm.

The children's hearings system formed only part of the new Act, which dealt also with a full spectrum of social work, including probation and the care of the elderly. The former, in the shape of the newly integrated probation service, came in for criticism.

'The courts were openly and forthrightly critical, seeing the new departments, with some justification, as the death knell of the highly valued specialist probation service. One Sheriff described the Act, 1968 as the most bungled piece of legislation; another speaking of the disastrous decline in service, described the new social workers as mini-skirted "Rosemarys and Gwendolines". The chairman of the parole board, a very revered gentleman, also troubled by mini-skirted supervision of men sentenced for rape, complained that reports were now based on hearsay and were worse than useless' (Murphy, 1992).

However, the social work profession and the structures for delivering welfare in Scotland have survived the criticisms of the world they were meant to serve, and have matured into a robust and respected service in the last twenty-five years. They have risen to the challenge of the major environmental changes which have taken place, especially during the last fifteen years. Whereas, prior to the Kilbrandon Report, welfare provision in Scotland tended to mirror developments in England and Wales, the Social Work (Scotland) Act 1968 gave Scotland the confidence to seek Scottish solutions to Scottish problems. It gave local government powers and duties to provide all citizens of whatever age and circumstances advice and assistance in solving their personal and social difficulties. Local authority social services were to be open to all in the same way as the National

Health Service. This was to be done through a 'single door' on which anyone might knock to ask for help, confident of getting it.

Ideological conflicts and the treatment paradigm

The children's hearings system sought to provide children with what was in the interests of their welfare. While this philosophy commanded wide support, and concepts of practical assistance, advice, counselling and guidance were generally understood, there was, as we have seen, no common understanding of what 'treatment' actually entailed. The most contentious arguments were around the 'spectrum' of treatment and focused largely on whether children could benefit most from residential treatment away from home or within the setting of foster carers based in the community or, best of all, at home with their own families.

Terminology also can be confusing. The term 'intermediate treatment', as we have mentioned, actually means little more than something between a home-based and a residential approach. The term 'compulsory measures of care' is also somewhat ambiguous; for many the notion of being 'in care' implied that the child had been placed away from his or her own family, which was not necessarily so. This explains the case for the change in terminology argued for in the Review of Child Care Law in Scotland (1990). The subsequent substitution of 'compulsory measures of supervision' adopted by the Children (Scotland) Act 1995 carried a quite different implication – not universally welcomed.[2]

Underlining and sometimes undermining the arguments for and against these various options was concern about the costs of child care, and of personal social service provision generally. Economic recession during the 1980s was becoming a reality, and reductions in spending were imposed on a wide range of public sector activities, including local authority personal social services. There was increasing emphasis on 'value for money' and 'cost effectiveness' – terms which were often bandied about but rarely defined. These were often wielded by social work managers and their committees as a protection against the materialist values of the 1980s.

There was only limited understanding of the real cost of residential care, foster care or treatment at home. There was a widespread belief that fostering was much more cost effective than residential treatment. A report from England and Wales at that time quoted an average cost per child based on the boarding-out allowance paid to families in respect of fostering and a *per capita* cost of residential care based on revenue expenditure, but it did not take account of capital costs.[3] The boarding-out costs probably included little more than the allowance paid by the authorities to foster parents. It therefore ignored the costs of social work support for foster families and the costs associated with recruiting, training and supporting foster placements. There was, and to some extent still is, a general belief that the

---

[2] See Chapters 6 and 7.
[3] The Provision of Child Care: A Study of Eight Local Authorities in England and Wales, Bristol District Auditors (1981).

boarding out of children is a cheaper and therefore a more cost effective means of providing 'away from home' care for children.

The Children (Scotland) Act 1995 requires local authorities to develop service plans for children in their area. Important elements are the services required for children subject to supervision requirements from children's hearings. Without a proper understanding of the cost effectiveness of the various options of residential care, foster care and various treatments at home, it is particularly difficult for local authorities to plan these services. There is danger that at times of economic recession, local authorities may have to bow to pressure to offer 'cheap and cheerful' options rather than more expensive and sophisticated solutions to complex dysfunctional patterns of behaviour displayed by children who appear before the hearings.

The development of residential care: statutory and voluntary initiatives

In discussing the workings of the children's hearings system it has been explained that the central criterion guiding the decision of the reporter was the judgment that 'compulsory measures' were indicated. This has meant that many situations referred to the reporter were not so considered, and either no further action was taken or the local authority was required to offer assistance to the child and the family, which they might accept or refuse on a voluntary basis. This initial step is the focus of current research, which is expected to throw light on the effectiveness of the reporter's decision-making and on the various measures offered by social work departments and other agencies.

As has been described in Chapter 1, Scotland has a long history of charitable and voluntary work on behalf of children. The activities of the Royal Scottish Society for the Prevention of Cruelty to Children[4] continue alongside those of the statutory bodies. Adoption and fostering are another field in which several charitable organisations have a long record of service. This contribution was recognised in the 1968 Act, which formalised the responsibility of each local authority to provide an adoption service or to oversee its provision by another agency. Voluntary organisations have always had particular merit in developing new lines of activity and, in the process, attracting funds from the public for such initiatives. This has applied particularly when responding to very specialised children's needs, as in the case of less common forms of developmental handicap.

Children, especially adolescents, with persistent and major behavioural problems causing severe stress in the family home, disruption at school and sometimes physical risk to themselves or others require special care and treatment. Health service provision in Scotland has not been able to provide adequate services for this group, and it may be unrealistic to expect that it should. In the 1960s several charitable bodies (eg, Barnardos and Save the Children) set up 'residential schools for maladjusted children' which provided safe and caring environments. They were, however, expensive to run and applications to local authorities for grants

---

[4] Now named Children First.

greatly exceeded available resources. As a result, several such schools were forced to close.

Moreover, 'care in the community' was becoming the watchword of social work and health provision. As a result, placement with foster families became an option preferred to residential care, and in many instances proved constructive. Yet there was a significant proportion of 'breakdowns' even by well-meaning, responsible carers. As in other countries, the lesson was being learned of the inherent necessity of ongoing, skilled support to foster parents. For many disturbed young people with histories of multiple placements, the environment least suited to their immediate needs was that of an ordinary caring family – an issue of importance in the Fife Inquiry. A consequence of this was that local authority children's homes, which had always been under-resourced in terms of trained staff, qualified staff and facilities, began to care for increasing numbers of children, and especially adolescents, with complex problems and needs.

Belatedly, a number of major authorities began to reinvest in residential care, recognising that some children's needs could best be met through good-quality residential care on which they could rely. The developments that were already in hand in some authorities which had residential child care action plans aimed at remedying many of the oversights and deficiencies of the previous decade were recognised by the government. Out of a sense of panic, because of specific criticisms of residential care in Scotland following upon serious deficiencies south of the border, the Scottish Office commissioned a report. Another Kind of Home (Skinner, 1992) focused on the need for good-quality residential care in smaller units with specialised functions. It also addressed key areas such as the training and qualifications of staff, the rights of children, the need to safeguard children who were in residential care, the compatibility of a residential care régime and individual children's care plans, and the improvement of practice.

The report recognised the central role of the local authority in providing residential care for children, but such recognition was not reflected in the allocation of guaranteed or ring-fenced resources. As a consequence, although the government gave additional funding to local authorities, which was to be used for residential child care, constraints on local government expenditure meant that residential care developments were piecemeal and hampered. However, the place of residential care as an essential element in a comprehensive child-care provision became re-established. The challenge for the future is to ensure that there is continuous improvement in the quality of residential care, and that young people who experience such care will be assisted in maximising their potential for personal development and independence. The limited experience of the smaller units that have been set up demonstrates that while there are some problems in staffing, features such as unauthorised absence and violence to staff have declined considerably.

Confronting the newly created social work departments, and continuing into the 1980s, was the rise of suspected cases of child abuse, sexual abuse and neglect. These particular problems demanded that special efforts be made to co-ordinate social work activities with other agencies. Judicial proceedings, both civil and criminal, made considerable demands, especially when the social worker was required to give evidence in court. Because of the dramatic nature of many such cases it was not possible to escape media publicity. It was hardly surprising, therefore, that social work departments developed detailed procedures in the management of care and protection situations, as a way of guarding themselves, and especially less experienced workers, often in the face of irrational criticism. These were stressful developments for social work departments, as they were for children's hearings, and especially as the resources that were required for assessment and treatment were in short supply and the social workers themselves were only very gradually acquiring the skills needed to face these tasks.

A particular initiative was that of the National Association for the Prevention Cruelty to Children which set up several special units in the UK to work with families in whom the physical abuse of children had occurred. One such unit was inaugurated in Glasgow by the RSSPCC as a pilot project supported by Strathclyde Regional Council, Greater Glasgow Health Board and the Scottish Office. The centre, which was founded in 1978, pioneered intensive work by a mixed-discipline team with a whole-family orientation. It rapidly developed educational programmes for a variety of disciplines and a consultation service to those who wished support and guidance in the task of dealing with difficult parent–child situations. At a later stage the focus moved to specialised work with sexually abused children and their families (RSSPCC, 1994).

The duty to promote social welfare
The maturity of a profession must be reflected in the values that it holds and in its ability to retain unshakeable faith in those values at a time when they are the subject of fierce onslaught. A cornerstone of the Social Work (Scotland) Act 1968 was that the state had a duty to provide for its citizens. This duty was enshrined in s 12(1) of the Act.

> 'It shall be the duty of every local authority to promote social welfare by making available advice, guidance and assistance on such a scale as may be appropriate for their area, and in that behalf to make arrangements and to provide or secure the provision of such facilities (including the provision or arranging for the provision of residential and other establishments) as they may consider suitable and adequate, and such assistance may be given to or, in respect of, the persons specified in the next following subsection in kind or in cash.'

Though this was a duty on the local authority as a whole, it was interpreted, and indeed enacted, as a duty that rested heavily on the shoulders of the social work department. The social work profession has used the statute imaginatively – at times pushing it to the limit by relying on it to support families experiencing enforced poverty.

This duty to promote welfare reflects the breadth of the 1968 Act and the generic range of services that it inspired, some focused on individuals, some on families and some on whole communities. The boundaries of section 12 payments were sometimes fudged in order to provide imaginative solutions to complex situations. Some social work departments funded a variety of approaches to solving youth delinquency, family poverty and social deprivation through their section 12 budgets and through grants to voluntary organisations. Although s 12 was to be the 'ignition key' to start the engine of the whole Act, the power to make financial payments predominated. In the years immediately after the Act was implemented, social work departments came under enormous pressure, to which many succumbed, to provide a financial safety net for every circumstance. For example, departments were involved in making payments to housing departments for rent arrears to avoid evictions (with the possibility that children would come into care); to the fuel boards to avoid discontinuation of essential supplies to vulnerable families; to those refused benefits by the government's income maintenance machinery; and to those left destitute as a consequence of industrial disputes. The responsibility of local authorities to deal with such problems, indeed their legal responsibilities to do so, were matters which created tensions and challenge. However, owing to the pressure created by the articulation of these conflicts by social work departments, codes of practice on fuel disconnection were introduced, case-law and legal advice defined responsibilities, and the Housing (Homeless Persons) Act 1977 laid the responsibility for dealing with homelessness on housing authorities.

In the wake of the economic crisis of the late 1980s there emerged an ideological attack on various social groups which were identified as challenging dominant values in society. A whole range of people were seen as undermining the family, law and order, and the authority of the state. Of particular significance, in the context of social work, was the attack on the poor, the unemployed and single parents. A concentrated media campaign against 'scroungers' and single parents was launched, based on the idea that these people were unjustifiably living off the state. The Institute of Economic Affairs, in a report issued in March 1995, proposed that the children of single parents who were dependent upon state welfare provision should be placed for adoption. This bastion of the 'new right' was concerned about the impact on society of the increasing number of children brought up by single mothers living on state benefit in poor housing. In particular, it feared that their rise would lead to a delinquent underclass. Not everyone can have money and wealth and not everyone can have children, so the ideology of the free market provided an elegant solution: 'The rich shall inherit the babies.'

Challenging injustice has been another cornerstone of social work. During the 1970s and 1980s community workers and community-based social workers played an invaluable role in empowering communities, confronting poor public service and providing high-quality advice on citizens' rights to welfare benefits. This aspect of Scottish social work has been 'crowded out' by the defunding of local government by central government, and also by local authorities' own ambivalence in having to deal with the organised response to inadequate local services. Local government has not always been comfortable when challenged about the quality of aspects of its service provision, particularly when the challenge is aided and abetted by its own funding. The portfolio of social work provision would be greatly enfeebled by the disappearance of community-based social work. Sadly, at a time of government-created financial crisis, preventive community work is fast becoming a casualty. Welfare-rights workers became the victims of their own success as the government introduced further restrictive legislation each time they successfully exploited the potential of the benefits system. The 1997 budget crisis in local government finance sounded the death knell of community-based social work in many of Scotland's local authorities. The portfolio of 'treatments' available to children's panels will be much enfeebled by the disappearance of community-based social work.

The Children (Scotland) Act 1995

The longevity of the 1968 Act is a testament to its strength and to the forward thinking of its creators. However, by the late 1980s there was beginning to be a radical rethinking about the way the social work profession specifically and society in general were responding to the needs of children and families. From the late 1970s child protection became a central activity of the social work profession, with a high priority being given to the initial investigation of allegations of child abuse. Research evidence suggests that the focus of concern was to establish what had happened: 'Who did what to whom?' And 'Was there enough evidence to prosecute?' It would appear that the strengths and weaknesses of the family and its broader needs for help and support were not given the kind of consideration they deserved (Gibbons *et al*, 1995).

The evolution of knowledge and the growth of experience relating to child protection, combined with the changing economic environment and a greater emphasis on the rights of children arising out of Britain's commitment to the United Nations Convention on the Rights of the Child, led to the need for a redefinition of the public and private law relating to children in Scotland. The Children (Scotland) Act 1995 is not a retuning of previous law. It is a major new body of law on the care of children which has evolved from an examination of existing law and reflects the values and principles of the society it serves. The Act has a number of new and radical features and is, by any standards, lengthy and necessarily complex. It replaces most of the sections relating to children in the Social Work (Scotland) Act 1968, and although many of the features of this Act are retained in the 1995 Act, local authorities and other agencies will have to make major changes in service delivery.

Local government reorganisation

The Children (Scotland) Act 1995, which is described fully in Chapter 7, was implemented as from 1st April 1997 by the unitary authorities set up in Scotland by local government reorganisation. Four major issues bear on its operation.

First, the 1995 Act is not a stand-alone and consolidated piece of legislation but requires fourteen sets of regulations and twelve sets of guidance to make it operational. It involves a massive implementation exercise – not least in staff training – at a time when the new authorities are still in the process of establishment.

Secondly, local government reorganisation was the result of political ideology and was not based on rational and empirical evidence that service delivery would be improved. In fact, counter-evidence was advanced that service would be impaired and costs increased.

Thirdly, the real costs of local government reorganisation are now becoming apparent. The miscalculation of such costs by the government, allied to political attacks on local government that have characterised central government's relationship with local government, has resulted in an underfunding of services on a massive scale. Many authorities are now forced into reducing their own services as well as cutting support to the private, independent and voluntary sectors.

Fourthly, the viability of the new authorities of all sizes has still to be tested. In the first year a number of authorities opted to combine departments such as social work and housing. The redeeming feature is the commitment of staff at all levels to make the new organisation effective.

Conclusion

The reader should take into account the fact that this chapter was written at a time when local government services in Scotland, including social work, were being cut for the second year running, and by unprecedented amounts. At the same time, neither of the main political parties was prepared to give a commitment to improvement over the next few years. The new unitary authorities had not had time to settle before they were forced to deal with major financial constraints. It is difficult to predict what the future holds for the social work services and what the implications will be for the children's hearings system.

During the past twenty-five years, the partnership between social work services and the children's hearings system has been based on a number of key elements: optimism; a belief in the hearings system; a belief in the values underpinning social work; a commitment to children and their families; a vision for improved, agreed goals; and a capacity to avoid being bound by traditional thinking or predetermined solutions.

10 : The Relationship Between Courts and Hearings

Brian Kearney

Separation of adjudication from disposal – the origins

'The shortcomings which cause dissatisfaction within the present juvenile court system (and this is no reflection on those who serve in such courts) seems to us to arise essentially from the fact that they seek to combine the characteristics of a court of criminal law with those of a specialised agency for the treatment of juvenile offenders, proceeding on a preventive and educational principle.... The underlying conflict between the two separate principles cannot fail in practice to create confusions and misconceptions which may be present, consciously or otherwise, in the minds of the bench; which are thus liable to be carried over to those appearing before such courts' (Kilbrandon, 1964, para 71).

In these words the Kilbrandon Report identified the heart of the problem. In the paragraph immediately following (Kilbrandon, 1964, para 72) the solution is proposed: 'Such considerations seem to us to point to the desirability of separating the two issues of (a) adjudication of the allegation issue, and (b) consideration of the measures to be applied.'

The practical working out of this solution is accomplished by requiring the hearing, where the grounds of referral are not accepted by the parents and child, or are not understood by the child, if it wishes to go ahead with the case, to direct the reporter 'to make application to the sheriff for a finding as to whether such grounds for referral' are established (1968 Act, s 42(2) and (7); 1995 Act, s 65 (7) and (8)). The reporter then has seven days to lodge the application in the sheriff court (Sheriff Court Procedure Rules 1971 ('the 1971 Rules', rule 4(1)); Act of Sederunt (Child Care and Maintenance Rules) 1997 ('the 1997 Rules', rule 3.45(1))). The application sets out the grounds of referral which were placed before the hearing, that is to say, the formal conditions of referral and the supporting statement of facts (1971 Rules, rule 4(2) and Form 1; 1997 Rules, rule 3.45(1) and Form 60) and a copy of any report made by a safeguarder appointed by the hearing (1971 Rules, rule 4(3); 1997 Rules, rule 3.45(2)). The application must be 'heard' by the sheriff within twenty-eight days of lodgement (1968 Act, s 42(4); 1995 Act, s 68(2)), although the hearing of evidence need not be concluded within this period (cf *H* v *Mearns* 1974 SC 152; 1974 SLT 184). In practice the grounds for referral accompanying the application have noted in the margin in handwriting those conditions and facts, if any, which were accepted at the hearing and those which were denied or not understood by the child.

The sheriff court
The sheriff in Scotland is the local professional judge, an advocate or solicitor of at
least ten years' standing, appointed by Royal Warrant and not removable from
office except after exacting statutory procedures (Sheriff Courts (Scotland) Act,
1971, s 12). The sheriff has extensive criminal jurisdiction. Sitting alone he or she
may try cases at the lower to middle range of seriousness and may impose terms of
imprisonment of up to six months and in certain circumstances twelve months as
well as the usual range of non-custodial disposals. Sitting with a jury, the sheriff
may try more serious cases and may impose up to three years' imprisonment, with
the power to remit to the High Court of Justiciary for sentence if three years
seems inadequate. In civil matters the sheriff has almost unlimited jurisdiction,
including actions for payment of any amount, actions for divorce, separation and
the custody of children. The sheriff also presides in fatal accident inquiries, acts as
appeal judge from the decisions of licensing justices and has numerous administrative responsibilities. In civil matters the sheriff may be appealed to the Sheriff
Principal of the sheriffdom and to the Court of Session in Edinburgh. In criminal
matters the appeal is to the High Court of Justiciary.

The Social Work (Scotland) Act 1968 enacted in Part III the principal
provisions introducing the children's hearings system and conferred two wholly
new jurisdictions upon the sheriff. Implementing the basic philosophy of Kilbrandon, the Act gave to the sheriff the duty of hearing the evidence which the
reporter relied upon in order to support the grounds of referral (1968 Act, s 42(6);
1995 Act, s 68(10)). The Act also conferred on the sheriff the power to hear
appeals at the instance of parents and children (but not the reporter) against
determinations of the hearings (1968 Act, s 49(1); 1995 Act, s 51(1)). This right of
appeal had been recommended by Kilbrandon (Kilbrandon Report, para 112).
The powers given to the sheriff on appeal were to refuse the appeal; to allow the
appeal and remit to the hearing with reasons so that the decision may be
reconsidered by the hearing; and to allow the appeal and discharge the referral.
The sheriff was also given power to grant warrant for the detention or apprehension of the child in certain circumstances (1968 Act, s 37(5A) and (5B), s 40(8A)
and (8B) and s 42(3); cf 1995 Act, s 67). All parties were given the right to appeal
to the Court of Session on a point of law against a decision of the sheriff (1968 Act,
s 50(1); cf 1995 Act, s 51(11)).

How the courts interpreted the powers of the sheriff
In one of the first cases to be reported, *D v Sinclair* 1973 SLT (Sh Ct) 47, the
sheriff considered the scope of the sheriff's appellate powers. The statute provides
that an appeal is to succeed 'where the sheriff is satisfied that the decision of the
children's hearing is not justified in all the circumstances of the case' (1968 Act,
s 49(5); 1995 Act, s 51(5)) and the sheriff is empowered to examine the reporter
and the authors of any reports which were before the hearing and is also entitled
'to call for any further reports which he considers may help him in deciding the
appeal' (1968 Act, s 49(3); cf 1995 Act, s 51(3), which additionally entitles the
sheriff to hear evidence during the appeal – see below for discussion). In spite of

these wide provisions for appeal, the sheriff in the case of *D* v *Sinclair* declared himself to be in effect limited to the approach appropriate to a court hearing an appeal from an administrative tribunal.

'In approaching this case I had the firm view that the procedure for appeals against determinations of a children's hearing made it clear that a sheriff should not interfere with the determination simply because he felt another form of treatment might be preferable. ... Accordingly, I consider that a sheriff should not allow an appeal unless there was some flaw in the procedure adopted by the hearing or he was satisfied that the hearing had not given proper consideration to some factor in the case.'

In a slightly later case, *K* v *Finlayson* 1974 SLT (Sh Ct) 51, the sheriff who had heard the evidence in an application under s 42 of the 1968 Act also heard an appeal by the parent against the ultimate decision of the hearing to place a child in a residential establishment. The sheriff recorded in her judgment in the appeal that in a note appended to her original decision (upholding the grounds of referral) she had indicated that her decision to uphold had been on a fairly narrow balance and she 'hoped that the panel would experiment for a period with supervision of the child in her own home'. The hearing, however, had not followed the sheriff's suggestion and indeed had paid attention to information which had not formed any significant part of the evidence which the sheriff had heard at the proof during the section 42 application. This information had convinced the hearing that an experimental period of home supervision would not be appropriate and they had made a residential requirement. The sheriff commented that it was unthinkable that a parent should be judged as unsuited to carry out part of her parental role 'on grounds which have not been stated as grounds of referral and which she has no opportunity of denying or having examined in court'. The sheriff then allowed the appeal and discharged the referral.

The approach of the sheriff in *D* v *Sinclair* has been generally followed by the sheriffs although in one case, *Humphries* v *S*, Inverness Sheriff Court, 8th September 1980 (unreported but noted in Kearney, 1987, p301), the sheriff rejected this approach and sustained an appeal by remitting to the hearing with his own suggestions as to disposal.

The 'pure' issue of the scope of the sheriff's powers on appeal does not seem to have been expressly addressed in any appeal to the Court of Session, but in cases wherein the appropriate method of dealing with appeals has arisen, the Court of Session has emphasised the autonomy of the hearing. In *H and H* v *McGregor* 1973 SC 152 (*sub nom H* v *McGregor* 1973 SLT 110) the child and the parent argued that the decision of a hearing not to discharge a referral and to direct the reporter to make application to the sheriff for proof of non-admitted grounds to the sheriff was a 'decision' which could be made the subject of an appeal under s 49 of the 1968 Act. The Court of Session firmly rejected this view and held that only final disposals were appealable. Lord Avonside commented:

'Even in the simple system envisaged in the Act there must occur numerous cases in which a hearing takes a "procedural decision". It surely was never the spirit or intention of the Act, which seeks to present a speedy and private method of dealing with children referred to the children's hearing, to envisage or permit all the delays necessarily inherent in appeals on points of procedure.'

The autonomy of the hearings system

The watershed in differentiating the law affecting the hearings system from the ordinary systems of civil and criminal pleading was the case of *McGregor* v *D* 1977 SC 330; 1977 SLT 182. The background to this case was an application to the sheriff in respect of grounds of referral alleging the commission of an offence by the child, including certain facts alleged in support of the condition and identifying, as the rules required, a particular offence as being the offence which the child had committed. Scottish lawyers are trained to scrutinise written pleadings with exacting care and Scottish civil courts may and not infrequently do dismiss cases in which the written pleadings do not state a case which, if proved, would establish the legal concept relied upon. The process by which this is carried through is known as a 'debate on the relevancy', which has some resemblance to the English legal process of demurrer. In *McGregor* v *D* it was argued on behalf of the child that the grounds averred by the reporter did not constitute a crime known to the law of Scotland and the sheriff allowed a debate on the relevancy. At this debate the reporter conceded that his case was irrelevant and asked for leave to amend so as to aver an offence which was a named crime known to the law of Scotland. The sheriff held that there was no power of amendment in these cases and consequently refused the motion to amend. He also held that no relevant case had been averred and accordingly dismissed the application and discharged the referral.

The reporter appealed to the Court of Session and this allowed Lord President Emslie and Lord Cameron to explain the scheme of the Act. Lord Cameron stated:

'I do not think it is appropriate or even competent to look outside the statute or the relevant rules to interpolate into the very simple procedural scheme the more elaborate and technical rules of formal process in the courts, be they civil or criminal.'

In a key passage of his opinion Lord Emslie stated:

'The scheme of the Act is the search for a solution which will be in the best interests of the delinquent child and other children in need of care. It is not surprising, therefore, to find that the body responsible for considering and disposing of a child's case is a lay body, that the reporters need not be lawyers, that the procedure, without pleadings or pleas on behalf of the child in question, may be conducted without the intervention of lawyers, and is intended to be quite informal. ... In no sense are proceedings under Part III of the Act criminal proceedings. They are, on the contrary, civil proceedings *sui generis*. ... To such proceedings accordingly, although the basic rules of evidence must be observed in the application before the sheriff, the ordinary codes of civil and criminal procedure do not apply.'

Lord Emslie stated further:

'An application to the sheriff is to secure a "finding" as to whether the grounds of referral, which have not been accepted in whole or in part, are or are not "established having regard to section 32 of this Act". This language, in my opinion, plainly envisages a finding upon evidence led and indicates clearly that the emphasis is laid upon an investigation of what a child is alleged to have done – a pure question of fact – before a decision is reached as to whether he has committed an "offence" and is accordingly in need of the care to which he is entitled.'

The court went on to hold that amendment was not competent within the rules, but the implication of what had already been said meant that amendment was unnecessary. The sheriff was entitled to find any offence justified by the evidence to have been committed even though, in attempting to obey the rules by naming a particular offence, the reporter had managed to name the wrong offence.

A subsequent case, *McGregor v A* 1982 SLT 45, decided that the power to make a finding in respect of any offence justified by the evidence, irrespective of the offence named in the grounds, applied equally to cases wherein an offence against the child was alleged. The case of *Sloan v B* 1991 SLT 530 (the Orkney case) reinforced the principle that the sheriff is bound to hear the evidence tendered by the reporter. Giving the opinion of the court, Lord President Hope said:

'So it was the sheriff's duty in this case to proceed to hear the evidence which was to be led by the reporter. Unless he was in a position to repel the plea [to the competency of the evidence] there and then he should have reserved his decision on it until he had made a finding based on the evidence as to whether or not the grounds for the referral were established.'

The autonomy of the hearings: the interface with the civil courts
The Court of Session and the sheriff courts have concurrent jurisdiction in actions of divorce which frequently have craves for custody and access to children, including interim custody and access. In *Aitken v Aitken* 1978 SC 297; 1978 SLT 183 the Court of Session had initially granted interim custody of a child to the pursuer in an action of divorce. Because of a deterioration in the mental condition of the pursuer, the reporter referred the child to a hearing, and the child was received into the care of the local authority. Before the hearing could dispose of the case, the defender applied to the Court of Session for the transfer of interim custody to himself and was successful. When the hearing came to dispose of the case, the decision was to make a supervision requirement with the condition that the child should reside with the mother – the pursuer in the divorce action. The local authority, which still had *de facto* care of the child, was uncertain what to do and wrote to the Deputy Principal Clerk of Session for guidance.

At a special hearing the Lord Ordinary, after expressing his own view that the authority of the Court of Session was paramount, nevertheless considered the matter as so important and novel as to merit reporting to the Inner House of the Court of Session for an authoritative determination, thus giving Lord President Emslie the opportunity of examining and ruling upon the relationship between a custody order granted by the court and a supervision requirement made by a hearing. The Lord President pointed out that the consideration that a parent had been granted access by the court did not entail that the parent was to enjoy the exercise of that custody irrespective of any inhibition which might be placed on that right by some competing order – for example, a child might be made subject to detention in terms of the criminal statutes, or he might, in those days, be subject to borstal training. The right of custody was a private right which might well be interrupted by the determination of a hearing.

> 'The existence of parental rights in relation to a child or of rights to his custody do not and cannot disable a children's hearing from making a supervision requirement in respect of a child who on any of the grounds specified in section 32(2) is in need of compulsory measures of care. The making of a supervision requirement does not deprive parents or a person to whom custody of a child has been awarded, of their rights in relation to the child. It is properly regarded as just another of those lawful orders which may temporarily prevent the exercise of those rights.'

Accordingly:

> 'The obligation of the regional council under the interlocutor of 3 February 1978 [which awarded custody to the father/pursuer] is accordingly in abeyance until such time as the supervision requirement of the children's hearing is discharged. In the meantime their duty under section 44(5) of the Act of 1968 is clear. They must give effect to the supervision requirement made by the children's hearing as long as it survives.'

The authority of the children's hearing to rule on access by a parent to a child who is the subject of a compulsory supervision requirement was asserted in the case of *D v Strathclyde Regional Council* 1984 SLT 114. In that case a child was subject to a supervision requirement which obliged him to reside in a local authority home and be amenable to its rules. The child's father was to be allowed a specified period of access. The father raised an action against the local authority seeking additional access. The Court of Session held the father's claim to be irrelevant, stating:

> 'In our view these submissions are ill-founded for a variety of reasons. The pursuer's crave is not one for access at large. It is a claim for residential access only at specified periods, and is directed against the defenders in respect of their legal control over the child. It is not an action seeking the extension of the hours of access in the home. What it seeks is in direct collision with what the defenders as managers of the home conceive to be in the best interests of the child. This runs contrary to the second condition attached to the supervision requirement. An order in relation to future access after the child has been removed from the care and control of the defenders would be irrelevant and inept in this process.'

In a recent sheriff court case the principle of access, as opposed to detailed access arrangements, was involved. In that case, *A v G (Party Minuters: Strathclyde Regional Council)* 1997 SCLR 186, Sheriff Principal N. D. MacLeod, QC, reversed in part the decision of the sheriff in *A v G* (Sh Ct) 1996 SCLR 787. The facts were that a child who had earlier been made the subject of an access order by the ordinary process of the court had thereafter been made the subject of a supervision requirement which excluded access by the father. The father attempted to use the ordinary court process to regain the right to access. The local authority argued that any decision on access was not a matter which it was open to the sheriff to decide since a supervision requirement affecting access was in force. The sheriff, founding upon the emphasis which he perceived in the case of *Aitken* on the distinction between the principle of access and access for a specified period, held that it was possible to hold a proof in the sheriff court at which the facts relevant to whether or not access should be allowed in principle could be explored. The local authority appealed to the Sheriff Principal who allowed the appeal and stated, in relation to the possibility of an order allowing access in principle:

'Such an order, although vague as to the exercise of a right of access, is none the less an order declaring a right of access. As such it would be an order declaratory of a right that would be in conflict with the statutory right of the local authority to determine access.'

The Sheriff Principal pointed out that the 1968 Act provided (s 47(1)) that a supervision requirement should not endure longer than was necessary and enabled the local authority to seek a review at any time. There was accordingly no need for recourse to the civil court. Commenting on the provisions of the 1968 Act as interpreted by the case-law, the Sheriff Principal commented: 'Indeed the scheme appears to be designed to be a self-contained system.'

The autonomy of the hearings: limited jurisdiction of sheriff on application and appeal

The decided cases have underlined the autonomy of the hearings in coming to their decisions. The Court of Session has maintained a searching scrutiny of the decisions of sheriffs. In the case of *M* v *McGregor* 1982 SLT 41 the Second Division, as well as reversing the sheriff on the facts as they appeared in the stated case, seemed to disapprove of the sheriff's having made an observation which tended to 'pre-empt the disposal of the case by the children's hearing by assuming that the child would be deprived of her mother's care which would be substituted by institutional mothering'.

As noted already (above, p158) the sheriff, under the powers conferred by the 1968 Act, was entitled to call for further reports which might assist him in deciding the appeal. The sheriff was entitled (1968 Act, s 49(3)) to allow the appeal if satisfied that the hearing's decision was not justified in all the circumstances of the case, and was required, when sustaining an appeal by remitting back, to state his reasons for so doing. In the case of *Kennedy* v *A* 1986 SLT 358 the sheriff, in sustaining an appeal by remitting to the hearing for reconsideration, made observations and gave directions as to how the hearing should dispose of the case after reconsideration, including a direction that the hearing must now proceed to make long-term decisions about the child's future. On appeal the Court of Session stated that the sheriff had 'clearly erred', adding:

'There is nothing in the Act or the rules to suggest that it is for the sheriff to make such observations or make such directions. ... [T]he sheriff is required to give reasons for his decision to the children's hearing for reconsideration of their decision. It is thus clear that the sheriff is required to give reasons for his decision, but it is one thing to give reasons for his decision and quite another to make observations or give directions. ... He is not in the same position as this court which is expressly empowered under section 50(3) of the Act of 1968 to remit the case back to the sheriff for disposal "in accordance with such directions as the court may give".'

The case of *Kennedy* v *A* also vindicated the integrity of the Hearings' Rules by holding that the sheriff had no power, in view of the existence of the rule (1971 Hearings Rules, rule 6(3)) that papers which are before the hearing must not be disclosed to any non-member of the hearing, to order disclosure of reports to the parties to the appeal. The concept that a case could be decided without parties having had access to the full reports which had been available to the deciding tribunal was to bring the hearings system into conflict with the UK's obligations under art 6 of the 1950 European Convention on Human Rights (*McMichael* v *United Kingdom* (1995) 20 EHRR 205 – see discussion below).

The autonomy of the hearings: position pending appeal
A recent small but important underlining of the authority of the order of a children's hearing occurred in the cases of *Kennedy* v *M* (IH) 1995 SCLR 88; 1995 SLT 717 and *Stirling* v *D* (IH) 1995 SCLR 460, both of which clarified the principle that an appeal against a sheriff's sustaining an appeal and discharging a referral leaves the hearing's decision standing, pending appeal to the Court of Session. In the case of *Stirling* v *D* it was said that the practice of reporters, reflected in the standard textbook (Kearney, 1987, pp366–367), was to treat the referral as discharged in such circumstances until it might be reinstated by the Court of Session. The comments on this by the Extra Division of the Court of Session, disapproving of the existing practice, seem to demonstrate a clear appreciation of the welfare philosophy of the system.

'If a child at risk is subject to a supervision requirement for its own protection, it does not seem to us to be in keeping with the purposes of the Act that, pending an appeal against the discharge of the requirement, there should be no supervision for the protection of the child.'

The autonomy of the hearings: the case of *O* v *Rae*
The calendar year 1991 produced two cases which brought into focus the issue of how far the ground stated for the referral should or should not be related to the disposal. The first of these was *M* v *Kennedy* (IH) 1991 SCLR 898; 1993 SLT 431. In that case the sheriff held as established a ground of referral based upon unlawful intercourse with the child under deletion of the words 'within the family home'. The hearing disposed of the case by requiring the child to live with foster parents upon the basis that the family home 'may have been the setting for any abuse'. On appeal to the Court of Session a special remit was made to the sheriff to clarify the finding and the sheriff confirmed that the abuse had not taken place in the family home. On receiving this clarification the Second Division sustained the appeal, stating:

'We are not persuaded that, in the light of the sheriff's findings, it is open to the children's hearing to disregard the sheriff's conclusion and to proceed upon the basis that the sexual intercourse may have taken place within the family home. For the children's hearing to proceed upon that basis would be inconsistent with and contradictory of the sheriff's conclusions.'

In December 1991 the First Division of the Court of Session decided the case of *O* v *Rae* (IH) 1992 SCLR 318; 1993 SLT 570. In that case children were referred to a hearing on grounds alleging various facts and circumstances inferring lack of parental care on the part of the mother and one allegation of sexual abuse by the father, Mr O. At the hearing O did not accept the grounds of referral and application was made to the sheriff for proof. When the case came before the sheriff the reporter deleted the reference to the alleged sexual abuse on the part of the father, O, and thereupon O accepted the grounds of referral and the matter was remitted to the hearing for disposal.

After sundry procedures before hearings, during which a safeguarder was appointed, the matter came to a hearing for disposal at a review hearing. The safeguarder's report included a narration that one of the children, a thirteen-year-old daughter of O, was maintaining allegations against O that he had abused her sexually. It was accepted that the girl was not a virgin and there was some suggestion that this fact of itself indicated a lack of due parental care. The safeguarder's report was available to the hearing and the safeguarder spoke to it. O, who was present with his solicitor, was heard on the report and protested his innocence in respect of the allegation of sexual abuse by him of his daughter. The hearing decided that none of the children should be returned to O and gave these reasons.

> 'The safeguarder has strongly recommended long-term fostering after consultation with the children. The children's lives have been disrupted long enough by the matrimonial discord. Mum is in agreement with long-term fostering. As long as the allegation of sexual abuse against father by his daughter [K] we cannot consider the children living with father.'

O appealed to the sheriff, who refused the appeal. He then appealed to the Court of Session where the opinion of the court was delivered by Lord President Hope. The Lord President referred to the provisions of s 43(1) of the 1968 Act, which deals with the functions of the hearing at the disposal stage and concludes with the words 'consider on what course they should decide in the best interests of the child', to s 48, which deals with reviews, and to rule 19 of the 1986 Children's Hearings Rules, which governs the conduct of the hearing on disposal and review and includes the obligation to take account of available reports, and the views of the child, parents and any safeguarder. The Lord President then stated:

> 'It is clear from a study of these provisions that the function of the children's hearing at this stage, once the grounds for referral have been accepted or established, is to consider the case of the child. The function of the hearing is to investigate the case so far as necessary to complete their consideration of what is in the child's best interests. The information to which they must have regard in terms of section 43(1) includes the grounds of referral accepted or established. But it may extend well beyond what may have been stated in these grounds. This is because the hearing must also have regard to a report obtained from the local authority in terms of section 39(4) on the child and his social background. As that subsection points out, this report may contain information

from any such person as the reporter or the local authority may think fit. Furthermore, they are entitled in terms of section 43(1) to have regard to "such other relevant information as may be available to them". Miss Raeburn [counsel for the appellant] said that this information must be confined to information which was relevant to the grounds for the referral, but in our opinion that interpretation is not consistent with the express purpose of the subsection. Its purpose is to enable the children's hearing to consider what is in the best interests of the child. The test of relevancy in this context, therefore, is whether the information is relevant to a consideration of what course should be taken in the child's best interests.'

The Lord President added:

'It can be seen therefore that the children's hearing have wide powers of investigation. As Mr Emslie [counsel for the reporter] pointed out, they are not just a disposing body, and their powers are not to be seen as confined within narrow limits determined by the grounds for the referral.'

As a consequence of the foregoing reasoning the First Division held that the decision of the sheriff in *K* v *Finlayson* (referred to above), with its presupposition that a fact which could have been a ground of referral but had not been relied on as such could not be a relevant factor in disposal, had been wrongly decided.

The *Scottish Civil Law Reports* (SCLR) carry commentaries by eminent lawyers in the relevant fields, and the commentary on *O* v *Rae* is written by the distinguished retired children's reporter, Alan Finlayson, (the respondent in *K* v *Finlayson*). Mr Finlayson generally welcomes the decision in *O* v *Rae*, commenting that the approach contained therein had already found favour throughout Scotland: '[F]or some time now it has been a matter of practice that hearings have gone well beyond the specific matters contained in the grounds for referral.' He also, however, sounds a warning against reporters being

'tempted to include the minimum of allegations required to establish grounds lest a subsequent children's hearing find themselves restricted in the information they were permitted to take into account in reaching their decision as a result of a finding at proof'.

Professor Norrie tells us in 'In Defence of *O* v *Rae*' 1995 SLT (News) 353 that the decision has been subject to much dispute and criticism. He mounts a spirited defence of the decision, pointing out that the hearings are well entitled to resolve differences of fact and he answers the critics by saying that they assume 'that a central role is played by the grounds of referral throughout the time in which the child is subject to the jurisdiction of the children's hearing', whereas 'the Act is plain that it is not the ground of referral that is to be considered by the children's hearing, but the child's case'.

The present writer and Professor Mapstone in the Report of the Inquiry into Child Care Policies in Fife (1992, para 27, p 598) observe, in relation to a reporter relying on an 'old' Schedule 1 offence in order to bring a child within the jurisdiction of the hearing:

'The reporter ultimately justified his department's action in founding on this "old" offence by averring that it was competent in law and in accord with the ordinary practice of reporters. While acknowledging this to be so, and noting in the recent case of *O* v *Rae*

1992 SCLR 318 the propriety of hearings taking into account matters not appearing on the grounds of referral is endorsed, we nevertheless think it is good practice for the reporters to aim to state the ground of referral most relevant to the child's needs. . . .'

Experience shows that failure to do this can skew the focus of the hearing, which must constantly remind itself that although the ground of referral relates to one specific matter, the main problem is elsewhere. This is of course recognised by Professor Norrie in his article.

'It is the professionalism of reporters that must be relied upon to ensure that all matters pertaining to the child's welfare are properly brought to the attention of the children's hearing, and that will involve, in appropriate cases, framing new or additional grounds of referral.'

The case of *O* v *Rae* has many interesting implications. Its prime importance for us here is that it represents an interpretation of the system by Scotland's Supreme Court which is consonant with the welfare philosophy of the system.

Procedural and evidential decisions
Space does not permit an examination of the many important cases whereby the peculiar requirements of children's cases have been imaginatively and sensitively examined by the courts. A few only must suffice.

In *W* v *Kennedy* 1988 SLT 583; (IH) 1988 SCLR 236 (*sub nom WW* v *Kennedy*) Lord Sutherland, delivering the opinion of the First Division admitting hearsay evidence which would not at the time have been admissible in an ordinary civil litigation, memorably stated:

'The detailed rules of evidence which may be appropriate in one form of proceeding may be wholly inappropriate in another form of proceeding. No doubt there is good reason for the strict rule relating to hearsay evidence in ordinary civil proceedings where parties have joined battle on the basis of written pleadings. It does not follow that the same rigidity would be necessarily appropriate in other circumstances.'

Later Lord Sutherland quoted with approval a dictum adopted by Lord Evershed in the English case, Re *K* [1965] AC 201. '[W]here the paramount purpose is the welfare of the infant, the procedure and rules of evidence should serve and certainly not thwart that purpose.'

The 'strict rule' excluding hearsay evidence in civil causes was abolished by the Civil Evidence (Scotland) Act 1988. The relevant provisions of this Act have been interpreted by the Court of Session in a number of cases, notably *F* v *Kennedy (No 2)* (IH) 1992 SCLR 750; 1993 SLT 1284 and *K* v *Kennedy* (IH) 1992 SCLR 386; 1993 SLT 1281, so as to make clear that what the child – provided he or she is proved to be a competent witness (see the following paragraph) – said to the social worker or the police may be competent evidence even if (as in *K* v *Kennedy*) the statement is retracted by the child in evidence.

In spite of all the relaxations of the rules of evidence the 'competency requirement' still obtains – that is, a child is presumed not to be able to testify unless he or she satisfies the judge that he or she is likely to give trustworthy evidence. Yet in interpreting this requirement the Court of Session has supported the approach of a sheriff who took several hours – spread over two consecutive days and involving communication with an elective mute by signs and notes – to satisfy himself that the child was competent to give evidence (*M* v *Kennedy* (IH) 1991 SCLR 898 (Notes); 1993 SLT 431).

Conclusions and a glance forward

The onset of the children's hearings system was greeted with some apprehension and perhaps some hostility by the legal profession, including the judiciary. In January 1973 the reviewer of Sheriff Gordon's fourth edition of Renton and Brown's *Criminal Procedure According to the Law of Scotland* observed in the *Scots Law Times*:

> 'Thirty-six pages of text are devoted to provisions relating to children, in which the Social Work (Scotland) Act 1968 and related statutory instruments bulk large. When the Act was published it was hailed as if it offered a vision of a New Jerusalem. Curiously, however, to attempt to read and understand it was to feel like a man who sets out to cross an estuary when the tide is out, trudges manfully through leagues of deepening sludge and retreats when the horizon seems just as distant.'

Yet the practice of the sheriffs and the decisions of the Court of Session have on the whole demonstrated a willingness to allow the system to work as an autonomous system aimed at securing the bests interests of children in a way which has maintained the original Kilbrandon philosophy.

The Children (Scotland) Act 1995

The Children (Scotland) Act 1995 contains provisions which affect the principle and the detail of the working of the system.

Under the 1968 Act there were generally two ways whereby the child was to be introduced into the system. In an emergency a constable or a person authorised by a court or a justice of the peace (who could grant a 'place of safety order') could take a child to a place of safety and the procedures would thereby be triggered (1968 Act, s 37). In a situation where no emergency was perceived, the reporter was empowered to arrange a hearing and require the child to attend (1968 Act, s 39(3) and s 40(1)). Largely as a consequence of Lord Clyde's recommendations in the Orkney Report place of safety orders have been replaced by child protection orders (1995 Act, s 57). The Act also introduces child assessment orders (s 55), which require the production of a child and may empower the local authority to restrict the liberty of the child for a period of up to seven days in order to carry out certain examinations of the child, and exclusion orders (s 76), which may exclude a suspected abuser from the house wherein the child is living. All these orders are granted by the sheriff. All have to be notified to the reporter, who must decide whether to take the case to a hearing. Procedures exist for the variation or recall of a child protection order within very short timescales – the earliest route would involve an application being lodged with the sheriff court before the second working day after the implementation of the order (s 59(2) when read with s 60(8)(a)). There is provision (s 60(10)) for the reporter to arrange a hearing to give advice to the sheriff on an application for variation or recall, but as the application for variation or recall has to be decided by the sheriff within three working days of its being lodged (s 60(8)), it may not often be practicable to set up such an advice hearing.

The 1995 Act further enlarges the power of the sheriffs by entitling the sheriff to hear additional evidence on appeal (s 51(3)) and entitling the sheriff when sustaining an appeal to substitute his or her own disposal for that imposed by the hearing (s 51(5)(c)(iii)).

The 1995 Act also makes explicit for the first time the basic principles which are to guide sheriffs and hearings in most of their deliberations. Section 16(1) of the Act states as the premier principle that the paramount consideration is to be 'the welfare of the child throughout his childhood'. Other basic principles, which apply to most although not all of hearings' and sheriffs' decisions, are the principle of having regard to the views of a child (taking account of age and maturity) who wishes to express such views (s 16(2)) and the principle of minimal intervention – ie, not making an order or requirement unless satisfied that doing so will benefit the child more than doing nothing at all (s 16(3)).

The Act also enacts a derogation from the welfare principle by providing that it may give way where the purpose is protecting members of the public from harm (whether or not physical harm (s 16(5)). The approach represented by this derogation was probably often given effect to in practice in applying the 1968 Act (eg, in *Humphries* v *S* 1986 SLT 683, wherein it was held to be in the child's own interests for a hearing to grant a warrant for his detention in order to prevent him from making his position worse by continuing to offend); but since the 1995 Act had for the first time elevated into law the paramountcy of the welfare principle, it was presumably thought necessary equally to make explicit the 'public safety' derogation from it. For the people of Scotland of today, as for the Romans of old, the safety of the people is the supreme law: *Salus populi suprema lex.*

Listening to the voice of the child – giving fair notice to all parties – the dilemma
The need to equate the children's hearings proceedings with the UK's obligations under the European Convention on Human Rights and the United Nations Convention on the Rights of the Child was no doubt part of the motivation in increasing judicial involvement in the system. The difficulty is that not all the provisions of these charters are mutually consistent. Article 12 of the UN Convention provides *inter alia*:

'States Parties shall assure to the child who is capable of forming his or her own views the right to express those views freely on all matters affecting the child, the views of the child being given due weight in accordance with the age and maturity of the child.'

Article 6 of the European Convention provides *inter alia*:

'In the determination of his civil rights and obligations or of any criminal charge against him, everyone is entitled to a fair and public hearing within a reasonable time by an impartial tribunal established by law.'

In *McMichael* v *United Kingdom* (1995) 20 EHRR 205 the above provision was held to have been contravened by the parents not having been given sight of reports which had informed the decision of the hearing. To overcome this, the Children's Hearings Rules of 1986 were amended in the terms now represented by rule 5(3) of the 1997 Rules which provides *inter alia* that the reporter is to supply to parents all reports and information which he provides for the hearing itself.

The difficulty is that the child may have something to say which he or she does not wish to be conveyed to the parent. What happens if a child 'confides' to a social worker information which he or she does not want to be thus passed on? His or her views, according to the UN Convention and the 1995 Act, are to be given due weight, but how are these views to be transmitted?

In proceedings before the sheriff there is provision for the sheriff to receive the views of the child to be sealed in a confidential packet for the eyes of a sheriff only (1997 Rules, rule 3.5(4)). If the sheriff is to make any use of these views, will this not contravene the principles of natural justice and also art 6 of the European Convention – as in the *McMichael* case? Yet, given that these provisions exist, is it not the duty of the sheriff to make the child aware of them and, if the child so wishes, allow him or her to express 'confidential' views?

Judicial scrutiny and minimal intervention
One of the 'lessons' of the Orkney case was seen to be the need to be more scrupulous in using the remedy of taking children from a home wherein abuse was suspected. To this end greater judicial scrutiny and the principle of minimal intervention have been introduced.

Whether greater judicial scrutiny will mean a dilution of the welfare principle remains to be seen. The case-law discussed in this chapter gives no reason to conclude that the judges and the sheriffs will be disposed to erode this principle or to seek to depart from the recognition of the primacy of the hearing illustrated by the approach of Lord President Emslie in *McGregor v D* and Lord President Hope in *O v Rae*.

It will be very interesting to see what will be the effect of the enactment of the principle of minimal intervention and of conferring upon the sheriff the responsibility for granting child protection and other orders. The advance perception was that social workers would be scrupulous in preparing and perhaps sparing in presenting applications for such orders. This perception has been so far vindicated. At the time of writing, exactly three months after the coming into force of the new child protection provisions, there have been fifteen CPO hearings before the sheriffs in Glasgow and Strathkelvin in relation to thirty-two children. All have been granted, but the hearings have lasted between half an hour and an hour, as opposed to the much shorter times taken, it is believed, in obtaining from justices of the peace 'place of safety orders' under s 37 of the Act of 1968. There has been one application for an exclusion order, which was granted. There have been three applications for recall of child protection orders, all of which have been refused. There has so far been no application for a child assessment order in Glasgow.

Exact statistical comparison is difficult because of the lack of congruence between reporters' areas and the area covered by the Sheriffdom of Glasgow and

Strathkelvin, but in the year before the new legislation took effect, ie, from 1st April 1996 to 31st March 1997, the reporter's records indicate that the number of children in respect of whom place of safety orders were granted in Glasgow was 257. The statistics do not convey how many hearings took place since sometimes, in multiple applications, the whole number of children involved was returned whereas some were counted as one. However, as we have seen, thirty-two children were made subject to CPOs in Glasgow during the first three months of the new legislation. Thirty-two per quarter is the equivalent of 128 a year, and accordingly the figures suggest a reduction of about 50 per cent. This *may* mean merely that happy children are no longer being taken from happy homes and that only necessary removals are now being effected. But does it?

11 : Towards a National Reporter Service

Sally Kuenssberg and Alan D. Miller

I N times of great change, it is often salutory to reflect that others have been there before. Speaking at a meeting of the Association of Reporters to Children's Panels in December 1975, Alastair Sinclair, then Reporter for Borders Region, reflected on

> 'the trauma caused for many by the reorganisation of local government which, so far as many reporters and panel members were concerned, seemed to strangle at birth the infant hearings system just at the time when it seemed to be growing into a healthy child. ... The structure has been changed ... many adjustments have to be made within the delicate network of the complex human relationships involved'.[1]

He concluded that reporters and others could best ensure the future of the system by reminding themselves of their shared commitment to the Kilbrandon philosophy. Much of this book is the story of how that 'infant' survived to maturity.

Twenty years on, in 1996, the next great convulsion affecting local government has seen the reverse process taking place, with regions once more being divided up into smaller unitary councils. For reporters, however, exactly the opposite has happened: their service has been removed from the local authority structure and combined into a new national body, the Scottish Children's Reporter Administration (henceforth SCRA or the Administration). Dramatic though this latest change has been, reporters have from the start of the hearings system shown themselves capable of responding to new circumstances. This chapter examines major issues in the history of the service and considers the challenges it faces in relation to the new national structure, the Children (Scotland) Act 1995 and the wider context of current debates about children's justice.

The office

The office known as the reporter and introduced in 1971 was paradoxical in a number of respects. A new element of a new system of juvenile justice yet the reporter's independent decision-making function could be compared to that of the procurator fiscal. Indeed David Cowperthwaite, Assistant Secretary of the Criminal Justice Division of the Scottish Home Department during the lead-up to the passing of the Social Work (Scotland) Act 1968, has suggested that

---

[1] Speech reprinted in *Social Work Today* (1976).

'but for the existence of the public prosecution system under the Lord Advocate, or, perhaps more especially, the existence of his local agent, the procurator fiscal, the concept of the reporter to the children's hearing might never have been entertained' (Cowperthwaite, 1988, pp 69–70).

At the same time, that independence had somehow to be reconciled with employment by the same local authority that would provide reports, recommendations and services through its service departments.[2] And despite the aspiration that the hearings system would reduce delinquency through the assessment and addressing of children's needs (Kilbrandon, 1964, para 12), little guidance was given on how these exacting expectations should actually be fulfilled. The reporter was, to some extent, to implement state policy, but with little direction or accountability as to how, or indeed how well, he or she should do so.

The core tasks to be undertaken by reporters were readily ascertainable from the 1968 Act and related secondary legislation: to receive and investigate information about children, reach a decision on each case referred, administer the hearing process, prepare grounds for referral, wherever necessary lead evidence before the sheriff, distribute information to those entitled to it and maintain statistical records. What was missing were clarity of detail of some significant elements, mechanisms for ensuring consistency and a coherent overview of the way in which reporters were expected to operate.

Nevertheless, at the dawn of a radical change of direction, what was never in doubt was that reporters should focus their efforts on improving the lot of children reported to them; and that the hearings system could be made to work for children to a degree that no court-based system could achieve. Whatever the professional background or working arrangements of the new reporters, as described in Chapter 3, the shared commitment to this 'mission' was palpable.

The service
Before addressing the developing nature of reporters' work, it is worth analysing some unusual features that have characterised the service from its inception.

First, the reporter service is very small. There are currently about 140 reporter posts, and about 160 posts dedicated directly to casework support. Although higher in absolute terms than at any time before, relatively speaking these are very small numbers, particularly for a specialist body that has no obvious counterparts within other systems.

Secondly, the service is geographically widespread. At present thirty-seven offices are staffed full-time, from Stranraer in the far south-west to Lerwick in Shetland. Apart from the national headquarters and the two main city offices, a 'typical' office is staffed by six people – three reporters and three support staff.

[2] The Kilbrandon Committee (para 102) had recommended that responsibility for appointment should rest with the sheriff.

A third feature is that the service has largely required to create its own path. From the outset, local government employers took their cue from the fact that the 1968 Act required them to appoint a reporter, but then entrusted all professional powers and duties direct to him or her. Scottish Office civil servants initially offered a significant and welcome level of support to the fledgling service, but adopted an increasingly 'hands-off' relationship after regionalisation in 1975 led to the creation of viable reporters' departments throughout mainland Scotland. For many years the only official guidance directed to reporters by the Secretary of State concerned the proper completion of statistical returns.

The combined effect of these factors has moulded the shape of the reporter service throughout its development. The vast majority of reporters are 'general practitioners'; there is little opportunity for specialisation. While this may result in individual skills not being fully exploited, the fact that most reporters follow most cases referred to them through to the finish supports a fundamentally child-centred focus rather than concentration on processing the case.

The professional diversity of the service continues to reflect the unique blend of tasks reporters are called upon to fulfil as case assessors, procurators and systems administrators. One reporter in two today has professional qualifications and experience in law; one in three has qualifications and/or experience in social work; and others bring skills and insights from a range of backgrounds, including teaching, child psychology, nursing, prison work, court administration and membership of a children's panel. Perhaps because of that very diversity, combined with the size and decentralisation of the service, training has tended to work best on an issue-by-issue basis rather than an integrated basis. More than one optimistic proposal for creation of a pre-entry qualification has died a lingering death on grounds of impracticality. The emphasis has increasingly been on good selection and induction training.

A more subtle result of the topography of the service is that concentration on local issues may have eclipsed a national perspective to some degree. Reporters have always – rightly – preached and practised the value of constructive inter-agency work at local and regional level. The development of national identity, strategic thinking and action has, to date, proved more elusive, though the Association of Children's Reporters was increasingly active in this regard from the late 1980s onwards.

The wherewithal now exists, in a national service structure, to develop appropriate consistency in culture, style and practice. The aim is to achieve a consistent platform for creative practice in individual cases that takes account of the underpinning policy of the new legislation, the realities of resource restraints and the need for demonstrable effectiveness of the system as a whole.

The work
Reporters have traditionally maintained an open-door attitude to referral of children's cases for investigation, believing it preferable that partner agencies should not feel unduly constricted with regard to the criteria employed for selecting cases for referral. While such an approach may admit the possibility of

over-use of formal powers of investigation, it nevertheless offers an important opportunity for objective reappraisal of the need and basis for action. It is far from unknown for reporters to bring together evidence to establish grounds for referral in cases thought by referring agencies to be highly concerning but unprovable. There is a fine balance here between respecting family privacy and parental responsibility and acting to secure the rights and interests of children.

The key may lie in flexible use of the reporter's wide discretion to investigate and seek information as is considered appropriate. At the extremes, investigation may range from one or two quick telephone calls to the commissioning of specialist reports and the tenacious tracking down of witnesses to a series of past incidents. Pitching investigation at an appropriate level requires sensitive judgments about the quality of information that may be available and the potential benefits and costs to the child and family. A further complication is that in some situations the child and family may not be aware that personal information has been sent to the reporter, necessitating careful consideration of whether and when to explain the reporter's involvement.

The information which the reporter receives through investigation, typically through school and health reports and a local authority social background report, may well contain a mixture of reported fact, observation, subjective opinion and professional assessment. Frequently there will be differences of emphasis – sometimes, outright conflict – between the professionals who have compiled reports. Out of that and the initial referral information, the reporter has to reach a clear view on three factors to inform a decision on the case.

- Is there sufficient reliable evidence to support at least one of the statutory grounds for referring a child to a hearing?
- Does it appear that the child's interests would be better protected and advanced through the provision of additional care, guidance or treatment?
- If yes, will an element of compulsion be required to secure that intervention?

A further source of information increasingly available to reporters, and used in decision-making, is contact with the child and the parents. While it is neither possible nor appropriate for the reporter in person to undertake a full social assessment, personal contact or communication can help to test out the reporter's developing perceptions, to provide relevant background and to identify possible ways forward in the child's interest.

It may be that reporters have historically differed in the priority given to communication with children and families. Part of the profound impact of the upsurge in child abuse referrals since the early 1980s, however, has been the necessity for reporters and others to be increasingly informed by the voice of the child victim. The realisation quickly dawned that, when seeking to help children pick up the pieces after traumatic experiences, well-intentioned but blundering intervention could reopen or even intensify deep emotional scars. The tension between the demands of due process and a busy case load on the one hand and the need to make the process work well for a particular child on the other is one to which every reporter is fully alive. It takes time and effort to ensure that communications and proceedings are managed in a way that is supportive for children and families – time that is increasingly scarce.

That tension is perhaps most acutely felt in those cases that proceed to proof before the sheriff and in which children are involved as witnesses and victims. No matter what effort is made by the sheriff, coming to court to be questioned about intimate, guilt-ridden matters is inevitably a highly distressing experience for a child. Somehow, the reporter must ensure that the child feels informed and supported, but without rehearsing the child's evidence so that it appears unconvincing or becomes open to charges of suggestibility.

At all stages of the case process, the mutual interdependence of the reporter and the partner agencies is evident. Reporters rely on information from other agencies as the basis for assessment of how to proceed in each case. While assessment of that information cannot but involve an element of 'assessment of the assessors', a reporter will be slow to disregard the view of a trustworthy professional whose report reflects much direct contact with the family.

Sharing case information is the most basic level of inter-agency work for reporters. The second level covers co-ordination of the powers and duties of the reporter and other agencies, including a multitude of issues about how information is shared, cases are progressed and services are offered.

There is a third level to this work which has been embraced more enthusiastically by some reporters than others: that is, to seek to work pro-actively with other agencies to identify ways of reducing the need for children ever to be referred to the reporter, or at least to a hearing, and to develop or redevelop services for those children. As a result of the increasing need to plan carefully the best use of resources for children, together with the opportunities for shared approaches and dialogue at all levels generated by the national structure, reporters are now increasingly engaging in this essential area of activity.

The legal framework

A different but equally significant developmental area for reporters has been the legal framework within which the children's hearings system operates. As with other fields of law, there has been an increasing tendency for decisions and actions to be subject to challenge through appeal and other means. Given that a single decision by the Inner House of the Court of Session on appeal from the sheriff can require existing practices or interpretations to be fundamentally changed, the appropriate defence of such appeals in a way that ensures the court can reach a well-informed decision has always been a high priority for reporters. But the reporter may also exercise a right of appeal from the sheriff's decision, whether on proof of grounds for referral or on appeal from a hearing. By that means the opportunity has been taken on various occasions to obtain authoritative interpretation of the law.

A fundamental theme in a number of cases has been the recognition by the courts of the special status of children's hearings proceedings. The starting-point was the clarification that the proceedings were 'civil proceedings *sui generis*' – that is, that they could not be classified neatly as civil or criminal proceedings (*McGregor v D* 1977 SC 330; 1977 SLT 182). One early practical effect of this formulation was the confirmation that a parent of a referred child could be called by the reporter to give evidence and be required to do so (*McGregor* v *T* 1975 SC 14; 1975 SLT 76). (A different decision could have created considerable difficulty where proof of certain grounds for referral, such as the child being beyond parental control, was required.) A further application of the same principle resulted in the assertion that hearing proceedings on 'care and protection' grounds for referral did not require to await the outcome of parallel criminal proceedings against the adult accused: except where clear and specific problems could be demonstrated, it could be assumed that the question of possible prejudice to the accused was not an issue of concern to the sheriff hearing the reporter's proof application.

Not surprisingly, the difficulties associated with taking evidence from vulnerable children who may have suffered traumatic experiences have featured with increasing prominence in recent years. Interestingly, most cases on this issue have been appeals taken against the reporter after evidence had been secured at the proof stage. The leading case is *M* v *Kennedy* (IH) 1991 SCLR 898; 1993 SLT 431 in which a twelve-year-old who had become electively mute as a reaction to severe abuse was enabled to give evidence that helped to establish the grounds for referral. The court recognised that hearsay evidence may be accepted where the child suffers particular communication problems which would prevent him or her being accepted as a competent witness (a significant departure from the normal approach to competency of evidence in civil proceedings). The case of *M* v *Ferguson* (IH) 1994 SCLR 487 offers a further example of this approach. The case of *Merrin* v *S* 1987 SLT 193 remains perhaps the most audacious attempt to redefine the legal framework of children's hearings. The case concerned a child under the age of criminal responsibility (eight years) who was nevertheless referred to a hearing on the grounds of having committed certain offences. The argument for the reporter was that the age of criminal responsibility was simply part of the statutory framework for criminal proceedings; there was no reason why it should necessarily apply in the hearings system. The majority of the court rejected that view, although Lord Dunpark issued a fascinating minority opinion based on the premises that the overriding concern of the children's hearing was the needs of the child; the 'deeds' reflected in the grounds for referral were no more than the doorway to consideration of the child's case. Despite the sympathetic tone and insight contained in this judgment, it must be concluded that the majority view was right in law and principle.

A national reporter service: the debate

Chapter 6 has placed the Finlayson Report (1992) in the context of a series of investigations and reports, partly provoked by crises, which exposed all aspects of the hearings system to searching scrutiny. Alan Finlayson concluded that on balance there was more to be lost through removing reporters from the local authority structure than would be gained by combining them into a national service. He did, however, outline a number of benefits which could flow from the national model, and the challenge for the new Administration will be to deliver the 'Finlayson agenda' while avoiding the negative developments against which he warned.

Despite Mr Finlayson's recommendation to the contrary, the White Paper, Scotland's Children (1993), made clear the government's intention to establish a national reporter service under the leadership of a 'Chief or Principal Reporter' and proposed the setting up of a new body to be responsible 'for the efficient running and management of the service' (Scotland's Children, 1993, para 6.13). The argument advanced was that the impending local government reform would lead to a significant increase in the number of local authorities (many of them small) and, consequently, in the number of reporters' departments. A proliferation of small departments would make it harder to achieve the stated aims of 'consistency and high standards of practice'.

Many misgivings about this development were expressed by MPs and others in the debates leading up to the Local Government etc (Scotland) Act 1994. There was concern that the removal of the reporter service from the local authority umbrella would threaten the delicate balance of the hearings system by undermining links between reporters, panel members and social work departments. Working relationships built up over many years might be severed. Regional reporters, hitherto chief officers of local authorities, would be likely to lose their influence over local resources and services for children. Alistair Kelly, formerly Regional Reporter for Fife, commented that 'the Kilbrandon concept of the community emphasis of care within the children's panel system will be that much more difficult to maintain' (Kelly, 1996, p25.) A black picture was painted of reporters being drafted to different parts of the country in the name of management efficiency, with families and panel members facing long journeys to large and anonymous centralised hearings centres. Fear was expressed that the person appointed to the post of Principal Reporter might be 'an administrator or an accountant' rather than a reporter (Strathclyde Children's Panel, 1994, para 1.8).

Valid though these concerns were, it can be argued that they were exacerbated by several factors. First, though the proposals were included in the White Paper, Scotland's Children, which laid the foundations for the Children (Scotland) Act 1995, for organisational reasons the change in the status of reporters had to be part of the restructuring of local government. The new Scottish Children's Reporter Administration thus became associated with the widespread hostility to the Local Government etc (Scotland) Act 1994. Secondly, the inclusion of arrangements for reporters in the legislation relating to local government rather than to children emphasised the impending split in the hearings system. Thirdly, the setting up of the SCRA as an executive non-departmental public body (NDPB) caused it to be subject, even before inception, to the widespread public suspicion with which 'quangos' of all kinds have been regarded over the last ten years, being seen as part of the political agenda to centralise powers previously held by local government.

The Scottish Children's Reporter Administration

Some of these misgivings were addressed in the planning stages and early months of the SCRA. The Principal Reporter, his two assistants and the majority of the senior managers of the new service come from the reporter service. The eight board members (who include the Principal Reporter) combine experience of the children's hearings system, the law, local government and the voluntary sector. The map of Scotland has not been redrawn for the new reporter service. Though the national headquarters are located in Stirling and the country has been divided into seven large territories for administrative purposes, the creation of the post of authority reporter for every new authority area is an explicit acknowledgement of the need to maintain links with councils and service departments. The vast majority of reporters and their support staff continue to work in the area teams in which they were previously based, and panel members are serving on hearings in the same premises as before. Children and families should have noticed no difference except for a different heading on the notepaper and a different sign on the door. The pattern of referrals under the new arrangements is being carefully monitored before decisions are made about the siting of reporters' offices in the small number of new authorities currently without them. Many hearings are, of course, already held in local centres which are separate from reporters' offices.

One aspect of the change which has given rise to particular concern has been the possible threat to reporters as independent decision-makers. Will the Principal Reporter, as professional head of the service, be likely to exert a constraining influence on the autonomy of individual reporters in an effort to achieve national consistency of practice? The debate about reporters' autonomy is not new. In 1976, John Grant summed up early anxieties about the unfettered nature of reporters' powers:

> 'It is less than satisfactory that reporters are subject to no external control and have no direct access to independent advice. ... The desirability of exercising some supervision over the work of officials performing quasi-judicial functions is obvious' (Grant, 1976, pp208–209).

Similarly, Martin and Murray (1976, p239) argued the need for research into all aspects of the system, but particularly the 'very considerable discretionary powers' exercised by reporters in the course of their decision-making. The results of the current research into reporters' decision-making commissioned by the Scottish Office are eagerly awaited.

While acknowledging the dangers of linking reporters with the *adult* criminal system, Alan Finlayson (1992, para 9.26) accepted that 'a national service would result in a uniform system of juvenile justice while preserving ... autonomy of decision-making' and foresaw that 'accountability to a central department would lead to consistency of decision-making based on experience and expertise'. Considering the possibility that the authority of a Principal Reporter might stifle individual autonomy, he pointed out (para 3.21) that under the previous structure regional reporters had in fact accepted ultimate responsibility for the professional decisions taken by the reporters in their departments, and had worked out various arrangements for the monitoring and support of their staff. Arguably the new extension of the line of authority through the seven reporter managers to the Principal Reporter will not make much difference to the day-to-day casework in area offices but should provide better opportunities for monitoring, debate and agreement about practice issues which can then be implemented consistently throughout the country. The foundation of this will be the systematic collection of data to allow for comparisons of practice in different areas in ways never possible before.

Although the Local Government etc (Scotland) Act 1994, s 128 (3) and (8) makes it clear that the purpose of the Administration is to 'facilitate' rather than to 'direct or guide' the Principal Reporter in the performance of his statutory 'functions', a further concern has been voiced that the board of the Administration might be tempted to exert pressure in the professional sphere, particularly in times of budgetary constraint. Again, the change is not so great as appears at first sight. The relationship between reporters and the SCRA is similar to that described by Mr Finlayson (1992, para 3.11) as existing between reporters and their employing authorities. 'The reporter is accountable to the local authority for administration purposes, including staffing, budgeting and accommodation, but is not accountable for professional decisions.' As he goes on to acknowledge, however (para 3.15), there were inevitable overlaps between the management role and professional practice and it is only realistic to assume that the same will be true under the SCRA.

It is important to recognise that the SCRA, though removed from the framework of local democratic accountability, is, in common with other NDPBs, subject to a high degree of public scrutiny and control. It is directly accountable for the management of the service to the Secretary of State and through him to Parliament. Its powers, and the limitations to these powers, are clearly set out in a series of framework documents. Progress towards the achievement of previously published targets will be described in an annual report and the Administration, with the Principal Reporter as its accounting officer, has responsibility to account for its use of public funds by publishing annual accounts. The SCRA responds directly to requests for information from MPs, councillors, members of the public and the press. Such requests are likely to increase following the transfer on 1st April 1997 from the Scottish Office to the Administration of the responsibility to maintain the national statistics relating to the hearings system. It is possible that the higher national profile may make the reporter service more accessible to public scrutiny and media pressure. Increased public interest and a higher profile may in turn enable the SCRA to enhance levels of knowledge about the hearings system – often surprisingly little understood by the Scottish public at large – and to defend its welfare principles when under attack.

The loss of one kind of accountability – to democratically elected councils – has perhaps been replaced by another – to the public at large. As a national body, the SCRA is obliged to adopt the principles of the Citizen's Charter, which emphasise its accountability to users of the service. In this respect, it is necessary to recognise that they are not 'clients' or 'customers' in the conventional sense because of the degree of compulsion which brings children and families into the hearings system and the confidentiality which must be observed in relation to specific cases. Nevertheless, the views of service users can be sought when possible on relevant aspects – for example, the quality of facilities in hearings centres, which will over time be upgraded to comply with basic national standards. The SCRA is obliged to introduce a clear complaints procedure and is subject to the authority of the Parliamentary Ombudsman who will adjudicate in cases of alleged maladministration.

In keeping with current trends towards openness and accessibility of information, one particular area of opportunity is the quality of the documentation sent by reporters to families. The reaction by a child or a parent to the initial letter from a reporter coming through the letter box can undoubtedly colour their view of how they are treated by the system as a whole, and the new emphasis in the Children (Scotland) Act 1995 on seeking views of children requires careful thought to be given to ways of communicating with them. One of the achievements of the Administration during its first year has been to agree a set of guidelines for communication with children and families which emphasise the need for an individual, personalised approach and the use of clear jargon-free language throughout.

The 1995 Act

Immediately following the transfer of responsibilities to the new Administration in April 1996, reporters had to focus their energies on preparation for the next major change, the implementation of the Children (Scotland) Act a year later. Though prolonging the period of stress inevitably associated with change, this has been seen as an opportunity to promote consistency of practice and to encourage reporters to work together towards the common goal, both internally and with other agencies.

Superficially, the greatest impact of the 1995 Act is at the level of detail. The Act radically reshapes some aspects of the hearings system, such as child-protection procedures, and introduces a wide range of detailed revisions to powers and procedures in other areas. It is notable, however, that all this has been achieved within the existing overall legal framework for hearings. The constitutional roles and interrelationships of the key agents in the system – the reporter, the hearing and the local authority – remain fundamentally untouched. So also do the scope of the system and the overall shape of its processes, while the powers of the hearing itself have been enhanced in a number of significant ways – for example, the powers to exclude relevant persons from hearings and to set a date for review of a child's case.

What then changes? First, the Act innovates by explicitly setting out underlying principles concerning the primacy of the child's welfare, the need to consider the child's views and the requirement not to intervene unless clearly for the better. Somewhat ironically, the Act does not seem specifically to require *reporters* to work to these principles, though it would clearly be impossible for them to do otherwise.

Nevertheless, principles can be something of a Pandora's box. It must be asked whether the Act as a whole consistently promotes the achievement of these principles in practice, and the answer is by no means clear cut. The drafting of the Act was certainly influenced by the children's rights language and philosophy of the United Nations Convention on the Rights of the Child. But alongside that lie provisions focusing on the paternalistic protection of children, and still others intended to protect the rights of parents and family privacy. Six months before the formal implementation of Part II of the Act, regulations were brought in to give parents full access to all papers being considered by children's hearings, including any statement by or on behalf of the child of personal views and wishes. Yet no mechanism has yet been identified to give the child in person any insight into the information on which decisions about his or her future may be based, nor any means by which the child may provide information in confidence to panel members. At the very least, this is indicative of tensions in the policy framework underlying the Act. Sometimes the rights of parents and children will, quite simply, be irreconcilable. In such situations the reporter's loyalty must be to the child's right to protection and support for his or her continued welfare and development.

A further issue here is whether the increased complexity in managing the hearing process, right from consideration of who should attend the hearing through to notification of the final outcome, will in itself prove difficult to reconcile with the underlying principles. The more complex the process, the greater the likelihood that time and attention will focus more on procedural matters than on the child whose interests lie at the heart of the matter.

Despite all these questions, it is clear that the 1995 Act marks a distinct change in tone from its predecessor. The language of welfare has been substantially modified by a new emphasis on bringing together care and justice for children. In this respect, the 1995 Act may be seen as somewhat closer to the spirit (if not the letter) of what is increasingly an international groundswell relating to the fundamental purposes and design of legal systems dealing with children's needs and deeds.

The future

It is a fascinating feature of the history of the reporter service that many of the basic questions it faced in 1971 are still alive today, albeit with a different emphasis. The scope for the professional creativity of the individual reporter, who is best placed to identify the individual child's needs, has remained a matter of concern throughout the period of regionalisation and on into the creation of a national service. Major variations in procedure are disappearing through the combined effects of internal practice guidance and new legislation. Systems of delegation and accountability are now being introduced that should achieve space for professional creativity within a consistent framework of guidance and support, and with appropriate answerability. In keeping with the Finlayson agenda, the national Administration will be able to provide greater opportunities for training and career development and harmonisation of pay and conditions for staff across the country.

Following a period of such major change, it will inevitably take time for reporters, panel members and local authority departments to become used to the new system. Reporters in local offices may feel disorientated, cut off from their old support systems and still not part of the new structure which may seem alien and remote. There is concern that the reporter, no longer present in the council chamber, may not now be listened to when speaking up for children's interests in the competition for scarce resources. It is comforting to note, however, that reporters are included in the list of agencies whom authorities are obliged to consult when preparing their children's services plans (Children (Scotland) Act 1995, s 19(5)(c)). The importance of joint working by child-care agencies is one of the dominant themes of the Act: indeed, the need for training on the new legislation has been used by many as an opportunity to maintain established links and cement new ones. It is likely that resource shortfalls, if nothing else, will increasingly focus efforts on strategic partnership in service development.

The removal of the service from the local authority framework has occurred at a time of unprecedented restrictions on available resources, for reporters and for other child-care agencies. At the same time demands for effectiveness in tackling youth offending have become common political and media currency, while public calls for effective child protection are always finely counterbalanced by pressures to respect privacy, support the family unit and intervene only when necessary. Somehow, all these issues need to be addressed within a philosophy that remains fundamentally welfare-oriented.

No simplistic panaceas are available to resolve these problems, but a possible temporary lowering of the reporter's profile at local level will be offset by the increased status of the service nationally. The Principal Reporter will be able to co-ordinate a national rather than a piecemeal response to suggested legislative changes, and the Administration will be well placed to enter national debates on issues about care and justice for children. This may help to uphold the participative, non-confrontational ethos of the hearings system in an increasingly litigious society.

There is no doubt that these difficult issues can be addressed satisfactorily only by the whole spectrum of interests in the children's hearings system working together to think strategically and act collaboratively. The timely creation of a national reporter service offers the best platform from which reporters can contribute constructively in the interests of Scotland's children.

12 : Panels and Hearings
Barbara Reid

The changing face of panel membership
Historical perspective
One of the major innovations of the children's hearings system was the formation of a children's panel in each local authority area. These panels were to consist of lay members of the community whose responsibility was to make decisions in the best interests of the children who appeared before children's hearings. That responsibility continues to this day.

From the outset it was anticipated that panels would in some way reflect the community from which the children who were referred to hearings came, though it was never an unambiguous objective. The only qualification for panel members indicated by the Kilbrandon Committee was that they should have 'knowledge or experience to consider children's problems' (Kilbrandon, 1964, para 92(a)). The 1966 White Paper, Social Work and the Community, suggested that panel members should be 'representative of the community' and these conceptions were combined in the criteria laid out in the Scottish Office circular which proposed that persons appointed should 'have knowledge and experience in dealing with children and families and be drawn from a wide range of neighbourhood, age group and income group' (Social Work Services Group (SWSG), 1969). However, the issue of what constitutes 'representativeness', and how this should be balanced against personal skills and attributes, has been the subject of debate throughout the twenty-five years of the hearings system.

Among the early research into the hearings system were studies which looked at the profile of those offering themselves for panel membership. It is worth noting that from the outset there were doubts as to whether in fact the Scottish public would actually offer themselves in sufficient numbers for the task. Despite some initial underestimates of the numbers required, there was never any shortage of applicants. During the past twenty-five years over 11,000 members of the public in Scotland have served as panel members; currently almost 2,300 people serve on the thirty-two children's panels throughout Scotland, which is more than at any time in the past. Panel members have been, and continue to be, recruited annually through open advertising campaigns which always attract considerably more applicants than can be appointed.

The early research into panel membership conducted by May and Smith in Aberdeen (1970) and Mapstone in Fife (1973) reached similar findings. Both studies showed that the outcome of the selection process was an over-representation of professional and managerial classes. May and Smith suggested that this led them to be too closely identified with social work rather than representatives of the communities from which their clients came. Mapstone, on the other hand, suggested that for the Children's Panel Advisory Committee (CPAC) 'individual suitability for the task' was the most important factor, and this was perfectly defensible. Rowe agreed with Mapstone that it was more important to have panel members who were 'articulate, imaginative, and sympathetic' than those who had the same background as 'clients', since the range of problems panels might expect to encounter would be beyond any individual's direct experience (Rowe, 1972).

After initial research and commentary on panel membership there was virtually no further informed discussion until the 1990s, when there was, first, the publication of the Scottish Consumer Council report, Can Anyone Get On One of These? (Jones and Adler, 1990), and then the research study on behalf of the Children's Panel Chairmen's Group (CPCG), Citizen's Service and Children's Panel Membership (Lockyer, 1992). The first looked at children's panels together with other voluntary tribunals. It made use of 1989 SWSG data on panel membership collected for the first time since the early 1970s. It claimed that hearings appointments were more 'open and representative' than other tribunals, but that those selected could be a wider cross-section if CPACs did not look for 'the right people' but were prepared to 'train up from scratch' anyone 'genuinely interested in children' (Jones and Adler, 1990, p114).

The CPCG study arose out of concerns among those responsible for the hearings rota about aspects of panel member service. In particular there were concerns in some regions and areas that

- the resignation level in early years of service was too high;
- some members' availability for service, especially for day-time hearings, was poor;
- the substitution of members on the hearings rota in some places too frequently occurred.

The main reason for these problems was thought to be the difficulty in getting time off work for some categories of members, and this in turn was associated with lack of understanding and appreciation among employers and others of the panel members' role (Lockyer, 1992, Ch 2).

The study sets out to examine and quantify all aspects of the background of panel members, their commitment to panel service, the problems which they have, and their attitudes to various aspects of their panel work. The profile of panel members, the issues and problems associated with panel membership are well documented by this study. The aim in what follows is to bring the picture up to date, and to give a panel-member perspective on current issues and difficulties.

Current membership
The CPCG report showed quite clearly that there had been a number of significant changes in the profile of panel members between 1971 and 1990 in relation to their age, sex, marital status, employment and social class. The extent

to which these characteristics were taken into account by CPACs when they carried out recruitment and selection is not known.

A significant finding of the CPCG report is that panel members in 1989 were generally older than their counterparts of 1971. In particular, the under-thirty age group had declined from 11 per cent of the membership to 6 per cent. Panel chairs generally considered it desirable to recruit in this age group because they were close in age to the parents who attended hearings. However, the latest figures from SWSG in 1997 indicate that this trend has been reversed. The under-thirty age group now accounts for 12 per cent of current panel members and, in the last intake of new members in 1996, they were over 22 per cent of those recruited. This indicates a willingness of CPACs to recruit younger members, if there is an opportunity to do so.[1]

The CPCG report also pointed out the low percentage of panel members at age sixty or over, and raised the question of whether or not it was desirable to make more use of this age group. In the interim the SWSG has made it clear that it did not regard sixty as the age limit for panel service. None the less, the percentage in this age bracket is only 2 per cent, which suggests that many CPACs still consider people at the top of the age range either out of touch or a bad investment to train. It could equally be that fewer older people consider themselves suitable to apply. However, the overall age profile continues to favour the forty to fifty-nine age group; in 1971 they were 58 per cent of the total membership, now they are 60 per cent. Significantly, this is the age group with school-age children; most panel members are in fact parents.

The indications are that there is a widening gap between the number of male and female panel members. In the early years there was very little difference in the proportion of male and female members. In 1992 45 per cent of panel members were male; in 1996 the figure was down to 42 per cent. The evidence from the early studies was that almost equal numbers of men and women applied, so the gender of applicants made no difference to the chance of being recruited. Although in recent years there has been no national data available on the gender distribution of applicants, it is well known that women generally have applied in greater numbers than men in most parts of the country. In some areas local recruitment advertising has been specifically aimed at men. Significantly, the percentage of men in the 1996 intake is only 37 per cent of the total.

The shifting profile of 'the family' in society at large is reflected to some extent in the make up of panels. As in 1971, most panel members today are married; the percentage unmarried (at the time of appointment) remained at 15 per cent for the first two decades; it has now increased to just over 21 per cent. In the early days very few panel members were recorded as being 'separated' or 'divorced'. In 1971 they were less than 1 per cent of the total; now they are recorded as almost 7 per cent. These figures do not give an especially reliable picture because then, as now, panel members in these categories may have described themselves as 'single'

---

[1] The statistics in this section derive from the CPCG report (Lockyer, 1992) and from unpublished SWSG figures.

and we do not of course know the number married more than once. The data, however, suggests that people who have experienced marriage breakdown are still under-represented, but not quite as notably as in the past.

As we have seen, some observers were critical of the social composition of the early panels, claiming that they were not sufficiently 'representative' of the people they served and suggesting that they were therefore less able to identify with, or understand, the problems of families. Without necessarily accepting the simplistic assumption behind this view, CPACs have generally acknowledged the desirability of widening the social mixture (although not to the same degree in all places). The CPCG study indicated that there has been a significant shift away from the professional and managerial groups since the early years of the system. Most panels now have a more representative profile – fewer higher professionals (less than 4 per cent), more manual and skilled members (together almost 47 per cent) and a small but increasing representation of unskilled groupings.

There are many complications and reservations that must be made about methods used in social classifications – including, for example, classifying those who are not in paid employment by spouses' occupation. However, Lockyer's finding in 1991 showed that panel members were still as 'upwardly mobile' as Higgins's 1972 study had shown them to be (Higgins, 1979). Given that they are now generally less socially 'high', their origins must be accordingly 'lower'. The significance which Lockyer draws from the fact that a large number of panel members (43 per cent in the CPCG study) have been upwardly mobile is not only that they have experience of a life style different from that which their current class indicates, but that they are likely to be optimistic about social improvement and have a positive view of what can be achieved through education. This is no bad thing if 'tempered with realism' (Lockyer, 1992, p46).

Availability
A key requirement for panel members is to have an understanding of children and the problems which affect them and their families. An equally important consideration to be weighed in their selection is the extent of their availability for service. This applies not only to hearings, but also to attendance at training, and giving time to prepare for hearings. Most panel members undertake two hearing sessions (which last on average three hours) each month. The majority of hearings are held in mornings and afternoons, and although some hearings are held in evenings, these have become a small proportion in most authorities. This means that panel members need to have day-time availability if they are to make a full contribution.

The 1992 CPCG study reports that three-quarters of panel members were in full-time or part-time employment – 60 per cent of women and 82 per cent of men. The majority in full-time employment require to take time off work for panel duties, although nearly half claim to make up time so that there is no loss to their employer. The hearings system demands and gets a fair measure of support from all categories of employers. However, about one in seven panel members report some difficulty associated with getting time off work.

The largest proportion of time devoted to panel duties is, however, not taken out of work, but time which could be devoted to leisure pursuits or spent with the family. On average, panel duties are estimated to take up about four hours every week; the largest proportion of time (43 per cent) being given over to reading case papers. The time spent on reading reports is likely to have been substantially reduced as a result of parental access to reports, which came into force in October 1996. The fact that all adult parties to hearings must receive copies of all documents sent to panel members has led to a dramatic reduction in the number of past reports being included in papers sent to panel members.

Of the remaining time, half again is devoted to training (22 per cent), which takes place in the evenings or at weekends; only 30 per cent is spent attending hearings (Lockyer, 1992, fig 6). These are panel members' estimates and there are of course significant individual and regional variations.

Training

Although there is no statutory requirement to train panel members it has always been considered that some training is necessary. Panel members' training is currently provided by the Children's Panel Training Organisers located in the Universities of Glasgow, Edinburgh, Aberdeen and St Andrews. Throughout the past twenty-five years the programmes offered by the training organisers in their divisions of the country have been developed relatively independently.

It has been universally accepted that newly recruited members must successfully complete a course of mandatory pre-service training. The recognition that what was offered across the country should bring all panel members to a similar basic standard, led to the publication in 1995 of the SWSG Core Curriculum for the Induction Training of Children's Panel Members. This sets out the content and expected outcomes of the initial *pre-service training* completed before serving on hearings, and also of *the new-member training* which is required to be completed during the first year of service.

Pre-service training and new-member training are no more than preparation and confirmation of the basic requirements for the panel members' tasks. Beyond this they are expected to attend in-service training both to improve their skills and to keep in touch with developments at local and national level. There has been an increasingly strongly held view that those panel members with poor attendance at in-service training should not be reappointed. CPACs have taken into account the extent of the member's training commitment when considering them for reappointment, though generally CPACs are reluctant to lose 'good panel members' whose attendance at training is poor.

The issue of training is particularly important at times when there are changes in legislation. Preparation for the implementation of the Children (Scotland) Act 1995 in April 1997 was just such a time. All serving panel members were required to retrain. For the great majority this was viewed as an opportunity to engage with the concepts and language of the new era, even though some old hands took the opportunity to retire gracefully.

However, the demand to meet the training requirement of the new legislation cannot be treated as an unique event, but has to be viewed in the context of the reorganisation of local government and the creation of new authorities, some of which have scant experience in supporting or providing for panel member service. The standard of training demanded by the panel members' tasks under the 1995 Act is likely to be greater than in the past, and, to begin with at least, harder to achieve within the new local authority structures. If the training needs are to be met and the standard of training is not to be compromised, additional resources will have to be found to enable training organisers to meet their obligations.

The future of panels

The capacity of the volunteer decision-makers to respond to the new demands made by the changes in legislation will in large measure determine their success. Children's Panel Advisory Committees and the Scottish Office have a major task in ensuring that those recruited are adequately trained, sufficiently supported and retained to provide the required level of service competence. The concept of a representative panel must continue to be secondary to recruiting those best able to meet the demands of the job.

Current trends suggest that one of the major areas of tension between the ideal composition of the panel and competence might relate to the male/female balance. We have noted that in recent years, despite efforts to target recruitment advertising, there remain significantly fewer men to choose from. Attempting to maintain a equal gender balance has the consequence that selectors must prefer less-able men to better-suited women.

This raises the question of whether it is desirable to continue to seek equal numbers of men and women. In the first place it may be possible to accept the norm of having one man and two women on most hearings, which would require that only one-third of each authority panel need be men. A more radical suggestions is to abandon the legal requirement to have a mixed gender of panel members on each hearing. The strongest reason for keeping at least one male on each hearing is not the special qualities men bring, but to give the sometimes important message to parents that child-care matters are the business of both sexes.

A major concern for those with the responsibility of preparing the hearing rota is to ensure that within each hearing there is sufficient experience. The practice in most authorities is that the hearing chairman must have served for a sufficient length of time and undergone specific in-service training in chairmanship. It was always anticipated that panel membership would be for limited periods. The need for 'new blood' was emphasised by Scottish Office circulars, and even (rather insensitively) in the letters sent out to ask whether members wished to renew their membership! Some CPACs impose time-limits on membership. However, more than sufficient 'new blood' is achieved in most places through 'natural wastage'; the greater problem is normally too high a rate of early retirement from service.

Among current membership 80 per cent have under six years' service and 27 per cent have less than a year's service. However, the largest proportion of members in any cohort are lost in the first two years of appointment. In 1992, according to the CPCG study, the average length of service was 4.76 years. Both the reorganisation of local government and the implementation of the Children (Scotland) Act 1995 precipitated resignations, so it is very likely that the average length of service has declined since 1992. In 1997 over 600 new recruits were appointed instead of the normal figure of under 400 a year.

There is no doubt that this created a significant deficit of experience when it was much needed; in some of the new authorities well over half the panel had less than two years' service. Shortage of experience among panel members remains a problem and efforts need to be redoubled to stem the flow of good people out of the system.

Local studies of reasons for resignation have shown that they are most commonly associated with the competing demands of paid employment (Lockyer, 1992, p12). One trend that has become more apparent in the last few years is the impact of new work practices which affect even those areas of employment which were once supportive to panel membership. The move to smaller and smaller work units or work cells in many industries and businesses – including the previous public utilities – means that although the company may have a policy of supporting time off for hearings, and panel membership is covered by the Employment Protection Act 1990, the reality is that the time taken away from work affects the targets and possibly bonuses of workmates. The more CPACs seek to have a cross-section of people in employment in all parts of the economy, the greater the potential problem of conflict between work and service. The hearings system's success in recruiting beyond the social and economic boundaries of traditional volunteers has created a greater need to convince employers, and others, of the importance of the work done, and generally to enhance the status of panel membership.

In many ways this issue is part of a wider problem, that of the profile of the children's hearings system itself. Most people do not come into contact with the children's reporter or with hearings. Unlike courts (whose business is endlessly portrayed in dramatic entertainment), little is known by the public at large about children's hearings or the juvenile justice system in Scotland. Despite twenty-five years of existence, panel membership is seen by many as 'just voluntary work', and not as part of the justice system of the country. Panel members lack the social status of magistrates. There is a need to raise the public profile of the children's hearings system and the part played in it by panel members.

The lack of public knowledge of the children's hearings system is in large measure the result of laudable restraint shown by all associated with its work to keep confidential the lives of the children and families with whom it deals. The fact that children cannot be identified has meant that publicity media have had little interest in the business of children's hearings. The hearings system did, however, receive unprecedented media notice in relation to Fife, Orkney and Ayrshire – mainly in the form of unfavourable publicity. The media have often given a distorted view of events, mostly through a lack of background knowledge, but little has been done through official channels to rectify this. Moreover, it is nowhere brought to public attention that panel members have been exonerated by the inquiries and Court of Session judgments associated with the above events, whereas sheriffs, social workers and other agencies have merited some criticism. Unlike the professional agencies, panel members have lacked a paid spokesperson of their own, and to date the Secretary of State's appointees have largely had to settle for words of private praise rather than robust public support.

The changing character of hearings

During the past twenty-five years perhaps the most significant change in relation to hearings has been through the nature of the cases referred. This subject is considered in other chapters of this book; here its impact on the work of the panel members is our concern. In much of the literature available in the 1970s the focus was on the delinquent child, although even then there was a small, but significant, number of care and protection cases. This focus was reflected in the training of panel members; subjects like 'Theories of Delinquency' and understanding 'Peer Group Sub-culture' were the stock in trade. The prominence of such topics has come to be replaced by topics associated with facets of child abuse. In the intervening period panel members and society at large have had to reach an understanding of 'battered babies', physical abuse and neglect, the sexually abused child, psychological abuse, and the child as the abuser.

At one level it is possible to exaggerate the effect of the change in cases considered by hearings. The focus remains the child's 'needs, not their deeds', and families remain the object of attention. In many ways this has meant that panel members have taken the changing grounds for referral in their stride. The shift in the balance of cases has meant that hearings have had to deal with many more young children at hearings. Generally this has been accommodated by some lessening of formality. Panel members have been willing to listen to children of any age and have normally wanted to see children with their parents, even when they have been too young to offer views.

It could be argued that emphasis given to child-protection work in social work departments and among social workers led to shift of resources away from older children and a relative neglect of what should be done to keep teenagers out of trouble and in education. The study initiated in 1988 by the CPCG on behalf of panel members themselves asked the question whether 'our proper concern for the safety and well being of the neglected and abused [has] led to the neglect of resources for other categories of children' (Lockyer, 1988 p28). It was suggested that there may be a danger of 'saving young children, to abandon them in their adolescence'.

It is fair to say that panel members have remained conscious of the importance of continuing to attend to the needs of all children who come before them. This has meant insisting on maintaining residential resources and on work being done with offenders throughout a period in the 1980s when local authority social work departments were inclined to put most of their efforts into child protection. While acknowledging the shift of emphasis to the protection of children from all kinds of abuse and neglect, panel members have recognised the importance of maintaining a credible capacity to provide care and control of offenders. This is necessary, if the Scottish system is to continue, to resist the popular clamour, which is periodically heard in England, for more Draconian measures to deal with youth crime. The representatives of the public in the Scottish system retain the belief that compulsory supervision, including working with families, is the best way of addressing delinquency effectively. It is important that child-protection work does not lead to turning a blind eye to young offenders.

Although panel members have resisted the conceptual separation of child protection and delinquency, and the domination of the former over the latter, it is true to say that the increasing number of child-protection cases has had an effect on the character of the 'typical hearing' and the demands of the panel member's task. Generally there are fewer easy and relaxed hearings; generally there are more hearings which require direct confrontation of difficult issues with parents. Dealing with cases of serious, sometimes unimaginable and horrendous, child-abuse cases provokes strong feelings, and indeed among panel members themselves. Supporting arrangements (and occasionally counselling of panel members) have been needed to augment in-service training on how to deal both with abused and abusers.

In child-protection cases it is much more common for the grounds for referral to be contested; therefore, a growing number of decisions made by hearings relate to protection arrangements prior to proof. This has taken panel members further into the area of risk assessment. Until the 1995 Act, hearings had very little power other than to approve or refuse place of safety orders, which gave the local authority great discretion – for example, as to where to place the child and the degree of parental access that was allowed. To scrutinise critically and approve or change proposed arrangements under child protection orders or warrants to keep children in places of safety are areas where the new legislation has increased the responsibility of hearings.

Changing structures
Local government reorganisation
The reorganisation of local government has had a significant effect on the hearings system. Perhaps the most important of the changes has been the removal of the reporter to the children's panel from local government to the Scottish Children's Reporter Administration (SCRA). There are great opportunities in the formation of a central organisation to set national standards for reporters' practice and to provide a national voice for part of the hearings system. However, there are also possible costs and disadvantages.

The working relationship with local authorities and local panels is less close. The loss of the reporter's influence in local authorities is the greater because it coincides with their reorganisation and a lack in some authorities of officers and elected members fully informed about the operational requirements of the hearings system and child-care needs.

Although for most panel members there appears to have been a seamless transition from a local to a national reporter service, for new-authority panel chairs the separation from the reporter has made a major difference. It has meant the loss of an important ally when child care or hearings business is being considered by the council. The panel chair can sometimes be the sole voice for the hearings system in the committees of the new council. Many councillors and officers with no experience of the hearings system find the independent position of the panel chair difficult to understand and, in some cases, to accept.

The problems faced by new-authority panel chairs are multiplied by the fact that Children's Panel Advisory Committees (CPACs) have lost some of their independence from local authorities. In some new authorities councillors appointed to serve on CPACs, and council officials who service them, have been inclined to act as if the CPAC were a committee of the council and its chair were the official voice of the system in the authority, with a duty to look after the interests of the authority. This has led to serious difficulties for some panel chairmen in acquiring the resources they need to carry out their functions effectively.

Under the 1995 Act the official duties of panel chairmen remain relatively unspecified. They are responsible for assigning panel members to hearings (usually by compiling a hearing rota); they must be consulted over the appointment of safeguarders; and about local authority children's service plans (this is the only new responsibility). However, the new-authority panel chairs have most of the practical responsibilities inherited from regional chairs in the past. They meet with the various agencies and organisations within and outside the hearings system locally and nationally. It is panel chairs who take up with local authorities issues relating to resources for hearings decisions – on occasion the non-implementation of decisions – and they have the task of investigating complaints by and against panel members. They also have a pastoral role towards members, ensuring that they receive the necessary training and support to fulfil their duties. Together with CPAC, panel chairs must ensure that there are sufficient members to conduct all the hearings that are scheduled. It would greatly assist panel office holders for these responsibilities to be specified by central government so that local authorities have a clear view of the panel chairs' functions and the support services they require. It would also help the standing of panel office holders – among panel members and among organs of the local authorities – if there were a specified, uniform and transparent procedure for their appointment.

A further consequence of the creation of the centralised SCRA is that the Principal Reporter at national level will tend to become *the* spokesperson of the hearings system, whereas the voice of panel members will tend to be lost. There is a need for reporters and panel members (and also CPACs) to retain their independent influence with the Scottish Office.

Budgets and resources
A further problem has arisen as a result of the disaggregation of budgets and resources. This has left some social work departments and panels dramatically short of the resources they need to enable them to make decisions in the best interests of children. In many councils there is active discouragement of the use of residential care and especially of 'out of authority' placements for children. In the

previous structure, both the reporter and the panel chairman were able to challenge policy and practice relating to resources. Although there were often perceived to be deficiencies, there were established mechanisms to deal with them. In many places, for the reasons indicated above, the loss of the reporter's influence has not been compensated for. The fear must be that the priorities set by the chief social work officer will not be able to be checked effectively or questioned within the authority. At a time of financial stringency, finding resources to meet the needs of individual children, as hearings define them, will inevitably be harder. This stringency is coming at a time when the formal and informal structure for resolving problems has been disrupted and an alternative voice to that of social work speaking for the hearings system is at its weakest. This is a potential recipe for the kind of conflict which occurred in Fife.[2]

The requirement under the 1995 Act to produce *child service plans* (s 19), and to do so in consultation with the panel chair, Principal Reporter and other parties, might go some way to allay some of the concerns expressed above. (It should be remembered that the recommendation to consult with panel chairs on resource issues came from the Fife Inquiry.) The fact that it is the local authority as a whole, rather than just the social work department, which now takes responsibility for children's services may in the longer term be beneficial. It is hoped that this will mean hearings will gain access to a wider range of authority services than previously. In particular it will be a most welcome change if educational resources are no longer beyond the reach of hearings.

Since the new local authorities have taken over responsibility for housing there is a further potential advantage from the fact that the 1995 Act makes the authority as a whole responsible for children's needs being met. Access to appropriate housing is often a critical issue in decisions about child welfare. Having the housing authority with a direct duty for children will be welcomed by panel members who have experienced the frustration of not being able to agree to a child staying with a parent because of their lack of suitable accommodation. Housing issues are also critically important for many of the sixteen- to eighteen-year-old age group: suitable housing is often a prerequisite of moving away from parents and beyond supervision. Children's service plans must take account of the accommodation needs of this age group. There will be teething problems for the new local authorities in coming to terms with providing and managing the range of resources required to meet children's and young people's needs and with the demands made upon them by the hearings system.

Access to reports

Prior to the implementation of the 1995 Act an amendment was made to the Children's Hearings Rules to give parties access to reports.[3] The change, which made all case papers available to parents of children coming to hearings, was generally welcomed by panel members. It was viewed as a desirable addition to

---

[2] See Chapter 6.
[3] Required by the finding of the European Court of Human Rights in *McMichael* v *United Kingdom* (1995) 20 EHRR 205.

openness and fairness. However, it does have a downside. It has led to some loss of information and a tendency for reports to be cautious in raising matters of concern which their authors cannot readily substantiate.

At the time of writing no decision has been made as to how children are to be given access to reports. Currently, the Children's Hearings Rules only require copies of reports to be sent to adults who have a right to attend hearings. The rules still require the hearing chairman to convey the substance of reports to children and 'relevant persons' (as under the 1968 Act), and the new legislation puts an onus on those producing reports and on panel members at hearings to seek the views of the child. Currently there is no way of allowing children to give information or express views directly or indirectly to hearings without their being made available to parents. (This contrasts with the position of the sheriff whose Court Rules allow confidential communications from a child.[4]) However, there is no major change in the extent to which matters pertinent to a decision can be kept confidential, since under the previous rules these must be included in the 'reasons for decision' given.

It is unlikely that the availability of reports to parties will have a major impact on hearings generally. Good social work practice has always held that the content of reports should usually be discussed with parents and children. Less time may be spent on checking information at hearings, but it will still be important for hearings chairmen, with assistance from the authors of the reports, to direct attention to the salient aspects of reports which might be relevant to decisions. There will be some cases where parents and their representatives may have prepared for the hearing by taking issue with detail in reports, which may serve to increase the adversarial character of these hearings. It will fall to the hearings chairmen to identify the important issues and to focus the discussion on them.

Instances where lawyer representatives appear at hearings are likely to continue to increase, but this should not alter the character of hearings so long as chairmen prevent inappropriate attempts at 'legal representation'. In fact, in recent years the legal profession has become aware of the difference between courts and hearings and most lawyers have adopted the discursive and constructive role required by the hearing forum. There may be an increase in the number of appeals against hearings' decisions as a result of families gaining access to reports, and reports may contain fewer unsustainable assertions – neither of these need be matters of regret.

The Children (Scotland) Act 1995

Although there were minor amendments and changes to the hearings system during the first twenty-five years there were no major changes in legislation to alter substantially the task of panel members. The introduction of secure accommodation, boarding out and fostering regulations and safeguarders each

---

[4] See Chapter 10.

required some adjustments of practice.[5] The main development of the period was not legal innovation but the gradual shift in the balance of grounds for referral, which has already been discussed. It could be argued that the changes in the 1995 Act were in large measure adjustments to the shifts in practice that had already taken place. Most of the sound alterations introduced by the 1995 Act were proposed by the Review of Child Care Law in Scotland, which reported in 1990.

The 1995 Act has some specific implications for hearings and panel members. Despite being firmly rooted in the previous legislation, there are areas of change which will create a greater demand for on-going panel member training than that initially required when the legislation was introduced.

The principles on which the new legislation is grounded are, in essence, already embodied in the Kilbrandon philosophy. The child's welfare being paramount, the requirement to seek and take account of children's views and to minimise intervention are each to be found embedded in established practice under the 1968 Act. To some extent, however, the 1995 Act detracts from principles already in operation. For example, the 1995 Act allows the paramountcy of the child's welfare to be set aside for the purpose of protecting the public from 'serious harm' (s 16 (5)). This is a major departure. To date, preventing harm to others has been a goal to be pursued as an aspect of the child's interest. Since no child can have a legitimate interest in harming others, and the long-term welfare of all children is served by preventing them from harming others, no great difference in practice is likely to follow. However, panel members already had the power to authorise secure accommodation to prevent children causing harm to others; taking account of others did not permit the welfare of the child to be set aside, or become secondary to public protection. This was preferable. There is now a concern, which may be unfounded, that unless panel members are seen to take sufficient account of the public interest, more offending children may be removed from the hearings system and directed to courts. This might be effected by the Lord Advocate instructing more offence cases ('persistent offenders' or any non-trivial offences) to the courts, or even by the removal of offence grounds from hearings' jurisdiction in response to a political or public panic about juvenile offenders.

The principle of seeking the views of the child, together with establishing the right of the child to attend his or her own hearing and the hearing's power to remove 'relevant persons' (parents), may enhance the child's feeling that his or her welfare is paramount. The arrangements which the Act makes for 'business meetings' (s 64) is an important means of improving transparency and uniformity of practice in deciding procedural matters. The business meeting can determine who is a 'relevant person' or otherwise has a relationship with the child such that he or she has a right to attend (and receive papers) and who, having an obligation

---

[5] The Health and Social Services and Social Security Adjudications Act 1983 was the legislative basis for the Secure Accommodation (Scotland) Regulations 1983 (SI 1983/1912) and of the Boarding-Out and Fostering of Children (Scotland) Regulations 1985 (SI 1985/1799). The Children Act 1975 was the source of the amendment to the 1968 Act introducing safeguarders. The Hearings Rules and the Sheriff Court Rules were amended by the Children's Hearings (Scotland) (Amendment – Safeguarders) Rules 1985 (SI 1985/843) and the Act of Sederunt (Social Work (Scotland) Act 1968) (Safeguarders) 1985 (SI 1985/780) respectively.

to attend, can reasonably be excused. These matters are decided after the reporter has submitted the views of interested parties. This is an increase of procedural formality, but one which will go a long way to rectify significant anomalies and unjustified variations in previous practice.

The power to exclude relevant persons and members of the press in order to seek the child's views, together with the duty to explain the substance of what took place to the relevant persons in their absence, gives the hearing members a major area of discretion to use with caution. They must balance the advantage to the child in speaking without an intimidating presence against the possible effect of the exclusion on the desired atmosphere of openness and co-operation. It is important not to give the child the assurance that what he or she says will be kept in confidence; the child must be made aware that anything he or she wishes to submit in writing, or to reveal to other writers of reports, will be made available to other parties. The provision does not afford children any new opportunity to express views confidentially, but it may assist in enabling some children to speak.

The new Act recognises that a hearing must consider the long-term care of the child subject to 'supervision requirements' (s 70(1)), even when he or she is also subject to court proceedings to consider who shall have parental responsibility. Children may now come to hearings in order to provide advice to the courts before final decisions about long-term care are taken. This in part recognises that a hearing is the best forum for listening to parents and seeking their co-operation. Even if the authority of the court is needed to finalise adoptions, where parental rights and freeing for adoption are concerned, it is hard to see why hearings are not making the decision, with the court available for appeals. Providing advice to sheriffs in relation to long-term decisions will require panel members to develop a facility for making succinct and persuasive reports.

The 1995 Act has the potential to alter somewhat the established relationship between hearings and courts. This is particularly so, given the sheriff's new power on appeal to substitute his or her own preferred disposal (s 51(5)(c)) – even though this power was not sought by sheriffs and the government envisaged that it would be rarely used. It remains to be seen whether, in practice, sheriffs will accept the Kilbrandon reasoning that courts are not the best forum for deciding on matters of disposal.

Courts and hearings have more interwoven roles to play in emergency protection. Child protection orders, issued by sheriffs, are reviewed by hearings on the second day after being implemented unless directly appealed against (s 59(3)). At these hearings there are no grounds for referral. An assessment of whether the conditions for the initial granting of the order still obtain is the sole issue for panel members. However, unlike the previous decisions relating to places of safety, hearings have to consider whether they require any subsidiary 'directions' – including, for example, those relating to contact – or whether the child's location should be known. The similar responsibility to consider specifying conditions or directions attaching to warrants to keep children in places of safety require hearings to adjudicate on matters of detail which were previously left to social work discretion. There is reason to believe that hearings might be better equipped than courts to agree a set of emergency arrangements which make some concessions to parents and gain their co-operation with interim measures.

Although most panel members are happy to accept the additional tasks and responsibilities which the new legislation brings, at present there are areas of practice largely untried and issues of practice largely unresolved. This creates a demand for more 'training' in the widest sense, including the opportunity to debate and explore flexible interpretation and innovative implementation.

As the hearings system enters the next millennium we can only hope that it receives the resources and support which ensure that it continues to meet children's needs.

13 : Rediscovering Juvenile Delinquency

Bill Whyte

THE conventional way of looking at changes in juvenile justice policy and practice is to see them as a reflection of changing perceptions of crime and of juvenile offenders. This, however, provides only a superficial picture. Modern states have legal structures that reflect the state's primary assumptions regarding the nature and value of the person and the value of property. Changes in legislation and systems of response to crime reflect social and political debates and are inextricably bound up with changes in social and economic order. Developments in juvenile justice have generally displayed pendulum-like movements, swinging between what is generally termed 'welfarism' or non-retributive and 'punishment' or retributive systems. The debate tends to be classified, rather simplistically and unhelpfully, as justice versus welfare.

Policies during much of the twentieth century have sought to create systems which erode the distinction between the young person in need and the delinquent. Once again these distinctions are subject to debate. Throughout Europe systems for dealing with young people who offend are under review and are associated with a shift in emphasis from social welfare intervention to punishment and individual responsibility, and it can be argued that this 'repoliticisation of youth' is part of a political strategy developed in response to economic problems. Whatever the underlying reasons, the consequence has been the 'rediscovery of the delinquent' (Tutt, 1981).

The renewed political emphasis in the United Kingdom on law and order and a growing public concern with crime, and with persistent young offenders in particular, coincided with a re-examination of perceived problems in the children's hearings system. The 1993 White Paper, Scotland's Children: Proposals for Child Care Policy and Law, led to legislative changes now included in the Children (Scotland) Act 1995 and Criminal Procedure (Scotland) Act 1995.

This chapter draws on studies from England and Wales and from North America, in addition to some limited Scottish data, to examine delinquency and to address the extent to which the unique Scottish provisions are suited, philosophically and practically, to dealing with juvenile offenders effectively.

The pattern of delinquency in Scotland and the United Kingdom
Much youth crime is invisible and goes unreported. Estimates in England and Wales indicate that between 1959 and 1977 crime in the fourteen-to-seventeen

age group rose by about 150 per cent and that since 1984 it has fallen by as much as 37 per cent (Hagell and Newburn, 1994). Only part of this reduction can be accounted for by demographic changes and by greater use of police discretion.

Probably the most important single fact about crime is that it is committed mainly by teenagers and young adults. The age-crime curve seems to have changed little over the century in the UK or elsewhere. The peak age of offending remains mid-to-late teens, reducing to a relatively small percentage by age twenty. The peak age for less serious recorded offences is around fifteen and a half and for more serious offences, particularly involving violence, the peak is between seventeen and nineteen.

Scotland seems to differ little from elsewhere in the UK with regard to patterns of recorded crime, with fifteen as the peak age of recorded offending for boys and girls (Scottish Office, 1995a). About 60 per cent of referrals (25,735) to reporters in Scotland in 1994 involved juveniles who were reported for an offence (Scottish Office, 1995a). Trends in the national figures show a drop in the rate of referrals of children who offend to 11.9 per 1,000 of this population in 1993 – the lowest in more than ten years (Scottish Office, 1994). The 1994 figures, however, show a rise of 11 per cent ending this downward trend. Only about a third of these referrals result in a children's hearing (Scottish Office, 1995a). There are regional variations.

Research suggests that in the eleven-to-sixteen age range most offences are minor and non-violent involving, typically, vandalism, theft from cars and shops. Graham and Bowling (1995) found that offending is widespread among this age group, with one in two males and one in three females admitting they had committed an offence at some time. The majority of offenders reported committing no more than one or two minor offences, with property offending more common than violent offences. They found overall that about 3 per cent of offenders accounted for approximately a quarter of all offences reported. The data support the view that a small group begin their criminal career around the age of twelve or thirteen and continue into their adult years. Although the age-crime curve is the most basic fact in criminology, its significance is not fully understood. While age as such cannot be used as an explanation for behavioural change, the constancy of the relationship indicates that it springs from some very basic feature of human development. Official statistics identify peak ages for first conviction as mid-adolescence, but this does not reflect activity or behaviour as such. In many jurisdictions children cannot be convicted of an offence until this age. For this reason, the wider concept of antisocial behaviour has been used as a measure.

The best explanation offered by developmentalists is that antisocial behaviour is treated as mischief in children, but as crime in adolescents; or that adolescent law-breaking is a different expression of the same antisocial tendency that was already present in childhood, reflecting changes within both the individual (maturation) and the environment.

Prospective longitudinal studies provide similar findings on the relationship between age and officially recorded offending (eg, Farrington and West's Cambridge study, 1977). Although the evidence demonstrates some continuity between antisocial behaviour in childhood, adolescence and adulthood, the results also reveal a substantial element of discontinuity. Robins has claimed that while adult antisocial behaviour is nearly always preceded by childhood antisocial behaviour, most antisocial children do not become antisocial adults (see Smith, 1995). Other research shows that although criminality is one of the symptoms of   *ros* antisocial personality, it is neither a necessary nor a sufficient condition. This conclusion has been strengthened by more recent results. Hence, although there is a considerable degree of continuity from one developmental stage to the next, the predictive power of behaviour problems in early childhood becomes diluted by other influences by the time of adolescence.

Smith (1995) suggests that such explanations are unconvincing as a general account of the relationship between age and antisocial behaviour because of the many types of antisocial behaviour, however measured, that rise to a peak in adolescence or early adulthood then fall sharply. A different kind of explanation might be developed from the social control theory elaborated by Sampson and Laub (1993). During adolescence, the young person is moving away from the restraining influence of parents and has not yet invested in reciprocal adult relationships that may in future be a restraining influence. For this reason, adolescents are unruly because they slip between the mechanisms of informal social control that are effective for children and for adults.

Recent re-analysis of longitudinal data from the 1940s and 1950s found a strong relationship between job stability, commitment to conventional educational, occupational roles and marital attachment and the chance of the later criminality. Research would indicate that the formation of social bonds is likely to be the central explanation for desistance from crime after adolescence.

Insofar as it is possible to generalise, data give support to the argument presented in Scotland's Children that in Scotland, as in other countries in the UK

- many young people, whatever their background, offend at some time, though not frequently;
- youth crime is not rising out of control (this is not to say that it is not a social problem);
- the range of crimes up to the age of seventeen tends not to be very serious;
- most young people who offend do not come to the attention of the authorities;
- most young people who offend stop without formal intervention.

Factors drawn from empirical research associated with offending behaviour tend to be drawn from recorded offending, which may tell us as much about those who get caught or who are processed through formal systems as it does about juvenile crime itself. In contrast to studies based on recorded crime, Graham and Bowling's self-report survey (1995) found only a weak relationship between social disadvantage, social class and offending. This relationship disappeared after controlling for family and school variables. Young people living in larger families were no more likely to offend than those in smaller families. However, young people living with both natural parents were found to be less likely to offend than those living with one parent or in a step family. The higher rate of juvenile offenders from lone-parent families was associated with issues of parental supervision and parent-child relations. Boys and girls who were less attached to their families were more likely to offend than those who were relatively content at home. Girls who reported disliking school and boys who reported regular truanting or school exclusion were more likely to offend than others.

Poor schooling, academic failure and being seen as 'troublesome' in school are consistently associated with delinquent activity. Anti-school peer groups can develop as a consequence of internal school activities which marginalise pupils, who then turn to alternative sources of approval and esteem. This is not to suggest that schools are to blame for delinquent activity but that through their ability to motivate, to integrate and to offer each young person a sense of achievement regardless of their ability, they can have an important influence on whether or not young people are diverted from delinquent activity. The role of schools is dealt with in Chapter 14.

There are significant gender differences in patterns of recorded crime in many studies, although it has been suggested that girls who become very frequent offenders may offend at similar rates to boys. A study of people born in 1953, 1957 and 1963 found that 30 per cent of males, as against 7 per cent of females, had been convicted at least once by age thirty-one, most offences being committed when they were juveniles (Home Office, 1985). Major differences between boys and girls are also true in Scotland. In 1994 only 21 per cent of referrals to reporters on offence grounds related to girls (Scottish Office, 1995a). Data suggest that among those who offend, a similar age-crime curve applies to females as to males. Girls are almost twice as likely to receive an official warning than boys and less likely to be referred to the children's hearings for minor offences (Samuels and Tisdale, 1996).

Data from England and Wales suggest that young black people are significantly more likely to offend than white. This may reflect differences in the rate and pattern of offending or a bias against black people. While there is evidence of bias at different stages of the criminal justice process, this offers only a partial explanation of the differences. Most commentators do not consider ethnicity as a causal factor but that racial predictors reflect environmental and socio-economic factors as well as child-rearing conditions and practices. There is no equivalent data available in Scotland. It can only be said that the vast majority of young people whose offences are recorded and who come within the children's hearings system seem to be white.

There are a few studies which shed additional information on the picture in Scotland. Anderson et al (1992) compared the less prosperous areas of Broughton and Wester Hailes in Edinburgh with the prosperous areas of Corstorphine and Marchmont. Just over two-thirds of all the young people contacted reported having committed at least one offence during the previous nine months, with a third of these reporting a serious offence. The study found no major differences relating to geography and, by implication, no major differences relating to socio-economic or class background in those who admitted offending in these different areas. The results of the study are similar to those of Graham and Bowling, supporting a view that offending may be more the norm than the exception among young people.

> 'In no sense, therefore, can "delinquency" be regarded as the preserve of any particular group or section of young people. On the contrary, rule breaking and petty crime would seem to be very much a normal feature of young people's lives, wherever they come from, and which ever school they go to' (p164).

In a study of families from three deprived areas of Glasgow, Laybourn (1986) used a checklist of 'social handicap', including social class, single-parent status, long-term unemployment, family size and quality of housing, to examine social factors associated with juvenile crime. 'Striking differences in child-rearing styles were found within a wholly working-class sample' (p 625). The research suggests that the best predictors of offending are factors related to parental supervision and care rather than factors relating to economic and material hardship *per se*. Parental attitudes towards crime and parents' expectations of the young person's behaviour were also seen as good predictors of juvenile offending. Young people from families where issues such as friendships, use of money, bedtime and behaviour were monitored carefully by parents were significantly less likely to be involved in delinquent activity.

In the main, the empirical evidence from Scotland supports the case for the maximum use of informal processes and diversion from prosecution when dealing with many children and young people who offend. In addition it suggests that any system seriously intent on addressing the problems of delinquency with a view to helping them change their behaviour needs to recognise and give special focus to parenting and family factors as well as those relating to the wider environment and the individual characteristics of the young person.

Persistent offenders

The 1990s have seen a growing public debate in the UK about the young person who persistently offends. Much public comment has been based on the widespread assumption that this group have special characteristics related to their offending and that special powers are needed to deal with them.

The debate has been hindered by the lack of any clear definition of persistence. Media discussion has focused on juveniles who, because of their persistent involvement in criminal activities, account for a large proportion of the offences committed by this age group. Politicians have seemed to focus on serious offenders and there has been a tendency to associate persistence with seriousness of offending. The media have claimed that these youngsters tend to be specialist criminals. It is often suggested that they should be removed from circulation into detention – this being seen as the most effective solution. Arguments have been used in Scotland to suggest that persistent offenders, particularly those aged between sixteen and eighteen, should be dealt with in the adult criminal justice system and not in the children's hearings system, in the belief that more punitive and restrictive measures can be brought to bear as an effective way of dealing with them. The Home Secretary in the Conservative administration proposed establishing secure training units for twelve-to-fourteen-year-olds in England and Wales on the basis of such views.

In a first attempt to identify the number of persistent young offenders in England and Wales, the Home Office conducted a study of all those under seventeen who had committed ten or more offences between April and June 1992. The study was incomplete as only thirty-three out of forty-three police services provided information. One hundred and six individuals were identified, of whom two-thirds were aged fifteen or sixteen and just over 7 per cent were aged ten and eleven. This left fewer than thirty twelve-to-fourteen-year-olds who had committed ten or more offences during the sample period.

A Home Office-commissioned study to establish common characteristics, if any, for the persistent offender provided more detailed evidence on the nature of the problem (Hagell and Newburn, 1994). From a sample of 531 ten-to-sixteen-year-olds who were arrested at least three times (convictions or alleged convictions) in 1992, the young people came from a range of backgrounds, lived in a variety of different types of home and gave a number of different accounts of their lifestyles. Girls represented only 16 per cent of the sample. The most common offences committed were traffic offences, theft from shops and car theft. Violent sexual offences and other serious violent crimes were rare. Self-report data from the group suggested that these young people were involved in a great deal of undetected or unreported crime, much of which was of a minor nature. Recorded drug offences were rare, although high levels of drug usage were reported. Most reported committing offences with others. Fifty-one percent of the whole sample were already known to social services, and patterns of familial disruption, alcohol and drug-misuse problems within their families were common, as was criminality. The researchers found that no two definitions of persistent delinquency led to the identification of the same children. An examination of common characteristics found few related to the offences themselves. There was little evidence of criminal specialism. Offences varied greatly. Patterns of offending were not continuous but tended to involve bursts of activity over short periods. However, some common themes emerged.

The commonality was less the young people's offending and more their adverse personal and social circumstances. Many had initially truanted, had then been excluded from schools and had subsequently left the education system permanently; many were not involved in education, training or employment; severe family disruption was common; the level of alcohol and drug use was high; and half those interviewed had received some form of psychological intervention or counselling. Few offended entirely on their own but usually with others they had met in care or elsewhere in the local area.

The research suggests that persistent offending is a fairly transient activity and that any definition will inevitably be arbitrary and lead to a significant degree of inequity should policy and practice be based on such a concept. The implications of the study are that if such a group are incapacitated and removed from the streets, they will quickly be replaced by a new group. Given the lack of a satisfactory definition, special provision aimed exclusively at one group is likely to miss the others.

Other research (Tarling, 1993) has challenged the proposition put by incapacitation models that identifying and removing the best-known juvenile offenders from a given area will reduce local and serious crime by anything up to 40 per cent. The evidence does not bear this out. The distribution of crime among young people seems so widespread and varied that removing a small group from a given area would make little difference to the local crime statistics.

In Scotland a study of 127 young people under the age of seventeen appearing in court found that they had many of the characteristics identified by Hagell and Newburn and Graham and Bowling (Kennedy and McIvor, 1992). They had been referred repeatedly to the reporter, had a 'lengthy history of prior social work involvement culminating in periods of ... supervision or care' and 'a range of family and personal problems'. Fifty-three per cent of the sample had made previous appearances in the children's hearings system (66 per cent of those sixteen and under and 42 per cent of those aged seventeen). Seventy per cent were unemployed; 62 per cent of seventeen-year-olds and 50 per cent of the younger group had no source of income; less than a third were raised by both natural parents; 40 per cent had a history of truancy. Eighty-three per cent left school without any qualifications and 27 per cent had been in residential care. While most had relatively stable living situations with parents, relatives or friends, 10 per cent were described as 'in transient accommodation or had no fixed address' (p 41). Eighteen per cent of those young people with a history of residential care received detention, compared with 3 per cent of others in the sample.

The study concludes that, in the hearings system, 'there is a lack of resources geared at addressing offending behaviour and the factors which surround it' (p 45) and suggests that the circumstances of some young people deteriorate following discharge from the system, particularly those who have been in residential care, placing them at high risk of custody.

Johnstone's study (1995) of sixteen-year-olds appearing in another court in Scotland found that almost 60 per cent had previously been involved in the hearings system. In only six cases was referral to the system suggested to the courts, and in only one case was a referral made.

These studies support the case that systems should address social adversity as well as provide effective help in reducing offending behaviour.

Effective intervention with young people who offend

Many politicians and professionals were influenced by the view promoted in the early 1970s that almost nothing works in reducing offending behaviour (Martinson, 1974). Since the mid-1980s a number of reviews of that research and later research have been undertaken using the statistical tool of meta-analysis. This method, while not without its limitations, has been developed to allow reviewers to combine the statistical results of a number of studies into a single database which allows the results to be expressed by common measures of effect size.

Garrett (1985) surveyed 111 experimental studies carried out between 1960 and 1983 in Europe and the USA, incorporating a total of more than 13,000 juvenile offenders. She found a significant overall effect of intervention on a variety of outcomes, including reoffending. 'The change was modest in some cases, substantial in others, but overwhelmingly in a positive direction' (p 293). The most powerful approaches were cognitive-behavioural, life skills and family approaches.

Gendreau and Ross (1987) carried out a series of detailed literature reviews on European and American studies published between 1971 and 1981 and further reviewed over 300 studies published between 1981 and 1987, most of which involved juvenile offenders. They presented evidence that 'reduction in recidivism, sometimes as substantial as 80%, had been achieved in a considerable number of well-controlled studies' (p350). They concluded:

> '[I]t is downright ridiculous to say "Nothing Works". This review attests that much is going on to indicate that offender rehabilitation has been, can be and will be achieved. The principles underlying effective rehabilitation generalise across far too many intervention strategies and offender samples to be dismissed as trivial' (p395).

Lipsey's review (1992a) of 400 experimental outcome studies published in English-speaking countries since 1950 included 40,000 offenders, mainly juveniles. He found that 65 per cent of the experiments showed positive effects in reducing reoffending. Behavioural, skill-oriented approaches and combinations of approaches (multimodal) had most impact. Deterrence or 'shock' approaches were associated with negative outcomes compared with control groups. When all types of programmes and outcomes were combined, reoffending averaged 9 to 12 per cent lower than for control groups. For multimodal behavioural and skill-oriented approaches, the reoffending rate was 20 to 32 per cent lower than for control groups.

Detailed findings of meta-analytic reviews are beyond the scope of this chapter. It should be noted, however, that the mean-effect size conceals wide variations and many studies have much larger reductions in reoffence rates. Some clear trends are emerging from the research concerning the content of intervention programmes with higher and lower levels of effectiveness in reducing offending.

Andrews *et al* (1990), in their meta-analysis of 150 research reports on juvenile and adult offenders, concluded that 'reviews of recidivism rates will reveal that, on average, appropriate treatment cut recidivism rates by about 50% (in fact the mean reduction was 53.06%)' (p385).

They suggest that the most effective forms of intervention conform to five broad principles.

Risk principle

Maximum levels of intervention should be reserved for the highest risk behaviour. Low-risk offending behaviour requires lower levels of intervention, with grades in between.

Criminogenic need principle

Intervention should focus on intermediate criminogenic (crime-related or crime-producing) targets which contribute to the risk of offending. The most promising intermediate targets include antisocial attitudes, habitual patterns of thought, personal control issues, peer associations and promoting familial affection.

Responsivity principle
Programmes of intervention should be matched to the way young people change and learn; this also requires matching staff skills to client need. The most successful programmes are, generally but not exclusively, directed by behavioural or social learning principles and include a cognitive component which focuses on challenging attitudes, values and beliefs that support antisocial behaviour, on modelling and skill development through rehearsal and role playing.

Community-based principle
The evidence for the effectiveness of community-based intervention is much stronger than that for residential or institutionally based intervention.

Programme integrity principle
Effective programmes have clear and stated aims and objectives; are carried out by staff who are specifically trained and skilled in the particular method; are adequately resourced and managed; the programme initiators are involved in all the management phases of the programme; and the programme is subjected to some form of evaluation.

The reviews conclude, in general, that effective intervention must be well focused, consistent and adapted both to the characteristics of the young person who offends and to the problem behaviour (offending) presented.

The evidence from such reviews offers cautious optimism that many approaches to working with young people who offend can be effective in reducing offending. It provides support for those who claim that juvenile offenders' antisocial attitudes can be amended, self-esteem can be boosted, skills can be acquired for making better prosocial decisions for resisting pressures to commit offences and for better self-management.

The most successful approaches offer scope for the involvement of significant family members in the decision-making and supervision process. Effective intervention is likely to combine work with individuals, with families and with groups. Some distinctions can be made between those approaches associated with significant positive effect and those that have very little or even negative effects.

The value of classical psychotherapeutic models has emerged as questionable. The programmes that were ineffective were those that were long-term in nature and frequently employed psychotherapy or group-therapy approaches (McGuire and Priestley, 1995). Similar findings apply to individual casework counselling. Sheldon (1994), while emphasising that counselling approaches in other fields of social work have produced positive gains, acknowledges

'that without undue pessimism ... rarely do we see offenders exposed to a therapeutic programme giving up criminal behaviour in large numbers in comparison with their control counterparts and maintaining these gains at two-year follow up' (p226).

Counselling methods seem to have a more positive effect when they are part of a multimodal approach. Russell (1991) suggests that, insofar as recent evaluations of casework counselling have been more encouraging, it is because more structured approaches, such as task-centred or behaviourally based methods, have been adopted within it.

The research indicates that effectiveness is greatest where there is

- a focus on the nature and consequences of the offending behaviour;
- an emphasis on problem solving and behaviour change, cognitive development, personal or social skills;
- a diversity of methods of intervention;
- use of positive authority;
- an emphasis on community integration.

The Scottish hearings system and the young offender

There is a growing consensus among commentators which recognises that a full understanding of the juvenile offender requires a knowledge of the background of crime, the social and moral context of opting for criminal behaviour, the situation of committing crime, its enactment in time and space, as well as the processes of detection and responses to the offender and to the victim.

Early intervention can assist children, families and communities to develop personal and cultural norms of social control through preventive measures. Research emphasises the importance of community-based and social-education approaches, which support the Kilbrandon Committee's contention (Kilbrandon, 1964) that attempting to define young people in criminal terms alone is an ineffective form of classification and that a key to helping young people address and change their offending behaviour lies in providing community-based preventive services focused on the individual and the family. The principles on which the hearings system are founded seem sound.

Scottish data support the view that the system operates effectively as a method of diversion for most children and young people in that about 60 per cent of referrals to reporters on grounds of offending are not brought before a hearing, with no obvious negative effects on the general picture of offending within the country. The picture in relation to serious or persistent offenders is much less clear.

Difficult and troubled young people, although small in number, present problems for all systems. However, the hallmark of a system built on child-centred, educational approaches to provision should be its ability to apply these principles in some measure to such young people. Nothing focuses more on the validity of the claims of a child-centred approach to intervention than the issue of child custody. Many euphemisms have grown up around resources used for controlling difficult children and young people, as if intent on softening the reality of locking up children in institutions especially designed for containment 'for their own good'. Kelly's detailed account of a secure unit (1992) highlights the tension between principle (or perhaps rhetoric) and practice in Scotland in dealing with the thorny problem of providing meaningful control and effective care.

It is difficult to get precise figures because of the nature of the activity, which can range from children being formally detained under criminal proceedings for serious offences, to those placed in secure care under the Social Work (Scotland) Act 1968 for their safety or the safety of others, to care practices such as close support, drug régimes in psychiatric units, and practices highlighted by 'pin down', all of which expose difficult and troubled children to many forms of control/incarceration with varying levels of public accountability for the acts.

Two legal principles drawn from the European and UN Conventions are intended to direct practice: every child deprived of liberty shall be separated from adults unless it is considered in the children's best interests not to do so; and secure care should be used as a measure of last resort and for the shortest appropriate period of time. A Scottish Office review of secure accommodation (SWSI, 1996a) states clearly that 'at the moment these two principles are not being met' in Scotland (para 73).

It estimated that Scotland has proportionately 30 per cent more secure places than England (para 85). They are generally full and in constant demand. Most places are used for young people aged fifteen to eighteen. The number of young people being kept in prison in Scotland is increasing (para 74). This seems directly related to a log jam in secure care. In addition, the review estimates that, in 1992–93, 500 young people were held in police custody on 'unruly' certificates when guidance indicates that these young people should have been in a place of safety under the care of the social work department.

Many of the children were already in the long-term care of the local authority when placed in secure care (para 51) and most were placed by children's hearings (para 35). Yet the review suggests, as have other commentators (Littlewood, 1996), that there are few apparent differences between many children in secure care and children in other forms of care.

Why should the Scottish youth population, which shows no distinctive features from other countries, require so many containment facilities?

Scarcity of normal resources has the knock-on effect that 'far from being used as a last resort, secure care is being used to make up for there being fewer residential school places' (para 77) and limited community-based alternatives to deal with difficult behaviour from its onset. The review, sensibly, avoids any knee-jerk reaction to recommend more secure care and confirms the view put by the 1993 White Paper, Scotland's Children, that there is 'considerable scope for improved local multi-agency collaboration in providing effective services for children who present special problems in the development of normal personal self-control' (para 7.26).

Good assessment is crucial if early intervention is to be effective and requires the existence of community-based projects which directly address offending and difficult behaviour by providing routinely available, intensive day programmes. Intensive community-based support units and well structured, adequately staffed residential units are required for these most difficult and vulnerable young people in our society.

The findings of the Scottish Office review do not, in themselves, undermine the principles of the hearings system but suggest that the system may not always be operating 'in the best interests' of the most difficult and troubled young people. The hearings system is built on a series of checks and balances. The gatekeepers to secure care – sheriffs, panel members, police and chief social work officers – must use consistent and explicit criteria for placement. An improved review system is required which promotes vigilance and allows justice and care to operate more effectively.

Scotland's Children refers specifically to the need for the system to use its existing powers to deal with more sixteen- and seventeen-year-olds in keeping with the spirit of the United Nations Convention on the Rights of the Child (1989), which emphasises the special status of this group and promotes special provisions for dealing with them (para 7.8). There are legal provisions in Scotland to facilitate this. In addition to requirements for courts to take the advice of hearings when dealing with any young person over sixteen and under eighteen subject to supervision, the Criminal Procedure (Scotland) Act 1995 (s 49) makes specific provision for courts to seek advice from the children's hearings on disposals when dealing with most young people under the age of eighteen and under certain circumstances to remit them directly to the hearings system for disposal if they so wish.

Empirical data discussed above give some weight to the view that the most persistent offenders are discharged prematurely from the hearings system only to face the full force of the adult system shortly afterwards. Statistical data show that the hearings system deals with very few young people in this age group. In 1994 of the 25,735 referrals to reporters on grounds of offences, only 325 related to sixteen-year-olds and 117 to seventeen-year-olds (Scottish Office, 1995b). There may be practical and legal reasons, as in car-related crime. However, the system would seem to be failing to recognise the special status of sixteen- and seventeen-year-old offenders by dealing routinely with them in the adult criminal courts. The adult court seldom refers or remits this age group to the hearings system except where required by law, and few social enquiry reports recommend this option to the summary courts.

This apparent failure of the courts to utilise fully the provisions in Scottish legislation may lie partly with the Crown Office. Procurators fiscal would seem to prosecute sixteen- and seventeen-year-olds unless special circumstances indicate that they should be dealt with by the hearings. It is likely that fiscals have insufficient information on the social circumstances of young people under eighteen years coming to their attention to allow them to apply the White Paper's 'test' of maturity or to assist them in making an appropriate decision in balancing public interest with the welfare of the young person. Section 66 of the Criminal Justice (Scotland) Act 1995 is intended to address this issue. It introduces a new provision in the Social Work (Scotland) Act 1968 (s 27(1)(ab)) which allows the Lord Advocate or procurators fiscal to seek reports from local authority social work departments on those aged sixteen to seventeen who come to their attention to assist their decision-making.

It is possible that some participants in the system believe that young people who offend are more effectively dealt with in the adult court. There is no research evidence to support the view that punitive, coercive or custodial responses have any positive effect on reducing crime among children and young people. Overall the evidence indicates that such approaches have a destructive and negative effect. Lipsey's review of punishment régimes (1992b), such as 'shock' incarceration, 'boot' camps and intensive surveillance, found that the average outcome was a 25 per cent increase in reoffence rates compared with control groups. The Audit Commission (1996) review of the youth justice system in England and Wales concluded that its 'arrangements are failing young people' (para 152) and that 'it would be better to prevent the offending behaviour in the first place' (para 79).

The commitment to community-based preventive intervention, emphasised by the hearings system, requires an optimism that services can be provided which will have a positive impact on the young person's life and which are seen to work in assisting them reduce their offending behaviour. This will require a multi-agency approach.

Although the evidence examined above is encouraging as regards the possibility of reducing reoffending, the same approaches do not necessarily work for all young people. There are considerable gaps in research on criminogenic needs to assist practitioners in understanding the factors influencing different types of offence behaviour and how best to respond to them. Evaluation of the effectiveness of service provision needs to be given priority.

Policy makers have a responsibility to ensure that sufficient resources are available through the hearings system for young people who are caught up in crime. The question of whether specialist child-care social workers are adequately equipped to intervene effectively with juvenile offenders needs to be addressed as a matter of some urgency.

The children's hearings system has many strengths, philosophically and practically, that are supported by research on juvenile offenders. Research findings on effective intervention are consistent with the social-education approach promoted by the Kilbrandon philosophy. The system requires to build on these strengths and to focus more of its effort on the serious and persistent juvenile offender, particularly those aged fifteen to eighteen, and to demonstrate that most 'rediscovered delinquents' can be assisted in addressing and reducing their offending within its framework.

14 : Reconstructing Social Education

Russell Forrest

Introductory reflections

The 'matching field organisation' envisaged by Kilbrandon in 1964 was to be one which would see the bringing together of all the services required to support children and families in the essential educational task of 'self-help and self-discovery': the concept underpinning this ideal was one of providing children and families with opportunities for a 'social education' or, more dynamically, an 'education for social living'. An eloquent analysis by Kilbrandon of the social conditions affecting children's development at home and at school gave rise to the idea that children, whether 'delinquent' or 'at risk', shared a common heritage as 'hostages to fortune' (Kilbrandon, 1964, para 251, p97).

The bringing together of children who were 'offenders' with those 'in need of care and protection' within a common dimension of need for social education was a major step forward in thinking about children's needs against the background of a divisive categorisation of children – for example, in terms of admission to industrial and reformatory schools and, later, to List D[1] and List G[2] schools.

Children's needs (a term disputed in educational language, as evidenced below) in respect of that assessment had, arguably, always been viewed schismatically by society, based on archaic images of 'classes', such as good and evil, poor and perishing, deprived and depraved.

Provision for delinquent children was characteristically influenced by provisions for adult criminals; even reforming spirits of the nineteenth century were still, to some extent, influenced by ideas of rescuing souls and applying restorative correction.

However, in Edinburgh in 1847 Dr Guthrie had expressed the view that 'children in need of care or protection, children beyond their parents' control, and truants ... should be committed to the care of the Education Authority and boarded out with foster parents'. His attitude to offenders was no less enlightened, arguing that 'these unhappy children are suffering for the crimes of their parents and the neglect of society' (Guthrie, 1847).

One hundred years later the Scottish Advisory Council in a report, Approved

[1] Formerly approved schools under the direction of the Scottish Office for children who were 'offenders' sentenced by juvenile courts in Scotland.
[2] Formerly schools for 'maladjusted' children (normally 'non-offenders'), usually managed by independent trusts or by the private sector. Both sets of schools are recognised on a list of schools registered by the Scottish Office, hence the terms List D and List G.

Schools, reflected that 'it cannot be assumed that the child who is an "offender" is *ipso facto* less worthy of sympathy, less in need of care and protection'.

> 'Children of both categories have usually come from similar environments and have been the victims of similar circumstances, and it is often merely fortuitous that one has appeared in court as an offender and the other as a child needing care or protection.'

Dr Guthrie's remedy in 1847 had been defined in terms of 'a good common and Christian Education and by training them to habits of regular industry ... and a reasonable allowance of time for play' (see also Chapter 1).

A major step in the right direction was also taken by Kilbrandon in 1964 in proposing that a child in need of these measures of social education could not be treated in isolation but rather 'as a member of a family unit in a particular environment'. The 'removal' of factors adverse to the child would involve a persuasive application of guidance in what was essentially 'an educational process for the child and his parents'. A comprehensive welfare strategy would be unfolded through the application of these measures, including elements of care, control, guidance, treatment, education, occupation and training. A radically different approach was anticipated by this proposal compared to the notions of individual deficit, pathology and psychopathology which had been derived from early medical studies of delinquents in prisons and which had given rise to the proposal of the existence of 'morbid varieties of mankind' (Maudsley, 1872, quoted in Ellis, 1890). It was said that it would not matter much whether delinquents were sentenced in *anger* and committed to the seclusion of prison, or sentenced in *sorrow* and committed to the seclusion of the asylum. The integration of feelings of anger and sorrow perhaps remains the challenge to all adults who work with troubled children. The old Norse linguistic root of both these feelings refers to a single condition which explains that the common meaning is through 'grief for the loss of a person'. It is instructive, given the later importance of 'self' and 'self-esteem' in reports on social education, and following again the roots of language, that the Celtic root of 'self' is 'selva', which means 'to possess one's own place'. For some educationalists (Dearden, 1968) 'self' has been identified as implying 'self-indulgence' and a desertion of 'traditional values' (perhaps especially, respect for authority) which require to be transmitted through the curriculum. And while Dr Guthrie's views were not derived from a perception of corrective discipline, the recommended response to such children in 'need' was defined without reference to birth-family rehabilitation or parental involvement (in that respect mirroring the general rationale of residential education (cf, Millham *et al*, 1975).

The responsibility for organising the new welfare-based, family-support model and 'matching field organisation' to underpin the children's panel was thought by Kilbrandon to lie best within Departments of Education under the direction of Directors of Education, but the Scottish Grand Committee[3] (July 1964) earnestly disagreed and argued, to the contrary, that such a disposition would be no less than 'disastrous'. That view, contradictory to Kilbrandon, put by Neil Carmichael,

---

[3] The Scottish Grand Committee is a special parliamentary committee of Scottish MPs who meet to discuss matters of particular relevance to Scotland.

MP for Glasgow Woodside (now Lord Carmichael), was based on his opinion that 'the didactic attitude to learning' in Scottish schools meant that 'our whole attitude to teaching in Scotland is not conducive to a proper integration of the problems in the family and in the school' (House of Commons Official Report, p76).

A related reason for rejecting the distinctive Kilbrandon proposal was to do with the 'question of staffing'. Neil Carmichael thought that it would take a very long time for teachers to 'slough off the classroom attitude which is so prevalent in Scotland ... and come to grips with the attitude which is necessary in successful work with individual delinquents'. In many ways, Carmichael's view could be regarded as something of an understatement given the fact that there were as yet no guidance teachers in schools, secondary schools were selective and more tellingly perhaps, schoolteachers still used corporal punishment as a sanction. It may be that Kilbrandon was influenced by an ideal of social education in schools boldly stated by the Advisory Council on Education in Scotland in 1947 when, in the Council's view, the supreme function of the mainstream school was to be 'the provision and the setting ... for ... progress toward social selfhood'. The 1947 Council, interestingly in view of the Approved School Report of 1947, also spoke of the adolescent's need for 'spiritual security', which was to be safeguarded by 'the encompassing presence of mature and balanced personalities, disinterestedly regardful of the child as a person and manifesting towards him a constant and active goodwill'. It is beyond the remit of this chapter to rehearse the background of advocacy by the Council of this kind of idealised relationship between teachers and children, but the proposal sits uneasily with modern concepts of 'negotiated' teacher–pupil relationships and the productive management of conflict of authorities (ie, between pupil and teacher, as evidenced in later reports which will be referenced below).

It might be argued that the changing nature of authority relations in families, between men and women, children and parents, and between the individual and the state in society at large (cf, Giddens, 1994), runs in parallel with an enduring and unchanged sense of the teacher, especially the head teacher, as being *in loco parentis* (cf, Handy and Aitken, 1990). Is this perhaps a lesson which has to be 'unlearned' from the assumptive 'male order' derived from the story of the Garden of Eden? The Children (Scotland) Act 1995 will require changes in this assumptive authority in the direction of *cum parentis*.

Aspects of social education in tune with Kilbrandon

In the primary sector (that is, in Scotland schools for children from five to twelve years old), however, anticipating the future emphasis to be placed on early intervention in the formative years, the Primary Memorandum of 1965 makes a significant public statement about the importance of children's needs and, by implication, defines the functions of teaching as including a form of 'specialised supplementary parenting'. The report encourages teachers to think of children's individual differences in growth and of their needs for guidance on social development, including the nature of adolescence.

It may be a telling reminder of possible reactions to such challenges to 'the establishment' (cf, Comfort, 1970), that a book contradicting this emphasis on children's needs in the Primary Memorandum of 1965, aimed at teachers in training, should be published only three years later (Dearden, 1968). Dearden reminds students that one of the original impulses of 'elementary education' was one of 'social utility', that is, 'what it is useful to teach the sons and daughters of the working classes', especially the teaching of reading, so that they should be able to read the Bible for themselves. Dearden, espousing the need (*sic*) for teachers to apply 'astringent intellectual scrutiny' to their daily task, argues that the Scottish Primary Memorandum betrayed serious errors of logic: the curriculum should not be driven by a psychology of needs, which, he deduces, are confused logically with wants, interests and desires, but rather by the transmission of values. There is not space here to do justice to the full intellectual rigour, almost surgical precision, applied by Dearden to his task, except to mark a further moment of schism in education between the needs of the child and the aims of the school and the curriculum, which are perhaps after all 'to gentle the masses', following the thesis of Freire (1996).

Adequate organisational structures to sustain such well-articulated commitments to children by primary school teachers, as argued in the Primary Memorandum, in the key areas of 'security ... freedom of choice and movement ... play and understanding ... quest for real life and imaginative [curricular] experiences ... beyond the bounds of the school', still remain to be put in place in primary schools.

An eloquent and comprehensive echo of the seminal 1965 Scottish report was given some twenty years later by an English educationalist (Bruce, 1987), who concluded that a child's education centres on an interaction between the child, others, the environment and knowledge itself.

Educational legislation in that respect of child-centredness has neither kept pace with nor is in accordance with social work legislation in facilitating, for example, the child's right to be heard. More will be said about this later in relation to school exclusion procedures, the recording of absence from school and the development of the Lothian Children's Family Charter (1992).

It was four years after the publication of the Kilbrandon Report that the Scottish Education Department paper, Guidance in Scottish Secondary Schools (SED, 1968), was published.

Young people are regarded in the report as facing new stresses in 'the increasing complexity of modern life', while '[t]he removal of certain fears and sanctions has made it easier for young people to assert themselves and challenge authority'. The 1968 paper goes on to adduce the need for young people to be provided with something akin to the 'spiritual security' envisaged by the Advisory Council in 1947 and to have compensatory guidance and personal advice from teachers in those schools where certain children and young people have a lack of such support at home. In this report reference is also made specifically to the importance for the pupil to 'know himself' – self-knowledge and the development of personhood, anticipating a significant report published later (The Heart of the

Matter, Scottish Consultative Committee on the Curriculum (SCCC, 1995), being the road to responsible membership of society.

And yet there is no explicit reference to Kilbrandon or to the anticipated needs of the children's panel system which would emerge in 1971 as Part III of the Social Work (Scotland) Act 1968. Education and family-care systems, as recognised by the Scottish Grand Committee, are not easily integrated. 'Maladjusted' children were traditionally more within the provenance of education services than were 'delinquents', as if the 'angry rejecting father', as head teacher, and the 'embattled caring mother', as social worker, were acting out an unconscious ritual in the question of blame for the production of what were in ancient times called 'unprofitable children'. Reason and emotion are still not well integrated in educational language: social workers and teachers can have very different views of 'the child'; differing perceptions based on differing work contexts, time-scales of intervention, theories of behaviour and experiences of working with parents.

Perhaps this schism is a deeply rooted element in Scottish culture, since it is Scots who have written *The Divided Self* (Laing, 1960), *The Strange Case of Dr Jekyll and Mr Hyde* (Stevenson, 1886) and *The Private Memoirs and Confessions of a Justified Sinner* (Hogg, 1824).

It is telling that the 1968 HMSO paper, Guidance in Scottish Secondary Schools, refers to young people challenging authority as 'a problem for society' and the need for 'a more sustained programme in the field of social and moral education'. It is also worthy of note that, in the later formulation of the five-to-fourteen curriculum in the 1990s, personal and social education was considered and reported on separately from moral and religious education. Perhaps more instinctively ironic, in terms of the missing reference to Kilbrandon and the Scottish Grand Committee's views on teachers, the paper takes the view that, given the need to engage young people in 'open-ended' group discussions on choices and values, it will not be an easy matter for the teacher, who has been accustomed to exercising a certain amount of authority, 'to step down, as it were, and encourage the expression of opinions that may run counter to his own'.

This theme concerning teachers' authority features in a number of other texts and papers on social education over the next twenty years, perhaps reaching its most critical moment when corporal punishment became illegal in 1986. In the meantime, it could be speculated that, in 1968, the paper on the introduction of guidance systems was closely associated with the raising of the school-leaving age from fifteen to sixteen years and with the anticipated introduction of comprehensive education in the early 1970s. It is also interesting to speculate whether any of the unstated agendas of the 1968 paper were related to an anticipated crisis in authority relations between adults and adolescents post-war. There is certainly mention in the paper of how desirable it would be to find 'some way of knitting the school (and society by implication) more closely together'.

The question of corporal punishment
Again, although there is no explicit reference to it in the 1968 paper, a Liaison Committee on Educational Matters produced in 1968 a Statement of Principles

and Code of Practice on the elimination of corporal punishment in schools. The code argued that children with special needs should not have corporal punishment inflicted upon them and advised teachers to look at behaviour problems as 'a possible symptom of maladjustment'. On the other hand, 'punishment of whatever kind should be appropriate to the blameworthiness of the child . . . and consistent . . . as regards attachment to particular categories of offences'. The proposed code did not argue for the elimination of corporal punishment, only that its use should be reduced until such time as it could be eliminated. As it turned out, the delay in time was nearly twenty years. It is interesting that the Liaison Committee felt able to agree that corporal punishment was undesirable for errors in spelling, or for infants, or for girls (especially by teachers of the opposite sex), and that certain other forms of sanction were also undesirable, such as the use of sarcasm, conduct marks, isolation and segregation, lines, and the detention of primary pupils after hours. It is as if children in mainstream schools in 1968 were, no less than others, 'hostages to fortune' in Kilbrandon's terms and perhaps through the ages (cf, De Mause, 1974).

It is instructive, in relation to the considerations and conclusions of the Scottish Grand Committee in 1964, to be reminded by this 1968 report of the extent to which schools and education managers were still responding to children within a corrective and punishment-based model of discipline, albeit mitigated by reference to special needs and vulnerable infants, but still fundamentally based on a model of child culpability and child deficit, perhaps even sinfulness – that is, a discipline 'directed to the punishment of the wrongdoer'. (It should be remarked in passing that these considerations are currently being played out all over again in Britain, notably in England, where there are proposals to 'tag' children electronically as offenders and to reintroduce corporal punishment in schools. In America one hears of retired army generals being appointed to run schools.)

On reflection, one wonders how Kilbrandon could ever have thought that a comprehensive support service as 'matching field organisation' to the entirely welfare-based children's hearings would be well and securely placed within the education service for schools.

Some local authorities moved more quickly than the law did in banning the use of corporal punishment (Education (No 2) Act 1986), which came into effect in 1987).

By 1968, of course, the Social Work (Scotland) Act was already in place, taking forward the Kilbrandon thesis of comprehensive family welfare and within Part III defining the terms of reference of the children's hearings system, which came into effect in 1971. The immediate effect of the 1968 Act on mainstream schools was minimal, but its effect on the approved schools under the administration of the Scottish Education Department, shortly to become List D schools under the Scottish Office's Social Work Services Group (see Introductory reflections above), was considerable.

Changes which would have a more significant impact on the pastoral structures and functions of mainstream schools were on their way, not through Kilbrandon but through the appointment of guidance teachers in secondary schools in the early 1970s. The 'new' guidance teachers, with responsibilities so eloquently addressed in the 1968 paper, as noted above, in terms of curricular and vocational guidance, and especially in terms of 'taking an interest in pupils as individuals', were in many schools allocated the task of administering corporal punishment. This could be regarded as truly ironic, none the more so given the statement in the 1968 paper that '[s]ome headmasters (sic) are reluctant to introduce any system of guidance because they fear it will rob them of some of the duties from which they derive the greatest satisfaction' (images of the 'angry father' at work? See above).

New visions of a social education

Help was on the way, however, in the form of reports on secondary schooling: the Munn Report (SED, 1977), and the Pack Report, Truancy and Indiscipline in Schools in Scotland (HMSO, 1977). Munn, while principally concerned with the overall aims of education in the formal curriculum and with the place of schools in the wider society, recovered the concept of balancing the formal with the informal curriculum (aims and needs, reason and emotion) and highlighted the contribution of both in helping pupils come to a responsible understanding of society. The report emphasised the importance of the 'affective development of pupils' and the development of social life in the so-called 'hidden [informal] curriculum'. A significant note of reservation in the report speaks of the importance of teaching children on an inter-subject basis how families work, including the 'family of man'.

In many ways it is unfortunate that the Pack Report, which could have been complementary to Munn, has come to be overly associated with the term 'sin bin', owing to the fact that, in matters relating to individual pupils, one of the major recommendations was that education authorities should set up 'day units' for seriously disruptive pupils and persistent truants. Many other of the Pack Committee recommendations would have been music to the ears of the 1964 Scottish Grand Committee debating Kilbrandon. Pack spoke of 'the greatest possible integration of each pupil with the school as a whole' and of other changes in the system which chime well with today's recurring dilemmas, if not practice: transition from primary to secondary education requiring serious attention; corporal punishment being phased out in secondary schools and eliminated immediately in primary schools; adequate staffing and support for staff in schools; in-service courses for teachers; avoidance of using guidance staff as 'dispensers of punishment'; social workers being attached to some schools; and the development of an interdisciplinary approach in the planning of teacher training (many of these ideas anticipating the recommendations of the Elton Committee in England in 1989).

With great insight the recommendations refer to the continuing importance of training for head teachers, of interdisciplinary co-operation in pupil support, and of the enhancement of parent and pupil participation. A statement of dissent by one of the committee members, however, challenges the absence of reference in the report to children's rights – a matter only obliquely evidenced by Kilbrandon and one which would have to await the United Nations Convention on the Rights of the Child 1989 and the Children (Scotland) Act 1995 to be more fully articulated in schools and education departments.

Echoes of concerns about the capacity of schools to deliver a fully child-centred education appeared again in 1984 when the SCCC published a position paper, *Social Education in Scottish Schools*. The report includes the statement that 'the involvement of pupils in school government in Scotland seems inadequate, space for diversity of views too restricted, the drive towards homogeneity of outlook and behaviour too powerful'. The report goes on to say also that '[t]eachers share heads' distaste for political activism or *the development of a critical attitude to authority*' (my italics). Here in 1984 was a straight reflection back, one might argue, to the 1968 Scottish Education Department report on guidance and the allusion there to problems a teacher might have in holding 'frank and open-ended' group discussions with pupils who might not share his opinions.

The development of a social education in the terms approved by Kilbrandon must surely forever remain beyond the grasp of Scottish schoolchildren if the system will not permit the proper exercise of 'critical attitudes to authority'. How else can children learn to exercise discretion and choice about their lives and come to achieve the promise of a social education whose aim is commended to be 'an education for the whole person', one advocating the 'democratic virtues ... tolerance, respect for reason and persuasion, hatred of cruelty and oppression, the willingness to surrender sectional privileges in the general interest ... and not least, an international temper of sympathy and understanding'? In 1984, when this SCCC paper was published, it was still lawful to administer corporal punishment to children at school.

The 1984 SCCC paper also argues that '[s]ocial education is concerned with the development ... of a person to function effectively as a member of many groups, eg, family, friendship, community, social and political groups'. The concept of reciprocal responsibility between the individual and the group and the attention given to 'attitudes and feelings' in a process of forming and reforming relationships defines the school as a place where children should be able to feel secure enough to make mistakes 'which are a necessary part of learning'. School management is to be about the business of facilitating 'mutual understanding'.

Interface issues between schools and the children's panel system
There are continuing operational difficulties, notwithstanding differences in value systems, in ensuring that this 'mutual understanding' is achieved 'face to face'. For example, teachers' vital attendance at hearings is now seriously constrained by budget reductions which formerly provided for 'cover' while teachers were absent from school. Such budgets have now been devolved to schools, making choices on how to spend it a matter for each head teacher. In England, the position is even more disadvantaged for children, many schools being no longer accountable to local authorities on policy matters of pupil support of any kind (cf, Blyth and Milner, 1996).

In Scotland, the ground of referral for *the child* to the children's hearings system, 'failure to attend school without reasonable excuse', is still a matter for debate where *the parents*, through educational legislation, can also be referred to attendance tribunals and onwards to court for failing to ensure regular attendance. Parents, albeit a very small number (ten out of some 12,000 referrals in one region), can be fined several hundreds of pounds while, at the same time, the child can be referred to a children's hearing as being in need of compulsory measures of care. The two systems are at odds with one another. Until the two sets of legislation are better harmonised, there will continue to be conflicting outcomes of this kind. Children in Scotland have no rights in administrative procedures defined by educational law.

There is no mention of children's hearings, however, in the SCCC paper of 1984, nor reference to that system in terms of social education and the values of welfare. While it would not be true across the board that schools failed to make much contribution to an understanding of children's needs in reports to children's panels at that time, given this degree of separation from its influence, it may well help to point up the extent to which some schoolteachers still expected that, thirteen years after the children's hearings system started, children appearing before a panel would actually be sentenced and punished in some way proportional to the 'offence'.

On the other hand, many teachers in Scotland had become members of the children's panel in their local area, and guidance teachers were undertaking sensitive work with children in terms of individual counselling. The quality of insight into children's needs available to hearings through guidance reports and through teachers attending hearings had undergone a sea change. The challenge remained for school reports to encompass 'the whole child' at school in a corporate report, as identified in an earlier book on children's hearings (Martin and Murray, 1976, p 111).

The Lothian Region youth strategy
It is of direct relevance to the progression of Kilbrandon's ideas that, in 1986, Lothian Regional Council formally adopted, through its Education and Social Work Committees, the formation of a Joint Sub-Committee on Youth Strategy to be led by the Chair of the Education Committee. The pioneering significance of this event could not have given a clearer signal that children's needs, in Kilbrandon's terms, were recognised as requiring the integration of care and education systems, working in partnership with others. The radical breakthrough achieved by the formation of the Joint Sub-Committee, apart from the key political significance of bringing together elected members from Social Work and Education Committees, lay in bringing together the main professional and voluntary support agencies for children and young people with social, emotional and behavioural difficulties, in close consultation with the children's panel, and with the lead role, following the Kilbrandon model in a quite explicit way, provided by the Chair of the Education Committee and the Education Department.

The principle of joint funding was also established at that time, ensuring, among other things, close interdepartmental planning of resource deployment. There can be no doubt that the success of the Lothian Youth Strategy policy was considerably enhanced by the political commitment to it by the Chair of the Education Committee and the extent to which she succeeded in increasing the budget for a wide variety of measures to support (the 'unprofitable') 'Kilbrandon's children'.

More significantly, from the point of view of social education, liaison groups were formed in every secondary school. These groups provided an interagency forum which advised head teachers and senior school management on the needs of the young people referred. With their own resources now enhanced, the schools could also bring into effect support programmes of various kinds in collaboration with other key agencies represented round the table: social work, psychological services, school health, community education, educational welfare, and local voluntary agencies. There was a clear readiness in 'the field' in Scotland for this kind of leadership of ideals and priorities building on existing good practice and on charismatic head teachers and staff, especially in areas of multiple social disadvantage.

It has not always been easy to convince observers that youth strategy policies are essentially about values and about valuing children and young people who traditionally were excluded from school, from their families and from their local communities to approved schools and their successors. The introduction of a full-blown welfare-based, policy-driven response to children must challenge schools and services related to schools when it is underpinned by justice-and-due-process type education legislation. Even today, the Scottish Office regards temporary exclusions as 'unauthorised absence', that is, as a matter of parental failure, while, by definition and according to a different interpretation of the same law,[4] the exclusion of a pupil from school by the head teacher surely must be accepted as a 'reasonable excuse' (that is an 'authorised absence') for that pupil not to be attending school and, facing the ultimate contradiction in law in these terms, children can be excluded from school for truancy.

There is no doubt that schools can be supported by welfare policies and programmes introduced by councils and can be more than willing in the 1990s to be receptive to the child-centred philosophies so well rooted in the Kilbrandon report of 1964. This is an especially compelling conclusion, bearing in mind that in England, given a 'free market' management style applied by the government to education, exclusions from day schools have risen by 30 per cent and more in some areas and are still rising, especially for Afro-Caribbean young people (Blyth and Milner, 1996).

There is not space here to describe in more detail the many productive initiatives which are being developed in youth strategy policies across Scotland (see below), only opportunity to mark the greater value to children of welfare over

---

[4] Reference is made here to the legal statutes: the Schools General (Scotland) Regulations 1975 (SI 1975/1135), as amended by the Education (School and Placing Information) (Scotland) Amendment Etc Regulations 1993 (SI 1993/1604); the Education (Scotland) Act 1980 (ss 35(2), 42(1)(c)).

punishment. It was Mary Carpenter, prison reformer in the nineteenth century, who said, "'Tis vain to look for change where the heart is not touched.' The development of youth strategy policies by education authorities in Scotland has also created the opportunity to witness, through direct experience, the close and interactive relations between difficult behaviour at school, early problems of literacy, truancy and economic and social disadvantage. It has highlighted the signal importance of working closely with colleagues in different sectors and departments, including pre-school services, primary and secondary schools, psychological services, community education, and services in social work departments and health services, as well as the reporters and chairs of children's panels. Meetings should be arranged systematically also to include senior personnel from the voluntary sector, housing, transport and the police. Early intervention must play a major role in a corporate strategy for children and families. The development of children's services plans under the requirements of the Children (Scotland) Act 1995 will provide a valuable opportunity to engage in this essentially collaborative process of strategic planning.

Schooling with a fresh sense of search for a social education

It is significant, as a result of the growing confidence in interagency approaches to young people 'at risk' by authorities in Scotland, that the Scottish Office felt it appropriate to mount a major conference on such work, perhaps in anticipation of local government reorganisation and certainly in contradistinction to what was happening generally in England. The conference brought together all the Scottish local authorities on an interdepartmental basis, was addressed by the Minister for Education at the Scottish Office, and resulted in the publication of Schooling with Care? – a major contribution to the whole enterprise of joint programming for children (Munn, ed, 1994). Perhaps the question mark is a telling one. More telling was the Minister's reference to the 'pioneering work in this area' by Lothian Regional Council and by other councils in Scotland.

Significant successes with this type of approach were reported by Tayside, Strathclyde, Fife, Central, Grampian and Lothian, and were identified with particular reference to the integration of policy, management, assessment, learning and teaching, and, perhaps more fundamentally, the importance of staff development (McLean, 1990). It is a matter of some significance that young people in care, from the Who Cares? organisation, made a great impact in the opening session of the conference in reporting directly to delegates what it felt like to be at school and 'in care' at the same time.

It has already become apparent (Blyth and Milner, 1996) that children in the formal care of councils are doubly disadvantaged in being greatly overrepresented in long-term exclusions from school; further research is required to consider in depth their invariably poor educational experience and achievement (cf, Francis and Thomson, 1995).

Scotland, in terms of its care and protection of children, especially owing to the influence since 1971 of children's hearings, is arguably ready for a resurgence of energy towards an 'education for social living' for all children, but it is still waiting for a 'matching field' in education to balance the 'social' half of the equation, particularly in terms of teacher training.

The fact that so many of the pupils presenting behavioural problems in secondary schools are picked up with learning difficulties in early primary and come from families where unemployment and related adversities are apparent reaffirms Kilbrandon's view of them as 'hostages to fortune'. Youth strategies serve to re-emphasise the critical part which school senior management can play in creating a coherent school ethos (cf, Ainscow, 1991; Schon, 1991), where schools become 'problem solving organisations' and teachers, after Schon, 'reflective practitioners'. The curriculum, however, is too crowded to allow this at the present time and the classroom teacher's task overly determined by 'paperwork'.

There is nothing new here for panel members, it might be said, responding since 1971 to the challenges of Kilbrandon and giving time to listen to children, but there is a considerable challenge to many professionals in education who are still coming to terms with the loss of the sanction of corporal punishment from the early 1980s onwards. This central issue of 'discipline' is a continuing factor not only in Scotland, as earlier described, but also in England, as noted above. In a seminal report on English primary education (Plowden, 1967), a note of reservation refers to a concern that, if corporal punishment is abolished, 'teachers in difficult areas will be placed in an impossible position if they are forbidden to use a reasonable amount of force by way of correction, *and if the children know that they are forbidden to do so*' (my italics).

Children's rights at the heart of the matter
Perhaps the most contentious programme to emerge from Scottish youth strategy initiatives is one which perhaps best encompasses all the strivings for excellence in services to children across Scotland, namely the programme deriving from the United Nations Convention on the Rights of the Child 1989, the Lothian Children's Family Charter (1992).

The value it added to all that was going on already was clearly twofold, one to do with the involvement and participation of pupils in school procedures and the other to do with creating an opportunity to locate children's rights directly in the personal and social development component of the five-to-fourteen curriculum. This particular approach has the potential to generate a 'personal and social matrix' for schools to use in co-ordinating the effects on the whole school and on the whole curriculum of child growth, health, well-being and personal safety/ protection initiatives of many different kinds.

Delegate conferences for P7 pupils in Lothian during 1994–95 allowed the process to be taken a step further. There are imaginative developments of this type of participation in one council in the West of Scotland where a pupil sits alongside politicians on the Education Committee and in Edinburgh where there is a proposal to hold a children's parliament.

The Lothian Children's Family Charter also brought into play for the first time anywhere in Britain (Buist *et al*, 1993) a children's adjudicator, who is to hear and report back to departments on complaints by children and young people that their entitlements under the charter have been infringed (Finlayson, 1996).

Reference must also be made to the contribution made by The Heart of the Matter, a further paper published by the SCCC in 1995. The language of the report is perhaps the most eloquent to date in its exposition of an education which will bring young people to 'ways of understanding and behaving which help to structure the inner self'. Central to the prospering of a just and democratic society are, according to the report, respect and caring for self; respect and caring for others; a sense of social responsibility; commitment to [life-long] learning; and a sense of belonging. Teaching is defined as 'a series of conversations' (ie, 'dialogical' rather than 'instrumental'). There is a clear definition of relationships which can take learner and teacher 'down unpredictable avenues of enquiry' (Kilbrandon's notion of 'self-discovery'?). Reports to hearings could then take a 'narrative' form, that is, where the child's story of school life is told from the child's point of view.

The Heart of the Matter concludes that 'it may well now be necessary to take a more coherent and co-ordinated view of the continuing professional development requirements of all teachers'. In that respect, once again, there is a compelling acknowledgement that, since the time of Dr Guthrie, the central task in being able to offer young people a truly social education has been argued to lie in the field of teacher training and staff development. Delegates at the Schooling with Care? Conference in 1994 unanimously agreed that it was time to undertake pre- and post-qualifying teacher training on an interagency basis.

And what of the structure of secondary schools? In any one day a teacher of eleven- and twelve-year-olds will meet some 200 pupils (seven classes of thirty), and the experience of four- and five-year-olds leaving nursery groups of ten to learn in classes of thirty-three will also have to be reconsidered. Scotland is nearly alone in Europe in sending children to primary school at four or five years of age. But a deeper understanding of the psychology of childhood must help inform the structures for learning that we provide, whether at four or five years of age, when children are challenged by absence of continuity of care by parents, or at eleven or twelve years of age, when children are challenged by puberty in their continuity of identity.

In addition to these psychodynamic pressures of the life cycle, head teachers in the new millenium will be faced with the demands of leading (or of being 'lead learner') in interactive 'management networks', where such management, 'after the experience of "direct rule", will feel like changing from power to sail, needing sensitivity rather than power, touch instead of force' (Ross, 1994). There could be no more appropriate metaphor for a comparison as between the organisation of the Scottish children's hearings and the juvenile courts.

15 : The Contribution of Research

Kathleen Murray

A LTHOUGH there has been no shortage of discussion and argument about the children's hearings system throughout its twenty-six-year history, the volume of serious research has remained fairly small. The system is not in this respect unique or even unusual. The various processes that shape British social legislation and administrative policies rarely involve systematic research. Unsurprisingly, therefore, the Kilbrandon Committee appears to have made no use of research findings in reaching its recommendations and neither the Social Work (Scotland) Act 1968 nor the Children (Scotland) Act 1995 was preceded by any large-scale investigation of the problems at which it was directed.

Changes in social policy tend to defy research penetration, partly because the objectives are rarely formulated with the precision and clarity which are needed for a systematic evaluation of performance. For example, the layman may wish to know whether the children's hearings system 'has worked' or 'has been a success', but these are not questions to which the research worker can give a direct answer. This is not because evasiveness holds any attractions but because there is no explicit or self-evident criterion of success; even if a criterion can be tentatively identified 'for the sake of argument' – for example, the reduction of delinquency – changes over time in the relevant measurements may be related to factors quite other than the operation of the justice system (Martin *et al*, 1981).

Yet research is not a mysterious or esoteric activity; it involves the systematic use of objective methods in order to construct an undistorted account of some aspect of our society. Through studies designed to illuminate the workings of justice systems it may be possible to achieve greater self-awareness and more thoughtful and effective practice on the part of the lay and professional participants. At the same time we should not harbour any illusions that research-based knowledge will necessarily prevail over emotional convictions and ideological prejudice.

The first enquiries
Varying practices
When Joe Curran carried out his review of research for the Scottish Office in 1977, the hearings system was in its sixth year (Curran, 1977). The twenty-three pieces of work he identified were of varying nature and quality but provided a

useful overview of the working of the system in different geographical areas. Some were small-scale investigations of particular aspects – for example, studies of actual hearings – others were wider-ranging descriptions of the ways in which children were processed through the various stages of the system. For example, a study by Allison Morris and Mary McIsaac, funded by the Scottish Office, illustrated the variations among reporters in the percentage of cases they referred to children's hearings and was able to show, at least in part, that variations were the result of differential use being made by police forces of the filter process of juvenile warnings (Morris with McIsaac, 1978). Curran considered that such findings lent support to the notion of juvenile justice as a system – influences at one stage of the process having implications, often unforeseen, for other stages. But the findings also suggest that not one but many systems may be in operation depending, perhaps, upon geographical variations (Curran, 1983). During subsequent years, the regional variations in reporters' practices continued to attract research attention (Martin *et al*, 1981; Lockyer, 1988; Finlayson, 1992).

A dual system
Curran (1983) cites the writing of John Croft (1981) who suggested that 'it is rare for one project to lead to or be identified positively with one policy decision; for the most part, the effect of research is cumulative and as much negative – the destruction of myths – as positive'. One such myth which developed in the early years of the hearings system was the result of the existence of the residual right to prosecute children in Scotland – a provision designed, in the public interest, when a very serious crime was involved and, in addition, when the needs of justice demanded a court hearing. The end result of this dual system – court or hearing – could often however be the same – residence in a List D school. The myth had it that those boys sent to List D schools by the courts created more problems for the schools than those offenders referred by a children's panel.

A detailed study of the social and offence characteristics of both groups of boys and of their behaviour in the schools suggested there was little reason to draw distinctions between them (Rushforth, 1977). This study helped to dispel a myth but perhaps almost as importantly drew attention both to the ambiguities and confusions created by a dual system for dealing with children who break the law and to the severely deprived backgrounds of both groups of boys. The research report was widely discussed at the time by children's panel members and social workers in training (Curran, 1983).

Care and control
During the first decade of the system there was a preoccupation with characterising the ideologies demonstrated by different participants in the hearing process. Both Morris and Giller (1983) and Asquith (1983) and other writers who examined the hearings system in its early years were instrumental in highlighting the tension between care and control, treatment and punishment that existed in the Kilbrandon Committee's report and in the subsequent White Paper (Asquith,

1977; May, 1971, 1977, 1979; Smith, 1977, 1978a, 1978b; May and Smith, 1970).
Curran (1983) wrote:

> 'If there was any complacency during these early years about the good intentions of the
> children's hearings system then the study by Morris and McIsaac surely had a salutary
> effect, emphasising as it did that the progress of a child through the various stages of the
> system and through the limited options open to the hearings was, in effect, governed by
> an implicit tariff system dictated by criteria such as the seriousness of the offence and
> the number of previous appearances' (pp5–6).

The new system, therefore, could be guilty of over-zealous intervention and
thinly disguised punitiveness. However, Stewart Asquith's comparative study of
juvenile justice in Scotland and England emphasised that the tariff identified by
Morris and McIsaac need not be seen as a negation of the welfare philosophy
underpinning the hearings system, if the seriousness of the offence and the
number of earlier appearances are interpreted by the reporter and by panel
members as indicators of need (Asquith, 1983). Furthermore, the studies carried
out by Martin *et al* (1981) revealed that the observed behavioural and attitudinal
realities of the hearings system were firmly in tune with the welfare principles.
Their findings provided strong empirical support for a critique of the 'Justice for
Children' lobby.

Ideological discussions were not limited to academic debate. A number of the
writers were members of children's panels and others participated in panel-
member training. They were therefore a forceful influence on the climate of
opinion that prevailed among the principal decision-makers.

Children's panel members
Social characteristics
The early research findings on the occupational class of panel members quickly
attracted widespread attention (Smith and May, 1971; Rowe, 1972; Mapstone,
1973; Moody, 1976). These studies all demonstrated the relatively high proportion
of panel members drawn from white-collar occupations in general and from
teaching in particular. They also found that manual workers constituted a minority
of applicants for panel membership and a slightly smaller minority of those
accepted. Such findings were discussed in terms of their compatibility with the
intentions underlying the creation of the new system. Although the 1966 White
Paper which preceded the Social Work (Scotland) Bill had emphasised the
desirability of panels being drawn from a wide range of occupational and income
groups, it had not suggested that they should constitute a representative cross-
section of Scottish society or of particular local communities. Nevertheless, in
terms of their socio-economic backgrounds at least, panel members were
considered far too middle-class to be seen as representatives of the Scottish
community. Curran (1983) notes: 'This finding in its solitary splendour drew a
reaction from the Scottish Office which sought to encourage those responsible for
the selection of panel members to cast their nets wider.'

By the time Jones and Adler (1990) carried out their research for the Scottish
Consumer Council in 1988, they found that other adjudicative systems involving

laymen had much to learn from the active recruitment strategies that were then being employed in the children's hearings system. They also commended the training of people responsible for selection that had been developed by a number of Children's Panel Advisory Committees.

Personal characteristics

Somewhat less controversial were the results of a small number of studies of the personal characteristics of panel members. Clark (1977) compared successful and unsuccessful applicants for panel membership in north-east Scotland, using Cattell's 16PF questionnaire, but found no significant differences between the two (small) groups. However, two non-significant tendencies were observed: for successful applicants to score higher on Factor C (emotionally stable, calm, mature) and lower on Factor L (trusting, adaptable, easy to get on with). Barrie (1977) used substantially the same method with a larger sample, and found that the selected applicants were in general more sociable, more assertive and independent.

Perhaps the most interesting finding was that of Higgins (1979), who gave the Eysenck Personality Inventory and the Marlowe-Crowne Social Desirability Scale to Scotland-wide samples of panel members, and showed them to be slightly above average with respect to introversion and prone to approval-seeking. The findings with respect to social desirability are particularly interesting in light of other research findings showing that high scorers tend to be susceptible to persuasion, responsive to perceived situational demands, reluctant to recognise failure and inclined to suppress their own aggression (Crowne and Marlowe, 1964).

Beliefs and attitudes to justice

Because panel members came from middle-class backgrounds it was argued that their values contrasted sharply with the values of the predominantly working-class delinquents on whom they sit in judgment. The expected result was a lack of understanding and empathy, an assumption that 'middle-class' values are the only valid ones, and to the imposition of measures of control which aim to achieve a shift from supposedly less desirable to more desirable social values. But as Martin and Murray (1981) pointed out, since these ideas were never subjected to empirical enquiry, they were no more than casual assertion.

Given the relative informality of children's hearings and the considerable measure of freedom with which panel members operate, it may be assumed that both the style of the proceedings and the decisions reached are influenced by the attitudes and values of the participants. The broad range of social attitudes, the variety of views on the causes of delinquency and on alternative ways of dealing with it which exist within panel membership were studied by means of questionnaire and personal interview (Martin *et al*, 1981). The authors concluded that whatever the respective influences of selection and training and initial self-selection, practising children's panel members share to a substantial extent a common body of values and beliefs.

'Such variations as exist are not patterned according to age, sex or occupational class. In this sense panel members resemble members of a political or social movement. However, their relatively high degree of acceptability in the eyes of their clients is achieved, at least in part, by some departure from strongly held principles when explicit adherence to them might generate tension or conflict' (p 159).

The attitudes of panel members towards justice were studied by Ollenburger (1987) by means of a questionnaire completed by a representative sample of 301 panel members. Panel members' attitudes towards punishment, crime causation and societal control of deviant behaviour were examined. The findings were that panel members as a group held less 'classical attitudes toward justice' than does the general population. The 'classical tradition' in criminology supports a strong deterrent element through the use of punishment, which reflects the assumption of 'free will' and rational choice on the part of the offender. This approach places its primary emphasis on choice and the responsibility of the juvenile offender. The social or 'non-classical tradition' looks to the community, family and social environment as responsible for criminal violations. This approach strongly reflects the welfare approach to the children's hearing, since it perceives juvenile delinquency and criminal behaviour as the result of a lack of proper socialisation and community controls. Ollenburger found that 'occupational status, educational achievement and gender were significant predictors of panel members' attitudes towards justice' (p372). The panel members without university degrees held the most classical attitudes towards justice. Gender was the next most significant correlate of attitudes, with men holding more classical attitudes towards justice than women. Panel members holding professional positions had the least classical attitudes, although this relationship was reduced in strength after controlling for education, sex and age. The findings had important implications for the decision-making bodies concerned with the recruitment, selection and training of panel members.

Panel members' service
Lockyer (1992), on behalf of the Children's Panel Chairmen's Group, carried out a questionnaire survey of panel members with a view to identifying the issues associated with panel membership and how their work could be supported and sustained. There was a long-standing concern among the panel chairmen that length of service and availability were negatively affected, possibly by difficulty with release from work, inadequate reimbursement and falling morale. Lockyer focused on the distinctive characteristics of panel members – their perception of the system itself and to what extent they derive satisfaction from the service they give; their time commitment and other costs; their other commitments and responsibilities.

The study concluded that panel members were less than fully satisfied with what had been accomplished and were eager that the system should progress as an agency for change. In particular they believed that if the system was better understood by the public at large, it would be more valued and supported. The study identified a major ambivalence among the panel membership. Panel members wanted to be seen as 'ordinary people' like the families they served, but they also wanted their work to be recognised and respected by those within the system, by their employers and by the wider public.

Quality of panel members' practice
No published study has been designed with the primary object of delineating strengths and weaknesses in the performance of panel members. However, in the course of a wide-ranging study of decision-making by hearings a number of inadequacies were revealed (Martin *et al*, 1981). Problems were observed to arise principally in the observance of procedural requirements, in an occasional tendency to block family participation by the use of particular modes of speech, and in a widespread avoidance of serious engagement with parents. All these observations had important implications for training.

In view of the recent upsurge of public interest in and concern about child abuse and neglect, surprisingly little research attention has been given to the problems raised for members of children's hearings by this group of referrals. The only systematic enquiry that has so far been reported drew on observation at forty-three such hearings (Martin *et al*, 1982).The key message from this research was that panel members are heavily dependent on social workers' recommendations, are reluctant to open up sensitive areas for discussion, even though they may be of central importance, and apparently lack curiosity about the arrangements made for children removed from their homes, and the implications of these. In general, it was concluded that the anxiety generated by child abuse and neglect prevented panel members from recognising the distinctive features of their role in the decision-making process and led them to fall back on an inappropriate model of practice derived from delinquency hearings. An alternative model of practice was proposed (Martin *et al*, 1982). The findings were the subject of a week-end school for panel members and were subsequently incorporated in a training video (Murray, 1981).

Reporters to the children's panel
Intake official
In the children's hearings system a central role has been allocated to the reporter, who may receive referrals from any source and has unfettered discretion to decide whether to retain the referral within the hearings system or to proceed no further. It has been evident since the first statistics on the system appeared that reporters exercise their discretion quite liberally, diverting from the system at least as many children as they keep within it.

The first study of the reporter's role (Morris with McIsaac, 1978) concluded that the child's prior record, the value of the property involved, where relevant, the number of offences involved in the current referral and, in the city, the nature of the offence were significant influences upon the decision whether to take or not to take formal action. Morris was conscious of the considerable volume of personal information that the reporter often has at his disposal and of its possible contribution to his thinking, but hesitated to assess the weight of that contribution.

Martin *et al* (1981) were especially interested in reporters' discretion. From an analysis of the factors affecting some 700 decisions by reporters it emerged that the decision to refer to a hearing was influenced, in the case of first referrals, by factors in the child's background, school attendance and whether or not there were problems at home or school. In the case of second or subsequent referrals, the reporters gave greater weight to the seriousness of the offence but were still significantly influenced by the child's social and family circumstances. The authors concluded:

> 'Incomplete and unstandardised though the information at their disposal undoubtedly is, reporters are concerned to derive from it the best estimate possible of both stresses and supports in the child's background as an essential component of their decisions' (Martin *et al*, 1981, p91).

Three out of every four children who were not proceeded with by reporters did not come to their attention on any subsequent occasion. Therefore, it appeared that reporters had developed considerable skill in identifying those children who had a good chance of getting through a patch of delinquent behaviour without recourse to compulsory measures of care.

Lockyer (1988) drew attention to widely different policies and practices between regions in the rate of referral from reporters to hearings in respect of different grounds. He speculated about the factors affecting the balance of cases coming to hearings, including institutional resources and sociological factors. He raised the question whether variations in referral rates to hearings are at all explicable by resource considerations (p51).

The role and function of the reporter were systematically examined in 1990 when Alan Finlayson, formerly Lothian Regional Reporter, was commissioned by the Social Work Services Group at the Scottish Office to carry out a review of the service (Finlayson, 1992). Although Mr Finlayson makes no reference to earlier studies of reporters' discretion, he nevertheless stresses the value of research in understanding fully the reporter's decision-making practice.

> 'Specific research focusing on this critical area could produce a more accurate picture of the children's hearings system in the future and could have a general beneficial effect on reporters' decision-making.'

More recently the Scottish Office commissioned a major research programme on the system, including a study of reporters' discretion, which is due to report shortly.

The reporter in the children's hearing

Martin *et al* (1981) were first to draw attention to the tendency of reporters to overlook a number of flaws in the adherence of panel members to the procedural rules that govern children's hearings. They defined the problem as 'one of attitude, and of human skills necessary to contribute to the proceedings appropriately, without obtrusiveness and without creating embarrassment' (p111).

Finlayson (1990) rejected the view that the reporter should act as an adviser or assessor, although he did consider there should be greater uniformity of approach to their role in the hearing. Mitchell (1997), on the other hand, views the reporter as the legal adviser to hearings who should assist the lay panel members, particularly in writing the reasons for the decision which in many cases will form the basis for consideration of whether there should be an appeal. To remove this flaw he proposes a 'children's court' or 'children's tribunal'.

Children's hearings
The hearing process
The dynamics of the hearing process have seldom been analysed, although study on these lines is essential to ensure a rounded understanding of the psychological processes that intervene between referral and disposal. Even such relatively simple questions as 'How often do panel members arrive at a hearing with a clear opinion as to the ultimate decision, and how often and in what circumstances do they change that opinion?' have rarely been formulated in an empirical inquiry. The national statistics demonstrate the extent of variation between panels in the frequency with which different decisions are made, but explanations of these differences remain wholly speculative (Lockyer, 1988).

Martin *et al* (1981) attempted to discover by what means panel members pursued their various formal and informal goals in hearings. They observed and recorded the actual events of 301 hearings (3 per cent of the total held annually), the topics introduced into the discussion, the styles of discourse and the attitudes adopted by panel members. They identified a number of trends and patterns of practice. The statutory objectives of hearings were less than adequately fulfilled. For example, assessment of the child's best interests and choice of the most appropriate course of action did not appear to be based on a framework of knowledge about the developmental process. By contrast, the informal goals adopted by panel members were relentlessly pursued.

> 'The dialogue of hearings was rich in examples of moral disapproval of the behaviour that resulted in the child's presence at the hearing and panel members were observed regularly to be warning the child about the dangers of a delinquent way of life. They were observed to communicate to the parents the importance of their exercising certain influences on the child's conduct but this tended to be done in a more indirect fashion avoiding any possible confrontation with the parents' (Martin *et al*, 1981, p138).

In a study of twenty-seven cases in which the child was committed to a List D school the decisions were examined with special reference to the objectives that the hearing members hoped to achieve (Martin and Murray, 1983). The study identified some significant inconsistencies between the system's ideology and the actual practice of its members. For example, residential disposals by children's hearings were not grounded in any realistic appraisal of likely benefits. Instead, the decisions either reflected a sense that all alternatives had been exhausted or aimed to ensure that the child was placed in an environment which would help resolve his personal or educational difficulties.

Consequences
Very little is known about the consequences of disposals in terms of subsequent history, though one would have supposed such information to be of critical interest in a system with a markedly consequentialist view of intervention. Studies of the 'careers' of those passing through the hearings system need, however, to be supplemented by closer examination of the implications of various 'disposals'. If hearings decide to take positive action, it is in the form of either social work supervision or admission to residential treatment. What these experiences mean for the various participants, and for the children in particular, is significantly under-researched.

What research has been done suggests that the way in which social workers implement supervision orders depends on the particular ideology about the hearings system which they adopt and their utilisation of multiple or conflicting ideologies out of which an 'operational philosophy' emerges (Smith, 1977). Ford (1982) refers to an interview study carried out by Vernon who concluded that social workers see supervision in a limited 'policing' way, differentiated, in some instances, from family problems which they did not feel equipped to deal with (Vernon, 1981).

Anstey (1976) studied some of the adjustment problems of girls in List D schools, and Newman and Mackintosh (1975) described in detail the various residential facilities provided in the east of Scotland. But there has been only one piece of participant observation of staff-pupil relations and attitudes (Walter, 1975), and no systematic attempt to characterise the régimes, psychological climates and day-to-day practices across the whole range of residential schools.

Resources
During the first decade there was a widespread tendency to see the potential of the hearings system as having been frustrated both by a shortage of the skills and facilities needed to implement the decisions reached at hearings and by the variable quality of those which were available. A good deal of scepticism was expressed about the quality of social work supervision. There was criticism of a lack of variety of residential accommodation and of the shortage of treatment facilities in the community. The lack of detailed research into service delivery and its consequences was a major handicap to systematic planning and even to intelligent discussion of the whole range of personal social services (Martin and Murray, 1976).

More than a decade later the paucity of knowledge on the deployment of resources became a major concern of the Children's Panel Chairmen's Group. They argued that local authority decisions about resources paid little regard to the requirement that local authorities must make provision to carry out the decisions of children's hearings. To gather evidence in support of their argument the Group planned and carried out a research survey. They aimed to give an overall estimate of the extent to which panel members at hearings saw themselves constrained in their decision-making by lack of resources, facilities or services which they could reasonably expect local authorities to provide (Lockyer, 1988). They found that

that hearings' decisions were perceived to be 'resource limited' in one in five cases. They also revealed that social workers were less likely to recommend compulsory intervention than hearings were to impose it, which was a reverse of the position found to be the case by earlier research (Martin *et al*, 1981).

Children and parents
Since a central objective of the system is to engender the involvement of child and parent in the hearing process, consideration of the users' perspective has from the outset been an important focus of research.

Willock (1973) interviewed a sample of parents and reported a relatively low level of criticism and complaint; in general, children's hearings were compared favourably with juvenile courts by those with experience of both systems.

A larger-scale and more sensitive examination of this complex area was made by Petch (1988) who explored 'how parents make sense of the hearing process, how they explain to themselves the fact of being referred, how they anticipate and then make sense of the actual routine of the hearings, and how they respond to the disposal which is the outcome of the decision-making process' (p 9). From hearing observation and interviews with 100 parents, Petch concluded that most parents whose children appear at a hearing were satisfied both with their own participation and with the outcome, although a minority were aggrieved.

In the most comprehensive study of children's views of the system so far conducted, Erickson (1982) found that most children attached considerable significance to the hearing event. She also described how children's reactions may be affected by the performance of panel members. While the potential of hearings to socialise children in a positive integrating way to community values was realised to some extent, the capacity to instil or reinforce feelings of rejection or alienation in youthful offenders was also documented. Suggestions to enhance the former capability, and reduce the more negative impact, were proposed for the practice of panel members.

Veitch (1995) examined the views of certain operators in the hearings system (panel members, social workers, reporters, guidance teachers and police officers) regarding the protection of the rights of children and parents in the system. Panel members and police officers were very positive whereas reporters and social workers were less inclined to believe that the rights of the family were adequately protected. Veitch also inquired into the improvements to procedures and practices that the respondents would like to see. In particular they were invited to comment on members of a hearing having a discretionary power to speak to children in the absence of their parents, on extending the role and use of safeguarders in hearings, on giving children and parents a right to see the reports available to the hearing, and on giving hearings the power to set a review date. All these suggestions received less support from reporters than from other members of the sample. The majority of the proposals have now been enacted by the Children (Scotland) Act 1995, and evaluating the implementation is being planned (Scottish Office, 1997).

An exploratory study of children's experience of anxiety before and during hearings was conducted by Howells *et al* (1996). They found that children were highly anxious about events to come, fearing in particular being removed from home, and some of the older children also worried about the demands of the hearing itself. Howells *et al* draw a parallel with child witness research and the fear of the unknown that is characteristic of children preparing to go to court. Their findings have important implications for the preparation of children who must attend hearings.

Safeguarders
The Children Act 1975 placed an obligation on the chairman of a children's hearing and on a sheriff determining the status of grounds of referral or hearing an appeal to consider whether there is or may be a conflict of interest between a child and parents on any matter relevant to the proceedings and, if so, whether it is necessary, in order to protect the interests of the child in the proceedings to appoint a person to act for that purpose. The title given to this unique role was 'safeguarder'.

A Scottish Office research study of the role of the safeguarder in children's hearings was carried out during the first twelve months following implementation in 1985 (Curran, 1989). This reported a low level of use, some confusion about the role but a growing acceptance among panel members and social workers of the value of the provision. Identifying a coherent and possible role for safeguarders then became 'an urgent theoretical and practical exercise' (Lockyer, 1994b).

The Children (Scotland) Act 1995 introduced a greatly enhanced role for safeguarders. The Scottish Office recently acknowledged the need to monitor the appointment of safeguarders and how they operate in the interests of children, including their role in conveying children's views (Scottish Office, 1997).

The scope of research
Comparative studies
With the exception of work by Asquith (1983) carried out in the early 1970s, there has been a significant absence of comparative research. Curran (1983) and others have observed that the major study of the hearings system, conducted at the request of the United States Department of Justice, unfortunately did not include a parallel study of the American system.

Both Curran (1983) and Martin (1983a) suggest that more comparative research is desirable, particularly to balance the claims for the welfare approach against those demanding a 'return to justice'. However, comparative studies are notoriously difficult to plan, to execute and to interpret. Many of the problems are conceptual and methodological, involving formulation of criteria and devices for assessing them. But even when tentative approaches to problems of design and interpretation have been worked out, there are sometimes obstacles of quite a different order which may block the way to comparative work. Political and administrative sensitivities are very easily aroused. It is inevitably assumed by those from whom rights of access must be sought that comparisons must be invidious, if not odious. One such proposal to embark on a comparative study of the English and Scottish systems of dealing with child-abuse cases provides an example.

> 'At the end [of a meeting convened specifically to discuss comparative research] it was made quite clear that there was no possibility of DHSS support for anything resembling a comparative study. And although no-one said so in as many words, I found it impossible to escape the conclusion that there was deep reluctance to embark on any investigation which might conceivably be interpreted as implying that there was anything useful to be learned from the barbarians in the North' (Martin, 1979).

Child witnesses

During the 1980s attention was drawn to a 'curious anomaly' in the Scottish legal system. For more than twenty years children who committed offences or were in need of care or protection had been dealt with in a sympathetic, understanding and constructive manner, whereas children who appeared as witnesses in the criminal courts often had scant attention paid to their needs or their fears (Nicholson and Murray, 1992). In contrast to the welfare-based children's hearings system whose central principle is the promotion of the child's best interests, the criminal justice system tended, until comparatively recently, to treat child witnesses much like any other witness, and made little attempt to alleviate the fear and anxiety which tend to be significantly more pronounced in child witnesses than in adult witnesses. However, unlike the changes made to the children's hearings system, the modifications to the criminal justice system have taken account of the findings of systematic research (Bull and Davies, 1996).

During recent times, psychological research has helped to reveal the main difficulties for children giving evidence in Scottish courts. These have included the more obvious stressors, such as the pre-trial interviews (Hutcheson *et al*, 1995) and confronting the accused (Montoya, 1995) or being cross-examined (McGough, 1994; Myers, 1992). Research has also identified potential stress arising from lack of knowledge (Mellor and Dent, 1994) and the effect of long delays (Flin *et al*, 1992).

A number of studies explored children's legal knowledge of criminal proceedings in Scotland (Flin *et al*, 1992). These demonstrated that children were ignorant of trial procedures and the role they would play if they were called to court as a witness. These research findings provided useful ammunition for child-care professionals and lawyers who believed that child witnesses were entitled to be given the necessary information to enable them to understand the form and purpose of court proceedings.

The introduction of a live television link in Scottish criminal courts was evaluated to assess its rate of use and its effectiveness in reducing the stress on child witnesses and enabling the delivery of clear and coherent testimony (Murray, 1995). As a result of that research the live television link was extended to all sheriffdoms in Scotland and a number of other changes were made in response to the findings. Currently a Child Witness Support Initiative is drawing on research to inform the setting up of a scheme that will appropriately prepare and support children who expect to appear as witnesses in Scottish courts (Plotnikoff and Woolfson, 1996).

Relevance of research

Reasoned commentary and constructive criticism that is enriched by the findings of systematic research provide the best chance of creating thoughtful debate about corrective action or change. Yet research contributions can often be seen as tiresome, in the sense that they run counter to ingrained preferences for vague, fudged, unsystematic formulations, and also create difficulties by threatening to upset vested interests of 'vocal' insiders. Several writers have suggested how the general impotence of the scientific method of influencing policy and practice in this area might be overcome (Asquith, 1987; Curran, 1983). They propose greater interaction and communication between practitioners and researchers, both at the planning stage and the execution stage of research, and more accessible dissemination of results.

Increasingly researchers have recognised the importance of recording directly the views of children (Sinclair, 1996). This reflects not only a respect for children but also acknowledges that children themselves are the most important source of evidence on how they experience the legal process and are subsequently affected by it. Effective channels of communication are needed to transfer the accumulating knowledge about children's reactions to those practitioners most likely to benefit. Research and practice that are more closely linked would have undoubted benefits for the children whose interests the system is expected to serve.

16 : Children's Hearings in an International Context

Stewart Asquith

I T is now over thirty years since the Kilbrandon Committee[1] – established to consider

'the provisions of the law of Scotland relating to the treatment of juvenile delinquents and juveniles in need of care or protection or beyond parental control and, in particular, the constitution, powers and procedures of the courts dealing with such juveniles' –

provided the basis for the introduction of the children's hearings system in Scotland. What is remarkable is that not only have the Scottish children's hearings remained a unique approach to dealing with children in need of care but that there have been relatively few changes to the way in which the children's hearings system has operated in that time. Any changes which have been made have been incremental and there have been no radical or fundamental changes to the very philosophy on which the system is based.

In relation to children who commit offences, with which this chapter is largely concerned, there have of course been regular attempts to introduce a more punitive approach to dealing with young offenders which have had their roots in developments south of the border but which have generally left the integrity of Kilbrandon substantially unchanged. Concern has been expressed (Asquith and Docherty, 1998) about the ways in which the adoption of a more punitive approach to dealing with children and young people who commit offences in England and Wales may find expression in proposals relating to what happens in Scotland. Two comments can be made here, however.

One is that the strength of reaction, now and in the past, to any suggestion that more punitive approaches be adopted in Scotland to children and young offenders, or that any radical change be made to the hearings system, suggests that the integrity of the Kilbrandon philosophy will continue. The other is that the wider international context provides a more appropriate background against which to appreciate current and future developments in Scotland for those children and young people who commit offences. In the view of this writer at least, for too long comparisons have been drawn between the children's hearings

---

[1] From hereon the Kilbrandon Committee and the Kilbrandon Report are referred to simply as Kilbrandon.

system and the juvenile justice system as it operates in England and Wales. This has had the effect of ignoring just how readily the philosophy and practice of the Scottish children's hearings system fits with wider European and international developments.

In this chapter, the children's hearings system is considered in the light of current international developments; and the implications that these may have for how we deal with children who commit offences will be discussed.

In placing the children's hearings system in an international context a number of themes will be considered.[2]

- Trends in offending by children and young people.
- Violence by children and young people.
- Juvenile courts and abolitionism.
- The age of criminal responsibility.
- Preventing delinquency.
- Rights and restorative justice.

Trends in offending by children and young people

In terms of the general trends in juvenile delinquency in Europe in the last decade or so, a clear distinction has to be drawn between those trends in Western Europe on the one hand and those relating to Central and Eastern Europe on the other. As for Western Europe, there is a considerable body of literature (Asquith, 1995) which charts the trends in juvenile delinquency since the Second World War and for that reason only general comments will be made here. A rather fuller statement will be given of trends in Central and Eastern Europe. The merit of considering in some detail what appears to be happening in Central and Eastern Europe is not simply that trends in juvenile delinquency are different from those in the West. Most Central and East European countries are currently reviewing their systems of juvenile justice in the light of current trends in juvenile delinquency *and* with reference to current debates in Western Europe as to the most appropriate means of dealing with young offenders. And because of the rapid social and economic transformation, developments in juvenile justice have to be seen in the light of future social and economic regeneration.

The main features of trends in juvenile delinquency in Western Europe (Asquith, 1992b) are that there was a general increase in offending by children and young people until the late 1980s, after which there was a reduction in the overall levels of offending behaviour. There has been a small but noticeable increase in most West European countries in more serious offences, including those involving violence. The vast majority of offences committed by children and young people are offences against property – such as theft and burglary. There has been a small increase in the involvement of girls in offending behaviour,

I am grateful to the Directorate of Legal Affairs of the Council of Europe for allowing me to draw on two of my reports: Social Reactions and Juvenile Delinquency in Europe (1995) and Juvenile Justice in Central and Eastern Europe (1996).

particularly in drug-related offences and fraud. Children appear to be entering an offending career earlier in age. What has to be noted of course is that juvenile delinquency is largely a male phenomenon and systems and measures considered appropriate for children and young people who offend are largely designed to deal with boys. This has a number of implications, to which we shall return later.

What is clearly the case is that although offences of violence by children and young people constitute a small proportion of the total number of offences they have increasingly become the focus of public and political attention in Western Europe. The Bulger case in particular has had a dramatic impact on the debate about future directions for juvenile justice systems, not only in the UK but also in the broader international arena. Again we shall return to this.

When trends in juvenile delinquency in Central and Eastern Europe are considered (Asquith, 1996), however, the profile presented is very different in a number of ways. A common feature is that there has been a substantial growth over the past ten years in the number of acts of delinquency and the numbers of delinquents caught up in formal systems of social control. This in itself is perhaps not surprising given the rapid social and economic change experienced in most of the countries involved.

Most Central and East European countries have joined countries in Western Europe in having high and increasing crime rates. What has to be noted, however, is that despite the increasing rates of offending by children and young people, the figures for most Central and East European countries have not yet reached West European levels. For example, delinquency has been on the increase in Estonia since independence though, as has been noted by other commentators,

> the rate of registered crime and delinquency per 1,000 inhabitants is not particularly high in Estonia. In 1993 the rate of registered crime was 24.8 per 1,000 inhabitants and for juveniles 14.9 per thousand in the age group 13–17. This is low compared to Estonia's Nordic neighbouring countries who are considered countries of low criminality. Norway has by comparison 57.4 investigated crimes per 1,000 inhabitants and for juveniles 17 per thousand in the age group 14–17 (Falck and Dunant, 1996, p11).

The general point to be made is that though there *has* been an increase in juvenile delinquency in most Central and East European countries, it has not yet reached the levels experienced by some countries in Western Europe.

Where the trends in Central and Eastern Europe do correspond with those in Western Europe it is in the fact that the majority of offences are committed by boys; most offences are property offences; offenders begin offending at a relatively young age; and there is an apparent increase in the numbers of girls involved in offending behaviour – especially in relation to drugs and prostitution. It is a matter of particular concern that girls are the victims of a variety of forms of sexual exploitation.

It is in relation to offences involving violence by children and young people that there is the most marked difference between Central and Eastern Europe and Western Europe. As we shall see, concern at increasing levels of violence by children and young people is much greater in the international arena than appears to be the case in the UK.

Violence by children and young people

Since the conviction in England in 1993 of the two young boys around the age of criminal responsibility (ten) for the murder of the toddler James Bulger, attention has concentrated on seeking answers to a number of rather simple questions. These have greatly influenced developments in juvenile justice in a number of countries – not just in the UK. The questions include:

- Are serious crimes of violence by children on the increase?
- What explanations of violent behaviour by young children are acceptable?
- At what age should children be held criminally responsible?
- How adequate are our juvenile and criminal justice systems in handling cases in which children have committed violent offences?
- Just how should we deal with children who commit violent offences, including murder?
- How might offences of violence by children be prevented?
- Can violence be explained differently from other forms of offending by children and young people?

Whether or not the numbers of serious or violent offences by children and young people have increased, there is increasing anxiety or, as Bailleau (1996) puts it, 'insecurity' about the threat posed to society by children and young people who commit violent offences.

The implications for juvenile justice systems is what might be referred to as a move to the penological right with, in England and Wales, a clear commitment from the Home Secretary to introduce more severe and punitive measures for dealing with young offenders (see Graham, 1996).

The whole issue of violence by children and young people has opened up consideration of the very philosophy, aims and objectives on which we wish to base our system of justice for children. It has prompted wide-ranging debate about the nature of childhood and the kind of life experiences we offer our children on their way to adulthood. In that respect, the charting of developments in other countries and jurisdictions, superficial though it may be in this short chapter, is important in considering what implications they may have for juvenile justice in Scotland.

The main questions, as outlined above, are whether current fears and concerns are valid and, if so, what is the most appropriate way in which to deal with those of our children who commit serious and violent offences, including murder. We have already noted that whereas there appears to have been a general reduction in juvenile delinquency in Western Europe in the past five years, there has been a slight increase in the number of offences involving violence by children and young people (see Asquith, 1992b, with reference to the Netherlands, Sweden and the UK; Walgrave, 1996, with reference to Western Europe generally).

In the wake of the Bulger case, concern has been expressed in Western Europe about the number of *murders* by children and young people, but it does not appear to be the case that there has been any increase. Referring to the UK, Cavadino (1996) argues that there has been no increase. Commenting on the European situation, Walgrave (1996) asserts that the figures may well reveal a degree of stability. Docherty (1997) points out that there is very little information on children who kill and that such information as is available is generally based on a case-study approach to analysis, thereby further inhibiting an accurate assessment of the extent of such behaviour. Docherty is able, though, to point to the fact that of all murders committed in the mid-1980s in the USA, 7 per cent were committed by adolescents (those aged between ten and seventeen) – a much higher percentage than for the UK or Western Europe in general. Docherty raises the question whether inferences drawn primarily from American material can be applied to a UK context. Implicit is the argument that they cannot and that there is great need for studies of murder by children and young people, as of violent offences generally, to be conducted in a specifically UK context from a socio-legal perspective. There must, however, be concern as to whether what is happening in the USA anticipates developments in the UK.

In a report to the Scottish Office (Asquith *et al*, 1996) the authors referred to the phenomenon of 'twin-tracking'. It is a fact that most offences by children and young people are less serious offences which need not necessarily warrant punitive or indeed formal intervention, but it is clear from the literature that the smaller number of more serious offences have influenced the philosophy and the development of juvenile justice systems. Indeed, it is argued (Asquith and Docherty, 1998) that the practices on which the Scottish system of juvenile justice is based could be threatened by the promotion of a more punitive philosophy and approach.

Although there does not appear to be a dramatic increase in offences involving violent behaviour in the UK and Western Europe, data from other sources suggest that this may not be the whole picture. What is worthy of particular note, given current concerns and preoccupations in Western Europe, is the increase in, or at the very least increasing concern about, the numbers of young offenders committing the most serious offences, especially those involving forms of violence, in Central and East European countries.

The situation regarding offences of violence, including murder by children and young people, is dramatically different from that in the West. In a number of countries, not only do there appear to be more acts of violence, there is also a substantial increase in murder by children, with cases of children and young people contracted to carry out murders. In Central and Eastern Europe offences involving violence may well be associated with drugs and organised crime. The situation there has to be seen in the context of social and economic change and the transition to the market economy.

Not only does murder by juveniles appear to be on the increase, there also appears to have been a qualitative change in the violence inflicted by juvenile offenders on their victims. A commentator in Latvia identifies the cruel nature of juvenile crime:

'The proportion of violent crime amongst minors is 4–8%. In 1994, the number of murders (+150%), robberies (+27%) and violent assaults (+21%) committed by minors increased dramatically. The cruelty of juvenile crime is rather alarming.'

The dramatic increase in some countries is best illustrated by Poland, where there were two homicides committed by juveniles in 1983 and 33 in 1994; 83 rapes in 1983 and 156 in 1994; 550 robberies in 1983 and 6,600 in 1994.

In terms of explanations for serious offending by children and young people, a number of international studies point to the significance of negative life experiences and in particular the fact that many serious offenders have been the subject of some form of abuse (Farrington and West, 1977; Boswell, 1995; Heide, 1993 and 1995; Docherty, 1997). Such studies indicate that where life experiences are negative, the effect can be amplified by other factors, including poverty, unemployment, divorce and domestic violence.

In the East as in the West, there are important issues of principle about how children who commit the more serious offences should be dealt with.

Juvenile courts and the 'abolitionists'

The position of those who might be referred to as the 'abolitionist' school falls to be considered. Given the high level of violence by children and young people in the USA and the increasing concern, whether real or supposed, about the threat they pose to personal and public safety, it is no surprise to find the argument that no distinction should be drawn between children who commit violent offences and adults who commit violent offences.

The abolitionists have argued that there should be no juvenile courts and that children should be subjected to the same punishments as adults. Thus, the criminal justice system should apply and be applied in the same way to children and to adults.

By extension this means that young offenders could be subject to the death penalty. This is a position the abolitionists would accept. In fact the past decade has seen a substantial increase in the number of juveniles on death row (Streib, 1994), and there have been claims that many of the judiciary would support the retention of the death penalty for juvenile offenders. The possibility of execution for young offenders has been a contributory factor in the failure of the US to ratify the United Nations Convention on the Rights of the Child.

The abolitionist argument is not particularly new, and the social and political reaction to the murder of James Bulger illustrated many of its elements. We can see elements of abolitionism in the use of more punitive approaches to children in England and Wales (Graham, 1996) and the proposal that young offenders be subject to electronic tagging. Even in Scotland there is concern (Asquith and Docherty, 1998) that ss 16(5) and 17(5) of the Children (Scotland) Act 1995, in which the threshold at which the wish to protect society rather than promote the interests of the child is lowered, suggest a gradual erosion of the distinction between adult offenders and children who offend.

Looking at the pan-European arena and beyond, it is clear that despite a commitment to a welfare and educative philosophy in most countries, the high level of violence by children and young people has contributed to a social and political reaction, calling for more punitive measures.

The age of criminal responsibility

The question of how to deal with children who commit violent offences has thrown the whole issue of the age of criminal responsibility into sharp relief. Although strong criticisms have been made by the United Nations Committee on the Rights of the Child regarding the low age of criminal responsibility in the UK, current demands from a number of quarters that it be raised may conflict with the move to a more punitive and judicially oriented approach for dealing with young offenders – particularly those who commit serious or violent offences. One of the effects of the Bulger case was that it probably thwarted any possibility that an appeal to increase the age of criminal responsibility would be successful either with the public or with the politicians. England and Wales and Scotland have amongst the lowest ages of criminal responsibility in the world, the ages being ten and eight respectively.

The age at which children are considered criminally responsible – whether described as 'children', 'juveniles' or 'minors' – varies widely in Europe and further afield, which means that it is difficult to make valid comparisons in terms of the levels of offending behaviour by children and young people.

Discussion of the age of criminal responsibility must take account of cultural, social, historical and legal specificity. It is impossible, for example, to appreciate why the age of criminal responsibility is thirteen in France and sixteen in the Ukraine without considering in the two jurisdictions the philosophy of childhood, the nature of the court system and the role of the judge.

As can be seen from the table, in a number of countries the age of criminal responsibility may be lowered if the offence is particularly serious.

In Western and Eastern Europe there seems to be little support for lowering the age of criminal responsibility; in the UK there is no concerted movement demanding the raising of the age.

In European countries, with the exception of the UK, the decision-making forum for young offenders at or above the age of criminal responsibility takes the form of a modified criminal court (Cavadino, 1996; Asquith, 1996). How it is constituted, how it operates and who presides differ from country to country, but it remains nevertheless a court of criminal law. The most favoured model is a modified court of criminal law presided over by a specially and professionally qualified judge assisted by two lay people, or what the French would call *assesseurs* (see Asquith, 1996, for different models of juvenile courts).

The court-based model has to be seen in the context of the fact that, because the age of criminal responsibility is high, offenders tend to be older than those who might attend hearings or the youth court in England and Wales. Children and young people under the age of criminal responsibility who commit serious offences do not appear in court and are not prosecuted. In Japan, for example, the age of criminal responsibility is fourteen, but no one under that age is prosecuted, no matter the seriousness of the offence (conversation with Takako Kumeda, a Japanese lawyer).

Age of Criminal Responsibility in Europe

Country	Age
Austria	14
Belgium	18
Bulgaria	14
Czech Republic	15
Croatia	14
England/Wales	10
Estonia	15 but may be lowered to 13
France	13
Germany	14
Hungary	14
Ireland	7
Latvia	16 but may be lowered to 14
Liechtenstein	7
Macedonia	16 but may be lowered to 14
Moldova	16 but may be lowered to 14
Poland	17 but may be lowered to 16
Portugal	16
Russia	16 but may be lowered to 14
Scandinavian countries (all)	15
Scotland	8
Slovak Republic	15
Slovenia	14
Spain	16
Switzerland	7
Ukraine	16 but may be lowered to 14

Note. As can be seen, the age of criminal responsibility varies greatly across Europe, but a rough rule can be applied – the further east, the higher the age of criminal responsibility.

In most European countries, the right of a child or young person to legal representation goes hand in hand with a judicial form of proceedings. The lack of adversarial legal representation in children's hearings is, for this reason, very difficult to understand for many of our European colleagues.

Referring back, however, to the age of criminal responsibility debate, the evidence from Dunkel (1991) is that in the European jurisdictions which have raised the age of criminal responsibility relatively recently, there has been no appreciable difference in the rates of offending. The issue may have to be addressed in Scotland, especially at a time when there is a threat to the integrity of the Kilbrandon philosophy from a more punitive approach to offending by children and young people (Asquith and Docherty, 1998).

Preventing delinquency
In the introduction to the 1996 White Paper on crime and punishment, the Secretary of State for Scotland emphasised the importance of crime prevention. The White Paper itself makes it clear that what is meant is the prevention of crime

largely by what might be referred to as 'target hardening' – that is, making it more difficult to commit crime through the use of such measures as closed circuit television (CCTV), electronic surveillance, neighbourhood watch and so on. There can be no disagreement that such initiatives have an impact on the prevention of specific crimes. However, a number of points should be made.

First, target-hardening preventive measures are usually directed at the older population of young offenders and may have more impact on those who are already caught up in a criminal career.

Secondly – and to return to what we discussed above – children appear to be entering offending careers at a much earlier age. Therefore, preventive strategies may have to be developed which focus on younger offenders.

Thirdly, if we are truly committed to preventing delinquency, in the way in which the Kilbrandon Committee had envisaged, preventive strategies must focus on the early life experiences of children, to reduce the risk of their becoming involved in delinquent behaviour at some time in their lives. Boswell (1995), for example, identifies the importance of negative aspects – in particular, abuse, violence, bereavement and loss – in the life experiences of children in England and Wales who commit the more serious offences.

Fourthly, international studies emphasise the importance of early intervention in the lives of children at risk of becoming offenders (Farrington, 1994). Developments in most European countries have been influenced by the commitment to addressing the social and life experiences of children, which have been expressed in a number of statements – for example, the Riyadh Guidelines (United Nations Minimum Guidelines on the Prevention of Delinquency, 1985), Recommendation No R(70) of the Council of Europe, and of course the United Nations Convention on the Rights of the Child which places on states the obligation to provide the necessary resources and services to allow children to develop healthily into adulthood.

The international studies, and the statements themselves, reveal that there is a degree of convergence in the explanations offered for offending by children and young people. They include abuse, ill-health, low self-esteem, failure to reach educational potential, poor social relationships, and association with depressive adults. Against this background the importance of a preventive policy is obvious:

> 'Any measure which reduces crime will probably also reduce alcohol abuse, drink driving, drug abuse, sexual promiscuity, family violence, truancy, school failure, unemployment, marital disharmony and divorce. It is clear that problem children grow up into problem adults' (Farrington, 1994, p26).

Internationally there is a movement towards early intervention in the lives of children to prevent delinquent behaviour and to protect those at risk, and a recognition of the need for a multifaceted, multidisciplinary policy to address the negative life experiences faced by many children (Asquith, 1995; 1996). The Riyadh Guidelines emphasised such a philosophy.

In a recent review of developments in juvenile justice in Central and Eastern Europe (Asquith, 1996), failure to implement preventive programmes was attributed not to a lack of political will (albeit that in many countries there is a vocal punishment lobby) but to a shortage of financial and other resources. There is a parallel situation in Scotland where the parlous state of local authority budgets undoubtedly inhibit the development and promotion of preventive strategies. This is particularly worrying, given that over thirty years ago the Kilbrandon Report provided a philosophy on which to base a preventive policy. It has never, however, been realistically implemented.

Despite the overwhelming evidence supporting the preventive approach, shortage of resources, and competing ideologies, will inevitably inhibit the implementation of such a policy.

Rights and restorative justice

Developments in child-care law and policy in Scotland, as in many other countries, have been greatly influenced by the UN Convention. It was a direct outcome of a growing movement to promote children's rights. One element of the movement was the Riyadh Guidelines regarding the ways in which juvenile delinquency might be prevented. Another element was the Beijing Rules, which are concerned with the protection of children once they are caught up in criminal and juvenile justice systems, by means of the provision of legal protection, the right to a fair hearing and respect for the right to privacy. (The right to privacy would be compromised in Scotland if the Secretary of State's suggestion permitting the identification of children caught up in the criminal justice system were implemented. Under Scots law, of course, information regarding the identity of children in the criminal justice system can be published *only* if it is in the public interest.)

Although most countries in Europe are committed to a preventive philosophy for dealing with children and young people who offend, the fact is that many have nevertheless retained some form of juvenile court structure (Asquith, 1996). Thus discussion about the rights of children generally centres on their rights *within* the juvenile justice and criminal justice systems – in particular, the right to legal protection. (Lockyer (1994a) and Duquette (1992) have discussed the nature of (whether it is necessary) representation of children in the children's hearings system.)

King (1997) and Walgrave (1996) allude to an increasing move to involve the law and judicial processes in welfare decisions about children. The fact that most European countries have retained some form of juvenile court suggests that, even where there is a commitment to welfare and education, there is considerable reluctance to forgo judicial procedure and the involvement of legally qualified persons.

King (1997) argues that the involvement of the law in welfare decisions about children was evident in what was then the Children (Scotland) Bill. More recently, the clause in the Criminal Justice (Scotland) Act 1995 which would have given the Crown the right to appeal could be construed as indicative of the trend (Asquith and Docherty, 1998).

In Europe, in the wake of the Bulger case, there is a questioning of juridical and punitive approaches on the one hand and of educative and welfare approaches on the other, as a basis for dealing with children and young people who offend. Walgrave (1996) and others in the 'restorative' movement refer to this swing between punishment and welfare in defining a new notion of justice and provide an alternative perspective on which to base measures for young offenders. (It should be noted, however, that the restorative justice movement is concerned with offenders in general, not only with young offenders. The main objective in dealing with offenders 'should not be to punish, not even to [re]educate, but to repair or to compensate for the harm caused by the offence' (Barnett, 1977).

As Walgrave illustrates, restorative justice has its roots in mediation, reparation and, in general, in those measures which involve some form of contact or communication between the victim of an offence and the offender through which an appropriate means of resolving the matter can be negotiated.[3]

Whereas mediation and reparation-based schemes are *added to* contemporary systems of juvenile justice, the advocates of restorative justice argue that such schemes can provide the basis for a completely new approach to dealing with children and young people who offend. The focus is not on the offence or the offender but on the wrong done to the individual as a victim or to the community as a victim. Punishment and educative techniques may be involved, but these are secondary to the need to resolve the wrong done.

Walgrave asserts that the restorative approach demands a type of society which acknowledges the importance of negotiation and empowerment as the basis for resolving conflicts – a type of society which seeks to integrate, not exclude, its young offenders.

The principles of restorative justice are that the victim is the central actor, not a secondary one; educative measures are less important than the righting of the wrong done; offenders are assisted in righting the wrong; and the integration of the offender back into the community is a main objective.

The restorative justice movement provides an alternative to the punishment or welfare approaches between which opinions, and systems, have traditionally swung. Mediation and reparation schemes have been applied across Europe in juvenile justice systems, but whether a truly restorative approach could be developed and how it might articulate with the Kilbrandon philosophy is another issue.

There have been relatively few changes in the way in which the children's hearings system has operated in regard to young offenders in the twenty-six years since it was introduced. Current preoccupations with the changing nature of offending and, in particular, with the increase in violent offending by young people, have prompted a reappraisal of the relative merits of punishment, welfare, mediation or reparation as the basis for a juvenile justice system. The proposal in the Kilbrandon Report for a 'social education (in the sense close to the French *l'education*)' department (later to become the social work department) reflected

---

[3] Restorative justice schemes south of the border, as applied to young offenders, have recently been commended by the Home Secretary.

the importance of European thinking on how to deal with young offenders. At a time when a more punitive approach is suggested by trends in juvenile justice in England and Wales, it is important that sight is not lost of the close relationship between children's hearings and wider pan-European developments.

SECTION III

Conclusion

Andrew Lockyer and Fred Stone

17 : Prospects

Andrew Lockyer and Fred Stone

W HEN the Kilbrandon Report (with Stone's introduction) was republished by HMSO in 1995 it was in the knowledge that the legislation to
which it had given rise was in the process of being replaced. Lord
Fraser of Carmyllie, Minister of Health and Home Affairs at the Scottish Office,
wrote in the foreword to the new edition that despite the 'many new provisions' in
the Children (Scotland) Bill it 'remains true to the original Kilbrandon principles'.
Whether this judgment can be accepted as a verdict on the Children (Scotland)
Act 1995 and on the system now in place is a critical question.[1]

Our view is that the legislators have left open the prospects of the Kilbrandon
legacy. The new framework has a dual potential which will allow the core
principles and institutions of the children's hearings system to be either maintained and strengthened or undermined. The future of the children's hearings
system will depend in the first instance on how participating actors (reporters,
social workers, panel members, sheriffs, and, in some measure, family members)
choose to exercise the discretion which the legislation permits and, in the second,
on what support there continues to be from politicians and the public for the
welfare approach to children in trouble.

Each of our contributors has reflected on issues which, directly or indirectly,
have a bearing on the future of the children's hearings system. In this concluding
chapter we review some of the factors which threaten the core principles of
Kilbrandon and some which may serve to sustain them. We will make suggestions
for the development of practice consistent with the welfare approach. Our
normative stance is that the Kilbrandon philosophy provides a valid value-basis for
the treatment of young people, and we hope to have shown that it has done so for
over twenty-five years.

Rights agenda

In the mid-1960s, when the Kilbrandon Committee formulated its Report,
children's rights were not part of the common language of social, political and
legal discourse. Although for two centuries there had been talk of all human
beings possessing rights not as privileges earned or inherited but as 'natural' – in
John Locke's words, what all mankind is 'born to' (Locke, 1687) – the imperative

---

[1] The continuing relevance of the Kilbrandon principles has recently been re-endorsed by the current
Secretary of State for Scotland (see the Preface).

to regard children as 'rights' holders had hardly been considered. When human rights were asserted to be universal – as, for example, by the 1948 Declaration of Human Rights (which, in article 21, claimed that 'everyone has a right to take part in the government of his country') – 'universal' often meant applying to 'everyone' once they become adults. In 1924 there was a League of Nations Geneva Declaration on the Rights of the Child and a similar UN Declaration in 1959. These exhorted states to adopt policies which nurtured and protected children within the family, rather than giving them rights of action, or rights that might challenge those of parents. In the 1970s there was a body of radical opinion in favour of extending all adult rights to children (the most notable child 'liberation-ists' were Farson, 1974, and Holt, 1975). This implied the attribution to children of adult responsibilities, although the liberationists usually neglected to point this out. Not until 1989 was there a fully articulated UN standard setting out rights specific to children, which included both rights to recipience (of welfare, education and protection) and rights to participate in, and have a voice in, determining where their interests lay – so-called 'autonomy rights'.[2]

The UK government's adoption of the United Nations Convention on the Rights of the Child in December 1991 had a substantial impact on the inquiries, reviews and White Paper on which the 1995 Act was based. This is not to say that the 1995 Act fully incorporates all the provisions of the UN Convention (Asquith, 1993; Cleland and Sutherland, 1996), or that the Convention strikes exactly the balance between welfare and autonomy rights (Alston *et al*, 1992; Hafen and Hafen, 1996). We have noted too the influence of the European Convention on Human Rights, although its impact is not entirely beneficial to the interests of children. The language of the Children (Scotland) Act 1995 speaks of adults' responsibilities rather than children's rights, the UN Convention provides much of the moral foundation upon which parental and local authority responsibilities are based.

To a considerable extent the Kilbrandon philosophy could be said to have anticipated a child-centred focus which naturally translates into children's rights. We have seen (in Chapter 7) that, with respect to giving priority to the child's welfare, the Social Work (Scotland) Act 1968 exceeds both the standard of the UN Convention and the principle of paramountcy in the 1995 Act, and that the right of children to have views taken into account is possibly better provided for (certainly for under-twelve-year-olds) by established practice at hearings. How-ever, there are aspects of the Kilbrandon approach which cannot readily be expressed in the language of individual rights, and an uncritical adoption of the international 'rights agenda' produces unwelcome effects.

There are features of the emphasis on rights which detract from the Kilbrandon principles, including the impetus to increase formality and promote uniformity. Arguably the aspect of the rights agenda most at odds with Kilbrandon is the tendency to assume, and in some measure to promote, adversarial contest rather

---

[2] The term 'autonomy rights' has become the common way of referring to those rights which invest the right-holder with authority to make choices which others must or ought to respect. These are also sometimes called 'rights of action' or 'choice rights'.

than consensus – that is, conforming to a court-based model of justice. This of course was the type of procedure that the Kilbrandon Committee was intent on replacing when it arrived at a course of action designed to assist children in trouble. As Stewart Asquith points out (in Chapter 16), the international children's rights agenda assumes that children will be dealt with in a court setting.

Rights and formality

It has been a long-standing criticism that hearings neglect 'due process' require-ments in the pursuit of informality. The right to a fair hearing has no doubt on occasion been compromised by hearings failing to observe procedural rules. Although there are no data to show that hearings are more lax in matters of procedure than courts in other juvenile justice systems, and there is no up-to-date evidence of hearings' observance of rules, we do know that panel members have consistently regarded procedural formality as less important than creating an ethos conducive to good communication and gaining the co-operation of families.

The rights agenda has been dominated by legal critics of the hearings system who have consistently viewed children's and parents' rights as an issue of 'due process'. Their proposed solutions to the deficiencies of hearings have consistently been to introduce more legally qualified people: reporters (McLean, 1983), hearing chair-men (Grant, 1975), representatives (Fox, 1991), or sheriffs with lay members – becoming in fact juvenile courts (Kelly, 1996; Mitchell, 1997). Without denying that procedural rights have importance, they are secondary rather than primary rights, a means to securing a just outcome, not ends in themselves.

The rights of children to be protected, to have their individual identity respected, to have their welfare promoted, to participate in decisions which affect them, to be treated according to their developmental needs and not with the same autonomy and culpability as adults (the list is not exhaustive) are all important primary and substantive rights. None are reducible to a duty to follow the rules, and none can be secured without the exercise of critical judgment which takes account of a child's individual characteristics.

There is no necessity for the rights agenda to be dominated by procedural rights. This is a minimalist approach which substitutes formal for substantive justice. However, it is a manifestation of what is sometimes called the paradigm of legal discourse which has increasingly come to dominate the operation of welfare systems. Nowhere is this more noticeable than in relation to what can be called the 'juridification' of social work practice. This widespread phenomenon can be seen to be linked with an increasing emphasis on 'court work' – particularly in regard to contested child-abuse allegations. King (1997) sees this process exempli-fied by events in Orkney and in the outcome of the Orkney Inquiry. In a climate of doubt about when to intervene in the lives of families, and where uncertainty of proof lays the worker and the authority open to litigious challenge, the disposition to seek security in bureaucratic process is overwhelming. The interposition of rules, guidance, forms and procedures, externally imposed upon social work and operating through internal management systems, comes close to deskilling the social worker by substituting process for professional discretion.

Representation

One of the reasons why the international rights agenda constitutes a threat to the Scottish system is that children's hearings are an atypical institution for deciding what should happen to children who have offended, or are victims, or are otherwise in need. The United Nations Convention on the Rights of the Child and the European Convention on Human Rights apparently presuppose that the characteristics of a court, or an equivalent 'competent legal authority' providing legal representation, provide the appropriate system for taking decisions which determine a child's liberty. Before the UK government became a signatory to the UN Convention, Sanford Fox warned that no account had been taken of the position of the hearings system – the UK representatives at Geneva, he tells us, were unaware of it (Fox, 1991). In his view there had to be legal representation at hearings to comply with art 37(d) of the Convention. His opinion was apparently shared by the UK government which, in ratifying the Convention, entered the reservation 'to continue the present operation of children's hearings ... having proved over the years to be a very effective way of dealing with the problems of children in a less formal, non-adversarial manner'.[3]

The case against legal representation at hearings is worth repeating, because it is frequently misunderstood. It is not an objection to the presence of lawyers at hearings, nor to representatives at hearings, nor even to lawyers acting as representatives at hearings. It is only *legal representation* which must be prohibited – that is, legal agents empowered to speak 'on behalf of' or instead of the child or 'relevant person' rather than all parties speaking for themselves, and speaking their minds. We have noted that the Children Hearings Rules under the 1995 Act have continued to characterise the representative as someone who 'may assist the person whom he represents in the discussion' (rule 11(2)). In essence this is the only limitation on the concept of representation required to sustain the distinctive model of the children's hearing. As Barbara Reid observes (Chapter 12) the legal profession has become aware of the difference between courts and hearings, and has generally modified its participation appropriately.

Whether or not parties to hearings are likely to benefit more from having a lawyer as a representative rather than a friend, colleague, neighbour, teacher or other professional assistant is an open question. Certainly, there ought to be no special advantage to family members in being assisted by a person with knowledge of the law relating to children's hearings, since the hearing chairman and the reporter have a duty to ensure that a hearing is conducted fairly and according to the rules. The limited role differentiation within hearings does not exclude any party from assisting children or other family members in expressing their views, or in defending their interests. In a sense all parties at a hearing have a responsibility to represent the interests of the child, beginning with parents. For this reason it is not essential to have anyone specifically designated as a 'representative', although more frequently than has happened to date, there is good reason for encouraging children to be accompanied by someone of their own choosing.

[3] For the argument against Fox's interpretation and therefore the need for the reservation, see Lockyer, 1994a.

The extension of the role of the safeguarder under the 1995 Act is a good example of the adaptation of new institution to the hearing process. Removing the 'conflict of interests' criterion recognises both the variety of circumstance where safeguarders may be used and their dual function in assisting children to express their views and in making an independent assessment of the children's interests. The fact that their appointment remains discretionary, despite the argument in favour of all children having an independent advocate, acknowledges that these functions are attached not only to this office. Safeguarders are an additional resource to be employed whenever there is doubt whether other parties can fulfil the safeguarding functions. There remains a need to monitor the use made of safeguarders by courts and hearings, not least by considering the views of young people to whose cases they are appointed.

Sheriff's power of disposal

The power under the 1995 Act permitting a sheriff on appeal to replace a decision of a hearing by any disposal which a hearing is empowered to make, is in principle the most far-reaching breach of the separation of functions at the heart of the Kilbrandon philosophy.

It was suggested by Lord James Douglas-Hamilton to the Scottish Standing Committee on 7th March 1995, speaking for the government, that the new provision was introduced to ensure that the legislation is not open to challenge under the European Convention on Human Rights, article 6(1) of which 'confers on all people the right to court proceedings in the determination of their civil rights'. It is far from clear whether the European Convention does require determination by a court. The relevant article says that everyone is entitled to 'a fair and public hearing within a reasonable time by an independent and impartial tribunal established by law'. It is a matter of serious concern if the government of the day was not convinced that a children's hearing could meet the standard of an independent and impartial tribunal. The only article in the Convention which refers specifically to a court is article 4, which says that 'everyone who is deprived of their liberty' is entitled to have the lawfulness of his detention 'decided speedily by a court'. But since the sheriff court has always had the power to 'liberate' a child on appeal from any requirement or 'warrant to detain', it is hard to see how this presents a problem. If the government is committed to the view that a tribunal other than a court is the appropriate forum to determine what course of treatment measures are needed, it ought at least to be prepared to argue the case.

There is, however, a real rights issue at the heart of the Kilbrandon Committee's separation of the role of the court and of the hearings which has practical implications. It was a commonly made criticism in the early days that the sheriffs' power to set aside hearings' disposals was inconsistent with the principle of separation. Accordingly, Sheriff Mowat's view that it was wrong for a sheriff to overturn a hearing's decision simply because he or she felt that another form of treatment might be preferable (*D v Sinclair* 1973 SLT (Sh Ct) 47) was generally followed. However, despite the decision of the Court of Session in *O v Rae* (IH)

1993 SCLR 318; 1993 SLT 570,[4] many, like Sheriff Mitchell, find serious fault in a system which allows hearings to base disposals on disputed information 'amounting to untested allegations' (Mitchell, 1997). It is correctly pointed out by Professor Norrie that the bases of hearings' decisions often have nothing to do with grounds for referral but involve judgments based on matters contained in reports and, after hearing from all parties, on the credibility of information presented to the hearings (Norrie, 1995). But if Professor Norrie is right in characterising hearings as resolving 'disputes of fact', the principle of separation could be said to be transgressed equally by hearings doing the job which Kilbrandon assigned to the courts.

Children's hearings are no more designed to hear evidence than courts are equipped to conduct a consensual discussion aimed at a treatment plan. But we believe it to be misleading to describe what hearings characteristically do as *resolving* disputes of fact. No doubt in the course of their decisions, hearings take cognisance of disputed accounts of events and make judgments about credibility, which often include believing or not believing factual assertions. We have argued that if a decision turns on specific disputed facts, this should be made clear in the hearing's reasons for decision, so that the sheriff may examine such matters on appeal.

Equally we argue that Lord Clyde was wrong to suggest that the judgment in *O* v *Rae* implied that a hearing should have considered reports relevant to whether the events asserted in the grounds had taken place (see Chapter 6). Decisions made by hearings prior to grounds being proved must be made in the light of facts accepted and what is disputed, including the fact of the local authority's and reporter's concerns and the facts of the family members' response to what is alleged. Compliance with Kilbrandon principles requires hearings to resist taking a preliminary view of the veracity of what is alleged, or attempting to resolve what is disputed.

In our view sheriffs should confine the exercise of their greater power on appeal to cases where they conclude that hearings have proceeded on mistaken facts, or given undue weight to factors which do not stand evidential test. The new provision to hear evidence on appeal facilitates this. Only where findings of fact clearly point to a specific disposal without requiring further discussion should the sheriff make a requirement rather than refer back to a hearing. The approach which the courts have taken in the past, as Sheriff Kearney has shown (in Chapter 10), has generally been to support the Kilbrandon principle of separation. The right to have the factual (or evidential) basis for a hearing's decision tested by the court endorses the Kilbrandon principle of separation if and only if sheriffs continue to respect the principle in their decision-making.

Welfare of offenders and non-offenders: the threat of disintegration

One of the key concepts in the Kilbrandon philosophy is that the child's welfare should be the sole criterion in matters of disposal whatever brings a child to public

[4] See Sheriff Kearney's discussion of this judgment in Chapter 10.

attention. Whether he or she is an offender or a victim of an offence, these considerations are relevant only with respect to the child's needs. The fundamental principle of not differentiating cases by grounds for referral for the purpose of disposal has survived, but it is under significant strain. This is partly because the international rights agenda presupposes a separation of rights of the accused from the rights of victims or of children in need, but also because public and political perceptions of what is deserved differentiate so markedly between children or young people, depending on how they are 'labelled'.

It has long been the practice to classify cases for statistical purposes by grounds for referral, and there is a growing inclination to speak of 'child-protection cases', 'child-abuse cases', 'young offenders' and 'delinquents' (as we have done) as separate types of case. The tendency to talk about 'child-protection procedures', or 'protection work', as distinct from 'working with offenders' is increasingly accepted in social work practice, which parallels a popular, idealised dichotomy of 'innocent' children who need protection and 'undeserving' youth from which society needs protection.

The introduction of the formal derogation from the paramountcy of the child's welfare for the purpose of protecting the public from serious harm is clearly a significant step away from the universal application of the welfare criterion, even though other people's 'safety' is, as Sheriff Kearney reminds us, implicit in the body of law which applies to all and is taken for granted when the welfare of children is assessed. We should notice that the Act does not reserve this derogation to cases where children are offenders; it can be applied to children too young to have committed an offence, though serious and persistent offenders are likely to be those whom the legislators had in mind.

Bill Whyte has shown us (in Chapter 13) the shortcomings of the assumption that there is such a readily definable category of delinquents. It will be recalled that the Kilbrandon Committee made provision for the most serious offenders to be prosecuted, and Lord Kilbrandon himself had early occasion to criticise the over-use of the provision (Kilbrandon, 1976). If considerations of public protection may now explicitly enter into the disposition of hearings, a case can be made for the Lord Advocate's directions to be reviewed. Kathleen Murray reminds us (in Chapter 15) that research evidence showed that children dealt with by courts rather than by hearings were indistinguishable in terms of most of their characteristics.

Stewart Asquith brings to our attention (in Chapter 16) the international context within which developments in Scotland must be viewed. He notes what appears to be a reduction in juvenile crime in Western Europe during the 1990s, albeit that the impact of the Bulger case in England and the high levels of juvenile crime in the newly capitalist countries of Central and Eastern Europe feed international concern about the most serious and persistent of young offenders. The 'move to the penological right', including the idea of subjecting children to the same punishment as adults if their offences are serious enough, makes the prospect of raising the age of criminal responsibility in the UK jurisdictions unlikely.

Equally, extending the jurisdiction of hearings over more serious young offenders, as advocates of the welfare approach have favoured, is unlikely to gain political approval. However, there may be more chance of persuading those members of the judiciary who are influenced by criminological research to refer appropriate cases for disposal to hearings, where they have discretion to do so. This prospect would be greatly improved by a positive demonstration by local authorities of their capacity to develop strategies of work with young offenders and their families, and a transfer of funds from the criminal justice system, too much of which still goes on custodial provision.

Presenting problems

'Children in trouble' was how Lord Kilbrandon described the clientele of the proposed new system (1966). Not all trouble which children get into is trouble of their own making. In brief, 'juvenile delinquency' and 'care or protection' covered the presenting problems. They are not mutually exclusive; both are prima facie evidence of something having gone wrong in the 'upbringing process'. As has been pointed out, the assertion seemed plausible – or true by definition – suggesting that there was no essential difference in the causal circumstances. The Kilbrandon Report was not at all explicit about what was involved in 'failure of upbringing'.

Thirty years later we still seek precise, confident explanations of what this might entail. From a sociological perspective Malcolm Hill identifies (in Chapter 8) two associated factors in problems of child care: discontinuity and poverty. No doubt explanations of particular problems must include psychological factors, and interpersonal dynamics, but as yet there is no diagnostic consensus to challenge the view taken by the Kilbrandon Committee that the capacity of the family to deal with 'problems', whatever their aetiology may be, is the key variable.

What is clear is the changing balance of the presenting problems referred to reporters and to hearings. In the early years, cases that could be classified as 'care and protection' were a small proportion of those dealt with; now they constitute at least half of the cases reaching hearings. Of these, until recently, a steadily increasing proportion were suspected cases of child abuse, including physical, sexual and, though infrequently cited, inescapably emotional abuse. It is not certain whether this reflected a rise in the prevalence of child abuse, or an increase in its recognition by the child-care agencies and a receptivity of reporters to such referrals. However, within the hearings system, as in the wider community, concern about child abuse, especially alleged sexual abuse, has become a major preoccupation.

In fact, sexual abuse, while deeply disturbing, is relatively uncommon compared with physical abuse and neglect; offences by children are still the most common basis for referral to the reporter. It can be argued that the public and professional focus on sexual abuse has had a distorting effect both on perceptions of the balance of child-care problems and on prioritising efforts to identify and confront them. The impact of a small number of severe but exceptional cases involving sexual abuse may have contributed unduly to the view that children's hearings handling child-abuse referrals are axiomatically different from those dealing with other presenting problems. That they are 'inherently complex' and require fundamental change to the standard form of the children's hearing, is the import of the Association of the Directors of Social Work's submission to the Orkney Inquiry (1992) and, in part, of Lord Clyde's response.

Most distinctive in cases of alleged sexual abuse is the difficulty of obtaining proof and the prevalence of denial (even after proof). It is largely from a court perspective that these types of case are especially problematic. Other forms of abuse and neglect can give rise to equally difficult hearings; cases involving offending and school refusal can be just as complex in arriving at a solution. All types of case coming to hearings have in common an initial judgment by a reporter that children face problems with which the family needs assistance. The focus of work with all childhood care and behaviour problems must, to varying degrees, be family-centred; this is obvious in cases of neglect and abuse, but indications from much of the research into delinquency suggests that early life experience and socialisation are critical. The international research (summarised by Bill Whyte in Chapter 13) suggests that a multi-strategy approach which includes harnessing the positive influence of 'relevant others' leads to a higher possibility of success.

The hearings system itself, it seems to us, provides a potentially rich learning opportunity for the elucidation of such matters as the ability to predict the likelihood of persistent offending and the effectiveness of forms of supervision that enlist family support – a resource which has scarcely been tapped.

A developmental perspective

We referred to the accepted view of two contrasting types of case – offenders and offended against – but it could be argued that in considering children's needs and welfare, it is a false dichotomy – that is, if we view the stages from infancy to adulthood as a continuum of growth and maturation: in short, if we adopt a developmental perspective.

We regard the substitution in the 1995 Act of the term 'relevant person' for 'parent', to cover persons legally recognised as having parental responsibilities and rights, as unnecessary and unhelpful. A more meaningful concept of 'relevant person', from the point of view of a children's hearing, is to identify the party or parties who are most important in the child's development. The relevant person in this sense may change: for the infant, the mother or mother substitute; for the toddler, the intimate family or play leader; for the young schoolchild, first friend or teacher; for the older child, neighbourhood pal or youth leader; and so on until the first intimacies of adolescence. Throughout this period, the roles of parents are also undergoing changes from stage to stage, with varying degrees of appropriateness and sensitivity.

Arguably, the different ages and degrees of maturity of children dealt with by hearings (and whether they are referred alone or with siblings) are as important as the presenting grounds. An advantage of children's hearings is that they have the flexibility to bring into their deliberations any parties who have something to contribute to resolving the problems which children are confronting.

At both ends of the age range issues arise in relation to participation in hearings.

The concept of a 'children's' hearing may need some modification for young people over the age of sixteen, especially for those living outside the parental home. Whether or not the obligation of parental attendance should be dispensed with must take account of the attitudes of family members, especially those of the young person. An appropriate perspective when dealing with adolescents is to recognise that they may already be parents themselves. In any case it may be more relevant to have such young persons accompanied at the hearing by a boyfriend or girlfriend, even if parents are still the legally 'relevant persons'.

One of the consequences of the higher proportion of care and protection grounds is that more young children are the subject of referrals to a hearing. There is a body of opinion that young children should not attend hearings, and it was a standing practice in some areas systematically to excuse them. We have argued that the presumption of twelve as the age at which children are normally sufficiently mature to 'form views' should not to be taken as a threshold for listening to children. If it is legal competence that has given us the age of twelve as a standard, we should note that Scottish courts have taken evidence from children as young as three years old. Seeing children and observing their interaction with parents can be quite as valuable as hearing what they say, and there can be virtue in children seeing themselves included in the decision-making.

The flexibility of children's hearings to modify their procedures to accommodate different developmental stages of children and young persons, and correspondingly different family formations, should not be undermined by the pursuit of uniformity.

Confidentiality

It may seem surprising that the issue of confidentiality has come to the fore after more than twenty-five years of practical experience. However, developments in the 1990s have in different ways brought it to prominence.

A new power which has received general approval is for hearings to speak to children in the absence of 'relevant persons' (and their representatives) but with the obligation to explain to the latter 'the substance of what has taken place' in their absence. As a means of allowing children to express their views it has its limitations. It is important that the chairman explains to the child in advance that the hearing cannot offer to keep the child's view secret. It seems probable that a child fearful of a parental reaction will not feel encouraged to speak, and the procedure runs the risk of compromising the child who has not properly understood the chairman's disclaimer. Our view is that the new power is of value but must be used with caution.

The question of confidentiality also arises in relation to the decision that copies of all reports and documents that are made available to panel members be supplied to all 'relevant persons' and other adults entitled to be present at hearings. As we have seen, this was a measure precipitately introduced by amendment to the Children's Hearings Rules in response to the judgment of the European Court of Justice in *McMichael* v *United Kingdom* (1995) 20 EHRR 205, but it was in line with the principle of openness embodied in the Access to Personal Files Act 1987 and endorsed by the Review of Child Care Law in Scotland (1990). Giving all parties to a hearing the same information and allowing all written submissions to be open to scrutiny is difficult to oppose in principle. However, as Sally Kuenssberg and Alan Miller point out (in Chapter 11), not only does this prevent the child from making any confidential written communication to the hearing similar to that which may be made to the sheriff (discussed by Sheriff Kearney in Chapter 10), but there is no mechanism yet identified to give the child the same information as other parties to the hearing. The new 'openness' runs the risk of enhancing the rights of parents, to the detriment of the interests of children.

At present the greatest concern is for the confidentiality of reports distributed to family members. Regrettably they are not covered by the strict rules which apply to panel members, safeguarders and other official parties for keeping secure and returning all case materials. The normal expectation is no doubt that parents will not wish to make public matters relating to their children, but experience has shown that parents have been less willing than professional participants, panel members and the press to keep children's hearings' business confidential, especially when they consider themselves to be aggrieved parties.

Confidentiality has always been an issue for professionals, especially those who may have a partly therapeutic or counselling relationship with clients or patients upon whom they also have, or acquire, obligations to make reports or give evidence. Where children are of an age to speak openly to trusted adults, but are not able to appreciate fully how information might be used, the ethical position is problematic. The increased emphasis on listening to children, together with the widening of the circle to whom reports for hearings are made available, accentuates the dilemma. How to prepare children for different forms of interview or examination and specifically how to decide what to include in reports to hearings and courts are matters requiring further consideration and guidance.

Resources

It is unfortunate, as several contributors have pointed out, that the reorganisation of local authorities into smaller unitary councils in the mid-1990s has been accompanied by major financial difficulties which have generally led to cuts in social services. An additional factor is the geographical distribution of resources, which has resulted in some of the new councils inheriting much poorer social provision than others, frustrating their ability to meet the requirements of the new legislation. In the most severely affected this may even delay the implementation of procedures as basic as those involving emergency protection of children. Those of our contributors who work for local authorities or in the child-care or hearings system suggest that access to appropriate resources is the central issue.

Potentially, however, the recast local authorities provide some positive aspects. It is now incumbent upon new councils to prepare and publish 'Children's Service Plans', in consultation with, among others, panel chairmen and the principal reporter. Local organisation permits a much greater flexibility than formerly, with opportunities to combine departments within and between authorities. The new authorities are no longer required to have separate social work departments with their own directors, but must provide social work services and have a chief officer responsible for them. An opportunity now exists, it would seem, to escape from the traditional barriers between education, social work and housing, to forge links with the child-health services, and to extend the partnership with the various providers of voluntary resources.

Malcolm Hill (in Chapter 8) has given a full account of the variety of resources which may be used with or without a compulsory requirement, and has indicated a range of value-perspectives which have influenced some of the shifts that have taken place in the types of resources demanded. We have noticed over two and a half decades the growing preference for children to remain in family homes, with one or both parents, or with substitute families rather than in institutional settings, despite the increasing numbers where neglect or abuse at home has been the reason for referral. The almost doctrinal opposition to the use of residential care, which developed in social work circles in the 1980s (never endorsed by panel members), has dissolved to a point where good-quality residential care is seen as a 'positive choice' for a limited number of children (see Chapter 9). There is even a large measure of acceptance of secure accommodation, especially if the educative and care régime it provides is the alternative to punitive custody. We believe that at present there are no great ideological differences between those who provide resources and propose their use and the panel members who make disposals, even though there will be disagreement about what is best for a particular child, especially in the absence of a desired resource.

Our contributors (in Chapters 8 and 9) have referred to the fact that hearings rely increasingly on social work supervision as the commonest resource, and it has been observed more than once that despite the accumulation of experience, exactly what supervision entails has lacked definition and specification. One approach has been to suggest that a treatment plan which specifies achievable goals is needed; another proposes setting standards for the amount of contact (following the model of probation); and most recently the emphasis has been on combining these with 'agreements' or written 'contracts' which set out the expectation upon children and parents as well as upon social workers.

There is little evidence that past guidance on supervision has had a significant effect on practice, and it is too early to judge whether the concept of agreements is helpful. The idea of standardising supervision on the probation model we do not endorse, since this misses the essential point that circumstances, problems and tasks in supporting children at home are widely diverse and demanding. Equally there must be reservation about the concept of 'contracts' with children, if taken too literally. What we do see as a positive step is the recognition that home supervision requires more than a commitment of social work time.

Experts and lay persons

The Kilbrandon Committee's proposal to place responsibility with lay people for deciding what should be done about 'children with problems' was, on the face of it, remarkable. Good reasons can be found for involving fellow citizens in addressing problems in their own communities – a fact which was first recognised in the 1966 White Paper, Social Work and the Community. In Chapter 2 we have presented the justification for the final decision on compulsory intervention lying with representatives of the public, albeit that this is not to be found in the Kilbrandon Report. The Committee's position, it could be argued, was based on the intuition that lay members with common sense were as likely as anyone else to know about 'the right upbringing' since there could be no reliable body of knowledge on the subject.

This contains an element of truth. Two things are clear. The Committee was aware that none of the recognised specialist disciplines dealing with children could be confident of diagnosing and treating all behavioural problems, and any possible improvement would require co-operation between disciplines and with family members. Adequate child care was not essentially a matter to be decided by experts, but this did not imply that there was no place for those with specialist training and skills. While nobody had a monopoly of wisdom, the expectation was that hearings would call upon the skills of trained panel members themselves and make use of 'specialist advisers' to supplement information contained in 'the initial social background report' (para 109).

For reasons that are unclear, hearings have seldom sought the additional assistance of specialist advisers, and where they have received specialist reports, their authors have not usually been invited to participate in hearings. School reports and social background reports have been the staple provision, especially for children whose removal from home is not under consideration. Multi-disciplinary assessments have been most commonly carried out in residential assessment centres, though in recent years more have been done without prior removal from home. To some extent 'case conferences' carried out in social work departments have become the forum for considering a diversity of opinion upon which recommendations to hearings are based, but these (subsequent to proof of grounds) have generally made little use of expertise beyond social work. At worst, case conferences and 'care reviews' have had the effect of keeping knowledge of professional disagreement from hearings and rendering the social worker at the hearing an inflexible delegate for an 'agreed' recommendation.

Martin, Murray and Millar, in their study of the conduct of hearings in child-abuse cases, observed in the early 1980s that panel members were inclined to be unprobing of the content of background reports and too heavily reliant on social work opinion (Martin et al, 1982). So long as hearings are presented with a single point of view with no alternatives, they will have a tendency simply to endorse what is proposed. The limitations of this have been more clearly recognised since the Fife Inquiry. Current guidance is to include and discuss alternatives in social background reports. In our view it is time for hearings to make greater use of their power to seek specialist opinions, to have readily available to them as a resource a variety of expertise in matters relating to children and families, and for there to be a normal expectation that authors of different reports will be invited to participate in hearings. Sheriffs could benefit similarly from a greater use of expert opinion.

Our concern is not simply to open up decisions to wider deliberation and scrutiny, but to broaden the resource base in assessing and assisting children and families. Many cases where there are complex problems – by no means confined to those of child abuse – involving the behaviour of children, adults, or both, could be assisted by specialists in psychology, psychiatry, child guidance and psychotherapy. At present these specialisms are largely to be found dispersed in branches of education and the health service, where they already have heavy commitments and are not able to provide a service readily accessible to reporters, social workers or hearings. In Scotland, as in many other countries, child mental health services remain poorly developed and unintegrated, with the result that some children go undiagnosed and unhelped.

As exemplified by the Lothian Youth Strategy referred to by Russell Forrest (in Chapter 14), some notably successful interdepartmental enterprises between education and social work occurred in the former regions. Too often, however, 'projects' or 'initiatives' which cross professional or disciplinary boundaries have lasted no longer than their short-term funding. Despite that, child-guidance and child-psychiatric units have several decades of experience using a multiprofessional approach to disturbed children and family relationships. They have established the worth of disciplines contributing their related but distinctive skills and orientation to an established team, as well as providing a supportive and learning opportunity for the less experienced.

In complex cases a multiprofessional team approach in working with children and parents needs to become the norm rather than an exception. Our hope is that the reorganisation of local authorities may have sufficiently loosened the departmental approach to children's services to bring interdisciplinary resources, professional expertise and the support services of volunteers into closer co-operation. It is just possible that this might also act as a catalyst for other innovations, such as the provision of child mental health services.

Training, social education and the Scottish dimension

In proposing the pooling and integration of professional services and disciplines, this is not to disregard the skills development in social work or to favour the specialist over the generalist. For twenty-five years, general social work practice has been at the heart of what has been achieved. As Donal Giltinan and Iain Gilmour suggest (in Chapter 9), social work practice has been 'continuously evolving' by learning from experience and, as Malcolm Hill shows (in Chapter 8), this has been accompanied by constant critical reflection on the role of social work in society. We must acknowledge too the extent of the changes that have taken place in social work training. A beginning has been made at joint professional in-service training, which we consider holds the key to the future of interdisciplinary work and interagency co-operation.[5]

There has been parallel progress in the training of other professional groups, but the central role of panel member training in the development of the hearings system merits particular notice. Some professional groups have been slow to

---

[5] The courses in child-care and child-protection work provided by the Department of Social Work at the University of Dundee are a model to be followed.

participate in joint training, but none have been reluctant to help train volunteers. From the beginning the training of panel members has been the meeting place of everyone with an interest, direct or indirect, in the children's hearings system. It is noteworthy that each of the contributors to this book has, to a greater or lesser extent, played a part in panel member training.

The decision of the Social Work Services Group to locate training organisers in the Adult Education Departments of four Scottish universities was a stroke of genius. It provided neutral and high-status arenas to be visited by those in professional practice, and it ensured the lively interest of that part of the Scottish academic community whose disciplines were touched by children, social policy and the justice system. Great credit must go to training organisers who showed no restraint in recruiting colleagues to inform, and in many cases to become, panel members. What the university base has ensured is that the children's hearings system has retained its critical, philosophical, and research-based edge.

Changes that have taken place in panel training have in large measure been led by practice. The establishment in 1995 of a national core curriculum for pre-service, mentioned by Barbara Reid (in Chapter 12), was long overdue. We endorse the principle, still only loosely applied, that continuing training ought to be regarded by Children's Panel Advisory Committees as a condition of continuing appointment. The word 'training' has always been a misnomer. Much of what has been provided by in-service events is the opportunity to share experience, debate issues with other agencies and renew and reinforce the commitment to service.

Vesting the final authority for state intervention in family life in citizen volunteers is the key both to ensuring the participation of family members in the decision process and to giving public credibility to the welfare approach. Just how typical a cross-section of the Scottish public panel members are has been much debated, here and elsewhere. The salient factor which distinguishes them from the public at large is their willingness to be involved in what they consistently view as 'helping' children. We have recalled Kathleen Murray's view of the social significance of educating a cross-section (in Chapter 3) of the Scottish public about those in their communities who have had 'less fortunate life experiences'. The main education is delivered by the experience of sitting on children's hearings rather than by training.

One measure of the success of the children's hearings system is its surviving for over twenty-five years, gaining rather than losing public confidence. Other measures of success are extremely difficult to judge. At worst, there are no indications that there are greater problems of juvenile delinquency, child abuse or family breakdown in Scotland than there are in England and Wales, but of course it is impossible to control for associated social and economic factors.[6] We remarked in the preface that the welfare approach has survived in Scotland despite an increasingly punitive climate elsewhere. It would be a mistake to claim

---

[6] A number of mentions have been made of two current research projects being conducted at the Universities of Stirling and Edinburgh, which aim to throw light on the effectiveness of decision-making. We look forward to the outcome of these studies.

that the population of Scotland is more humane and tolerant than the rest of Britain, or that the different political culture in Scotland demonstrates a greater sympathy and understanding for the juvenile offender or the failing parent.

The Scottish children's hearings system was the product of an enlightened report, from a deceptively conservative-looking committee. It passed into legislation with the support of some inspiring individuals and (to summarise Cowperthwaite, 1988) by good fortune and solid administration. It has become an established Scottish institution – a distinction due in no small measure to the high level of public involvement. In the context of the UK, respect for distinctive Scottish institutions – the legal system, education and the church – is a condition of the Union. Once the children's hearings system became part of the national furniture, it drew to itself much of the support which belongs to other longer-established institutions bound up with Scottish identity.

If our emphasis on the Scottish dimension seems exaggerated, it is because this book has perhaps not sufficiently conveyed the enthusiasm, dedication and commitment which the children's hearings system has invoked among those associated with it. Especially important has been the vocal, sometimes passionate, support of the citizen volunteers themselves. The survey of panel members showed not only an unequivocal commitment to the Kilbrandon principles, but also a high level of pride in their 'Scottishness' (Lockyer, 1992).

It is now clear that Scotland is soon to have its own Parliament, which will give Scottish politicians and the electorate a greater say in distinctively Scottish affairs. The Children (Scotland) Act 1995 will provide the legal framework into the twenty-first century. Scottish children and their families will continue to be dealt with by the arrangements we have discussed. Whether the spirit of Kilbrandon will continue to provide the basis for future development is less certain, though we have more reason to be optimistic as a consequence of the creation of a new constitutional structure in Scotland. But those who have inherited, supported and nurtured the Kilbrandon approach will need to continue to argue for it. This will mean seeking to have their views fully represented in the new political forum, and insisting on the resources required to give the best possible deal to the children and families that the system is designed to help.

Authors

Authors and Editors

Andrew Lockyer is a Senior Lecturer in the Department of Politics at the University of Glasgow. He lectures in political and social philosophy. He was a children's panel member for seventeen years and Chairman of the Strathclyde Panel from 1987 to 1992. His writings include various publications on the hearings system.

Fred Stone is Emeritus Professor of Child and Adolescent Psychiatry at the University of Glasgow. He was a member of the Kilbrandon Committee and Chairman of the Children's Panel Advisory Committee in Strathclyde from 1989 to 1994. He was awarded an OBE for his services to children in 1993. In 1995 he gave the Second Kilbrandon Lecture at Glasgow and wrote the introduction to the republished Kilbrandon Report.

Contributors

Stewart Asquith holds the St Kentigern Chair in the Centre for the Child and Society at the University of Glasgow. He is currently also head of the Department of Social Policy and Social Work. He has written widely on the children's hearings system and juvenile justice within and beyond Scotland, particularly in Central and Eastern Europe. He is engaged in promoting child welfare and research on children and justice with various international organisations.

Russell Forrest is an educational psychologist recently retired from the post of Pupil Support Manager for the Edinburgh City Council Education Department. He was formerly principal psychologist with responsibility for the development of the Youth Strategy and the Children's Family Charter in Lothian Region. He served on the Children's Panel Advisory Committee in Lothian, and has previously published on education and the hearings system.

Iain Gilmour is Senior Depute Director of Social Work for Glasgow City Council. He has wide experience in social work, with particular responsibilities for directing child-care policy and practice. He was formerly Depute Director (Child Care) for Strathclyde Regional Council, a member of the Child Care Law Review in Scotland and he has been president of the Association of Directors of Social Work.

Donal Giltinan is Scottish Director of the British Agencies for Adoption and Fostering. He has played a major role in providing training for social workers, lawyers and others responsible for child care. He was a member of the Child Care Law Review in Scotland and has written on child-care law and professional practice.

Malcolm Hill is Director of the Centre for the Child and Society and Professor of Social Work in the Department of Social Policy and Social Work at the University of Glasgow. His background is in social work practice and education, in which he has international experience. He has carried out research and published extensively on children and families, adoption, children in care and social work.

Brian Kearney is a solicitor and senior sheriff in the Sheriffdom of Glasgow and Strathkelvin. He has written widely on child-care law and on the relationship between children's hearings and the courts in Scotland. He is the author of the main reference book used in practice. He presided over the Inquiry in Child Care Policies in Fife (reporting in 1992). He has advised the government and has had a leading role in lecturing to sheriffs on current legislation.

Sally Kuenssberg was appointed the first Chairman of the Scottish Children's Reporter Administration in 1995. She is a linguist with a background in adult education. She served as a panel member in Glasgow between 1984 and 1990 and subsequently worked for five years as a Children's Panel Training Organiser based in the Department of Adult and Continuing Education at the University of Glasgow.

Alan Miller is the Principal Children's Reporter in Scotland, the first person to occupy this post. He has the leading executive responsibility for the Children's Reporter Service in Scotland. He was previously the Regional Reporter in Dumfries and Galloway, and Secretary of the Association of Children's Reporters. He is qualified in law.

Kathleen Murray is an Honorary Senior Research Fellow in the Centre for the Child and Society at the University of Glasgow. Her involvement in practice and in academic research relating to the hearings system has been extensive. As one of the originally appointed organisers of panel training, she was involved in much of the written work on the hearings system during the first two decades. Recently she has conducted major research on children as witnesses and has written a review of the literature on the prevention of child abuse.

Barbara Reid is a lecturer responsible for children's panel training in the Department of Adult and Continuing Education at the University of Glasgow. She was Depute Chairman of Strathclyde Children's Panel from 1987 to 1992 and Chairman from 1992 to 1996, in which roles she was involved in research on panel members and in consultation on the implementation of legislation. She was a panel member for twenty years and, in 1996, received an OBE for her services.

Bill Whyte is a Senior Lecturer and Programme Director of Advanced Social Work Studies in Criminal Justice at the Universities of Edinburgh and Stirling. He has a social work and research background and has made a major contribution to training social workers and panel members. He is currently involved in research commissioned by the Scottish Office to evaluate the effectiveness of the children's hearings system.

References

(Articles, books, reports and White Papers, etc)

Adler, R M (1985), *Taking Juvenile Justice Seriously*, Scottish Academic Press.

Advisory Council on Education in Scotland (1947), Report on Secondary Education.

Ainscow, M (1991), 'Effective schools for all: An alternative approach to special needs in education', *Educational and Child Psychology*, 82.

Aldgate, J, Bradley, M and Hawley, D (1996), 'Respite accommodation: A case study of partnership under the Children Act 1989' in Hill, M and Aldgate, J (eds) *Child Welfare Services*, Jessica Kingsley.

Allen, F (1973), 'Criminal justice, legal values and the rehabilitative ideal' in Murphy, J (ed) *Punishment and Rehabilitation*, Wadsworth, Belmont, California.

Alston P, Parker, S and Seymour, J (1992), *Children, Rights and the Law*, Clarendon Press.

Amato, P R and Keith, B (1991), 'Parental divorce and well-being of children: A meta-analysis', *Psychological Bulletin*, 110: 1.

Anderson, R, Kinsey, R, Loader, I and Smith, C (1992), *Cautionary Tales*, University of Edinburgh Centre for Criminology.

Andrews, D, Zinger, I, Hoge, R, Bonta, J, Gendreau, P and Cullen, F (1990), 'Does correctional treatment work? A clinically relevant and psychologically informed meta-analysis', *Criminology*, 28: 3

Anstey, S C F (1976), A study of List D schools for girls, their modes of treatment and some of their effects on girls, PhD thesis, Department of Social Administration, University of Edinburgh (unpublished).

Asquith, S (1977), 'Relevance and lay participation in juvenile justice', *British Journal of Law and Society*, 4, 1.

Asquith, S (1981), 'Justice for children: a black outlook', *The Hearing: Bulletin of the Panel Training Resource Centre*, 3, University of Glasgow.

Asquith, S (1983), *Children and Justice: Decision-Making in Children's Hearings and Juvenile Courts*, Edinburgh University Press.

Asquith, S (1987), 'Children's hearings: The research contribution', *Scottish Concern, Journal of the National Children's Bureau Scottish Group*, 13.

Asquith, S (1992a), 'Coming of age: 21 years of the children's hearings system', in Paterson, C and McCrone, D (eds) *Scottish Government Yearbook 1992*, Unit for the Study of Government in Scotland, Edinburgh.

Asquith, S (1992b), 'Natura ed evoluzione della criminalita minorile nell'Europa occidentale' in Palomba, F (ed) *Esperienze di giustizia minorile*, Roma.

Asquith, S (ed) (1993), Protecting Children: Cleveland to Orkney: More Lessons to Learn, HMSO, Edinburgh.

Asquith, S (1995), Analysis of Provisions for Young Offenders in Member States of the Council of Europe, Council of Europe.

Asquith, S (1996), 'Juvenile justice in Central and Eastern Europe', Council of Europe.

Asquith, S, Buist, M, Loughran, N, MacAulay, C and Montgomery, M (1996), Children, Young People and Offending in Scotland, The Scottish Office.

Asquith, S and Docherty, M (1998, forthcoming), 'Preventing offending by children and young people in Scotland: A Utopian response?' *Journal of Scottish Affairs*.

Asquith, S and Hill, M (eds) (1994), *Justice for Children*, Kluwer.
Association of the Directors of Social Work (1992), Child Protection: Policy, Practice and Procedure, HMSO, Edinburgh.
Audit Commission (1996), *Misspent Youth*, London.
Ayalon, O and Flasher, A (1993), *Chain Reaction: Children and Divorce*, Jessica Kingsley.
Bailleau, F (1996), *Les jeunes face à la justice penale*, Syros, Paris.
Ballantyne, N (1995), 'Diversion at the point of entry to the Scottish children's hearings system: Area team resource groups' in Fuller, R and Petch, A (eds) *Practitioner Research*, Open University Press, Bristol.
Barnett, R (1977), 'Restoration: A new paradigm of criminal justice' in Barnett, R and Hagel, J (eds) *Assessing the Criminal*, Ballenger, Cambridge.
Barrie, C (1977), An investigation into personality characteristics of panel members, MAppSc thesis, University of Glasgow.
Bebbington, A R and Miles, J (1989), 'The background of children who enter local authority care', *British Journal of Social Work*, 19.
Becker, H (1963), *Outsiders*, Free Press, New York.
Berridge, D and Cleaver, H (1987), *Foster Home Breakdown*, Blackwell.
Biehal, N, Clayden, J, Stein, M and Wade, J (1995), Moving On: Young People and Leaving Care Schemes, HMSO, London.
Bilson, A and Thorpe, D (1987), *Care Careers and their Management*, Fife Regional Council, Glenrothes.
Bissett-Johnson, A (1994), 'Cost of Orkney and Fife Inquiries', *Journal of Social Welfare Law and Family Law*.
Black, Lord (1979), Report of the Children and Young Persons Review Group (Black Report), HMSO, Belfast.
Blyth, E and Milner, J (1996), *Exclusion from School: Inter Professional Issues for Policy and Practice*, Routledge.
Borland, M, O'Hara, G and Triseliotis, J (1991), 'Placement outcomes for children with special needs', *Adoption and Fostering*, 15: 2.
Borowski, E (1981), 'Looking-glass justice', *The Hearing: Bulletin of the Panel Training Resource Centre*, 2, University of Glasgow.
Borowski, E (1982), 'Honesty: the best policy', *The Hearing: Bulletin of the Panel Training Resource Centre*, 6, University of Glasgow.
Boswell, D G (1995), *Violent Victims, The Prevalence of Abuse and Loss in the Lives of Section 53 Offenders*, The Prince's Trust, London.
Bottoms, A *et al* (1990), Intermediate Treatment and Juvenile Justice, HMSO, London.
Boushel, M (1994), 'The protective environment of children: towards a framework for anti-oppressive, cross-cultural and cross-national understanding', *British Journal of Social Work*, 24.
Bowlby, J (1951), Maternal Care and Mental Health, WHO, Geneva; HMSO, London.
Bowlby, J (1979), *The Making and Breaking of Affectional Bonds*, Tavistock.
Bristol District Auditors (1981), The Provision of Child Care: A Study of Eight Local Authorities in England and Wales.
Brown, P (1979), 'The hearing process: Telling it like it is' in Brown, P and Bloomfield, T (eds) *Legality and Community*, Aberdeen People's Press.
Bruce, T (1987), *Early Childhood Education*, Hodder & Stoughton.
Bruce, N (1982), Interagency Cooperation in the Primary School, University of Edinburgh (report sponsored by SED and SWSG).
Buist M, MacPherson, M and Asquith, S (1993), Lothian Region's Children's Family Charter, Centre for the Study of the Child and Society, University of Glasgow.
Bull, R and Davies, G (1996), 'The effect of child witness research on legislation in Great Britain' in Bottoms, B L and Goodman, G S (eds) *International Perspectives on Child Abuse and Children's Testimony*, Sage.
Bullock, R, Little, M and Millham, S (1993), *Going Home*, Dartmouth.

Butler-Sloss, Lord (1988), Report of the Inquiry into Child Abuse in Cleveland 1987, (Cleveland Inquiry Report) HMSO, London.

Butler-Sloss, Lord (1993), 'From Cleveland to Orkney' in Asquith, S (ed) Protecting Children: Cleveland to Orkney: More Lessons to Learn, HMSO, Edinburgh.

Campion, M J (1995), *Who's Fit to be a Parent?*, Routledge.

Catton, K and Erickson, P G (1975), 'The juvenile's perception of the role of defence council in juvenile court', Centre for Criminolgy, Working Paper Series, Toronto.

Cavadino, P (1996), *Children Who Kill*, British Juvenile Family Court Magistrates Association.

Change (1980), Papers given at the 7th Children's Panel Summer School, August 1980, University of Edinburgh (unpublished).

Child, the Family and the Young Offender, The (1965) (White Paper), Cmnd 2742, HMSO, London.

Children in Trouble (1968) (White Paper), Cmnd 3601, HMSO, London.

Clark, D F (1977), 'Personality characteristics of applicants and members of children's panels', *British Journal of Criminology*, 17.

Cleaver, H (1996), Focus on Teenagers, Department of Health, HMSO, London.

Cleland, A (1995), *Guide to the Children (Scotland) Act 1995*, Scottish Child Law Centre, Glasgow.

Cleland, A and Sutherland, E (1996) (eds) *Children's Rights in Scotland*, W Green.

Clyde, Lord (1946), Report of the Committee on Homeless Children, (J L Clyde Report), Cmnd 6991, HMSO, Edinburgh.

Clyde, Lord (1992), The Report of the Inquiry into the Removal of Children from Orkney in February 1991 (Orkney Inquiry Report), HMSO, Edinburgh.

Cochran, M, Larner, D, Riley, D, Gunnarson, L and Henderson, C R (1990), *Extending Families: The Social Networks of Parents and Their Children*, Cambridge University Press.

Cohen, A (1966), *Deviance and Control*, Prentice Hall.

Cohen, B (1995), *Childcare Services for Rural Families*, European Commission, Brussels.

Comfort, A (1970), *Authority and Delinquency*, Sphere Books.

Committee of Enquiry into Discipline in Schools (1989) (Elton Report).

Consultative Memorandum on Powers and Procedures (1980).

Cowperthwaite, D J (1988), *The Emergence of the Scottish Children's Hearings System*, Institute of Criminal Justice, University of Southampton.

Crime and Punishment (1996) (White Paper), Cm 3302, HMSO, Edinburgh.

Croft, J (1981), Managing Criminological Research, Home Office Research Study, No 69, Home Office, London.

Crowne, D P and Marlow, D (1964), *The Approval Motive*, John Wiley.

Curran, J H (1977), The Children's Hearing System: A Review of Research, HMSO, Edinburgh (supplementary mimeo, 1979).

Curran, J H (1983), The relevance of research to the working of the juvenile justice system in Scotland, paper presented at a Scottish Office Central Research Unit seminar, 24th March 1983.

Curran, J H (1989), Safeguarders in the Children's Hearings System, Central Research Unit, SWSG, Edinburgh.

Curtis, M (1946), Care of Children Committee (Curtis Report), HMSO.

Davidson, R (1991), 'Financial assistance from social workers' in Davidson, R and Erskine, A (eds) *Social Work Response to Poverty and Deprivation*, Jessica Kingsley.

De Mause, L (ed) (1974), *The History of Childhood*, Psychohistory Press, New York.

Dearden, R F (1968), *The Philosophy of Primary Education*, Routledge.

Department of Health (1991), Patterns and Outcomes in Child Placement, HMSO, London.

Docherty, M (1997), Parricide by Children and Young People, Centre for the Child and Society, University of Glasgow (occasional paper).

Donnison, D V (1954), *The Neglected Child and the Social Services*, Manchester University Press.

Dunkel, F (1991), 'Legal differences in juvenile criminology in Europe' in Booth, T (ed) *Juvenile Justice in the New Europe*, Social Services Monograph: Research in Practice, Sheffield.

Dunpark, Lord (1977), Reparation by the Offender to the Victim in Scotland, (Dunpark Report), Cmnd 6802, HMSO, Edinburgh.

Duquette, D N (1992), 'Scottish children's hearings and representation for the child' in Asquith, S and Hill, M (eds) *Justice for Children*, Martinus Nijhoff.

Ellis, H (ed) (1890), *The Criminal*, Walter Scott.

Erickson, P G (1982), 'The client's perspective' in Martin, F M and Murray, K (eds) *The Scottish Juvenile Justice System*, Scottish Academic Press.

European Convention on Human Rights (ratified 1953) in Brownlie, I (ed) (1971) *Basic Documents on Human Rights*, Clarendon Press.

Fahlberg, V (1994), *A Child's Journey Through Placement*, British Agencies for Adoption and Fostering, London.

Falck, A and Dunant, A (1996), *Juvenile Delinquency in Estonia*, Council of Europe.

Farrington, D (1994), 'Early developmental prevention of juvenile delinquency', *RSA Journal*.

Farrington, D and West, D (1977), *The Delinquent Way of Life*, Heinemann.

Farson, D (1974), *Birthrights*, Collier Macmillan.

Fenyo, A, Knapp, M and Baines, B (1991), Foster Care Breakdown: A Study of a Special Teenager Fostering Scheme, PSSRU, University of Kent.

Ferri, E (ed) (1993), *Life at 33*, National Children's Bureau, London.

Finlayson, A (1992), Reporters to the Children's Panels: Their Role, Function and Accountability (Finlayson Report), SWSG, The Scottish Office, HMSO, Edinburgh.

Finlayson, A F (1996), Lothian Children's Family Charter: Third Annual Report by Adjudicator, Lothian Regional Council.

Flin, R H, Boon, J, Knox, A and Bull, R (1992), 'The effects of a five-month delay on children's and adults' eyewitness memory', *British Journal of Psychology*, 83.

Fonagy, P, Steele, M, Steele, H, Higgitt, A and Target, M (1994), 'The theory and practice of resilience' *Journal of Child Psychology and Psychiatry*, 35: 2.

Ford, R (1982), 'Consequences' in Martin, F M and Murray, K (eds) *The Scottish Juvenile Justice System*, Scottish Academic Press.

Fox, L M (1982), 'Two value positions in recent child care law and practice', *British Journal of Social Work*, 12: 2.

Fox, S (1974), 'Juvenile justice: Reform innovations in Scotland', *American Criminal Law Review*, 12: 1.

Fox, S (1991), Children's Hearings and the International Community, The Kilbrandon Child Care Lecture, HMSO, Edinburgh.

Fox Harding, L M (1991), *Perspectives in Child Care Policy*, Longman.

Fox Harding, L M (1996), *Family, State and Social Policy*, Macmillan.

Francis, J and Thomson, G (1995), The Quality of the Educational Experience of Children in Care, University of Edinburgh (unpublished report).

Fraser, Lord (1993), 'Legislating for child protection' in Asquith, S (ed) Protecting Children: Cleveland to Orkney: More Lessons to Learn, HMSO, Edinburgh.

Freeman, I, Morrison, A, Lockhart, F and Swanson, M (1996), 'Consulting service users: The views of young people' in Hill, M and Aldgate, J (eds) *Child Welfare Services*, Jessica Kingsley.

Freire, P (1996), *Pedagogy of the Oppressed*, Pelican.

Garrett, C J (1985), 'Effects of residential treatment on adjudicated delinquents: A meta-analysis', *Journal of Research in Crime and Delinquency*, 22.

Gendreau, P and Ross, R (1987), 'Revivification or rehabilitation: evidence from the 1980s', *Justice Quarterly*, 4: 3.

Gibbons, J (1995), 'Family support in child protection' in Hill, M, Kirk, R H and Part, D (eds) Supporting Families, HMSO, Edinburgh.

Gibbons, J, Gallagher, B, Bell, C and Gordon, D (1995), After Physical Abuse in Early Childhood: A follow-up study of children on Protection Registers, HMSO.

Giddens, A (1994), *Beyond Left and Right: The Future of Radical Politics*, Polity Press.

Gilligan, R (1997), 'Beyond permanence: The importance of resilience in child placement practice and learning', *Adoption and Fostering*, 21: 1.

Godwin, C (1976) 'The Rules of Procedure' in Martin, F M and Murray, K (eds) *Children's Hearings*, Scottish Academic Press.

Goffman, E (1968), *Stigma: Notes on the management of spoiled identity*, Pelican.

Gordon, G (1976), 'The role of the courts' in Martin, F M and Murray, K (eds) *Children's Hearings*, Scottish Academic Press.

Graham, J (1996), 'The organisation and functioning of juvenile justice in England and Wales' in Asquith, S (ed) *Children and Crime*, Jessica Kingsley.

Graham, J and Bowling, B (1995), Young People and Crime, Research Findings No 24, Home Office, London.

Grant, J (1975), 'The legal safeguards for the rights of the child and parents in children's hearings', *Juridical Review*, 209.

Grant, J (1976), 'Protecting the rights of the child' in Martin, F M and Murray, K (eds) *Children's Hearings*, Scottish Academic Press.

Grant, J (1982) 'The role of the hearing procedural aspects' in Martin, F M and Murray, K (eds) *The Scottish Juvenile Justice System*, Scottish Academic Press.

Grieve, W (1981), 'Reflections on the Annual Conference of the Reporters' Association, March 1981' *The Hearing: Bulletin of the Panel Training Resource Centre*, June, University of Glasgow.

Grieve, W (1993) 'A Report on the Seminar on the Role of the Safeguarder', Save the Children, Edinburgh (unpublished).

Guthrie, T (1847), 'First plea for ragged schools' in *The Centenary Celebration of Dr Guthrie's School for Boys and Girls* (1947), Stewart & Co, Edinburgh.

Hafen, B and Hafen, J (1996), 'Abandoning children to their autonomy: The United Nations Convention on the Rights of the Child', *Harvard International Law Journal*, 37: 2.

Hagell, A and Newburn, T (1994), The Persistent Offender, Policy Studies Institute, London.

Halsey, A H (1993), 'Changes in the family' in Pugh, G (ed) *30 Years of Change*, National Children's Bureau, London.

Handy, C and Aitken, R (1990), *Understanding Schools as Organisations*, Penguin.

Hardiker, P, Exton, K and Barker, M (1991), *Policies and Practices in Preventive Child Care*, Avebury.

Hart, H L A and Honore, A M (1959), *Causation in the Law*, Clarendon Press.

Heide, K (1993), 'Parents who get killed and the children who kill them', *Journal of Interpersonal Violence* 8 (4th December).

Heide, K (1995), *Why Kids Kill Their Parents: Child Abuse and Homicide*, Sage.

Hendrick, H (1994), *Child Welfare: England 1872–1989*, Routledge.

Higgins, L (1979), 'Personality characteristics of children's panel members and members of other voluntary organisations', PhD thesis, University of Glasgow (unpublished).

Hill, M (1987), *Sharing Child Care in Early Parenthood*, Routledge & Kegan Paul.

Hill, M, Kirk, R H and Part, D (1995), 'Supporting families: changes, challenges and dilemmas' in Hill, M, Kirk, R H and Part, D (eds) Supporting Families, HMSO, Edinburgh.

Hill, M, Lambert, L and Triseliotis, J (1989), *Achieving Adoption with Love and Money*, National Children's Bureau, London.

Hill, M, Murray, K and Rankin, J (1991), 'The early history of Scottish child welfare', *Children and Society*, 5: 2, 182–195.

Hill, M, Murray, K and Tisdall, K (1997), 'Children's services' in English, J (ed) *Social Services in Scotland*, Mercat Press.

Hill, M, Triseliotis, J, Borland, M and Lambert, L (1996), 'Outcomes for teenagers on supervision and in care' in Hill, M and Aldgate, J (eds) *Child Welfare in the United Kingdom and Ireland*, Jessica Kingsley.

Holman, B (1988), *Putting Families First*, Macmillan.

Holman, B (1996), 'Fifty years ago: The Curtis and Clyde Reports', *Children and Society*, 10.

Holt, J (1975), *Escape from Childhood*, Penguin.

Home Office Statistical Bulletin (1985), Criminal Careers of Those Born in 1953, 1958 and 1963, Home Office, London.

Howe, D (1996), *Adopters on Adoption*, British Agencies for Adoption and Fostering, London.

Howells, J (1974), *Remember Maria*, Butterworths.

Howells, L A L, Furnell, J R G, Puckering, C and Harris, J (1996), 'Children's experiences of the children's hearings system: A preliminary study of anxiety', *Legal and Criminological Psychology*, 1.

Hutcheson, G, Baxter, J, Telfer, K and Warden, D (1995), 'Child witness statement quality: Question type and errors of omission', *Law and Human Behaviour*, 19.

Ingleby, Lord (1960), Report of the Committee on Children and Young Persons (Ingleby Report), Cmnd 1191, HMSO, London.

Institute of Economic Affairs (1995), reported in the *Independent on Sunday*, 5th March 1995.

Intermediate Treatment Resource Centre (1986), Review of IT in Scotland, ITRC, Glasgow.

Jenkins, J M and Smith, M A (1991), 'Marital disharmony and children's behaviour problems: Aspects of a poor marriage that affect children adversely', *Journal of Child Psychology and Psychiatry*, 32: 5.

Johnstone, H (1995), Interface of the Children's Hearing System and the Criminal Justice System, MSc thesis, University of Edinburgh (unpublished).

Jones, C and Adler, M (1990), *Can Anyone Get On One of These? A Study of the Systems of Appointment and Training of Justices of the Peace and Members of Social Security Appeals Tribunals and Children's Panels in Scotland*, Scottish Consumer Council, Glasgow.

Jones, G and Wallace, C (1992), *Youth, Family and Citizenship*, Open University Press, Buckingham.

Jones, H E and Gallagher, J (1985), Intermediate Treatment in Scotland, The Scottish Office.

Kearney, B (1987), *Children's Hearings and the Sheriff Court*, Butterworths.

Kearney, B (1992), The Report of the Inquiry into Child Care Policies in Fife (Fife Inquiry Report), HMSO, Edinburgh.

Kearney, B (1997), 'Children's hearings, child protection *and* the Children (Scotland) Act 1995, *SCOLAG Legal Journal*, 243.

Kelly, A (1996), *Introduction to the Scottish Children's Panel*, Waterstone Press.

Kelly, D (1992), *Children Inside: Rhetoric and Practice in a Locked Institution for Children*, Routledge.

Kempe, C H *et al* (1962), 'The battered child syndrome', *Journal of the American Medical Association*, 181.

Kendrick, A (1995a), 'Residential Care in the Integration of Child Care Services', *Research Findings No 5*, The Scottish Office Central Research Unit.

Kendrick, A (1995b), 'Supporting families through inter-agency work: Youth strategies in Scotland' in Hill, M, Kirk, R H and Part, D (eds) Supporting Families, HMSO, Edinburgh.

Kendrick, A and Mapstone, E (1992), 'Reviewing practice in two Scottish social work departments' in Batty, D and Robson, J (eds) *Statutory Reviews in Practice*, British Agencies for Adoption and Fostering, London.

Kennedy, R and McIvor, G (1992), Young Offenders in the Children's Hearing and

Criminal Justice Systems: A Comparative Analysis, Tayside Regional Council (unpublished report).

Kiernan, K (1992), 'The impact of family disruption in childhood on transitions made in young adult life', *Population Studies*, 46.

Kiernan, K and Wicks, M (1990), Family Change and Future Policy, Family Policy Studies Centre, London.

Kilbrandon, Lord (1964), Report of the Committee on Children and Young Persons. Scotland (Kilbrandon Report), Cmnd 2306, HMSO; republished 1995 with Stone, F 'Introduction', Children in Society Series, HMSO, Edinburgh.

Kilbrandon, Lord (1966), 'Children in Trouble', *British Journal of Criminology*, 6.

Kilbrandon, Lord (1976), Foreword to Martin, F M and Murray, K (eds) *Children's Hearings*, Scottish Academic Press.

King, M (1997) *A Better World for Children: Explorations in Morality and Authority*, Routledge.

Kirk, R H (1995), 'Social support and early years centres' in Hill, M, Kirk, R H and Part, D (eds) Supporting Families, HMSO, Edinburgh.

Knight, B (1993), *Voluntary Action*, Centris.

Kosonen, M (1993), Evaluation of Foster and Adoptive Care Services in Tayside, Tayside Regional Council, Dundee.

Kuenssberg, S (ed) (1996), *A Distinctive Task: Reflections on the Reporter Service 1970–1996*, The Scottish Children's Reporter Association.

Kumar, V (1993), *Poverty and Inequality in the UK: The Effects on Children*, National Children's Bureau, London.

Lambert, L, Buist, M, Triseliotis, J and Hill, M (1991), *Freeing Children for Adoption*, British Agencies for Adoption and Fostering, London.

Laybourn, A (1986), 'Traditional strict working class parenting – an undervalued system', *British Journal of Social Work*, 16: 6.

League of Nations Geneva Declaration on the Rights of the Child (1924).

Lipsey, M (1992a), 'Juvenile delinquency treatment: A meta-analytical inquiry into the viability of effects' in Cook, T *et al*, *Meta-analysis for Explanation*, Sage, New York.

Lipsey, M (1992b), 'The effects of treatment of juvenile delinquents: Results from meta-analysis' in Losel, F *et al* (eds) *Psychology and Law: International Perspectives*, De Gruyer, Berlin.

Littlewood, P (1996), 'Secure Units' in Asquith, S (ed) *Children and Young People in Conflict with the Law*, Research Highlights in Social Work 30, Jessica Kingsley.

Locke, J (1687) *Second Treatise on Government* in Laslett, P (ed) (1967) Cambridge University Press.

Lockyer, A (1982), 'Justice and welfare' in Martin, F and Murray, K (eds) *The Scottish Juvenile Justice System*, Scottish Academic Press.

Lockyer, A (1983), 'Training by observation and discussion', *The Hearing: Bulletin of the Panel Training Resource Centre*, 9.

Lockyer, A (1988), Study of Children's Hearings' Disposals in Relation to Resources, Children's Panel Chairmen's Group, Macdonald Lindsay.

Lockyer, A (1989), 'The Scottish children's hearings system: Community or state control?' in Hudson, J and Galloway, B *The State as Parent: International Research Perspectives on Interventions with Young Persons*, NATO ASI Series, Kluwer.

Lockyer, A (1992), Citizen's Service and Children's Panel Membership, Children's Panel Chairmen's Group, Edinburgh; The Scottish Office Social Work Services Group.

Lockyer, A (1994a), 'The Scottish children's hearings system: internal developments and the UN Convention' in Asquith, S and Hill, M (eds) *Justice for Children*, Kluwer.

Lockyer, A (1994b), Interests and advocacy: Identifying the role of safeguarders in the Scottish children's hearings system', *Children & Society*, 8: 1.

Long, G (1995), 'Family poverty and the role of family support work' in Hill, M, Kirk, R H and Part, D (eds) Supporting Families, HMSO, Edinburgh.

Longford, Lord (1964), Crime: A Challenge To Us All (Longford Report), Labour Party Study Group.

Longitudinal Study (1980), Children and Hearings: A Longitudinal Study of Children Referred to Reporters, Statistics Branch, Social Work Services Group, Edinburgh.

Lord Chancellor's Department (1984), Justices of the Peace in England and Wales: Their Appointment and Duties Explained, Central Office of Information, HMSO, London.

Lothian Region (1994), Children's Record System – June 1994, Social Work Department, Edinburgh.

Lothian Regional Council (1992), The Lothian Children's Family Charter, HMSO, Edinburgh.

McBoyle, Lord (1963), Report of the Committee on the Prevention of Neglect of Children (McBoyle Report), Cmnd 1466, HMSO, London.

MacDonald, G and Roberts, H (1995), *What Works in the Early Years*, Barnardo's, London.

McGhee, J, Waterhouse, L and Whyte, B (1996), 'Children's hearings and children in trouble' in Asquith, S (ed) *Children and Young People in Conflict with the Law*, Jessica Kingsley.

McGough, L (1994), *Fragile Voices: The Child Witness in American Courts*, Yale University Press.

McGuire, J and Priestley, P (1995), 'Reviewing "What Works": past, present and future' in McGuire, J (ed) *What Works: Research and Practice on the Reduction of Re-Offending*, John Wiley.

McKay, M (1980), 'Planning for permanent placement', *Adoption and Fostering*, 4: 1.

McLanahan, S and Booth, K (1989), 'Mother-only families: Problems, prospects and politics', *Journal for Marriage and the Family*, 51.

McLean, A (1990), Promoting Positive Behaviour in the Primary/Secondary School, Strathclyde Regional Council.

McLean, S (1983), 'Professionalism and Juvenile Justice', *Journal of Social Welfare Law*, 3.

McMichael, P (1974), 'After-care, family relationships and reconviction in Scottish approved schools', *British Journal of Criminology*, 14: 3.

Mack, J (1953), *Family and Community*, Carnegie United Kingdom Trust.

Maluccio, A, Fein, E and Olmstead, K A (1986), *Permanency Planning for Children*, Tavistock.

Mapstone, E, (1973), 'The selection of the children's panel for the County of Fife', *British Journal of Social Work*, 3, 4.

Marshall, K (1994), 'Looking after Scotland's children in the twenty-first century', *Adoption and Fostering*, 18: 3.

Marshall, K (1992), Submission to the Orkney Inquiry, Scottish Child Law Centre (unpublished).

Martin, F M (1976), 'The Social Work Department' in Martin, F M and Murray, K (eds) *Children's Hearings*, Scottish Academic Press.

Martin, F M (1979), 'Comparative social policy research and the components of the United Kingdom', Paper presented at the SSRC Workshop on Comparative Social Policy Research, September 1979, Edinburgh.

Martin, F M (1982a), 'Reparation in theory and in practice', *The Hearing: Bulletin of the Panel Training Resource Centre*, 7.

Martin, F M (1982b), 'The role of the hearings: Decisions' in Martin, F M and Murray, K (eds) *The Scottish Juvenile Justice System*, Scottish Academic Press.

Martin, F M (1983a), 'Regions Caesar never knew', *The Hearing: Bulletin of the Panel Training Resource Centre*, February.

Martin, F M (1983b), 'Curators ad Litem – ad Infinitum', in *The Hearing: Bulletin of the Panel Training Resource Centre*, 9.

Martin, F M and Murray, K (1976), 'Achievements, issues and prospects' in Martin, F M and Murray, K (eds) *Children's Hearings*, Scottish Academic Press.

Martin, F M and Murray, K (1981), 'The lay component in Scottish juvenile justice', *Law and Human Behaviour*, 5, 2/3.

Martin, F M and Murray, K (1983), 'The end of the road: Residential disposals in the Scottish children's hearings system', *Journal of Adolescence*, 6.

Martin, F M, Murray, K, and Millar, H (1982), 'The role of children's hearings in child abuse and neglect', *Child Abuse and Neglect*, 6.

Martin, F, Fox, S and Murray, K (1981), *Children Out of Court*. Scottish Academic Press.

Martinson, R (1974), 'What Works? Questions and answers about prison reform', *The Public Interest*, 10.

Maudsley, H (1872), 'Responsibility in mental disease', King, London.

May, D (1971), 'Delinquency control and the treatment model: Some implications of recent legislation', *British Journal of Criminology*, 11: 4.

May, D (1977), 'Rhetoric and reality: The consequences of unacknowledged ambiguity in the children's panel system', *British Journal of Criminology*, 17: 3.

May, D (1979), 'The children's hearing system, Part 1. The limits of legislative action', Part 2, 'The limits to social work influences', *Journal of Social Welfare Law*, 1, 1.

May, D and Smith, G (1970), 'Policy interpretation and the children's panels', *Journal of Applied Social Studies*, 2.

May, D and Smith, G (1971), 'The appointment of the Aberdeen City Children's Panel', *British Journal of Social Work*, 1, 1.

May, D and Smith, G (1980), 'Gentleman v Players: Lay-professional relations in the administration of juvenile justice', *British Journal of Social Work*, 10.

Meek, R (1982), *The Hearing: Bulletin of the Panel Training Resource Centre*, February.

Mellor, A and Dent, H (1994), 'Preparation of the child witness for court', *Child Abuse Review*, 3.

Middleton, S Ashworth, K and Walker, R (eds) (1994), *Family Fortunes: Pressures on Parents and Children in the 1990s*, Children's Poverty Action Group, London.

Millham, S *et al* (1975), *After Grace Teeth*, Human Context Books.

Mitchell, A (1985), *Children in the Middle*, Tavistock.

Mitchell, J K (1997), 'The Children's hearing system and the Children (Scotland) Act 1995', *SCOLAG Legal Journal*, 240.

Montoya, J (1995), 'Lessons from Akiki and Michaels on shielding child witnesses', *Psychology, Public Policy and Law*, 1.

Moody, S R (1976), Survey of the Background of Current Panel Members, Scottish Home and Health Department mimeo.

Morris, A and Giller, H (1977), 'The juvenile court – the client's perspective', *Criminal Law Review*.

Morris, A and Giller, H (1983), *Understanding Juvenile Justice*, Croom Helm.

Morris, A and McIsaac, M (1978), *Juvenile Justice?*, Heinemann.

Morris, A, Giller, H, Szwed, E, and Geach, H (1980), *Justice for Children*, Macmillan.

Morrison, M (1996), 'Permanency planning' in *The Children (Scotland) Act 1995: A Training Programme*, British Agencies for Adoption and Fostering, London.

Munn, J (1977), The Structure of the Curriculum in the Third and Fourth Years of the Scottish Secondary School (Munn Report), SED, HMSO, Edinburgh.

Munn, P (ed) (1994), *Schooling with Care?*, Scottish Council for Research in Education, Edinburgh.

Murphy J (1992), *British Social Services. The Scottish Dimension*, Scottish Academic Press.

Murray, K (1976) 'The children's panel' in Martin, F M and Murray K (eds) *Children's Hearings*, Scottish Academic Press.

Murray, K, (1980), 'Attitudes to change in the children's hearings system', *The Hearing Bulletin of the Panel Training Resource Centre*, 1.

Murray, K (1981), 'Children at Risk. The Management of Child Abuse and Neglect in the Children's Hearings System', Proceedings of the 1981 Children's Panel Summer School, University of Glasgow.

Murray, K (1995), Live Television Link: An Evaluation of its Use by Child Witnesses in Scottish Criminal Trials, The Scottish Office Central Research Unit, Edinburgh.

Myers, J E B (1992), 'Steps toward forensically relevant research' in Goodman, G, Taub, E, Jones, D, England, P, Port, L, Rudy, L and Prado, L (eds) Testifying in Criminal Court: Emotional Effects on Child Sexual Abuse Victims, monograph of the Society for Research in Child Development, 57: 5.

Nelson, S (1995), 'Locking up Pandora's Box', *Scottish Child*, April/May.

Newman, N and Mackintosh, H (1975), *A Roof Over Their Heads?* Department of Social Administration, University of Edinburgh.

Nicholson, G and Murray, K (1992), 'The child witness in Scotland', in Dent, H and Flin, R (eds) *Children as Witnesses*, John Wiley.

Noller, P and Callan, V (1991), *The Adolescent in the Family*, Routledge.

Norrie, K (1995), *Children (Scotland) Act 1995*, W. Green.

Norrie, K, 'In Defence *of O* v *Rae*', 1995 SLT (News) 353.

Norrie, K (1997), *Children's Hearings in Scotland*, W. Green.

O'Hara, G and Hoggan, P (1988), 'Permanent substitute family care in Lothian – placement outcome', *Adoption and Fostering*, 12: 3.

Oliver, A (1982), 'Progress made since the Secretary of State's statement on 19th May 1981', *The Hearing: Bulletin of the Panel Training Resource Centre*, 5.

Ollenburger, J C (1986), 'Panel members' attitudes towards justice', *British Journal of Criminology*, 26.

Pack, D (1977), Truancy and Indiscipline in Schools in Scotland (Pack Report), HMSO, Edinburgh.

Packman, J, Randall, J and Jacques, N (1986), *Who Needs Care?*, Blackwell.

Petch, A (1988) 'Answering back: Parental perspectives on the children's hearings system', *British Journal of Social Work*, 18.

Phillips, R and McWilliam, E (1996), *After Adoption*, British Agencies for Adoption and Fostering, London.

Pitts, J (1988), *The Politics of Juvenile Crime*, Sage.

Plotnikoff, J and Woolfson, R (1996), The Child Witness Support Initiative, paper presented at the Fourth Conference on Socio-Legal Research in the Scottish Courts, 7th October.

Plowden, Lady (1967), Children and Their Primary Schools (Plowden Report), Central Advisory Council for Education, HMSO, London.

Ramsay, D (1996), 'Recruiting and retaining foster carers: Implications of a professional service in Fife', *Adoption and Fostering*, 20: 1.

Richards, M (1994), 'The Interests of Children at Divorce', paper presented at the Conference on Families and Justice, Brussels.

Richards, M (1995), 'Changing Families' in Hill, M, Kirk, R H and Part, D (eds) Supporting Families, HMSO, Edinburgh.

Riyadh Guidelines (1985). United Nations Minimum Guidelines on the Prevention of Delinquency.

Robertson, A and McClintock, D (1996), 'The community-based alternative: Intermediate treatment for young offenders' in Asquith, S (ed) *Children and Young People in Conflict with the Law*, Jessica Kingsley.

Robertson, J (1952), *A Two-year Old Goes to Hospital*, Tavistock Research Unit, London (film).

Rodger, J J (1996), *Family Life and Social Control*, Macmillan.

Ross, M (1994), 'The culture of conversation', *Educational and Child Psychology*, 11: 4.

Rowe, A (1972), *Initial Selection for Children's Panels in Scotland*, Bookstall Publications.

Rowe, J and Lambert, L (1973), *Children Who Wait*, ABAA, London.

Rowe, J, Hundleby, M and Garnett, L (1989), *Child Care Now: A Survey of Placement Patterns*, British Agencies for Adoption and Fostering, London.

Royal Scottish Society for the Prevention of Cruelty to Children (1994), Child Sexual Abuse, Overnewton Centre, Glasgow, HMSO, Edinburgh.

Rushforth, M (1977), Committal to Residential Care, HMSO, Edinburgh.

Rushton, A and Rushton, A (1995), 'Adoption and fostering: New perspectives, new research, new practice' in Sigston, A, Curran, P, Labram, A and Wolfendale, S (eds) *Psychology in Practice with Young People, Families and Schools*, David Fulton.

Russell, M N (1991), *Clinical Social Work*, Sage.

Ryburn, M (ed) (1994) *Contested Adoptions*, Arena.

Sampson, R J and Laub J H (1993), *Crime in the Making: Pathways and Turning Points Through Life*, Harvard University Press.

Samuels, E and Tisdale, K (1996), 'Female offenders in Scotland: Implications for theory' in Asquith, S (ed) *Children, Young People in Conflict with the Law*, Research Highlights in Social Work 30, Jessica Kingsley.

Scarr, S and Dunn, J (1987), *Mother Care Other Care*, Pelican.

Schaffer, H R (1990), *Making Decisions About Children*, Blackwell.

Schon, D A (1991), *The Reflective Practitioner*, Avebury.

Scotland's Children: Proposals for Child Care Policy and Law (1993), (White Paper) Cmnd 2286, HMSO, Edinburgh.

Scottish Advisory Council (1947), Approved Schools Report, Edinburgh.

Scottish Advisory Council on Child Care (1961), Remand Homes, Report of the Remand Homes Committee, Cmnd 1588, The Scottish Office, HMSO, Edinburgh.

Scottish Consultative Committee on the Curriculum (1984), Social Education in Scottish Schools.

Scottish Consultative Committee on the Curriculum (1995), The Heart of the Matter.

Scottish Education Department (1968), Guidance in Scottish Secondary Schools, HMSO, Edinburgh.

Scottish Grand Committee (1964), Parliamentary Debates: Kilbrandon Report, House of Commons Official Report, 23rd July 1964, HMSO, London.

Scottish Law Commission Report (1992), Report on Family Law, SLC 135.

Scottish Office (1990), Review of Child Care Law in Scotland: Report of Review Group Appointed by the Secretary of State, HMSO, Edinburgh.

Scottish Office (1994, 1995a), Statistical Bulletin, Children's Hearings Series, The Scottish Office.

Scottish Office (1995b), Statistical Bulletin, Criminal Justice Series, The Scottish Office.

Scottish Office (1996), Scotland's Children: Implementation Newsletter 2, The Scottish Office.

Scottish Office (1997), Scotland's Children: Research Programme on the Children (Scotland) Act 1995, The Scottish Office Central Research Unit.

Seebohm, Lord (1968), Report of the Committee on Local Authority and Allied Personal Services (Seebohm Report), Cmnd 3703, HMSO, London.

Sheldon, B (1994), 'Social work effectiveness research: Implications for probation and juvenile justice services', *Howard Journal*, 33: 3.

Sinclair, A (1975), Speech to the Association of Reporters to Children's Panels, *Social Work Today*, 7: 5, May 1976.

Sinclair, R (1996), Editorial, *Children and Society*, 10.

Skinner, A (1992), Another Kind of Home (Skinner Report on Residential Care in Scotland), The Scottish Office, HMSO, Edinburgh.

Smith, D J (1995), 'Youth crime and conduct disorders: Trends, patterns, and causal explanations' in Rutter, M and Smith D J (eds) *Psychosocial Disorders in Young People* John Wiley.

Smith, G (1977), 'The place of "professional ideology" in the analysis of "social policy"

Some theoretical conclusions from a pilot study of the children's panels', *The Sociological Review*, 25.

Smith, G (1978a), 'Little kiddies and criminal acts: The role of social work in the children's hearings system', *British Journal of Social Work*, 7.

Smith, G (1978b), 'The meaning of "success" in social policy', *Public Administration*, 56.

Smith, P (1991), Ethnic Minorities in Scotland, The Scottish Office.

Smith, S (1995), 'Permanence revisited – some practice dilemmas', *Adoption and Fostering*, 19: 3.

Social Work and the Community (1966) (White Paper), Cmnd 3065, HMSO, Edinburgh.

Social Work Services Group (1969), Guidance to Children's Panel Advisory Groups, SW7/69, The Scottish Office.

Social Work Services Group (1971), Assessment of Children, SW2/75, The Scottish Office.

Social Work Services Group (1980), Consultative Memorandum on Part III of the Social Work (Scotland) Act 1968: Powers and Procedures, The Scottish Office.

Social Work Services Group (1982), Powers and Procedures of Children's Hearings: Use of Voluntary Reparation as a Method of Treatment (Consultation), The Scottish Office.

Social Work Services Group (1985), Safeguarding the Interests of Children in Proceedings before Children's Hearings and Sheriffs: Notes for Guidance for Persons Appointed as Safeguarders, SW7/85, The Scottish Office.

Social Work Services Group (1992), Emergency Protection of Children in Scotland: Consultation Paper on Proposals for Change, The Scottish Office.

Social Work Services Group (1993), The Future of Adoption Law in Scotland, Scottish Office.

Social Work Services Group (1994), Children in Care or Under Supervision 1990 and 1991, Statistical Bulletin, The Scottish Office.

Social Work Services Group (1995a), Services for Children 1993, Statistical Bulletin, The Scottish Office.

Social Work Services Group (1995b) Core Curriculum for the Induction Training of Children's Panel Members, The Scottish Office.

Social Work Services Inspectorate (1995a), Caring for Scotland's Children, The Scottish Office.

Social Work Services Inspectorate (1995b), Fife Child Care Services, The Scottish Office.

Social Work Services Inspectorate (1996a), A Secure Remedy. A review of the role, availability, and quality of secure accommodation for children in Scotland, The Scottish Office.

Social Work Services Inspectorate (1996b), Consultation on Guidance on Home Supervision and Contracts, The Scottish Office.

Spalding, S (1976), 'Social Work Supervision' in Martin, F M and Murray, K (eds) *Children's Hearings*, Scottish Academic Press.

Stone, F (1995), Children's Hearings, The 1995 Kilbrandon Child Care Lecture, The Scottish Office, HMSO, Edinburgh

Strathclyde Children's Panel (1994), Children Come First, Glasgow.

Streib, V (1994), *The Juvenile Death Penalty Today*, Cleveland State University.

Sutherland, E (1995), 'The role of the safeguarder' in Listening to the Voice of the Child, Scottish Child Law Centre.

Sutherland, E (1995), 'Scotland: child care law reform at last!' in Bainham, A, *International Survey of Family Law*, Martinus Nijhoff.

Swanson, M (1988), 'Preventing reception into care: Monitoring a short-stay refuge for older children' in Freeman, I and Montgomery, S (eds) Child Care, Jessica Kingsley.

Sweeting, H and West, P (1995), 'Family life and health in adolescence: A role for culture in the health inequalities debate?' *Social Science and Medicine*, 40: 2.

Tarling, R (1993), Analysing Offending: Data, Models and Interpretations, HMSO, London.

Tisdall, E K M and Donaghie, E (1995), Scotland's Families Today: Children in Scotland, HMSO, Edinburgh.

Triseliotis, J (1989), 'Foster care outcomes', Adoption and Fostering, 13: 3.

Triseliotis, J, Borland, M, Hill, M and Lambert, L (1995a), Teenagers and the Social Work Services, HMSO, London.

Triseliotis, J, Sellick, C and Short, R (1995b), Foster Care Theory and Practice, Batsford.

Triseliotis, J, Shireman, J and Hundleby, M (1997), Adoption: Theory, Policy and Practice, Cassell.

Tunstill, J (1995), 'The concept of children in need: The answer or the problem for family support?' Children and Youth Services Review, 17, 5: 6.

Tunstill, J (1996), 'Family support: past, present and future challenges', Child and Family Social Work, 1: 3.

Tutt, N (1981), 'A decade of policy', British Journal of Criminology, 21: 4.

United Nations Convention on the Rights of the Child (1989) UNICEF, Calouste Gulbenkian, UNA.

United Nations Declaration on the Rights of the Child (1959).

United Nations Standard Minimum Rules for the Administration of Juvenile Justice (Beijing Rules), General Assembly Resolution 40/33 of 29th November 1985.

Universal Declaration of Human Rights, adopted by the United Nations General Assembly on 10th December 1948.

Veitch, W (1995), 'Rights and the children's hearings system', Children and Society, 9: 3.

Vernon, J (1981), Report to Social Work Services Group (unpublished).

Wagner, Lady (1988), A Positive Choice (Wagner Report), HMSO, London.

Walgrave, L (1996), 'Restorative justice: A way to restore justice in Western European Systems' in Asquith, S (ed) Children and Crime, Jessica Kingsley.

Walter, T (1975), Delinquents in a Treatment Situation: The Processing of Boys in a List D School, University of Aberdeen (unpublished).

Waterhouse, S (1992), 'How carers view contact', Adoption and Fostering, 16: 2.

Watson, D (1980), 'Children's hearings: Care and control', Journal of Social Welfare Law 1.

Watson, D (1982), 'Recommendations, decisions and rubber stamps', The Hearing: Bulletin of the Panel Training Resource Centre, 7.

Werner, E E and Smith, R S (1992), Overcoming the Odds, Cornell University Press.

Willock, I (1973), Dundee Children's Panel Parental Attitudes Survey, mimeo, University of Dundee.

Wilson, H and Herbert, G W (1978), Parents and Children in the Inner City, Routledge & Kegan Paul.

Wootton, B (1959), Social Science and Social Pathology, Allen & Unwin.

Young, M E (1995), Early Childhood Development: Investing in the Future, World Bank.

Younghusband Report, The (1959), HMSO, Edinburgh.

Index